MARX MATTERS

Studies in Critical Social Sciences Book Series

Haymarket Books is proud to be working with Brill Academic Publishers (www.brill.nl) to republish the *Studies in Critical Social Sciences* book series in paperback editions. This peer-reviewed book series offers insights into our current reality by exploring the content and consequences of power relationships under capitalism, and by considering the spaces of opposition and resistance to these changes that have been defining our new age. Our full catalog of *SCSS* volumes can be viewed at https://www.haymarketbooks .org/series_collections/4-studies-in-critical-social-sciences.

MARX MATTERS

EDITED BY
DAVID FASENFEST

Haymarket Books
Chicago, IL

First published in 2022 by Brill Academic Publishers, The Netherlands
© 2022 Koninklijke Brill NV, Leiden, The Netherlands

Published in paperback in 2023 by
Haymarket Books
P.O. Box 180165
Chicago, IL 60618
773-583-7884
www.haymarketbooks.org

ISBN: 978-1-64259-815-5

Distributed to the trade in the US through Consortium Book Sales and
Distribution (www.cbsd.com) and internationally through Ingram Publisher
Services International (www.ingramcontent.com).

This book was published with the generous support of Lannan Foundation and
Wallace Action Fund.

Special discounts are available for bulk purchases by organizations and
institutions. Please call 773-583-7884 or email info@haymarketbooks.org for more
information.

Cover design by Jamie Kerry and Ragina Johnson.

Printed in the United States.

10 9 8 7 6 5 4 3 2 1

Library of Congress Cataloging-in-Publication data is available.

Contents

Acknowledgements

Many people participate, knowingly and unknowingly, in the creative process of any work, and I am sure I cannot name everyone who provided input, suggestions and advice. If I did not listen, it was due to stubbornness or confusion on my part. I would like to thank Penelope Ciancanelli for many conversations that have helped me clarify my thinking about what a book like this should accomplish, and Alfredo Saad-Filho for his regular input and collaboration over the past several years that has brought new energy and enthusiasm for a long-held project of promoting critical scholarship. In addition, I am indebted to the many contributors to this volume from whom I have learned much, both in the completion of this collection and over the years of our interactions.

Finally, but not least, I want to thank Heidi Gottfried for her intellectual curiosity that pushes me onward, her necessary criticism of my work, and her companionship and constant support over more than four decades. It should be obvious that I alone am responsible for any mistakes I may have made over the years.

Notes on Contributors

José Bell Lara
is Professor at the University of Havana and researcher of the Latin American Faculty of Social Sciences (FLACSO-Cuba). He was one of the original editors of the revolutionary Cuban journal *Pensamiento Crítico*. He has authored and co-authored numerous texts about Cuba and Latin America, including *Fidel in the Cuban Socialist Revolution* (with T. Caram León and D. L. López-Garcia, Brill, 2020); *Cuban Socialism within Globalization* (Editorial José Martí, 2008); *Imperialism, Neoliberalism and Social Struggles in Latin America* (with R. A. Dello Buono, Brill, 2006); and *Cuba in the 21st Century: Realities and Perspectives* (with R. A. Dello Buono, Editorial José Martí, 2006).

Ashley J. Bohrer
is Assistant Professor of Gender and Peace Studies at the University of Notre Dame. A philosopher by training, her research focuses on structural violence under capitalism and social movements' attempts to contest it. Her recent book, *Marxism and Intersectionality: Race, Gender, Class, and Sexuality under Contemporary Capitalism* (2019) is available from Transcript Verlag, Pluto Press, and Columbia University Press. In addition to her academic work, she organizes across various feminist, anti-racist, and anti-colonial social movements.

Tom Brass
formerly lectured in the Social and Political Sciences Faculty at Cambridge University, and directed studies in SPS for Queens' College. He carried out fieldwork research in Latin America and India during the 1970s and 1980s and is the second-longest serving editor of *The Journal of Peasant Studies* (1990–2008). His books include *New Farmers' Movements in India* (1995), *Free and Unfree Labour: The Debate Continues* (1997), *Towards a Comparative Political Economy of Unfree Labour* (1999), *Peasants, Populism and Postmodernism* (2000), *Latin American Peasants* (2003), *Labour Regime Change in the Twenty-First Century* (2011), *Class, Culture and the Agrarian Myth* (2014), *Labour Markets, Identities, Controversies* (2017), and *Revolution and Its Alternatives* (2019) and *Marxism Missing, Missing Marxism* (2021).

Rose M. Brewer
is an activist scholar, sociologist, and The Morse Alumni Distinguished Teaching Professor of African American & African Studies at the University of Minnesota-Twin Cities. She writes extensively on gender, race, class, Black radicalism and

political change, publishing over 80 articles, book chapters and essays as well as several books and edited volumes. Her most recent co-edited book is *Rod Bush: Lessons from a Radical Black Scholar on Liberation, Love, and Justice* (2019). She was a founding board member of Project South: Institute for the Elimination of Poverty and Genocide, a founding member of the Black Radical Congress, organizer of U.S. Social Forums in 2007, 2010 and 2015 and is a member of the People's Strike network. She has a long history of fighting for Black lives and radical political change in Minneapolis, MN, nationally and internationally.

William K. Carroll

is a Professor in the Sociology Department at the University of Victoria since 1981 and founding Director of the University of Victoria's interdisciplinary program in Social Justice Studies. His research interests are in the political economy of corporate capitalism, social movements and social change, and critical social theory and method. Carroll's books include *Regime of Obstruction: How Corporate Power Blocks Energy Democracy, Organizing the 1%: How Corporate Power Works* (with J.P. Sapinski), *Expose, Oppose, Propose: Alternative Policy Groups and the Struggle for Global Justice, A World to Win: Contemporary Social Movements and Counter-Hegemony* (with Kanchan Sarker), and *The Making of a Transnational Capitalist Class and Corporate Power in a Globalizing World.*

Penelope Ciancanelli

is a political economist who has specialized in banking, finance, and accounting. Her academic research has explored the role of financial institutions (banks, accountancy bodies and regulatory agencies) in facilitating the expansion of capitalism, particularly its commodification of such public goods as scholarly knowledge dissemination. Her most recent work, appearing in *Global Labor Migration: New Directions* (forthcoming, University of Illinois Press), explores the scale and pathways of remittance payments associated with contemporary global labor migration. Ciancanelli is on the International Advisory Board of *Critical Sociology.* She retired as a Senior Lecturer from Strathclyde University in Glasgow, UK and maintains a part-time appointment at Glasgow University in the Adam Smith School of Business.

Raju J Das

is Professor at York University, Toronto. His teaching and research interests are in political economy, globalization, and the capitalist state and international development. His recent books include *Marxist Class Theory for a Skeptical World* (Brill, 2017). He has published journal articles on topics such as uneven development, dispossession, agrarian change, child labour, identity politics, state-society relations, and social capital. He is currently completing a two-volume manuscript on Marx's Capital Volume 1 and engaged in a multi-year research project on capitalist industrialization and class relations in India. He serves on the editorial board and on the manuscript collective of *Science and Society: A Journal of Marxist Thought and Analysis.*

Ricardo A. Dello Buono

is Professor of Sociology at Manhattan College in New York City. His books and articles have spanned across a broad range of social problems and the sociology of development, with a regional emphasis on Latin America. He is co-author of *Social Change, Resistance, and Social Practices* (with D. Fasenfest, Brill, 2010); *Latin America after the Neoliberal Debacle: Another Region is Possible* (with X. de la Barra, Rowman and Littlefield, 2009) and *Social Problems, Law and Society* (with W. J. Chambliss and A. K. Stout, Rowman and Littlefield, 2004). He is active in the Society for the Study of Social Problems (SSSP), the Association for Humanist Sociology (AHS), the International Sociological Association (ISA) and the Latin American Studies Association (LASA).

David Fasenfest

is Associate Professor of Sociology, Wayne State University, the editor of *Critical Sociology* and editor of the book series *Studies in Critical Social Science* and *New Scholarship in Political Economy* (with Alfredo Saad-Filho), both with Brill Publishers. Fasenfest is the recipient of a Lifetime Achievement Award from the Marxist Section of the American Sociological Association. His research focuses on inequality, urban development, and Marxism. Recent publications include "Emergency Management in Michigan: A Misguided Policy Initiative" (2018) in Ashley Nickels and Jason Rivera (eds.) *Community Development and Public Administration Theory: Empowerment through the Enhancement of Democratic Principles*, London: Routledge; "A Neoliberal Response to an Urban Crisis: Emergency Management in Flint, MI" (2018) in *Critical Sociology*; "Monsieur Le Capital and Madame La Terre on the Brink" (with P. Ciancanelli, 2017) in Molly Scott Cato and Peter North (eds.) *Towards Just and Sustainable Economies: Comparing Social and Solidarity Economy in the North and South,* Policy Press; "The Cooperative City: Building Economic Democracy" (2015), in Michael Peter Smith and Lucas Owen Kirkpatrick (eds.), *Reinventing Detroit*, Transaction Books.

Ben Fine

is Emeritus Professor of Economics at the School of Oriental and African Studies, University of London, UK, and Visiting Professor, Wits School of

Governance, University of Witwatersrand, South Africa. He has published around 300 articles and 30 books and has been in receipt of both the Deutscher and Myrdal book prizes. His most recent books include *Material Cultures of Financialisation,* co-edited with K. Bayliss and M. Robertson, Routledge, 2018; *Race, Class and the Post-Apartheid Democratic State,* co-edited with John Reynolds and Robert van Niekerk, University of KwaZulu-Natal Press, 2019; and *A Guide to the Systems of Provision Approach: Who Gets What, How and Why*, with K. Bayliss, Palgrave, 2020. He is Chair of the International Initiative for Promoting Political Economy (http://iippe.org).

Lauren Langman

is emeritus professor of sociology at Loyola University of Chicago. He has long worked in the Marxist tradition of the Frankfurt School of Critical Theory, especially nationalism and reactionary movements, relationships between culture, identity and politics/political movements He is the past Chair of Marxist Sociology of the American Sociological Assassination where he recently received the Lifetime Achievement Award, Past President of Alienation Research and Theory, Research Committee 36, of the International Sociological Association. He a founding and board member of the Global Studies Association and the International Herbert Marcuse Society. Recent publications deal with globalization, alienation, global justice movements, the Tea Party, the body, nationalism, and national character. His publications include *Trauma Promise and Millennium: The Evolution of Alienation*, with Devorah Kalekin, *Alienation and Carnivalization* with Jerome Braun and a special issue of *Current Sociology* on Arab Spring, the Indignados and Occupy. His latest books are on *American Character* (with George Lundskow), *God, Guns, Gold and Glory* (Brill/Haymarket) and (with David Alan Smith) *Inequality in the 21st C: Marx, Piketty and Beyond* (Brill). He serves on several editorial boards, including *Critical Sociology, Current Perspectives in Social Theory* and *Populism.*

Alfredo Saad-Filho

is Professor of Political Economy and International Development at King's College London. Previously, he was Professor of Political Economy at SOAS University of London, and Senior Economic Affairs Officer at the United Nations Conference on Trade and Development. Saad-Filho has degrees in Economics from the Universities of Brasília (Brazil) and London (SOAS) and has taught in universities and research institutions in Brazil, Canada, Germany, Italy, Japan, Mozambique, Switzerland and the UK. He recently published *Brazil: Neoliberalism versus Democracy* (2018, with Lecio Morais, Pluto Press). His interests include the political economy of development, industrial policy, neoliberalism, democracy, alternative economic policies, Latin American political and economic development, inflation and stabilization, and the labor theory of value and its applications.

Vishwas Satgar

is an Associate Professor of International Relations, University of the Witwatersrand, South Africa. He is the principal investigator for Emancipatory Futures Studies in the Anthropocene and editor of the *Democratic Marxism* series. He recently edited BRICS *and the New American Imperialism: Global Rivalry and Resistance*, 2020. Open-source access: https://library.oapen.org/ handle/20.500.12657/22401 and *Cooperatives in South Africa – Advancing Solidarity Economy Pathways from Below*, UKZN Press, 2019. A veteran activist, he recently co-founded the South African Food Sovereignty Campaign and the Climate Justice Charter process.

William K. Tabb

is Professor Emeritus, Queens College and of Sociology, Political Science and Economics at the Graduate Center of the City University of New York. Recent publications include *The Restructuring of Capitalism in Our Time* (2012) and *Economic Governance in the Age of Globalization* (2004, Columbia University Press). His books are listed on his Amazon Author's Page and many of his articles can be downloaded from his Academia.edu and Google pages.

CHAPTER 1

The Once and Future Marx

David Fasenfest

But the old man was tired and muddled with his backsight, and dreams were in his noddle. He thought it would do in the morning – could not remember whether he was in the future or the past.
WHITE, 1994: 262

∙∙∙

If it mattered to express in few words what Marx did for the contemporary working class, then one could say: Marx has uncovered the modern working class as historical category, that is, as a class with particular historical conditions of existence and laws of motion.
ROSA LUXEMBURG cited in FUCHS, 2022: 227

∙∙
∙

The ideas for this volume began during the anniversary of the birth of Marx, living in a world in which it seems capitalism was victorious even as the financial crash of 2008, what Tooze (2018) called the first crisis of the global age, changed the world. The capitalist globe was struggling with neoliberalism and austerity (Blyth, 2013), in a period of growing unrest and frustration with the levels of inequality between regions of the North and South, between Souths within Norths and Norths within Souths (see Horner 2020). During the past decade or so, popular discontent created anger and populist movements on the left and right (see Lonergan and Blyth, 2020). How, then, to understand the ongoing importance of Marx was percolating in me for some time. Simply put, why indeed did Marx matter?

First, I tried to address the growing human rights agenda by considering how Marx dealt with this question, concluding that for Marx there was no real political freedom until there was economic freedom (Fasenfest, 2013, 2016). By the 200th anniversary of his birth I asked whether Marx was still relevant to deal with contemporary problems, and answered I believe he was (Fasenfest,

2018). I became more drawn into providing an understanding of Marx, and was given the chance to work out some questions during the Second and Third World Congresses on Marxism held at Peking University.[1] First, Raju Das and I explored how Marx informed development in the Global South, in the context of China's Belt and Road Initiative (Fasenfest and Das, 2018) – was there a path to development that did not bring with it the kinds of abuses found in the colonial and neo-colonial expansion by capitalist nations? More recently, with Alfredo Saad-Filho (Fasenfest and Saad-Filho, 2021) we addressed the role Marx plays in our understanding of the emergence and implementation of technology in capitalist societies for economic development, and how any benefits are appropriated rather than put into the service of the people in developing nations.

At the same time, I began discussions with scholars whose work highlighted Marx and demonstrated the utility of Marxism in dealing with a range of contemporary social problems. These discussions led to commitments for chapters discussing why Marx matters today, but the rapid spread of COVID-19 forced people to change their habits and adjust to new working patterns. The pandemic intensified known fractures and revealed how truly fragile it turns out the global capitalist system really is. Production in industrial countries stumbled as workshops and factories in China supplying component parts to Western industries shut down due to COVID-19. And as China began to recover and its factories reopened, there was a global decline in demand for goods leaving parts from reopened factories stacked up in ports throughout Asia. People everywhere were imagining what a new society and economy would look like as everything was going to change, and the promise of a new beginning filled both progressive and conservative imaginaries.

Like Merlyn in White's Arthurian novel, guiding the hero in the present yet having unfailing knowledge of the sadness that was to come, Marx was both a careful observer and analyst of the emergence of capitalism during his life, while also providing a model of how a capitalist world will develop in the future. Marx is dismissed as a man of his time and place whose insights, however correct, have become less important. Alternatively, he is lauded as a visionary whose methods of analysis and expositions of the workings of a vibrant economic system serve as the foundation of any present day understanding of capitalism. This volume brings Marx to the fore, reaffirms the relevance of Marx, and demonstrates how we can use Marx to investigate and

---

1   By the Third World Congress the pandemic dictated that we would be attending virtually.

unpack contemporary social issues. In other words, as Cornell West (1993) maintained for race, this volume argues that Marx matters.

The defense of Marx's relevance is not new.[2] Capitalism today is booming, and yet capitalism is in crisis. How do we understand the contradictions inherent in this reality? Understanding Marx is a complicated project because of the many different texts written by him over time. Making it a bit more complicated is the way we understand the texts and who translated Marx's words, not to mention how Marx uses terms in different tomes. As Ollman (1976: 3) famously points out (in Chapter 1 entitled, *With Words That Appear Like Bats*), "The most formidable hurdle facing all readers of Marx is his 'peculiar' use of words … [citing Pareto] Marx's words are like bats: one can see in them both birds and mice." In other words, Marx presents us with concepts that are both new and not always consistent with common usage. As Engels points out, according to Ollman, in Marx's terminology one can find "the same word meaning different things at different times" (1976: 4).

Why does Marx matter? Three major contributions in Marx's writings are central to understanding contemporary society. They are that crisis is systemic and offers opportunities for change, that there is a fundamental collective nature of human society driving social structure of work and the environment; and that an historical understanding of the development of productive forces is central to understanding the social, political and economic transformation within any epoch. For this volume, there are several themes: Class matters, Race matters, and Gender matters. The contribution of these essays is through their exploration of how these factors interrelate and are co-dependent.

> … Marx's theory penetrates and enlightens everything – the moral power, by which we overcome perils; our tactics of struggle, even its last details; our critique of opponents; our everyday agitation, by which we win the masses; our entire work down to the tips of the fingers. And if we here and there indulge in the illusion that our politics is today with all its inner power independent from Marx's theory, then this only shows that our praxis speaks in Marx's terms although we do not know it, just like Molière's bourgeois spoke in prose.
>
> LUXEMBURG cited in FUCHS 2022: 230

---

2   See Dobb 2001 for an earlier discussion of the importance of Marx for linking ideas to economic conditions.

Reviewing the importance of Marx for the social sciences is a regular activity.[3] McLaren and Jaramillo (2010) resurrect Marx for a critical pedagogy in the face of variants that have emerged. Marxism reveals "... the natural yet illusionary relations of human beings under capitalism ..." (2010: 256). Sinha and Varma demonstrate the continued importance of Marx's work in connection to the growth of postcolonial theory: "... both Marxism and postcolonial theory have been remarkably versatile in terms of responding to new critical challenges" (2017: 553). Further, Pradella, reflecting on whether Marx is only analyzing developments in a particular historical juncture in Britain, argues that "... the labour theory of value is not restricted to a self-enclosed national economy but encompasses capitalism as an imperialist system, and provides us with tools for developing an immanent critique of Eurocentrism" (Pradella, 2017: 574).

For the 200th anniversary of his birth, Foster (2018) maintained that the strength and relevance of Marx for contemporary society is precisely because Marx's work and analysis found in his publications are incomplete. That is, they are living analyses of the workings and impact of capitalism at a particular point in time. What matters is the methods employed, and how they can be used to analyze contemporary capitalism. A good example of the importance of applying Marx to understanding both the generalities and specificities of capitalist development, in this case in Japan, is the work of Hideo Aoki (2021).

There have been many challenges to the notion that Karl Marx was still (or even ever) relevant; Alvin Gouldner set the tone for many with his rejection of Marx. In his *The Coming Crisis of Western Sociology*, Gouldner notes that a version of the US Academic Sociology had emerged in the Soviet Union, concluding "(t)his development has been intellectually troublesome to those radicals who, out of a rote Marxism, have concluded that American Academic Sociology is an instrument of American corporate capitalism. For clearly the conservative character of American sociology cannot be attributed to its subservience to corporate capitalism if an essentially similar sociology has emerged where, as in the Soviet Union, there is no corporate capitalism" (1970: 9). Where were academic Marxists? He points out:

> Marxism was borne by unattached intelligentsia, by political groups and parties oriented to lower strata groups who were in rebellion against an emerging bourgeois society that excluded them. Academic Sociology was developed in the United States by university academicians who were

3   See Elster's 1983 negative assessment of 100 years of Marx, pointing out that contrary to economic theory that assumes preferences are given, Marx makes the case that these are both causes and effects of the dominant economic structure in which agents act.

oriented to the established middle class, and who sought pragmatically
to reform rather than systematically to rebel against the status quo.

GOULDNER, 1970:20

Throughout, Gouldner speaks of Academic Sociology and Marxism as if they
are distinct forms of scholarship, in which the latter has no real place in the
former. In the spirit of the Cold War, American Sociology is "for all practical
purposes, the model of Academic Sociology throughout the world" (Gouldner,
1970: 23) while Marxism is the product of the Soviet Union. Anticipating his
conclusions later on (Gouldner, 1980), he states that "world sociology underwent a binary fission; one "half" of it became Academic Sociology, in which
the Functionalist tradition finally became the dominant theoretical synthesis,
while the other "half" of world sociology became Marxist" (Gouldner, 1970: 447).
In the end, Gouldner envisioned two Marxisms, Critical and Scientific, the first
represented by the Frankfurt School with a potential for understanding society
able to avoid the pitfall of the second reflecting a devolution to what he considered to be Soviet socialism.

> What, then, are Marxism's nightmares? There are at least two. Implicit
> in its repression of idealism and utopianism, as well as in its sublimation
> of millenarianism into scientism, there is the lurking fear that it is not a
> truly "scientific socialism," not a theory about society or of the objective
> conditions that will change it, but only another disguise of the political
> will, an old utopian project masquerading as new science. In other words,
> one nightmare of Marxism is that it is another religion of the oppressed-
> a revolutionary messianism, as Georg Lukacs once described his own
> Marxism. This nightmare broke into the theorizing of Critical Marxism,
> which is nucleated with utopianism, and, at the political level, emerged
> openly in Maoism ... Yet there is another Marxist nightmare, an even
> deeper dragon of the mind that stirs fitfully within it. It is, most basically,
> this: Marxism emerged in a society whose middle classes had proudly
> insisted that private property and those having it were the foundation of
> civilization itself ...
>
> GOULDNER 1980: 381

At the end of the day, however, Gouldner served an important role in the development of a more critical sociology. His analysis of sociology to that point,
with its reliance on a Parsonian structural functionalism, had come to an
end and opened the doors to a more critical assault on mainstream sociology

in America. "Alvin Gouldner who correctly diagnosed the coming crisis of Western sociology had prefigured the Marxist assault" (Burawoy, 2003: 196).

What followed was a reinvigoration of a Marxist sociology, one that was predicated on understanding how capitalism developed, explored the contradictory nature of capitalist reproduction, and plotted the emergence of an emancipatory alternative to a capitalist society. Burawoy and Wright (2006: 463–4) identify three fundamental theses, derived from an understanding of causal mechanisms at work, informing Marxist theory. They are: (1) the non-sustainability of capitalism; (2) the intensification of anti-capitalist class struggle; and (3) the natural transition to socialism. What is central to sociological Marxism are the concepts of class as exploitation, labor process, world systems theory, Marxist feminism, and racial formations. Wright (2019) outlines the arguments found in Marx, in the context of the empirical trajectory of capitalism, to conclude that capitalism as a system is detrimental to human development. Therefore, it is essential that we turn to Marx in order to form a strategic agenda that will transform and transcend capitalism in the 21st Century.[4]

A return to Marx challenged the hegemonic view of society informed by Durkheim (social psychology, norms, social Darwinism) and Weber (social stratification, bureaucracy, rationalization), and it disrupted the narrow apologetic view of American society. As Burawoy (2005: 316) points out,

> ... stratification gave way to class analysis and later more broadly to the study of inequality, conditions of liberal democracy gave way to studies of states and revolution, social psychological adaptation to work gave way to theories of alienation and the transformation of work, sex roles gave way to gender domination, value consensus turned into the diffusion of ruling ideologies through school and media, irrational collective behavior became the politics of social movements.

This volume unfolds in two parts, an examination and application of Marx's political economy followed by an excavation of how Marx influences and enriches our understanding of the problems of the day. But first, Tabb introduces the collection of chapters by asking how Marx can provide insights to help us understand the present. Marx's reflections on the politics of his era can inform an analysis of our own era's political developments. As the economic fortunes of workers decline and the promise of prosperity for the well-educated

---

4 Also see articles by Panitch and Gindlin and by Hudis discussing capitalist crisis and the nature of class struggle in Vidal et al. (2018).

dry up, Marx's discussion of the crisis in France during the closing decades of the 19th Century informs an understanding of the reactionary politics in the US more recently. Tabb reviews macroeconomic trends, financialization and the roots of environmental crises made more critical in an environment that curtails and constrains social knowledge. The power of Marx's method and theory examining the capitalist system necessitates a return to Marx in order to understand today's central theoretical and political issues.

In Part 1, *Marx's Political Economy for the Present*, this volume examines some of the technical aspects of Marx's theories to set the stage for applying Marx today. Chapters by Fine, Saad-Filho, Das and Ciancanelli review the nature of finance, the meaning of money, value and capital, and the relationship between capital accumulation and social oppression in the way our understanding of the contemporary context of each is both influenced and revealed by the work of Marx. Fine asks how does the political economy of Marx inform our understanding of financialization, and what questions still need to be answered regarding its role in capitalism? Ciancanelli examines the way money is both a medium of exchange and a socially constructed substance, and in its fetishized form is both a solution and a problem. Saad-Filho returns to Marx's theory of value to unpack how, as a theory of class, class relations and exploitation, concepts in Marx are central to contemporary analyses. He concludes that what Marx offers is not simply a theory explaining how producers are separated from the means of production, nor is it merely an explanation how commodities exchange and the allocation of labor. Rather, Marx highlights the social form of economic activities leading to the reproduction of social structures that support capitalism. By applying Marx, Saad-Filho argues, we can overcome the divisions and fragmentation leading to exploitation. This leads us to Das, who revisits how Marx informs inquiries into the causes and extent of social oppression. He argues that only by returning to a class analysis, by bringing class relations to the fore and not resorting to identity politics, can we begin to end exploitation and oppression. As Filc and Ram (2014) argue, Marx provides concepts of class and the formation of political subjectivities making it central to an understanding of how to conceive of an emancipatory political subject.

Brass explores how our understanding of the reserve army of labor, what Marx calls surplus to the needs of production, helps us figure out how to differentiate the variations in recent migration streams into the centers of capitalist production. He points out that recent populist initiatives see a "great replacement" of immigrants displacing the traditional labor force. He calls for understanding this labor flow in terms of the needs for capital accumulation. One must, Brass argues, understand the populist rhetoric juxtaposed to the political and economic analysis afforded by Marx's theories of the reserve army of labor. This chapter takes us to the point of understanding how Marx's ideas were instrumental in the transformation of society.

In Part 2, *Marx and a Changing Society*, authors provide instances when the application of Marx supports efforts at social change. Dello Buono and Bell Lara excavate Marx's positions against colonialism and European imperialism to understand the important of "Carlos" Marx for the development of Latin America. They document how Marx's writings were important in debates and analyses in Mexico at the same time Paris was engaged in defending its commune. Latin American scholars trained in Europe, like José Mariátequi influenced by Gramsci, returned and brought with them a commitment to form a united front against the contradictions of a neocolonial dependent capitalism. They discuss how Marx's writing on Ireland illustrated the contradictory role anticolonial struggles had in the development of capitalism. The Latin American experiences with Marx led to transnational global justice movements in Mexico and a renewal of the Bolivarian Revolution in Venezuela. They outline how the Latin American search for self-determination and its anti-colonial anti-neocolonial struggles was informed by and evolved out of the reading of Marx.

Satgar returns to Marx through an exploration into his thinking about the commons, arguing that for Marx the critique of capitalism was also a critique of the destruction of the commons, to craft a movement to restore the commons in the service of what Satgar calls democratic eco-socialism. The destruction of the commons was central to the appropriation of social capital and transferring communal property into private property. The long-term consequence of this process has been both the obliterations of the conditions necessary to sustain life outside capitalist profit and surplus extraction, and the way private capitalist property is anti-ecological. By highlighting how Marx thought about the commons, Satgar posits a Marxist ecological theory of the commons to promote and support climate justice struggles.

Like Satgar, Carroll provides us with an example of how Marxism can simultaneously inform both scholarship and political practice. He focuses on how fossil capitalism organized successive eras of neoliberal polices to protect their revenue streams and prevent positive social change. Carroll explores the causal relationships between consumption of fossil fuels, greenhouse gas emission and global temperature increases, pointing out that this relationship was clearly understood for decades but little was done to mitigate the extreme weather events, ocean acidification and the loss of biodiversity as a result. Relying on the works of Marx and Gramsci, Carroll is part of a research agenda whose goals is to expose and problematize corporate power, provide data in support of progressive movement and provide policy analyses to promote feasible climate justice initiatives. Echoing the social agenda outlined by Satgar in this volume, Carroll advocates praxis-based action research to advance the climate justice movement.

Chapters by Brewer and Bohrer reflect on the nature of a racist and sexist capitalist society, and how Marx informs an understanding of its persistence. Brewer looks at the Black struggle for justice and equity, and how systematic dispossession is based on what she calls a capitalist heteropatriarchal system of white supremacy in the US. Racialization of society informs not only state policies but also the very institutions of civil society.[5] For evidence Brewer points to the findings of the Kerner Commission in response to the urban rebellions of the 1960s, findings opposed by Southern Democrats essential for President Johnson's ruling coalition. The capitalist racial state manages Black discontent by containment, cooptation, duplicity, and as the recent history has demonstrated, by violent oppression.

Embracing Marxist-feminist critiques of intersectionality, Bohrer seeks to address claims that traditional Marxism, with a primary focus on class, ignores other forms of oppression. The approach of Marxist-feminists is to engage with the specifics of class relations to unpack a holistic critique of heteronormative capitalism. Rather than situate intersectionality as a static assignment of race, gender and class, Brewer (2010) talks about intersectionality as the process of society being gendered, raced and classed – that is, one's position is not static but the result of forces that reflect and influence capitalist social relations over time. Through a review of both intersectional criticisms and Marxist-feminist approaches, Bohrer seeks to develop what she calls an intersectional Marxism, a Marxist theory of intersectionality if you will. She concluded by arguing that each needs the other to fully engage in understanding the matrix of domination that is contemporary capitalism. In other words, to borrow from Audre Lorde, there is no hierarchy of oppression[6] and so no one should benefit from resistance to one kind of oppression and ignore all the others. As a poor Black lesbian woman, Lourde states that whether the attack on her is based on class, race, sexual orientation or gender, there is no space to argue one is worse. Truly, for Bohrer there is a matrix of oppression, requiring an analysis that, borrowing from Marx, must speak about real historical people, their real identities and the social locations produced by those identities.

---

5   See, for example, Malcolm X explaining the role of white supremacy on the self-perceptions of Black people as a way to undermine their aspirations and goals, (https://www.youtube .com/watch?v=gH3vtiEb1RY). His 1962 speech about police violence (https://www.youtube .com/watch?v=6_uYWDyYNUg&t=13s) is a harbinger of the messages from the Black Lives Movement arising from the murder of George Floyd.
6   Listen to Lorde reading her essay (https://www.youtube.com/watch?v=i1pNsLsHsfs).

The volume closes with chapters by Brass and Langman, seeking to unravel the reasons behind the rising populist movements. Populism is generally a difficult concept to nail down, especially as it takes on so-called "left" and "right" populist movements.[7] It seems to be at the same time a democratic impulse and an authoritarian movement. Brass turns to Marx's position on the peasantry to re-evaluate the peasant movements in the Russian (then) and Indian (now) countryside. This is important, says Brass, if we are to understand the currents of contemporary agrarian populism. Pointing to the work by Engels following Marx, Brass links peasant populism with efforts to restore aristocratic rule. The key is that at each historical moment when the proletariat advances their political aims, the peasantry allies with the bourgeoisie. This pattern identified by Engels appears in those Russian and Indian peasant movements. For Brass, Marxism is the alternative to the cultural turn of reactionary populism[8]. In the end, it is the way peasant economic activity is tied to capitalist development that calls for the utilization of Marx in any analysis. That is the only way to confront a globally resurgent right-wing populism.

Coming at the nature of populism from a social movement perspective, Langman turns to Marx, Gramsci and the Frankfurt School to delve into the motivations of popular unrest. Pointing to movements from the left and right, he asks how cultural factors coupled with the political economy shape the targets and objectives of this range of protests. Using Marx and Gramsci, Langman argues that while cultural movements do not appear to be materially based, there is a material foundation in the way individuals engage in dealing with grievances. Like Das earlier in this book, Langman excavates Marx's ideas around alienation and domination to frame the cultural motivations for protest. Marx points out, in his writings about the Paris Commune and civil wars in France, that Bonapartism attracts the support of an aggrieved public and, like Brass, that support often turns conservative as people seek a return to a time when life was not so precarious. Gramsci's analysis of the interregnum is, as Langman puts it, very prescient in helping us understand the rise of populist autocrats in democratic societies – leaders like Trump in the US, Bolsonaro in Brazil, Modi in India and to a lesser extent Johnson in the UK. Each mobilizes grievances in the service of right-wing agendas, capturing state power in the process. But Langman takes his analysis one step further by turning to the traditions out of the Frankfurt School

---

7   The journal *Thesis Eleven* has devoted two issues to trying to come to an understanding of the concept in theory and in practice (see Issue #149 December 2018 and Issue #164, June 2021).
8   Here Brass returns to the role of the industrial reserve army as discussed in his earlier chapter.

to also add social, cultural and psychological factors that are as important and salient as socio-economic factors for any analysis of populist movements whether left or right-wing. He ends with a discussion of generational changes in goals and attitudes along with shifting historical conditions which points to how reactionary agendas fly in the face of existential threats for this new cohort. By contrast, the supporters of conservative social movements focus on retaining and defending past privileged social positions, in the US and perhaps in other advanced capitalist countries. With this, Langman leaves us with the expectation that a new generation will work for a more progressive and equitable future.

Taken together these chapters outline how the works of Marx, and those that follow in this tradition, offer insights and perspectives that were certainly derived from an analysis by Marx in his time and place, but also useful in applying Marx's methods as we grapple with issues central to the current state of affairs. In that way, we can argue that certainly Marx matters.

References

Aoki, Hideo (2021) Marxism and the Debate on the Transition to Capitalism in Prewar Japan, *Critical Sociology*, 47: 1: 17–36.

Blyth, Mark (2013) *Austerity: The History of a Dangerous Idea*, Oxford: Oxford University Press.

Brewer, Rose M. (2010) Black Radical Theory and Practice: Gender, Race and Class, *Socialism and Democracy*, 17: 1: 109–122.

Burawoy, Michael (2003) For a Sociological Marxism: The Complementary Convergence of Antonio Gramsci and Karl Polanyi, *Politics & Society*, 31: 2:193–261.

Burawoy, Michael (2005) The Critical Turn to Public Sociology, *Critical Sociology*, 31: 3: 313–326.

Burawoy, Michael and Wright Erik Olin (2006) Sociological Marxism, in J. H. Turner (ed) *Handbook of Sociological Theory*, pp 459–486, New York: Springer.

Dobb, Maurice (2001/1947–48) Marxism and Social Sciences, *Monthly Review*, 53: 4 (September) Available at https://monthlyreview.org/2001/09/01/marxism-and-the-social-sciences/.

Elster, Jon (1983) One Hundred Years of Marxist Social Science, *London Review of Books*, June 19. 5: 11. Available at https://www.lrb.co.uk/the-paper/v05/n11/jon-elster/one-hundred-years-of-marxist-social-science.

Fasenfest, David (2013) Marxist Sociology and Human Rights, in David L. Brusma, et al. (eds.) *Handbook of Sociology and Human Rights*, pp 440–448, Herndon, VA: Paradigm Publishers.

Fasenfest, David (2016) Marx, Marxism and Human Rights, *Critical Sociology*, 42: 6: 777–779.

Fasenfest, David (2018) Is Marx Still Relevant, *Critical Sociology*, 44: 6: 851–855.

Fasenfest, David and Raju Das (2018) Marx, the Global South and China's Belt and Road Initiative, presented at the *Second World Congress of Marxism*, May 5–6, Peking University. Beijing, China.

Fasenfest, David and Alfredo Saad-Filho, (2021) Marx, Technology, and Limits on Economic Development, presented at the *Third World Congress of Marxism*, July 17–18, Peking University. Beijing, China.

Filc, Dani and Uri Ram (2014) Marxism after Postmodernity: Rethinking the Emancipatory Political Subject, *Current Sociology*, 62: 3: 295–313.

Foster, John Bellamy (2018) Marx's Open-Ended Critique, *Monthly Review* May, Available at https://monthlyreview.org/2018/05/01/marxs-open-ended-critique/.

Fuchs, Christian (2022) *Foundations of Critical Theory*, New York and Milton Park: Routledge.

Gouldner, Alvin. (1970) *The Coming Crisis in American Sociology*, London: Heinemann.

Gouldner, Alvin. (1980) *The Two Marxisms: Contradictions and Anomalies in the Development of Theory*, London: MacMillan Press, Ltd.

Horner, Rory (2020) Towards a New Paradigm of Global Development? Beyond the Limits of International Development, *Progress in Human Geography*, 44: 3: 415–436.

Lonergan, Eric and Mark Blyth (2020) *Angrynomics*, Newcastle upon Tyne: Agenda Publishing.

Luxemburg, Rosa. (1903/2020). Karl Marx. *Vorwärts* 62: 1–2, in Christian Fuchs *Foundations of Critical Theory*, New York and Milton Park: Routledge.

McLaren, Peter and Nathalia E. Jaramillo (2010) Not Neo-Marist, Not Post-Marxist, Not Marxian, Not Autonomist Marxism: Reflections of a Revolutionary (Marxist) Critical Theory, *Cultural Studies <-> Critical Methodologies*, 10: 3: 251–262.

Ollman, Bertell (1976) *Alienation: Marx's Conception of Man in a Capitalist Society*, 2nd edition, Cambridge: Cambridge University Press.

Pradella, Lucia (2017) Postcolonial Theory and the Making of the World Working Class, *Critical Sociology*, 43: 4–5: 573–586.

Sinha, Subir and Rashmi Varma (2017) Marxism and Postcolonial Theory: What's Left of the Debate? *Critical Sociology*, 43: 4–5: 545–558.

Tooze, Adam (2018) *Crashed: How a Decade of Financial Crises Changed the World*, New York: Viking.

Vidal, Matt, Tomás Rotta, Tony Smith and Paul Prew (eds.) (2018) *The Oxford Handbook of Karl Marx*, Oxford: Oxford University Press.

West, Cornel (2001/1993) *Race Matters*, Boston, MA: Beacon Press.

White, T.H. (1994) *The Once and Future King*, New York, NY: Harper Collins.

Wright, Erik Olin (2019) The Continuing Relevance of the Marxist Tradition for Transcending Capitalism, in Vidal et al. (eds) *The Oxford Handbook of Karl Marx*, Oxford: Oxford University Press, Available at https://www.oxfordhandbooks.com/view/10.1093/oxfordhb/9780190695545.001.0001/oxfordhb-9780190695545-e-48.

CHAPTER 2

What Marx Anticipated That Is, or Should Be, Central to Political Economy Today

William K. Tabb

Many of the concerns, central to what are understood to be failings of early 21st Century capitalism, were remarkably well understood by Marx. It is not however our intention here to explain what Marx "really meant," but to look to him for insights into what is going on now and the ways his work implicitly and sometimes explicitly helps analysts understand our fraught present. There are many areas where his insights are useful. Here we focus on the structural tendency to inequality of income, wealth and power, the middle class being pushed downward to the ranks of the proletarians, the manner in which control of technology and the organization of production and the social relations in production are designed to exploit the energies of the workers, the concentration and centralization of capital, the resulting inadequacy of demand for goods and (non-financial) services that lead to an imbalance between what can be produced and what can be sold profitably, the extraction of surplus from productive activities that finds its way into the overproduction of fictitious capital and the financial collapses that are part of capital's nature, along with the behavior of swindlers and speculators, even his expectation regarding social knowledge.

This chapter discusses some of the important ways the contemporary debate is informed by Marx's understanding of political economy and to suggest that even his understanding of the politics of his era echoes our own. The task is to show the extent to which Marx's understandings have become central to much of contemporary social science. This is especially the case of those for whom Marx's insight into the contradictions of the system that prompt its crises and point to its eventual demise have become once again topics of discussion for a new generation. In terms of the system's inability to reproduce itself on a sustainable basis, the constant revolutionizing of the means of production has set the terms for new class awarenesses. There is anger by those whose livelihoods have been taken from them as they have been displaced by the way technological change has proceeded. For others, who have sought and achieved education to a greater extent but find themselves unfulfilled and not compensated to the extent they expected, their place in the 21st Century is unsatisfactory as well. The former tends to look back to a cherished past while the latter to a different deployment of the existing and emergent forces of production.

These factions of the working class having been differently impacted, the former's role no longer part of the then historically progressive manufacturing of an earlier stage of capitalist development in the centers of the world capitalist system responded in significant number by accepting a reactionary understanding of who and what was to blame. The latter looked to a different future that capitalism's advances made possible. The extent to which the social relations of production are inhibiting the potential to use the social knowledge that should be the common inheritance of humankind and for the young especially, awareness of the need to deploy resources and intelligence to meet the climate emergency in ways that must challenge the power of capital, are creating a socialist constituency for whom his ideas seem fresh in relation to a tired capitalist liberalism that has brought austerity and increased inequality.

How can Marx help us understand the contemporary situation? The elements of his thought that we would bring together are the following. It will be argued that the dominant explanation by political scientists regarding the election of Donald Trump, and by extension that of Bonapartism in Europe and the strength of hard right parties comes from racism in the form of anti-immigrant beliefs on the part of working class voters and also the understanding of economists that automation is producing less demand for labor and that government debt is the reason to fear new downturns are not the best ways of understanding the dramatic changes in politics and the economy. Rather, the lack of aggregate demand is slowing growth as inequality has grown as a result of political choices and the surplus appropriated by Occupy's 1%, and within that the one percent of the 1%, has led to a situation of global overcapacity and the overaccumulation of capital, has found outlet in dangerous levels of asset speculation that when bubbles collapse produce economic crises that will continue to be resolved by, as the expression goes, saving Wall Street but not Main Street.

In doing so, in choosing to manipulate asset prices to indemnify financiers for losses rather than addressing the crisis through public investment in needed infrastructure and green jobs to meet the climate emergency the existing masters of the political economy undermined the legitimacy of the system for both those on the right and the left. The populist right grew strong as people lost homes and jobs grew fearful, and so looked for a savior and accepted scapegoating to blame immigrants and racial minorities as taking too much and leaving less for them instead of seeing the capitalist class and especially its financial segment as the enemy as the left did. Scapegoating the weak becomes prominent in periods in which the working class feels pinched and becomes desperate as economic insecurity increases. It is not that the racism is not real, it is rather that it becomes virulent under the stimulus of working-class loss and rising fear of the future that capitalism imposes on them. It is overcapacity on a world scale that produces the political economy in which we live.

While, as this is written, the stock market is at a record high and real wages for workers in the United States are rising after a long period of stagnation there is a tremendous overaccumulation of capital that is structurally problematic. During the Bill Clinton administration in the 1990s the 1 percent garnered 45 percent of the increase in disposable national income. In the 2000s under George W. Bush the 1 percent received 73 percent of the increase in disposable income. The surplus went to asset speculation and was the basis for the financial collapse 2007–8. From 1975 to 2015, the share of the nation's total income going to labor fell from 61 percent to 57 percent. The 1 percent came to have more private net wealth than the bottom 90 percent of Americans. It also pays a lower percentage of their income than does the working class. The Federal Reserve's Distributive Financial Accounts show that between 1989 and 2018 the top 1 percent increased its total net worth by $21 trillion. These are surely too many more numbers, so let us just go with: "Top 1% Up $21 Trillion. Bottom 50% Down $900 Billion" (see Bruenig 2019). While not as extreme in most other countries the appropriation by the capitalist classes had not only led to legitimacy crises and the need for the center right to partner with the most reactionary political tendencies but has brought on a worldwide uprising against corruption and the growth of inequality.[1]

The growth of inequality and the exposure of the extent of systemic corruption has other consequences that are beginning to attract needed attention. The system in our time is unable to reproduce itself on anything like a healthy basis is a result of a complex, intertwined set of developments. Debt, public and private has increased substantially forcing monetary authorities to pursue low and in many places negative interest rate policies to prevent defaults that would bring on financial collapse. The government policies of lowering taxes on the rich, transnational corporations and international finance in a race to the bottom does not go to meaningful levels of decent jobs as the workers of the world are thrown into more intense competition. Given the limited purchasing power of the working class, overaccumulation of capital results and capitalists not seeing productive uses of the surplus extracted the wealth finds its way into asset speculation. The system becomes more prone to financial crises which become harder to address within the confines of traditional policy

---

1   https://en.wikipedia.org/wiki/Protests_of_2019 .

in what Bank of England's executive director for financial stability warns is a "doom loop" (Tabb 2021). The financial sector is rescued by regulators to prevent economic disaster and becomes bigger and able to take on larger risks, must be bailed out and the size of the problem grows inexorably (Haldane 2012). In understanding why this is the case Marx can be helpful.

1   Macroeconomic Imbalance and Secular Stagnation

Marx, following Quesnay understood the circular flow that today is the centerpiece of Keynesian economics, the need for macroeconomic balance between consumption and investment, what Marx called Departments 1 and 2 (Mandel 1978). In the current stage of capitalist development, "accumulate, accumulate," remains "the Moses and the Prophets," the religion of capitalists. The power of the ruling class is such that extracting value from productive capital cannot be reinvested to generate greater output of goods and non-financial services because of the imbalance between the departments that interferes with smooth reproduction of the system. This is not uncommon in capitalism an anarchical system after all and creates economic crises that produce suffering for working people.

In our time there is a surplus of capital, overaccumulation in the hands of large corporate entities and at the top of the income distribution. It is called "the savings glut" by former Fed chair Ben Bernanke. This surplus capital has fed asset speculation and the collapse of financial bubbles has for some time produced economic downturns. The tendency to crisis comes from the growth of fictitious capital that outruns the returns that can be expected bring first financial bubbles and then their collapse. An essential element of this tendency is excessive risk taking was also of course grasped by Marx who analyzed the credit crises of his day, arguing that a banking system "subordinated" to capital accumulation would produce financial expansions that were inherently unstable and would overshoot because of "over-speculation" and "credit swindles."[2] He saw that a "large part of the social capital is employed by people who do not own it and who consequently tackle things quite differently than the owner." They would overreach, take excessive risks with rentier class monies. Credit growth would stop, debt would come due and nervous bankers would scramble mostly unsuccessfully for liquidity (Krause 2018). Marx

---

2   See Marx (1863–1883) Volume III, Part V.

described the corruption of bankers who walked away from such crises with great wealth, avoiding punishment after their reckless behavior and swindles.

In the *Monthly Review* usage, secular stagnation can be defined as the tendency to long-term sluggishness in the private accumulation process of the capitalist economy, manifest in rising unemployment, excess capacity, and a slowdown of growth. A key part of this definition is that it is a tendency. That is, it is not a phenomenon only of business cycles but is potentially present all the time. Monopoly capital can appropriate surplus that cannot be profitably reinvested in productive activities. This surplus needs to be absorbed in advertising, product obsolescence, war and preparation for war, and financial speculation, or more constructively, "epoch-making innovations" offering capitalism growth opportunities. But the normal state of capitalism was one of overaccumulation. Capital received more of the social surplus than it could profitably invest hence the tendency to wasteful uses. The editors of *Monthly Review* saw a rising rate of exploitation in monopoly capitalism as opposed to the earlier competitive stage of the system as well as the significant expansion of finance in the mid-1970s well before most observers (Sweezy 1994).

The claim of secular stagnation theorists is that factors limiting growth can prevail over countertrends, that the potential of the economy is not being reached, and that the composition of growth can be wasteful and in major respects harmful. The possible (unproductive) outlets for the surplus based on their work was explored by Paul Sweezy and Paul Baran (1966) in their classic *Monopoly Capital: An Essay on the American Economic and Social Order*. It was, they argued based on the work of Michal Kalecki and Josef Stendl (Hein 2014), that "monopoly capitalism is a self-contradictory system."[3] Its irrationality produces waste in the midst of social need and it required major breakthroughs, opened new vistas for growth, create new industries, epoch-making innovation – the railroad, the automobile, that produced different spatial fixes that required huge investment in the built environment that offset the tendency to stagnation.

In the 1980s, Harry Magdoff and Sweezy (1987) saw the growth of financialization as resulting from economic stagnation and that financial over-leveraging produces unsustainable household, public and business indebtedness, instability and crisis, declining real income and greater inequality. This occurred because the obvious offset – using the surplus to meet human need – is not

---

3   The famous quote is included in a useful book review by a then future editor of *Monthly Review*, see Magdoff (1967).

profitable within the terms of capitalism. In the decades since, financialization has absorbed more and more of the social surplus even as it has produced a debt peonage society for most Americans, to invoke Paul Krugman's (2005) descriptor.

2   21st Century Finance Capital

Fictitious capital and the extractions of surplus that finds its way into speculation is central to what today is the triumph of the 21st Century version of Finance Capitalism.

Marx deploys the concept of fictitious capital, paper claims on future earnings that may not be realized, to explain what we now know as the Keynes-Minsky understanding of business cycles. According to Marx, when the extent of fictitious capital so exceeds the potential valuations that people begin to doubt their plausibility, the prices of assets can suddenly and dramatically fall. Fictitious capital does not have an assured material basis in commodities or productive activity. Instead, it relies on the anticipated future value that will be created to justify its exchange. This optimism prompts the extension of credit and, as Keynes and before him Marx explained, uncertainty is always present. The buying and selling of claims to wealth can become a self-levitation process in which, as prices of paper claims rise the assets can be used as collateral to borrow to purchase more assets driving prices higher in a seemingly endless loop. It is endless that is until it unceremoniously ends leaving many disappointed players who thought they would be able to sell and get out before the collapse. The more naïve are left holding devalued assets facing severe losses.

The incentives to dishonest opportunism remain central to capitalism even as people think of these misdeeds only in terms of the extended present. There is little doubt that were Marx alive today he would record with interest the way hedge funds make money by manufacturing company defaults in what *Bloomberg Businessweek* calls "Wall Street Bloodsport." That publication quotes one observer as saying, "The participants in this CDS [credit default swap] market are all incredibly sophisticated, with wonderful lawyers."[4] They speak to what financialization has wrought, dirty tricks generating riches from maneuvers that have no socially redeeming value. Marx understood the essentials that are only now beginning to tentatively penetrate mainstream financial

---

4   "Wall Street Bloodsport," *Bloomberg Businessweek, April 22.*

economics thanks in significant measure to renewed interest in the work of Keynes and Minsky.[5]

Financialization describes an increase in the size and importance of the financial sector relative to the overall economy and of "the increasing role of financial motives, financial markets, financial actors and financial institutions in the operation of the domestic and international economies," as Gerald Epstein (2006, 3) writes.[6] Mike Konczal and Nell Abernathy add a political perspective, seeing financialization as "the growth of the financial sector, its increased power over the real economy, the explosion in the power of wealth, and the reduction of all of society to the realm of finance" (2015, 4).[7] In keeping with our understanding, Lenore Palladino suggests what we are talking about is corporate financialization, "the increasing share of profits earned from *financial activity* and the increasing *flow of profits to shareholders*" [emphasis in original], which "is a key driver of this economic inequality." She understands corporate financialization as the mechanism for such capture, specifically through the rise of financial activities within firms. The firms are holding a rising proportion of financial assets and earn an increasing percentage of their total profit from such assets (versus the profit that they earn from their normal business activity of making and selling commodities). Their profits are increasingly used for stock buybacks or loans rather than being spent on labor or physical capital. Companies have themselves been borrowing large amounts to buy back their own stock.[8]

This pattern represents what Palladino (2018) calls "the economic puzzle," the combination of record corporate profits and share prices and low corporate investment and wage growth. It may seem to go against the expectations of economic logic, but it is not a puzzle. Corporate financialization is facilitated because companies with a great deal of market power (the concentration and centralization of capital which Marx foresaw even in the early stage of industrial capitalism) are able to extract large rents on a continuing basis. They see

---

5   For those interested in the relation of Marx to the later economists referenced here and others see these essays that appeared in *European Journal of Economics and Economic Policies*, 16(2) evaluating the relation between Marx, and Keynes and post-Keynesians. See essays there by Eckhard Hein, "Karl Marx: an early post-Keynesian? A comparison of Marx's economics with the contributions by Sraffa, Keynes, Kalecki and Minsky" and Fritz Helmedag, "Marx and Keynes: from exploitation to employment"; and Hansjörg Herr "Karl Marx's thoughts on functional income distribution: a critical analysis from a Keynesian and Kaleckian perspective."

6   Also see Tabb (2012) Chapters 1 and 2.

7   See also Van der Zwan (2014) who surveyed a decade of literature on financialization; Orhangazi (2011).

8   "Borrowing Billions to Buy Stock, Not Invest," *Bloomberg Businessweek*, August 12.

little reason to reinvest in job creation or paying their workers more. The monopsony power of the employer class and the legal terrain when it comes to the enforcement of labor rights have meant they can keep their costs down and find outlets outside the sphere of production for the surplus they appropriate. This in essence has not changed since Marx's time. For these reasons, part of the necessary analysis requires looking at the context within which business choices are made and this inescapably includes the class nature of capitalism, the struggle between capital and labor, and the ways financialization functions in a particular historic conjuncture.

What is now called financialization, Hyman Minsky called money-manager capitalism. He saw it becoming a reality in the 1980s well before the dramatic expansion described. Money managers are judged by how well they maximize the value of the investments made for those whose moneys they hold in their portfolios. They push business leaders to increase short-term profits and stock market valuation so that while in the era of managerial capitalism corporate CEOs were the overseers of the private economy. By the 1980s money managers were its masters. Firms under pressure from stockholders and corporate raiders increased dividends, borrow themselves to avoid being a cash cow takeover target and in doing so become cash poor and risked insolvency in a downturn. Mergers, acquisitions, leveraged buyouts and stock buybacks grew as money managers came to sit astride American capitalism. The rise of institutional investors provided a ready pool of buyers for securitized loans and commercial paper. Minsky saw the system going global, as it has, so that short-term returns have come to dominate for financial institutions almost everywhere (see Whalen 1999). Marx grasped the beginning of these developments from his observation of mid-19th Century capitalism.

Heterodox economists see a new stage of capitalism characterized variously as "monopoly-finance capital" (Foster 2006) and "the Finance-Dominated Accumulation Regime" (Stockhammer 2004). The reason is not simply the dramatic growth in the size and significance of finance but the changed nature it plays in the contemporary economy. There is an escalation of leveraged buyouts by private equity and hedge funds which use investor and borrowed money to directly purchased control of large companies. Between 2011 and 2017, private-equity, hedge funds and other large investors[9] spent $36 billion to buy more than 200,000 homes in collapsed real estate markets across the country. Some observers (see, for example, Semuels 2019) found it ironic that

---

9   On the differences between hedge funds, private equity and other categories of deep-pocketed investment vehicles for the potential fund traders among readers see *Investopedia* for a quick lesson.

some of the same investment firms that had played a part in the housing crisis were to profit from the mess they had made. These money manager capitalists bought up hospitals, purchased to consolidated markets, including ambulatory surgery, hospitalist staffing, and home health, undertaking more than $50 billion in total transactions, according to a 2018 McKinsey report (Patel, Foo and Sutaria 2018). The list of industries that private equity entered and transformed almost always to the detriment of consumers and honest competition is a long one.

The private equity industry has attracted trillions of dollars in a world with very low interest rates. Since they claimed 13 percent annual returns over the past quarter of a century, far more than the S&P 500, investors found the sector appealing although there is some concern that the industry games its returns (Parmar and Kelly 2019). They buy up all manner of businesses with borrowed money, cut costs with ruthless layoffs and contributing to job polarization (Olsson and Tåg 2017). They sell company assets, especially the valuable real estate of retailers. They buy to extract value and then sell the acquired firms off, often saddled with large debts. Elizabeth Warren has likened them to vampires.

While collateralized debt obligations and credit default swaps may be new, in their essence they would not have seemed strange to Marx who wrote: "With the development of interest-bearing capital and the credit system, all capital seems to double itself, and sometimes treble itself, by the various modes in which the same capital, or perhaps even the same claim on a debt, appears in different forms in different hands. The greater portion of this 'money-capital' is purely fictitious."[10] The sudden repricing of assets used in overnight repurchase agreements are well reflected in Marx's description of sudden collapse of price "acting like a feather which when added to the weight of the scales, suffices to tip the oscillating balance definitely."[11] This is certainly not a bad portrayal of more recent events, and surely the key point Marx makes is about fictitious capital – that claims to future income need not, or as the bubble inflates which lead to the crisis certainly are not, related to any productive activity.

Looking at the problems of financialization as an accumulation strategy Wolfgang Streeck sees three stages, each of which worked for perhaps a decade before the contradictions it produced grew to dangerous proportions. These are inflation in the 1970s that gave the illusion of working people being better off – until they became wise to money illusion (the reality that higher monetary wages did not mean a higher standard of living because price increases

---

10   See Marx (1971[1894]) chapter 29.
11   *Ibid.*

were robbing their dollars of purchasing power). The second was the use of increased public debt to pay for growth. It reached its limits, governments having to abandon expanding the public sector and adopt austerity measures. The third was private debt, increased borrowing to finance more spending and maintain standards of living that also reached its limits as the debt burden became too great. Growth from privatized Keynesianism was thought to be a good thing since the economy expanded and such lending by financial institutions was after all a market phenomenon, albeit one allowed and encouraged by government policy. But debt fed asset speculation and produced bubbles as has been discussed. Each of these deterrents bought time hiding the secular stagnation that followed the end of the postwar growth spurt.

Streeck sees the exhaustion of the stratagems after each temporarily expedient revived the system producing the very serious legitimation crisis the system now faces. He writes, "What I feel sure about is that the clock is ticking for democracy as we have come to know it." Streeck further raises what "must remain an open question ... whether the clock is also ticking for capitalism." Neoliberalism, austerity, privatization, and growing inequality take a toll on the legitimation capitalism needs to sustain its ideological hegemony. This in turn raises the alternative of a capitalism without democracy, "or at least the capitalism we know" (Streeck 2017, 5 and 173). Using existing policy measures there is a serious problem. The system needs to create more debt to fuel growth. But interest rates can hardly be lowered below zero and a great deal of bad dept is present in almost all economies, very much including Market-Leninist China. The size and fragility of the debt leads to calls for its reduction. This would be a disaster since aggregate demand would fall, unemployment and corporate bankruptcies would rise and a new and possibly even more severe financial crisis would result. As a result, central banks, in the case of the United States the Federal Reserve System, must buy trillions of dollars of the paper of firms to hold up the value of their remaining obligations. The market no longer determines value, for if it did valuations would collapse bringing on another great depression.

In such an economy the "old call on governments to reduce debt and to back down in favor of companies is now more than obsolete; it is outright stupid," Heiner Flassbeck and Paul Steinhardt (2018, 77) write. They conclude in somewhat apocalyptical terms, although if the road were to be taken they are not wrong, that persisting with the existing regime of accumulation puts the capitalist system "on a direct road to collapse worldwide."[12] In agreeing with these analysts, one can suggest that mainstream economists need to rethink

---

12   Flassbeck is the Director of the Division on Globalization and Development Strategies of the United Nations Conference on Trade and Development (UNCTAD). He is the principal

their methodology and models and what amounts to their "delusional ideologies," a term these authors apply to political systems, but might be applied to now dominant, but increasingly contested schools of economic policy thinking as well. It the failure of the analysis and policy advice they offer that has brought us not only to the pain of the, what is called, Great Recession in the U.S. and elsewhere the Global Financial Crisis. With COVID-19 shutdowns years of stagnant working-class income threaten politics of an order not seen since the 1920s and 1930s in Europe.

3   Bonapartism Is One Response to the Crisis of 21st Century Capitalism

Donald Trump's promise to Make America Great Again resonated with many who had lost faith in establishment politicians. Karl Marx had thoughts on the character of the times in which such a figure rises to prominence. In the preface to the second edition of *The Eighteenth Brumaire of Louis Napoleon* he explained that his short book was written to demonstrate how the class struggle in France created circumstances and relationships "that made it possible for a grotesque mediocrity to play a hero's part." Marx described the vast economic and social upheavals that Europe was undergoing in the middle of the 19th Century – the rapid technological changes, population movements, dislocations, and the misery they created for the masses – and the undemocratic character of governments unable to deal with these developments in a manner citizen found acceptable.

Marx is helpful in his insight that extreme turbulence can bring an unlikely personality to the top. In a time when what is thought of as normal politics loses legitimacy, the dominant fractions of the ruling class are forced to accede to such a figure. Marx describes Bonapartism as a popular form of government by personal rule that can occur when the system cannot reproduce itself on a sustained basis, resulting in a stalemate with "the capitalist class too divided, and the working class too disorganized to instruct or inform the government. The result was a degree of relative state autonomy, one expressing, even as it masked, a deadlock between social classes."[13] In this regard, the specifics of

---

author and the leader of the team preparing UNCTAD's Trade and Development Report, a source Marx would no doubt refer to extensively were in writing in the present period. It is a most radical and useful document in its current incarnation.

13   Karl Marx, *The Eighteenth Brumaire of Louis Bonaparte*, https://www.marxists.org/arch ive/marx/works/1852/18th-brumaire/.

Louis-Napoléon Bonaparte himself are not without interest. The events leading to his coup d'état in 1851 may sound familiar, as is his promise to bring back the good old days of "order" and "prosperity". This Bonaparte determined to free himself from dependence on the Party of Order, which had won the parliamentary elections of May 1849. He imposed censorship and harsh repressive measures against opponents and appointed a cabinet consisting of men dependent on him and not the parties in the National Assembly. Barred by the Constitution and Parliament from running for a second term he organized a *coup d'état* assuming the throne on December 2, 1852. As Napoleon III he travelled the country, rallying an enthusiastic following. He used the disfranchisement of 3,000,000 electors by the National Assembly in 1850 and an economic recession in 1851 as pretext for harsh denunciation of traditional parties and to present himself as the "strong man" who could save the country from the danger of a nonexistent revolution.[14] This Bonaparte was deposed after he made some bad decisions, the nature of which need not concern us here. That Trump was not reelected may bring some comfort, but the factors that led to his Electoral College victory in 2016 have not been overcome (at this writing it is not clear whether Trump will run again in 2024).

Writing of the parallels in style and substance between Donald Trump and leaders such as Vladimir Putin, Modi, Erdoğan and Viktor Orbán, Rana Dasgupta points to the waning of the nation state, "its inability to withstand countervailing 21st-Century forces, and its calamitous loss of influence over human circumstance." National political authority is in decline and, "since we do not know any other sort, it feels like the end of the world. This is why a strange brand of apocalyptic nationalism is so widely in vogue." It is a reassertion of sovereignty of those seen as belonging to the nation against enemies defined by a supreme leader. This explains "the current appeal of machismo as political style, the wall-building and xenophobia, the mythology and race theory, the fantastical promises of national restoration – these are not cures but symptoms" (Dasgupta 2018). The cause of the rise of such men is the social structure of accumulation of 21st Century globalized neoliberal capitalism, not the venality and stupidity of centrist politicians who knew no better than to provide what transnational capital and international finance demanded of them. They may be to a significant extent venal and stupid in terms of the contradictions of the system their policies made worse engendering both a legitimation crisis and in the short-sighted rush to discipline labor and redistribute wealth to the 1% produce conditions that slow growth and invite new crises. The economic insecurity created leads to scapegoating, as it did in the

---

14   https://www.britannica.com/biography/Napoleon-III-emperor-of-France.

1920s and 1930s in Nazi Germany where defeat in World War I and the economic crisis that followed could be blamed on Jews and claims of racial superiority could be used by Hitler to achieve power.

As in the 1930s, a weakened capitalist class finds it must make deals with such figures. Rather than focus on parallels between the weaknesses of capitalism that produced the Great Depression and the present moment this essay now turns to how the successful developments of the forces of production and those nascent in the contemporary period point to a prediction Marx made which has been for the most part ignored, but that comes into its own in the contemporary period when we ask why so many people are angry and why 21st Century capitalism has disappointed so many.

4   The Knowledge Commons

In addition to explaining capitalism's tendency to the greater monopolization in the economy, the concentration and centralization of capital as he phrased it, Marx made the remarkable forecast that labor time would cease to be the measure of value as he and other Classical Economists assumed in their models of the capitalism of their time. That social knowledge was captured by capitalists in the 21st Century has so extensively meant humanity's potential is held back by the social relations of production, of the class monopoly of ownership and control within the 1%. For Klaus Schwab (2016), founder and Executive Chairman of the World Economic Forum and the Davos elite a natural evolution of capitalism, one they will benefit from and control, was anticipated by Marx.

In 2012, five years after the financial collapse Schwab at that group's annual gathering declared: "Capitalism, in its current form, no longer fits the world around us." Such a remark brings to mind Terry Eagleton's *bon mot*, "Whenever you hear capitalists talking about capitalism, you know the system is in trouble." But by the 2016 Forum, the conference theme was "Mastering the Fourth Industrial Revolution." Such a revolution in technology impacting many areas of importance is not implausible, but whether if one occurs it would in some automatic fashion create an economic future that will satisfy an angry and divided electorate would remain to be seen. The logic seemed credible. Keynes for example in a 1930 lecture, "The Economic Possibilities for Our Grandchildren," worried about technological unemployment, a phrase that has been invoked much of late, and predicted that in the future, around 2030 he estimated, the production problem would be solved and there would be enough for everyone. Machines (robots, he thought) would cause technological unemployment and jobs might be scarce. The problem would no longer be scarcity, but how to use abundance. Such a hope is what might be called structurally naïve. And it is here Marx should not be far from people's thinking about class appropriation of the surplus created.

Capitalism as a revolutionary economic system was celebrated by Marx, (even as he condemned its "drinking blood from the skulls of its victims") and called for a workers' revolution so that the potential the system had created could be appropriated by the working class for the working class (Tabb 1999). At a future stage of its development, Marx thought, its "powerful effectiveness" would become "out of all proportion to the direct labor time spent in production but depends rather on the general state of science and the progress of technology or the application of science to production" (1971[1857], 706). This is an idea we hear echoed by students of 21st Century associative intelligence. The stage at which Marx thought "labor comes to relate more as watchman and regulator of the production process" and at last the prospect of "the artistic, scientific, etc., development of the individuals in the time set free, and with the means created, for all of them" (1971[1857], 704–6). When this happens the contradictions of capitalist social relations act to inhibit rather than promote development and become a fetter on subsequent human potential.

With the liberation of social knowledge in the hands of a socialist society as a goal, we can ask if we have now reached the "Keynes point," where "indeed enough is produced by the economy, both physical and virtual, for all of us," (1971[1857], 704–6) (or more accurately could be produced if it were not for the realization problem that would arise if potential output were attempted under existing class relations) if not yet the flowering of the expected "Marx moment," when the workers of the world aware of what is holding back the dawn of human freedom the conditions for which capitalism has created, a different struggle in the political sphere arises over the control of the means of production and the application of social knowledge, the shared inheritance of humanity that is being enclosed by capital.

Marx argued that at such a point the revolutionary potential of capitalism goes unrealized because of the social relations of capitalism (Tabb 1999). To put this in terms relevant to the discussion today, monopolists want to appropriate rents in production based on social knowledge, to enclose the scientific commons, selling things that can be produced at low or zero marginal costs at high prices and limit access to them and extending free services in exchange for valuable personal data. The design of algorithms to maximize profit in dishonest applications have been shown to be surprisingly common.

The ownership of 21st Century means of production allows owners of social knowledge to employ fewer people than the giants of the 20th Century so that more workers are crowded into low paying tasks not only in the gig economy, but most jobs come to resemble non-traditional work that lacks good pay and benefits. Using data from the Well-Being and Basic Needs Survey to examine changes in material hardship between 2017 and 2018 in contrast to the rise in the stock market to gauge the success of the U.S. economy, Michael Karpman, Stephen Zuckerman and Dulce Gonzalez (2019) find that, despite what was seen as a strong labor market there was only modest progress in families' ability to meet basic needs. Nearly 4 in 10 nonelderly American adults reported that in 2018, their families "had trouble paying or were unable to pay for housing, utilities, food, or medical care at some point during the year." While the official unemployment rate reached a 50-year low level, the purchasing power of the average wage was only beginning to show any advance after decades of stagnation. There was a persistently high rates of hardship among adults in low-income families, including "unexpected income losses, inadequate savings, household members with disabilities, lack of health insurance, and high housing costs relative to income." Such findings offered a depressing picture of a record long "recovery" that had favored the few and not the many. The class power of capital that controls the way technologies are deployed are weapons in the class struggle.

Those who are hired for a task on a platform to walk dogs or park cars for busy more affluent people accept compensation that reveals two aspects of contemporary American capitalism, its extreme income inequality that makes these deals as common as they are and it reveals the fetishism of commodities, exchange between individuals in which one is able to exploit another without this being necessarily apparent. The two aspects are of course closely related. Capitalism as a system of exploitation and class division has always allowed the rich to have servants. Technology enables the merely better-off to buy the service of servants on a piecemeal basis through the intermediation of the platform firm. Upper middle-income persons can receive services from those who are forced by economic circumstance to do this poorly rewarded work. Their time has little market value because of the way the society organizes and rewards participants in the economy. The app makes these new forms of exploitation possible in a context in which labor as a class has lost strength. The interface companies profit from this situation.

Such realities lead us to ask: When placing hope for a better future on technology we need to further ask, would breakthrough technologies be patented property of a small elite? Would it create good jobs providing a comfortable livelihood? Would the Fourth Industrial Revolution be purposed for the good of all by the private sector, as Schwab's reformed capitalism presumed? The broad question of ownership of the future is one to which we will return. It is one on which Marx's answer was unequivocal. Under capitalism the exploit-ing class claimed ownership of the political economy. The class struggle would determine the future. If present social relations continue to hold it will be a relatively small number of firms and their major stockholders who will benefit. They will own the future unless a new wave of popular mobilization demands economic democracy and public decision making as to the uses of social knowledge.

While others place their faith in technology to provide abundance, Zac Tate writes (on the website of the World Economic Forum) regarding "the fun-damental challenge" presented by the sense of injustice most people in the advanced economies feel in reaction to bank bailouts, years of austerity, cor-porate scandals, and that "the growing awareness in the rich world that most of the benefits of technology and globalization flow to people who own investible capital and to the well-educated," while the costs are "borne by unskilled work-ers, local producers and people who have little property and savings," suggests that the problem "is not capitalism itself. Instead, the issue lies with policies that extended the role of the free market beyond sensible limits" (Tate 2017). In his view, a view many of the elite's thinkers have concluded, the rawer forms of capitalism are unsustainable. "[I]f too many people do not have capital," restoring faith in the system requires "making amends," and rethinking how capitalism "not only creates but distributes value." That is, capitalism's apolo-gists who take this viewpoint are hardly advocating a workers' commonwealth where capital is owned by the workers themselves. The viewpoint is rather, beyond immediate maximization of profits, stability of their control in the face of a legitimacy crisis requires thinking about what concessions granted from the top will diminish opposition and prevent the maturing of the class consciousness of those they oppress and exploit.

The imperative to maximize profit at all cost is producing too many wasteful commodities whose manufacture is absorbing too many resources and adding mightily to global warming while creating the asset bubbles discussed. It has led to the rise of the angry hard right as it sees the base of the Democratic Party moving left and formerly marginalized groups gaining standing in the society. The white nationalism that has driven the rise of Trump and other anti-globalization nationalisms that have grown strong elsewhere is rejecting liberal democracy. This is a concern widely shared among elite reformers. It is behind calls for guaranteed income plans to support losers (and subsidize employers of low wage workers). These proposals often include a guaranteed income replacing other social spending and paid for by more borrowing and out of general revenues, not new taxes on the wealthy and transnational capi-tal and finance in the face of a presumed coming robot apocalypse, labor being replaced on a large scale by artificial intelligence – a thing to be widely feared in a capitalist system as the great increase in the unhappy reserve army of the unemployed had political implications.

But analytically the reason for the increase in inequality has been the market power and increasing returns to size that are characteristic of the most profitable parts of the economy. Most of this is based on the appropriation of technologies developed in universities, by workers trained at public expense and much of it under government funded research. A successful business model that takes off and reaching critical mass the combination of first mover and network effects that allows for the exercise of market power buying out potential competitors or crushing them with unfair and often illegal business practices. The implications of the way this economy now functions are less hidden but there is still not a broad awareness of causes and consequences.

It may help to know that "No social order ever perishes before all the productive forces for which there is room in it have developed; and new, higher relations of production never appear before the material conditions of their existence have matured in the womb of the old society itself," as Marx wrote and that therefore "mankind always sets itself only such tasks as it can solve; since, looking at the matter more closely, it will always be found that the tasks itself arises only when the material conditions of its solution already exist or are at least in the process of formation."[15] The argument here is that the material basis to solve today's problems are available. The increased powers that capitalism has produced can be repurposed for a socialist transition, one in which socialization of production grows within the framework of a transforming capitalism. Knowing what is needed and worth fighting for requires judgments of how to be both red and expert, so to speak, to judge which reforms satisfy movements for basic change, non-reformist reforms. We shall suggest a focus on two areas that in addition to the workers' struggles for a greater share of what they produce: on the financialization of 21st Century capitalism and on the climate emergency taking on board the prospect of the social appropriation of science and of technological developments.

Joseph Schumpeter, one of Marx's important interlocutors, is best known for his concept of "creative destruction," the idea that capitalism grows through a process in which innovation destroys the value of existing companies by introducing better ways of producing goods and services and developing new and better products that replace existing ones. The older companies seem well-protected, but the innovation is radically different, a major improvement,

---

15   In his Preface *A Contribution to the Critique of Political Economy*.

and so shakes up and undermines the old methods, products, and companies. The railroad replaces the wagon and the pony express for shipping goods and delivering the mail across great distances, latter music downloads displace CDs which had replaced taped sources that made vinyl records history in wide usage. Creative destruction is the dynamo that makes capitalism grow, not perfect competition as other economists maintained (see Schumpeter 1942, Chapter 7). We might think of the capacities of artificial intelligence, 5G networks and other major developments in such terms.

Schumpeter's explanation of how major breakthroughs destroy the value of existing companies and stimulate the long-term growth of capitalism is found in his 1942 book, *Socialism, Capitalism and Democracy*. Its great theme that goes undiscussed is that the success of capitalism creates fewer larger corporations that control technology and markets. This would seem to be today's inescapable conventional wisdom; market power is excessive. Schumpeter's next logical step in this work is generally ignored. An intellectual climate, its author believed, will develop in which creation of a better welfare state would be demanded by serious analysts making a critique of capitalism and the crises it produces. A popular understanding would develop that uncontrolled markets and private property in production had to be superseded.

Schumpeter did not prefer socialism. He did however predict capitalism's demise saying, "If a doctor predicts that his patient will die presently this does not mean that he desires it" (1942, 61). He thought a planned economy along Soviet lines incompatible with democracy. The question was: how can socialism and democracy be made compatible? That, Schumpeter wrote, depends on what we mean by socialism and what we mean by democracy.[16] This aspect of Schumpeter's thinking comes back to prominence in the contemporary period when it is possible to envision shared plenty even as there is widely fear of intensified scarcity due to the impacts of climate change and as the destructive contradictions of capitalism have ripened pushing so many workers into low-paid marginal and insecure jobs. Capitalism stands athwart human progress saying, "no looking beyond this point of technocratic necessity" and "no trespassing" on the terrain of surveillance capitalism (Zuboff 2019). This is historically regressive. While Marx, Engels and others were overly optimistic about the revolution that would expropriate the expropriators today the contradictions of the system have reached new heights. Politically there is reliance

---

16   There is also a rather strange discussion in the literature over whether Schumpeter was a Marxist. This too, like most such discourse is a question of definition, in this case what it means to be a Marxist and their shared approach to technology. For this such essays are not without interest. See Rosenberg (2011); Lazonick (2011); and Kurz (2013).

on Bonapartist figures because establishment politicians and incremental progress have been exposed as shilling for a system than fails the working class that has grown poorer in proportion to the enrichment of the capitalists is producing movements for change, the potential of which Marx would celebrate.

History, as Marx and Engels (1846) wrote is "nothing but the succession of the separate generations, each of which exploits the materials, the capital funds, the productive forces handed down to it by all preceding generations, and thus, on the one hand, continues the traditional activity in completely changed circumstances and, on the other, modifies the old circumstances with a completely changed activity." Like them, although starting from a position temporally removed from theirs, we can see an economy capable of producing abundance for all being impeded from doing so by the social relations of production. This is a position that has gained support from economists including W. Brian Arthur, credited with developing the modern approach to increasing returns who writes on the relation of complexity theory, technology, and financial markets. In his view the economy has arrived at a point where it produces enough in principle for everyone, but where the means of access to these services, products, and jobs is "steadily tightening. This new period we are entering is not so much about production anymore – how much is produced; it is about distribution – how people get a share in what is produced." Without overtly entering the realm of specific policy advocacy it is clear to him that "[e]verything from trade policies to government projects to commercial regulations will in the future be evaluated by distribution. Politics will change, free-market beliefs will change, social structures will change." He sees us at the start of this historic shift.

In Marx's political economy perspective, the context of ownership claims, choices of goals, and intentions in which political decisions are made are uppermost. The virtual economy is not just an Internet of Things, it is a source of intelligent action external to human workers Intelligence no longer housed internally in the brains of human workers has moved into the virtual economy, into the conversation among artificial intelligence algorithms (Marx and Engels, 1846). As the associative intelligence is privatized it more closely controls workers on the job, monitoring and coercing their actions in the factory, the warehouse and in the office. The power capital wields further diminishes democratic practice to a shadow of even its present diminished form. It need not be this way. Revolutionary innovation in social knowledge can also empower people if it is not captured and enclosed by a privatization from which owners can extract rents from users. The opportunities it offers can move what had been limited and private into the realm of the commons, providing greater returns widely shared.

5   Glimpsing the Realm of Freedom

The underutilization of social knowledge, its enclosure and enforced scarcity, is now slowing human development and promoting illiberal democracies and undemocratic capitalisms. The consequences of the further development of contradictions between human potential and the actuality of austerity and unnecessary suffering depend on what citizens as active agents of their own history do and fail to do. The easiest, laziest choice is to attempt to muddle through under centrist leaders offering bromides of stability something most voters are no longer inclined to do. New breakthroughs with broad application could create opportunities that would absorb surplus capital in other ways, a point Baran and Sweezy stress. Surplus can be absorbed by a Green New Deal, an immense and necessary undertaking that could play the role of other waves of innovation that can offset stagnation in the past in the United States. As, the automobile made suburbanization possible with its construction boom and sale of white goods and was a major consumer of steel, rubber, glass and other sectors, every new breakthrough of such significance reshapes society and its politics testing the confines of the norms and accommodations of its existing institutions.

We live in the age of the fast-moving Anthracene in which "production" is destroying the planet as we have known it. Geological time has been dangerously speeded up and this latest stage great acceleration challenges the optimism of such socio-economic understanding. While Marx's circular flows reproduction schemes do not deal with nature and the environment (Burkett 2004), Marx himself was greatly concerned with such issues and drew on wide relevant literatures in developing what had until this century been an important, overlooked aspect of his work.[17] Today, viable social and economic reproduction very much centers on environmental limits (see the chapter in this book by Vishwas Satgar). It is also central to thinking about the next social structure of accumulation, and macroeconomic policy, finance and a host of other issues, some of which have been the concern of this essay. While it is a longer argument, proposals for a Green New Deal that would create good jobs and redeploy the social surplus to meet the climate emergency would solve two problems. One is the obvious environmental collapse that faces us. The other is addressing the overaccumulation of capital, the cycles of debt creating and excessive risk taking that produces financial collapse.

---

17   The Marxist who has done most to explore Marx's research on nature and the environment and its relation to his economic analysis of capitalism has written numerous books and articles. See Foster (2000); Foster (2020) and everything he has written in between.

It is the democratic socialists that have the potential to challenge the centrist Democrats and Republicans on capitalism and democracy going together, that capitalism supported individual freedom, and so on. They gain a hearing to the extent that Americans increasingly have learned to dislike and even hate the oil companies, the pharmaceutical giants, the insurance companies, the banks. Today's capitalist paragons seem to many criminal enterprises that extort customers and oppress workers and liberals in Washington have been hesitant to take on these powerful interests. But as socialists in the extended present are being created by awareness of the workings of actually existing capitalism, they are more open to a system critique and their numbers are growing. "These days you can't swing a dead kulak without hitting someone who's really, really into socialism, or at least giving it a longer look," writes Nick Gillespie (2018) in the libertarian publication, *Reason*. He offers the instance of movie star Jim Carrey saying on a major TV network (On *Real Time with Bill Maher*) that "We have to say *yes* to socialism, to the word and everything. ... We have to stop *apologizing*." Gillespie responded, arguing that the market is synonymous with freedom. But when socialists hear "the market" they "think of the anxious parent, desperate not to offend the insurance representative on the phone, lest he decree that the policy she paid for doesn't cover her child's appendectomy," writes Corey Robin (2018) on the opinion page of *The New York Times* no less. The socialist argument against capitalism isn't that it makes us poor, he tells us. "It's that it makes us unfree. When my well-being depends upon your whim, when the basic needs of life compel submission to the market and subjugation at work, we live not in freedom but in domination."

Here too is the echo of Marx who believed "The realm of freedom actually begins only where labour which is determined by necessity and mundane considerations ceases; thus, in the very nature of things it lies beyond the sphere of actual material production." What separates Marx and Engels from other analysts who saw the contradictions of capitalism was that they did not think these could be overcome with reforms but required did not claim only that capitalist development engenders its own contradictions, but also that those contradictions could be overcome only through the "forcible overthrow of all existing social conditions." These start with the enforced division of labor and extent to all realms of social existence.

The promise of the application of social knowledge to production suggests the potential for this to happen. "Freedom in this field can only consist in socialised man, the associated producers, rationally regulating their interchange with Nature, bringing it under their common control, instead of being ruled by it as by the blind forces of Nature; and achieving this with the least expenditure of energy and under conditions most favourable to, and worthy of, their human nature." Earlier Marx saw the "development of human energy, which is an end in itself, the true realm of freedom, which, however, can blossom forth only with this realm of necessity as its basis. The shortening of the working-day is its basic prerequisite."[18] In this well-known passage from the third volume of *Capital*, Marx opposes the "true realm of freedom" to the "realm of necessity" which has produced a lively discussion (see James 2017). The distinction which cannot concern us here is part of a larger discussion interrelated types of freedom that are central to Marx's critique of capitalism and the promise of socialism (Klagge 1986) or as he called it communism (a term that has fallen into disrepute after the Soviet experience, a system much at variance with Marx's goals).

As always with Marx the philosopher the choice of terms and their meaning can be a matter of contestation. The political Marx of the 1875 *Critique of the Gotha Program* tells us more simply that "In the highest phase of communist society, after the enslaving subordination of the individual to the division of labour, and therefore the antithesis between mental and physical labor, has vanished; after labour has become not only a means of life but life's want; after the productive forces have also increased with the all-round development of the individual, and all the springs of co-operative wealth flow more abundantly – only then can the narrow horizon of bourgeois right be crossed in its entirety and society inscribe on its banners: from each according to his ability, to each according to his need."

In our moment, Kate Aronoff, Alyssa Battistoni, Daniel Aldana Cohen, and Theo Riofrancos (2019) write: "For decades, the Right has claimed the language of freedom. But their vision of freedom as your right as an individual to do whatever you want – so long as you can pay for it – is a recipe for disaster in the twenty-first century, when it's clearer than ever that all our fates are bound up together." These writers too make the essential point, "Freedom has to mean something more than the capitalist's freedom to invest or the consumer's freedom to buy." Just as FDR called for freedom from fear, they write that "we also must transform our built environment to grant us freedom from fear of the physical changes that already locked-in global warming will bring: fire and hurricanes, extreme temperatures, sea level rise and storm surges – and freedom from the fear that those dangers will grow exponentially worse." In the appeal to defend the commons we hear a demand for embedding markets in a moral society. The work to save the planet extends to a questioning of claims to intellectual "property" that are an enclosing of the social knowledge commons

---

18   See Marx (1978 [1863–1883]) Volume III, Part VII, Chapter 48.

and the abrogation of responsibility of those who escape taxes and pressure governments as special interests representing companies and industries that invest in politics and politicians to establish rules that violate societal responsibilities and as they greenwash reputations.

The contradictions of financialization of 21st Century capitalism and the impacts of the climate emergency will force dramatic change. The likelihood of more productive outcomes is increased, it has become painfully more obvious if the work of Karl Marx accompanies analyses of contemporary capitalism, both its moral critique and its materialist analysis can inspire and inform today's socialists and the wider penumbra giving socialism and the anti-capitalist critique "a second look." When the god-like director in the 1998 film "The Truman Show" played by Ed Harris explains "we accept the world with which we're presented, it's that simple," the everyman played by Jim Carrey none the less having gotten wise to the falseness of the world that has been created for him learns to fight with all his might to get free. Marx thought capitalism creates a world for us and human freedom begins with understanding (s)he is confined and unfree and takes action to change the human fate.

The realm of freedom lies on the other side of capitalism, after the climate emergency has been addressed due to the struggles of dedicated social movements composed of people who may not call themselves socialists but will find that capitalism stands in their way, its greenwashers and false friends needing to be confronted and their power stripped away so that another world that is possible can be born. The climate emergency must be met by the growth of unalienated human intelligence dedicating all areas of work to changing what is produced, how it is produced and to what ends labor time is devoted.

References

Aronoff, Kate, Alyssa Battistoni, Daniel Aldana Cohen, and Theo Riofrancos (2019) "The Green New Deal's Five Freedoms," *Jacobin*, February 6.

Bruenig, Matt (2019) "Top 1% Up $21 Trillion. Bottom 50% Down $900 Billion," *People's Policy Project*, June 14.

Burkett, Paul (2004) "Marx's Reproduction Schemes and the Environment," *Ecological Economics*, 49(4).

Dasgupta, Rana (2018) "After Decades of Globalisation, Our Political System Has Become Obsolete – and Spasms of Resurgent Nationalism Are a Sign of its Irreversible Decline," *The Guardian*, April 5.

Epstein, Gerald A. (2006) "Introduction: Financialization and the World Economy." In Gerald Epstein, *Financialization and the World Economy*, Northampton: Edward Elgar.

Flassbeck, Heiner and Paul Steinhardt (2018) "Corporate Power and the Self-Destruction of Neoliberalism," *American Affairs*, 11:4 (Winter): 66–78.

Foster, John Bellamy (2000) *Marx's Ecology: Materialism and Nature,* New York: Monthly Review Press.

Foster, John Bellamy (2006) "Monopoly-Finance Capital," *Monthly Review*, 58(7).

Foster, John Bellamy (2020) *The Return of Nature: Socialism and Ecology,* New York: Monthly Review Press.

Gillespie, Nick (2018) "What We Talk About When We Talk About Socialism," *Reason*, September 12.

Haldane, Andrew (2012) "The Doom Loop," *London Review of Books*, 34(4).

Hein, Eckhard (2014) "Post-Keynesian Distribution and Growth Theories II: Kalecki and Stendl," Chapter 5 in Eckhard Hein, *Distribution and Growth after Keynes; A Post-Keynesian Guide*, Northampton: Edward Elgar.

James, David (2017) "The Compatibility of Freedom and Necessity in Marx's Idea of Communist Society," *European Journal of Philosophy*, 25(2).

Karpman, Michael, Stephen Zuckerman and Dulce Gonzalez (2019) "Labor Market Gains in 2018, There Were Only Modest Improvements in Families' Ability to Meet Basic Needs," *Urban Institute*, May 13.

Klagge, James C. (1986) "Marx's Realms of 'Freedom' and 'Necessity'," *Canadian Journal of Philosophy*, 16(4): 769–777.

Konczal, Mike and Nell Abernathy (2015) "Defining Financialization," Roosevelt Institute, https://rooseveltinstitute.org/wp-content/uploads/2020/07/RI-Defining-Financialization-201507.pdf.

Krause, Laurence A. (2018), Marx on Credit, Agency Problems, and Crises, World Economics Association (WEA) Conferences, No. 2, "The 2008 Economic Crisis Ten Years On.".

Krugman, Paul (2005) "The Debt Peonage Society," *New York Times*, March 8.

Kurz, Heinz D. (2013) "Schumpeter and Marx: A Comment on a Debate," *Industrial and Corporate Change*, 22(3).

Lazonick, William (2011) "Comment on Nathan Rosenberg, "Was Schumpeter a Marxist?" *Industrial and Corporate Change*, 20(4).

Magdoff, Harry (1967) "Reviewed Work: Monopoly Capital by Paul A. Baran, Paul M. Sweezy," *Economic Development and Cultural Change*, 16(1).

Magdoff, Harry and Paul M. Sweezy (1987) *Stagnation and the Financial Explosion,* New York: Monthly Review Press.

Mandel, Ernest (1978) "Introduction." In Karl Marx *Capital*, Volume II. London: Penguin Books.

Marx, Karl (1978 [1863–1883]) *Capital* (Volume III), edited by Friedrich Engels, London: Penguin Books.

Marx, Karl (1971[1857]) *Grundrisse, Foundation of the Critique of Political Economy,* London: Penguin Books.

Marx, Karl (1971[1894]) *Capital; A Critique of Political Economy,* Volume III, edited by F. Engels, London: Penguin Books.

Marx, Karl and Friedrich Engels (1846) "The Illusion of an Epoch," *The German Ideology,* https://www.marxists.org/archive/marx/works/1845/german-ideology/cho1b.htm.

Marx, Karl, *The Eighteenth Brumaire of Louis Bonaparte,* https://www.marxists.org/archive/marx/works/1852/18th-brumaire/.

Olsson, Martin and Joacim Tåg (2017) "Private Equity, Layoffs, and Job Polarization," *Journal of Labor Economics,* 35(3).

Orhangazi, Özgür (2011) " 'Financial' vs. 'Real': An Overview of the Contradictory Role and Place of Finance in the Modern Economy," *Research in Political Economy,* 27.

Palladino, Lenore (2018) *Corporate Financialization and Worker Prosperity: A Broken Line,* Roosevelt Institute, https://rooseveltinstitute.org/wp-content/uploads/2020/07/RI-Financialization-Primer-201801.pdf.

Parmar, Hema and Jason Kelly (2019) "The Returns Are Spectacular. But There Are Catches," *Bloomberg Businessweek,* October 7.

Patel, Neha, Lisa Foo and Saum Sutaria (2018) "The Silent Shapers of Healthcare Services," https://www.mckinsey.com/industries/healthcare-systems-and-services/our-insights/the-silent-shapers-of-healthcare-services# .

Robin, Corey (2018) "The New Socialists," *New York Times,* August 24.

Rosenberg, Nathan (2011) "Was Schumpeter a Marxist?" *Industrial and Corporate Change,* 20(4).

Schumpeter, Joseph A. (1942) *Capitalism, Socialism and Democracy,* New York: Harper & Brothers.

Schwab, Klaus (2016) *The Fourth Industrial Revolution,* Geneva: World Economic Forum.

Semuels, Alana (2019) "When Wall Street Is Your Landlord," *The Atlantic,* February 13.

Stockhammer, Engelbert (2004) "Financialization and the Slowdown of Accumulation," *Cambridge Journal of Economics,* 28(5).

Streeck, Wolfgang (2017) *Buying Time: The Delayed Crisis of Democratic Capitalism,* Second Edition, New York: Verso.

Sweezy, Paul and Paul Baran (1966) *Monopoly Capital: An Essay on the American Economic and Social Order,* New York: Monthly Review Press.

Sweezy, Paul M. (1994) "The Triumph of Finance Capital," *Monthly Review,* 46(2).

Tabb, William K. (1999) "Marx and the Long Run," in William K. Tabb, *Reconstructing Political Economy: The Great Divide in Economic Thought,* New York: Routledge.

Tabb, William K. (2012) *The Restructuring of Capitalism in Our Time,* New York: Columbia University Press.

Tabb, William K. (2022) "Financialization, A Key Contradiction of the Neoliberal Social Structure of Accumulation," in Terrence McDonough, David M. Kotz and

Cian McMahon (eds.) *Handbook of Social Structure of Accumulation Theory,* London: Edward Elgar.

Tate, Zac (2017) "What Democrats Can Learn from the Democratic Socialists About Rebuilding the Left," www.weforum.org/, November 16.

Van der Zwan, Natascha (2014) Making Sense of Financialization. *Socio-Economic Review*, 12(1).

Whalen, Charles J. (1999) "Hyman Minsky's Theory of Capitalist Development," Working Paper No 277, Levy Economics Institute, http://www.levyinstitute.org/pubs/wp277.pdf.

Zuboff, Shoshana (2019) *The Age of Surveillance Capitalism: The Fight for a Human Future at the Frontier of Power,* New York: Public Affairs.

PART 1

Marx's Political Economy for the Present

∵

From Marxist Political Economy to Financialization or Is It the Other Way About?

Ben Fine

1   Introduction[1]

So penetrating is Marx's analysis of capitalist production in Volume I of *Capital* that it is easily overlooked that its subtitle is *Critique of Political Economy*. In this vein, this chapter seeks to make a contribution to the understanding of financialization, a concept that has become increasingly prominent over the last two decades. Whilst there have been significant analyses of financialization from within the Marxist tradition, and even sharp disputes,[2] the greater weight of literature derives from non-Marxist schools of heterodox economics, as well as from other social science disciplines addressing the topic from their own concerns.

As a result, in the next section, I seek to assess not only the contribution made by political economy (and more) to the understanding of financialization but also to tease out the sorts of questions that still need to be resolved. In section 3, I address these questions by deploying Marxist political economy, thereby seeking to provide a framework through which the role of financialization, both within political economy and in contemporary capitalism, can be critically assessed.

2   From Fuzz and Buzz ...

The "financialization"[3] literature has a number of key characteristics that I will first delineate. First, it is a concept that has exploded across the social sciences.

---

1   This contribution is based upon Fine (2018).

2   For my own engagement in these, see Fine (2010a and 2014) and Christophers and Fine (2020).

3   Put here for the first and last time in inverted commas to indicate that the term is a real phenomenon reflected in varieties of conceptualisations that are more or less, and variously, attached to that reality. The different uses in what follows should be clear.

Although it was in use prior to the Global Financial Crisis, GFC, its popularity
has since soared in analytical discourses even if with a lesser presence in popular and political discourses. The latter may reflect the extent to which the
term is currently owned by progressive and critical stances. It has meant that
financialization has become a buzzword and fuzzword.[4] What is meant by this
is that its use has become commonplace at least within its received circles (the
buzz) but, in doing so, the concept has been victim to multiple, potentially
inconsistent and incoherent collective meanings (the fuzz). Now, clearly buzz
and fuzz have some pejorative connotations, but this does not mean that correspondingly endowed concepts should be rejected. Without offering justification here, I like imperialism, neoliberalism, globalization and financialization
primarily because the buzz and fuzz shift scholarship and potentially ideology
and practice in progressive directions although this is a matter of judgement.
By the same token I dislike social capital, modernization and almost anything
that comes out of, or is promoted or appropriated by, World Bank speak. The
reason for my support for financialization in particular is that it captures the
distinctive nature of contemporary capitalism, or neoliberalism, a theme to be
taken up later from the perspective of Marxist political economy.

Second, by the same token, finnbuzz and finnfuzz have been common
across all of the social sciences,[5] if unevenly by timing, extent and focus, but
also with the notable exception of mainstream economics where it is essentially precluded by some combination of its commitment to methodological
individualism and its corresponding incapacity for genuinely systemic analysis. This explosion across the social sciences is a reflection of Epstein's (2005,
p. 3) early, ever-cited and all-encompassing definition as "the increasing role
of financial motives, markets, actors and institutions in the operation of the
domestic and international economies." Motives, markets, actors and institutions, plus domestic and international economies – I am not sure this leaves
out anything, and is an open invitation for different topics, methods, concep-
tualizations, and theories, let alone open season on what might be termed "follow the money" or "financialization is as financialization does". As Davis (2017,
p. 1333/4) puts it in her survey of the finnvestment nexus:

> first, important to recognize that the definition of financialisation
> remains nebulous and often varies substantially across papers. This vari-
> ance in definition has both advantages and disadvantages. On the one

---

4 See especially Cornwall and Eade (eds.) (2010).
5 I will use finnX to denote the coupling of financialization with the factor X, where X itself
   may be a readily identifiable acronym – and finn itself will stand for financialization.

hand, financialisation summarizes a broad, wide-reaching process of structural change, and there is no a priori reason to expect all aspects of this phenomenon affect investment analogously. A range of empirical indicators, thus, has the advantage of capturing different aspects of financialisation. On the other hand, the term 'financialisation' is often applied differentially across analyses despite an often-implicit pretense that the same phenomenon is analysed. As such, it is increasingly unclear what is meant when one concludes that 'financialisation' does or does not depress investment. More specifically, within countries different empirical measures are used to draw different conclusions about financialisation and investment, without clear reference to distinctions between the indicators used. Across countries, conclusions from one country – for example, regarding shareholder ideology in the USA – are sometimes also applied to other countries despite vastly different institutional settings. One contribution of this survey is, thus, a delineation of distinctions between studies that claim to otherwise study the same thing: 'financialisation' and investment.

Much the same is true across a much broader canvas, with Epstein's definition far from innocent in having spread its reach across the weight, presence, forms, and impact of finance, precisely in a world where its reach has expanded both intensively and extensively – the fuzz and buzz have some purchase on realism.

Third, then, the finn literature, finnlit, has been extraordinarily rich and wide-ranging – far beyond the finnvestment nexus – especially in empirically identifying the role played by finn, so much so that we already have surveys, dividing it into categories, spanning the functioning of the economy in each and every one of its aspects to each and every aspect of everyday life.[6] Studies along the lines of the more the presence of finance the more the impact on variable X, finnX studies, are legion.[7] On the basis of Epstein's definition we now know an enormous amount about finn. This has a number of implications from the grand narrative and posture to the multiplicities of the more mundane.

For, fourth, one theme of the finnlit, rarely a focus but occasionally subject to passing commentary, is to relate finn to the contemporary nature of capitalism. Does it signify a cyclical movement or a break with the past and, if the

---

6   For most recent overview, see Mader et al. (eds.) (2020).
7   See also Powell (2018, p. 14) observing that, "in the growing diversity of the literature there comes the risk that financialization will become a meaningless term ('take x, add finance'), used more to obfuscate than to illuminate."

latter, does it indeed represent a new, financialised stage, and how does this relate to neoliberalism (if this is itself a legitimate category beyond its own fuzz and buzz). Such commentary, though, tends to be dominated by reducing finncapitalism to a marrying of more influence from finance with erstwhile understandings that originate within the post-war boom, generally designated as Keynesianism[8] – so we have post Keynesianism with finn, finnPK, and similarly with Varieties of Capitalism, the Developmental State Paradigm, the Developing and Emerging Economies, the Social Compacting Paradigm, the Welfare Regime Approach, ie finnVoC, finnDSP, finnDEE, finnSCP, finnWRA,[9] respectively, and so on such as shareholder capitalism, and including finno, the contribution from mainstream economics as well as finnull (that the notion of finn is to be rejected altogether because of finnbuzz and finnfuzz or because it is not historically unprecedented).[10] Far more common, though, than finncapitalism, as already indicated are finnX studies with X as variable not world view or theoretical predisposition.

Fifth, then, such endeavors have not only added to our empirical knowledge but have, in doing so, led to the one certainty that finn matters, but it does so across both a wide range of economic and social phenomena and unevenly by time, place and sector. Overviews of the proliferation of corresponding empirical investigations have increasingly come to emphasize how differentiated is the nature of finn and its effects, what has been appropriately termed variegation, Brown et al. (2017). Accordingly, Karwowski et al. (2016, p. 18) propose "a variegated financialisation approach:"[11]

---

8   As should be apparent, Keynesianism is a misnomer for the post-war boom from the perspective of the restructuring of capital, for which much more and more important is involved than demand management – such as internationalisation of capital across all its forms, as well as state intervention in industrial policy, etc., including key roles played through nationalised industries and promotion of health, education and welfare.

9   For critique of the inability of these paradigms to deal with, occasionally even to address finn, see Fine (2016). See also Ward et al. (2018) and Ashman and Fine (2013) for critique of finnVoC, and Fine and Pollen (2018) and Fine (2020) for finndevt. Note also, with exception of the now discredited microfinance, finn and the social capital paradigm have never intersected in light of the neglect of the rich and the powerful in its paradigm, Fine (2010b) even though finance is arguably the single major source of "social capital", apart possibly from the state which is equally subject to neglect, so wedded is the social capital paradigm to civil society for the many as opposed to (conflict with) the power of the few.

10   For finnull, see Michell and Toporowski (2014) and Christophers (2015a and b), and responses to him. Note, though, that, despite being a substantive critic, Christophers (2018) finds it convenient to deploy the term in his account of land privatisation in the UK! See Fasianos et al. (2018) for the historical comings and goings of finn.

11   See also Karwowski and Stockhammer (2016) for similar for emerging economies. Perversely, although they write of such variegation primarily from a post Keynesian

financialisation is not a single process that occurs across all economic sectors simultaneously. Rather sectoral financialisation processes are distinct and relatively independent. They proceed for different reasons and, potentially, with different effects. The financialisation of households, businesses and the financial sector has distinct causes. Moreover, these sectoral financialisation processes can have effects on the economy as a whole that work in opposite directions. The financialisation of non-financial firms has been found to dampen investment expenditure … whereas households' financialisation is likely to increase consumption financed by credit. While the former phenomenon has a negative effect on aggregate demand, the latter has a positive one.

Thus, more broadly and in historical vein, finn has been associated with the wide-ranging dysfunction, not only of the financial system itself but also through its multifarious effects, especially rising and dramatic reversal of trends in inequalities, in income and wealth, in social provisioning from pensions to housing, and through volatilities in particular markets such as food and energy.[12] Yet, such dysfunction is far from even and universal.

Sixth, such conundrums can only be resolved with application of theory as the means with which to address them. Initially observe finnlit is no longer in its infancy. After all, it cannot be both fuzz and buzz, and have taught us so much empirically, be subject to survey articles, and been around for nearly two decades, and still claim to be novel even though, of course, it does move onto pastures new, partly as a result of finance's own expanding reach as well as the greater or lesser lethargy with which different disciplines and topics have taken it up. More generally, new concepts do tend to have some degree of common trajectory, with both strengths and weaknesses and their own peculiarities depending upon both their subject matter and their context. The starting

---

perspective, that approach has tended to reduce finn to crushing countries into (the more numerous) wage-led and (less numerous) profit-led regimes with correspondingly bad and good results as a consequence of finn (for effects on aggregate demand and more). For the notion of variegated social reproduction, more on which later, see Bakker and Gill (2019).

12 Note that such volatilities are not confined to the markets but, with neoliberal's rolling back of progressive institutional representation, and its rolling out of more centralised and authoritarian forms of governance in part in conformity to financialization, political and ideological life has also become more volatile, especially in terms of the squeezing of traditional forms of participating, and dissenting, and the greater influence of (social) media in electoral campaigning. This all tends to favour the right if not uniformly so, see Boffo et al. (2018).

point is almost always what I have already designated as finnX ... here is some research I have done before but I can publish it again with refurbishment and finn added, I get a REFable[13] if I am lucky and even a major research grant. The next stages can be to complain about this, to decry the new concept, to defend it, to deplore that it has overlooked particular aspects (gender, and possibly race, usually to the fore here, if not so much in case of finn, for finngender[14] has been remarkably muted other than for, or even within, consideration of poverty and the household, despite healthy literatures on finnclusion, finndebtedness, even finnsterity although, perversely, feminist macro is alive and well). And, eventually, we get to the point where it is acknowledged that there is need for theoretical renewal if not innovation to put the buzz and fuzz in order.

Whilst finnlit has arrived at this cusp, it has yet to go much beyond it. Most finntheory draws directly or extrapolates from the role of finn in promoting speculative short-termism at the expense of the real economy and in underpinning dysfunction, finn is bad for X in finnX studies, whether X be investment, productivity, innovation, wages, equality, growth, social provisioning, poverty alleviation, and so on. There are a number of reasons for finnlit's hesitation and lethargy in moving beyond such theoretically limited if empirically informative studies. One is that finnlit can take impoverished mainstream economics as critical point of departure without really reconstructing the theory of money and finance, instead relying upon adding variables, insights or structured relations that readily distinguishes finnlit from the extremities of the Efficient Market Hypothesis.[15] Another reason is the absence of a theory of value upon which to base the roles played by finn. There is certainly acknowledgement that finance appropriates more than previously and more than it should for reasons of efficacy and justice, and so that this might be dysfunctional with the effect of less to distribute. But where the dividing line is to be drawn between producing and appropriating (surplus) value has been left vague if not unaddressed altogether.[16] And a final reason for lack of

---

13   REF is the UK system of submitting articles for consideration for ranking academics for their research record, as a symbolic assessment of quality and as the means to allocate general research funding to institutions.

14   For an exception, if primarily falling back upon macro, see Young (2019).

15   And what might be termed the Inefficient Market Hypothesis of financial markets, in which information available to, and/or behaviours of, individuals are the basis for suggesting finance works less than perfectly, i.e., no structures, power or conflicts as such.

16   For an insightful exception that proves the rule but does not resolve it, see Mazzucato (2018). Thus, p. 128: To ignore the question of value in relation to finance is, then, highly irresponsible. But in the end, the real challenge is not to label finance as value-creating or value-extracting, but to fundamentally transform it so that it *is* genuinely value-creating. In contrast see discussion between Christophers and Fine (2020).

theoretical development around finn is that its attachment to the state has tended to run along well-worn lines, not least macroeconomic policy (and the inclination within political economy towards emphasizing finnsterity) or microeconomic policy (as financial deregulation with or without macro effects), without situating the role of the state more holistically, as opposed to collections of fragmentary accounts of the nature of the state and finn across other disciplines.

Seventh, then, not only does finn tend to burst its scope outside of its traditional boundaries, so does its relationships with the state, rendering traditional divisions between macro and micro, and monetary and financial policy increasingly arbitrary. Unconventional monetary policy, such as quantitative easing, is not simply expansion of the money supply at low, even negative, rates of interest, but specific and (alongside) selective interventions on behalf of the financial sector.

Drawing conceptual boundaries for analytical convenience or as a mimic of conventional approaches is inappropriate. There is no division between the monetary and the financial, as has been neatly brought out by the study of Fastenrath et al. (2017) who focus specifically on the shifting financialization of state finances, seen as "a shift from hierarchies and networks towards financial markets as a governance mechanism ... shared by all countries in our sample, but with different country-specific trajectories" (p. 284).

To some extent, this issue has begun to be broached by asking whether the state's dealings with financial markets are better characterized in terms of its being player or victim, and whether and how the state itself is being financialized. The most significant development is the extent to which government debt is privately traded to a greater extent and in new forms. As Fastenrath et al. (2017, p. 287) put it:[17]

> Do sovereigns use markets by making choices and do they still have autonomy ... or do markets use governments ...? With reference to this, our analysis provides evidence that one needs to take into account both arguments.

Yes, but this does not suffice since it is necessary to go much further not least as they also observe that, "the relationship between finance capital and governments in the SDM (sovereign debt management) is complex, by no means one-sided and in flux" (p. 287). Indeed, p. 286:

---

17   See also Powell (2018, p. 6).

Whether it is regarding a shift from hierarchies and networks to financial
markets as governance mechanisms, or concerning the substitution of
macroeconomics with financial economics as underlying sense-making
frameworks, financialisation is a mega trend affecting all political economies and their SDM. Of course, this does not mean that we rule out distinct trajectories or even stark differences. What we want to stress instead
is that one must always reflect them against the common background of
financialisation.

My point is that such commonalities and differences cannot be captured by
traditional distinctions between macro and micro, and monetary and financial, rather than through increasingly financialized economic and social
restructuring, to be taken up later. This is both theoretical and empirical for, as
Ward et al. (2018, p. 17) observe, we need to frame that:[18]

> As the banking bailout occurred through the purchase of shares in fail-
> ing banks, it is also reflected in the large jump in state equity ... This is
> perhaps the most flagrant illustration of the sort of political-economic
> restructuring that neoliberalisation and financialisation has entailed: the
> equity held by central government is no longer that of owners of hospi-
> tals, schools and other service provision infrastructure; but shares in the
> banking sector.

In this respect, nor is it appropriate to perceive the state as some relatively
autonomous or embedded agent (to coin a phrase) that does well or badly
out of the financial markets. Rather, the state offers a contested terrain in
which the pressures to promote financialization are as important as the need
to play alongside or with it. Nor is this confined to the national stage as the
adjustments across peripheral Europe so amply demonstrate, let alone how
finnternationalization is attached to "a structured and hierarchic international
monetary system which fundamentally distinguishes exchange rate drivers
in emerging economies from those in developed ones", Kaltenbrunner (2018,
p. 1315), but see below.

Thus, for, finnstate. precisely because each of the state and financialization
are so increasingly pervasive, the state being such despite neoliberal ideology to the contrary, so are their intersections, as is recognized, primarily in a

---

18   For case studies of New Zealand, Spain and Italy, see Trampusch (2019), Masso (2016) and
      Lagna (2016). And, of course, Greek's debt adjustment was initially about rescuing over-
      exposed German and French banks.

piecemeal fashion other than at the level of grand posturing. This is acknowledged in burgeoning literatures on finnhousing, finnwelfare (social policy) and finnclusion, finnfrastructure, finnpower, finnland and so on. This indicates and reflects the need to take both a holistic and a contextualized, focused approach to finn, one which can tease out the shifting forms and balances of power, and the means and institutions through which it is both exercised and contested. Studies such as CRESC (2009), detailing the role of British finance in reviewing itself, are relatively rare but are crucial to understanding what I presume are the embedded imperatives of finance within and between the organs of state and governance, including the media,[19] and on a global scale.[20]

3   … To Value and Beyond

The review of finnlit has presented a series of knowledges and challenges from which Marxist political economy can draw and which it can meet, respectively. First off is value theory. Mainstream economics, and even some supportive as well as some dismissive if sympathetic accounts, tends to view Marxist value theory in quantitative terms alone, with value defined as an analytical instrument by (Ricardian) labour-time embodied and, as such, either to be inventively reconstructed to gain a valid theory of (equilibrium) price or rejected altogether as incapable of, or unnecessary for, doing so.[21]

This inevitably leads to the rejection of Marx's Law of the Tendency of the Rate of Profit to Fall (and Counteracting Tendencies), however understood, as well as his theories of landed property (and rent) and distinctions between productive and unproductive labor. Significantly, his theory of finance, which occupies a major part of the unfinished Volume III of *Capital*, as well as his

---

19   See Davis and Walsh (2016, p. 680): It was *financial market* thinking as much as *free market* thinking that provided the rationale and directive parameters for 'Big Bang', privatisation, deregulation of finance and trade, and evolving corporate governance and takeover regimes. These not only shifted economic conditions in favour of international finance and against manufacturing, they helped to pass UK industry more overtly into the hands of the financial sector.

   See also Lai and Daniels (2015) for revolving doors and state-led financialization in case of Singapore, and Happer (2017) for finnmedia and Bayliss et al (eds) (2018) for finnculture more generally.

20   Finnlit's neglect of finnstate has its counterpart in insufficient histories of how finn came about and forged the strongest of links with globalisation and neoliberalism. We do have histories, if insufficient, but these need to be strengthened and reinterpreted in light of the evolving understandings and trajectories of finn itself.

21   For recent responses to such endeavours, see Fine (2017) and Fine and Saad Filho (2018).

theory of circulation (most of Volume II) other than as an interpretation of intersectoral equilibrium conditions, have received little critical, if more by way of benign neglect than critical acceptance.

The position adopted here is totally different, emphasizing both quantitative and qualitative aspects of Marx's value theory and their irreducible attachment to one another in examining the capitalist "economy" and society as a totality. More specifically, if still abstractly, value theory is about how surplus value is produced and circulated, accumulated and distributed, with dynamic and contested effects and interactions across time and place, in increasingly complex forms, whether these are reflected in corresponding relations, structures, processes or agencies of production, distribution and exchange, and the corresponding powers and conflicts that they engender. Marxist political economy is replete with analyses of these issues and, most important for my purposes, provides both logical specification of the forms and effects of capital in constituting a totality, as well as lessons on how to engage with these as they historically and contextually are manifested.

In my own work in engaging such matters both theoretically and empirically,[22] value theory has been attached to how the accumulation of capital (and its crises) necessarily embodies the restructuring of capital across all its forms, alongside corresponding economic and social reproduction and transformation. This is not the place to rehearse such analyses in detail. Rather, it is to observe that Marxist political economy can take the finnlit and the multiple finnX studies as critical point of departure, what is to be explained rather than as explanations in and of themselves, finndoneit as it were.

Indeed, as observed, most notably absent from discussion of financialization has been any renewal of what surely must underpin it, a theory of money although, inevitably, money is everywhere in the finnlit as if a natural phenomenon to be taken for granted. Here, I would take as a starting point, the role of money as the commodity form taken by social exchangeability. To paraphrase the starting point of the very opening of Volume I of *Capital*:

> The wealth of those societies in which the capitalist mode of production prevails, presents itself as "an immense accumulation of financial assets," its unit being a single commodity.

22   This originates theoretically in Fine and Saad Filho (2016a), now in its sixth edition with first of 1975, and empirically especially with work on the British and South African economies, Fine and Harris (1985) and Fine and Rustomjee (1997). For some updating for these economies in light of finn, see Fine (2019), Ashman et al. (2018) and Fine and Saad-Filho (2019).

This raises the question, if not for the first time,[23] other than in the context of finn, of whether Marx's value theory and associated theory of money (itself also first presented at the beginning of Volume I of *Capital*) remains relevant for contemporary capitalism even if presumed relevant for his own time. My own view is that it does remain valid, subject to interpretation, although it can be better expressed.

I am not going to run through Marx's theory of money, as derived from the logical exposition of the commodity form, and the functions of money, nor am I particularly interested in whether we start with wealth, commodity or money, nor with whether we work with a commodity money, gold or otherwise, and its relative or absolute displacement by other forms or symbols of money as capitalism develops. Rather, my concern is with how to understand world money in Marx's theory, a concept which remarkably appears even before capital itself, and, indeed, an account even of the world. In other words, world money as such is an abstract category, not an empirical specification. My argument is that, at least initially and faithful to Marx's approach, world money is about the form of money which incorporates exchangeability, liquidity if you wish, maximally across its different functions.

Necessarily, in the context of no capital and no countries even, this is abstract, general and logical. What does it mean? For Marx, it is gold in practice, possibly silver for bimetallism (significant for my theory of world money as maximal since silver serves as money in some locations as opposed to gold). This is indicative that money as exchangeability is a binary relation and, as formal logic informs us, such a binary relationship need not yield a unique maximal element. There need not be the commodity that will only exchange with money at one extreme, and a perfect money at the other that can buy anything. Dollars and gold are not acceptable everywhere, gold hardly at all. So, there can be pockets, deep or otherwise, where different moneys function as world money, in the sense that they can exchange where others cannot, even though, and this is where the dollar and other currencies are relevant, some have much greater scope than others. In short, world money is not a thing, gold in the past, the dollar now, but a structured set of hierarchical relations expressing the potential for exchangeability in practice.

So what? This is admittedly highly formalistic although it reveals that monetary relations are hierarchical before they are financialized (however we understand this). The formalism is a shallow starting point until those hierarchical relations around world money are given some substantive underpinnings. This

---

23   See Fine et al. (2010).

itself has two aspects. One, which is Marx's immediately following concern in *Capital* after the opening chapters, is what are the social relations being expressed by these monetary relations. Marx reaches both backwards to production from acts of exchange and forward to the exchange relations themselves from production, both in quantitative, more exactly material, and in qualitative, symbolic terms. In reaching backwards, his concern is to specify value relations, the production of surplus value. In reaching forwards, his concern is how that surplus value is appropriated through exchangeability, and so, as a second aspect, the different forms of monetary relations are vital but integral with the first aspect.[24]

In this light, Marx has a tight, if disputed, distinction between productive and unproductive labor, with the productive located exclusively within the process of profitable production of commodities, and structurally distinct from (wage and other) labor engaged in circulation. The capital attached to such labor is amenable to concentration and centralization through accumulation and engages in the production of both absolute and relative surplus value. By contrast, labor (and corresponding capital) in circulation is not productive, however much necessary for the wheels of commerce, and depends upon the surplus value created by productive labor for any surplus it appropriates.[25]

But how and why and with effects do we move forward from the creation to the appropriation of surplus value? This is exactly the question addressed by Marx in his theory of circulation (laid out in Volume II of *Capital*) and finance, primarily in Volume III. For the latter, the distinction is first drawn between capital in production that creates (surplus) value, and capital in exchange that circulates it. But, within exchange itself, the logical distinction is also drawn between capital that merely circulates commodities, and money capital itself as a commodity that is bought and sold for interest, but which has the use value of being able to create and/or appropriate surplus value. This he calls interest bearing capital, IBC. And IBC for the lender creates a claim on surplus value that can be independently traded as what Marx calls fictitious capital. Marx then goes round and round in circles asking the question, when is an

---

24   Hence, refining quote from Kaltenbrunner above, which is correct but limited insofar as world money as a set of hierarchical relations is attached merely to the forms of money as opposed to the production relations that underpin them. This absence has been conducive to the notion of peripheral or subordinate finn, with affinities to World System theory, with some tensions over whether finnglob is rigidly structured or variegated. On subordinate/(semi-)peripheral finn, see Powell (2018), Bonizzi et al. (2019), Kaltenbrunner and Panceira (2018), Barradas et al. (2018) and Santos and Teles (eds.) (2020).

25   Hence the difference with Mazzacuto, quoted above, for whom finance is value-creating if made so (by and for whom and by what criteria other than her own subjectivities?).

accumulation of fictitious capital an accumulation of real capital.[26] We know it need not be given booms and busts.

Marx does not answer his question because he cannot; the answer cannot be found in the logical and practical differences between real and fictitious accumulation. Nor is it primarily let alone exclusively a function of individual actions and intentions as opposed to systemic functioning. Investment may fail for any number of reasons, but they will also create markets for other investments that succeed, as will (state) expenditures that are not necessarily geared towards generating profit directly. At the level of aggregate demand, this is the thrust of Keynesian stimulus. But effective demand as such is not the only nor necessarily the driving factor behind closing the gap between the accumulation of fictitious and real accumulation. And, of course, we are only too aware that there is and has been a huge gap between real and fictitious capital, driven by financialization and, equally, driving finnlit itself.

In short, Marx's political economy provides a logical derivation of the different forms taken by capital in production and capital in exchange and how they interact with one another to give rise to what I have previously designated as economic restructuring and reproduction. In passing, I might add that my longstanding view is that Marx's theory of the tendency of the rate of profit to fall, and counteracting tendencies, is a theory over how such restructuring takes place, in accommodating the tensions between developments in the production and circulation of (surplus) value as opposed to crude reductions to whether the rate of profit falls or not. This renders redundant much of the discussion over whether finance is a response to falling profitability or a contributory factor. This is not what it is about but, in the finnage, how finance is increasingly present in economic (and social) restructuring – indicating, equally, the irrelevance of the idea that the restructuring from the end of the post-war boom (the Brenner hypothesis and beyond) has yet to be satisfactorily broached – once we take a look at just how much restructuring has taken place and, equally and increasingly important, how, the most important aspect to which the finnlit contributes.[27]

This, then, points to the need to move from the logic of value theory (and of money and finance) to the historical specification of finn and its relationship to contemporary capitalism. I first place considerable emphasis on just

---

26   For a more extended account of Marx's theory of capital in exchange, and the various categories involved, see Fine and Saad-Filho (2016a). See also Fine (1985/86 and 1988).

27   See Fine et al. (2005) for this in the context of steel. By the same token, finance is not an epiphenomenon in the law of the tendency of the rate of profit to fall but, increasingly, the form through which it is expressed.

how favorable have been conditions for capital accumulation since the end of the post-war boom – the decline of the strength and organization of the working class and progressive movements in terms of trade unionism, political parties and the growth of the world labor force with entry of China into global markets, female labor market participation, the collapse of the Soviet bloc, the containment of economic and social wages through austerity, and a whole sequence of wide-ranging and even revolutionary technological innovations. Yet we have experienced the worst recession since the 1930s with inability to restore sustained growth without this in any way being able to be blamed upon working class militancy or rewards.

Such observations unavoidably point to the need both to identify the contemporary as a new stage of capitalism, with finn occupying a central if not necessarily exclusive role. In short, we have to acknowledge that neoliberalism has now outlasted the Keynesian period, and I would claim that neoliberalism as the current stage of capitalism is itself underpinned by finn, Fine (2012), Fine and Saad-Filho (2016b), Boffo et al. (2018) and Bayliss et al. (2020). This involves deep methodological and theoretical issues over how we understand capitalism let alone its periodization into different stages, for which the most prominent contributor has always been Lenin and his followers. For me, periodization is based upon how economic restructuring and reproduction occurs in the accumulation and circulation of (surplus) value, and how that economic restructuring and reproduction is embedded within social restructuring and reproduction. As so ably demonstrated by the finnlit, neoliberalism is marked by the increasing presence of finance in economic and social reproduction and restructuring, both quantitatively and qualitatively.

Significantly, the piecemeal understanding offered by finnlit, and its relationship to neoliberalism, has led to a large extent to the neglect of the global restructuring of production increasingly through finance – as a result of the confinement of studies by methodological nationalism to intra-country methods, and whether one country, or a group of countries, is more or less financialized than another and, if so, in what ways. Significantly, this has been captured by *econophysicists* in their study of global inter-corporate networks and who have identified the extent to which the state and a few hundred global corporations, the vast majority financial, run the world through their mutual ownerships and connections, Vitali et al. (2011).[28]

---

28   Note also that the Global Production Network literature, derived from the Global Commodity/Value Chains approach, has tended to overlook finn as it is not a source of intra-network/chain value transfer or its governance. For a recent exception, see Auvray

Putting this observation to the fore is paramount in understanding why finn should be variegated, including dysfunctions that reflect excessive accumulation as with energy (and climate change) and food consumption (with the malnourished through overweight now exceeding the undernourished on a global scale). Finn drives accumulation as well as constraining it, and unevenly, even if the weight of speculative short-termism is disproportionate. So variegated financialization is not just differentiation due to different variables and contexts being present but because of the complex interaction of underlying forces. Here, then, emphasis must be placed upon the different forms and extent of financialization as such, as well as correspondingly different effects across time, place and sector. This is well put as follows, Ward et al. (2018, p. 3):

> The contribution of the term 'variegated financialisation' ... does not lie in merely mirroring the concept of 'variegated neoliberalisation'. Rather, it invites us to consider how these two era-defining processes have been entwined, complementary and contradictory.

Indeed, p. 3:

> The key problem for those studying financialisation with an international purview is how to conceptualise the highly hetereogenous manner in which different political-economic institutional configurations have incorporated common pressures associated with the rise of global finance.

Further, it can be argued that neoliberalism has gone through two **previous** phases (with the current, third, soon to be specified) which, in the realm of scholarship at least, conform neatly to the distinction between Washington and post Washington Consensus and, politically, to Reaganism/Thatcherism and Blairism/Third Wayism, respectively. I also emphasize, though, that neither ideology nor policy in practice necessarily conform to scholarship but each has a shifting and complicated relationship to the others, differing over time, place and issue, Bayliss et al. (eds.) (2011). The current, tentatively delineated third, phase of neoliberalism is marked by three features. One is the impact of the Global Financial Crisis to which the response was unprecedented, and telling, measures to sustain national and global finance. Another is the stunning

---

and Rabinovich (2019). Note also neglect of relationship between finn and the labor process, Hanlon and Harney (2019) for an exception.

failure to be able to renew sustained accumulation despite what have been the most favourable conditions over the entire neoliberal period. And, last, the third, new phase of neoliberalism is one of intensified if uneven collaboration between finance, industry and the state to renew accumulation, not least through state support for new industrial policy, and economic and social infrastructure.[29] Nothing could better illustrate the inconsistencies between neoliberal ideology and practice, with the state essentially using its resources to support the role of private finance in public provisioning and to purvey the ideology that the market is superior to the state.

Whilst it is appropriate that the definition of neoliberalism should be focused on globalized and financialized economic reproduction, the latter is itself embedded within a much more wide-ranging social reproduction on which it has profound influences and interactions. This is precisely what has inspired the wide-ranging buzz and fuzz of finnlit. It has also had the effect, following Epstein's definition of finn, of categorizing a wide range of phenomena as falling under such a broad definition. This is unacceptable since, through accompanying fuzz and buzz, the inevitable empirical presence of finn is taken, more or less tautologically, as causal of any other outcome with which it is associated in light of the limited distinction between the nature of finn and its effects. Everything is or has been caused by finn where any sort of monetary relations, institutions or even ethos is detected. Instead, as suggested here in following Marx's political economy, there is the option of taking a narrow and precise definition of finn, as interest bearing capital.

This, then, offers a dialectical relationship between IBC and fictitious capital, FC, and whether their expansion is or is not in line with one another, overall and in relation to uneven development. The result is highly diverse in substance, incidence and impact, and its influence is both direct and indirect especially in relation to both economic performance and social, political and ideological outcomes. Consequently, whilst these are general propositions drawn from the nature of IBC, including the relationship with other capitals in production, distribution and circulation during economic restructuring, they can also be rooted historically in defining the current period of capitalism, (globalized) neoliberalism, as one in which finn has been so extensively embedded, that it has increasingly dominated the processes of economic and social reproduction.

---

29   Or finnfrastructure for which there is currently a rapidly expanding literature, with PPPs
      to the fore, of some quantitative significance but much more symbolic of the third phase
      of neoliberalism as detailed. For the more general picture, see Haberly and Wójcik (2016).

In short, in part in response to its critics for being fuzz and buzz, neoliberalism by its nature and in its dependence upon financialization is not homogenizing towards what remains a virtual model of (free) market provision. Rather, financialization can do its work where full privatization of state industry, for example, has taken hold, and corresponding streams of revenue can be securitized for the purposes of creating financial assets to be traded and on which to borrow. This is what I term commodification with a big C. But, and in order to address the much broader range of phenomena attached to the finnlit, C is complemented by provisioning that may not be fully commodified, as in contracting out for fees or subject to user charges that may be regulated and/or subsidized rather than being primarily determined by private market provision. This I term Commodity Form, CF, and corresponding revenues can also be securitized as the basis for tradeable financial assets. In addition, the increasing influence of financialization is to be felt by, if not occurring with, the imposition of commercial logics on provision even if monetary exchange does not actually occur. It is, or is not, worth (the state or its institutions) doing this, that or the other according to commercial criteria even though commerce is not directly involved. This I call commodity calculation, CC, e.g., central state allocation to lower-level budgets for health and education on basis of indices of need irrespective of whether used for such purposes or not. This is not financialization as such, but the latter's influence can be heavily felt in political, ideological and policy terms. Mimic some notion of the (financialized) market.

This is already beginning to specify framing the relationship between the grand theory – of finn as IBC and as underpinning neoliberalism as the contemporary stage of capitalism – and the more specific, and variegated outcomes to which it is attached. To some degree, C, CF, and CC are often rounded up together as simply C, whether in terms of privatization, new public management or NE liberalization and so on. There is some merit in this insofar as globalized, financialized NL has witnessed a dynamic in which there tends to be a move from CC to CF, and from CF to C. But matters are far from so simple as brought out by the example of supposedly decommodifying health care by the state paying for public access free, as it were, at the point of delivery. As such, it is nothing of the sort; indeed, it is the commodification of health care even if the major customer is the state. More generally, the relations across CCFCC are complex and contradictory, not least because commodification tends to exclude those who are unable to pay, leaving the state in a residual and even expanding role. A neat example of this is housing benefit to support those in rented accommodation, which has mushroomed across Europe at the expense of state housing provision, even as mortgaged owner-occupation has simultaneously grown through heavy promotion.[30] Similar tensions around both promoting financialization and dealing with those residualized as a result are to be found across almost every aspect of everyday life – highly and randomly selectively: pensions, Bonizzi and Churchill (2018); SMEs, Mertens and Thiemann (2018); higher education, Eaton et al. (2016); public land, Christophers (2018) and housing, Appleyard et al. (2016); intangible assets, Bryan et al. (2017) and Orhangazi (2018); Ahlers and Merme (2016) and Bayliss (2014) for water; credit as heavily exposed by the finnclusion literature, Bateman et al. (2018), Gabor and Brooks (2017) and Mader (2018); and so on.

Elsewhere, with colleagues, I have proposed to deal with these conundrums of attaching grand narratives to contradictory diversity through the system of provision, or SoP, approach. Here is emphasized that economic and social reproduction is in part disaggregated into different systems, whether for private or public consumption or some mix between the two. The housing, health and education systems differ from one another in and of themselves and across countries by virtue of the different structures, processes, relations and agencies through which the chain of activities underpinning provisioning accrues in practice, reproducing or transforming patterns of who gets what and how, and to be specified through the analytical framings just delineated. And it is within and across these SoPs that the state plays a leading role, even if of neglect, as the leading agency promoting social reproduction and economic within it. Bayliss and Fine (2020).

Over time, and in part in response to continuing developments within neoliberalism and its scholarly and ideological trajectories, the SoP approach has itself been refined and operationalized (i.e., how to deploy). First up is to attach SoPs to identifiable (ie to be identified), Social Norms, these to be understood in sophisticated and complex forms not only of who gets what by socio-economic, cultural variables such as income, location, gender, race, etc,[31] but also how with obvious differences between public and private provisioning and their privileging. Attaching norms to SoPs in this way is a crucial aspect of laying out what has to be explained (not what is explained) and breaching

---

30   See National Housing Federation (2017).

31   Significantly, social norms in the sense suggested here have been the focus implicitly of much recent work and renewal of interest in social reproduction, under the rubric of intersectionality. See Bhattacharya (ed.) (2017) for example. Much of this work tends to confine such social reproduction to that of labor power (as opposed to other classes and aspects), as a result of its origins in redressing the neglect of household labor; and there also tends to be an interactive dualism between economic and social reproduction rather than the former being embedded within the latter – economic is contained within social reproduction.

with individualistic methodologies that take social determinants as individual characteristics, sufficiently explicable as such in and of themselves (i.e., poverty and gender as causal rather than socially constructed both materially and culturally). I do not want to open sores over whether financialization is a complementary source of exploitation, appropriation or whatever.[32] Rather the point is to emphasize the role of globalized, neoliberalized, financialized, CCFCC in transforming what are social norms in terms of what is delivered, to whom, and in what ways with shifting meanings whether it be around rights, entitlements, or whatever, or from citizen to client/consumer. More specific to neoliberalism, and especially its post-GFC phase, is that provisioning, in part by virtue of financialization, both directly and indirectly, is subject to what might be abbreviated as V^3; it is subject to variegated and volatile vulnerabilities as in the diverse vagaries of the incidence and impact of financialization and the policy responses to it, in part in light of increasingly fragmented and weakened forms and effects of protest and struggles for alternatives.

And, finally, let me address explicitly the ideational factors and the nature of the relationship between continuing provision and the struggle for alternatives. Here, the SoP approach appeals to what has been designated as the 10Cs – in brief, that provisioning is Constructed, Construed, Contradictory, Commodified, Conforming, Closed, Contested, Contextual, Collective and Chaotic. These are loosely divided between those material factors that condition the what and the how of culture/ideational factors, and the nature of corresponding meanings, etc. Thus, ideas eg of what we mean by Universal Health Care or the relative merits of public and private is Contested; but who gets to contest and how is constrained (Closed even) and in what Context, is highly contextual (not least with Commodification and the Constructed superiority of private provisioning through state support). And so on. The SoP approach seeks to identify how provisioning and cultures of provisioning mutually interact, not least in the globalized, financialized and neoliberalized conditions of contemporary capitalism.

With the current phase of NL, increasingly oriented to use the state to support, even finance, private finance itself to finance private investment, there will be opportunities to expose the material and cultural deficiencies of how provisioning is being reproduced, and to unite around alternatives, going beyond financing to the provisioning itself, by whom for whom. I have become increasingly mindful, not least in the wake of the GFC and its continuing stagnation, that the current phase of NL has, to some degree, leapfrogged, the

---

See especially Lapavitsas (2013) and Fine (2010a and 2014) for wide-ranging critique.

basket cases for privatization and financialization to the front of the queue – let's make money out of health, the railways, education and so on. This is our cue to offer detailed and situated alternatives to serve those at the rough end of these developments.

References

Ahlers, R. and V. Merme (2016) "Financialisation, Water Governance, and Uneven Development", *WIRES Water*, vol 3, no 6, pp. 766–74.

Appleyard, L., Rowlingson, K. and Gardner, J. (2016), 'Variegated financialization of sub-prime credit markets' *Competition & Change*, 20, 5, 297–313.

Ashman, S. and B. Fine (2013) "Neo-liberalism, Varieties of Capitalism, and the Shifting Contours of South Africa's Financial System", *Transformation*, no 81/2, pp. 144–78.

Ashman, S., E. Karwowski and B. Fine (2018) "Introduction to the Special Section 'Financialization in South Africa'", *Competition & Change*, vol 22, no 4, pp. 383–87.

Auvray, T. and J. Rabinovich (2019) "The Financialisation-Offshoring Nexus and the Capital Accumulation of U.S. Nonfinancial Firms", *Cambridge Journal of Economics*, vol 43, no 5, pp. 1183–1218.

Bakker, I. and S. Gill (2019) "Rethinking Power, Production, and Social Reproduction: Toward Variegated Social Reproduction", *Capital and Class*, vol 43, no 4, pp. 503–23.

Barradas, R., S. Lagoa, E. Leão and R. Mamede (2018) "Financialization in the European Periphery and the Sovereign Debt Crisis: The Portuguese Case", *Journal of Economic Issues,* vol 52, no 4, pp. 1056–1083.

Bateman, M., S. Blankenburg and R. Kozul-Wright (2018) *The Rise and Fall of Global Microcredit: Development, Debt and Disillusion,* London: Routledge.

Bayliss, K. (2014) "The Financialization of Water", *Review of Radical Political Economics*, vol 14, no 3, pp. 292–307.

Bayliss, K. and B. Fine (2020) *A Guide to the Systems of Provision Approach: Who Gets What, How and Why*, Basingstoke: Palgrave MacMillan.

Bayliss, K., B. Fine, M. Robertson and A. Saad Filho (2020) *Neoliberalism, Financialisation and Welfare: The Political Economy of Social Provision in the UK*, Cheltenham: Edward Elgar, in preparation.

Bayliss, K., B. Fine and E. Van Waeyenberge (eds) (2011) *The Political Economy of Development: The World Bank, Neoliberalism and Development Research*, London: Pluto.

Bayliss, K., B. Fine and R. Robertson (eds) (2018) *Material Cultures of Financialisation*, London: Routledge.

Bhattacharya, T. (ed) (2017) *Social Reproduction Theory: Remapping Class, Recentering Oppression,* London: Pluto.

Boffo, M., Brown, A. & Spencer, D. (2017). From happiness to social provisioning: addressing well-being in times of crisis. *New Political Economy,* 22(4), 450–62, reproduced in Bayliss, K., Fine, B. & Robertson, M. (Eds.) (2018) *Material cultures of financialisation,* London: Routledge, pp. 96-108.

Boffo, M., B. Fine and A. Saad-Filho (2018) "Neoliberal Capitalism: The Authoritarian Turn", with M., in L. Panitch and G. Albo *A World Turned Upside Down?*, Socialist Register, 2019, London: Merlin Press, pp. 247–70.

Bonizzi, B., A. Kaltenbrunner and J. Powell (2019) "Subordinate Financialization in Emerging Capitalist Economies", *Greenwich Papers in Political Economy,* no 23044, https://gala.gre.ac.uk/id/eprint/23044/13/23044%20POWELL%20Subordin ate%20financialisation%20GPERC%20WP%20BKP%20v2%20050319.pdf.

Christophers, B. (2015a), "'The Limits to Financialization'", *Dialogues in Human Geography,* vol 5, no 2, pp. 183–200.

Christophers, B. (2015b) "From Financialization to Finance: For 'De-Financialization'", *Dialogues in Human Geography,* vol 5, no 2, pp. 229–32..

Christophers, B. (2018) *The New Enclosure: The Appropriation of Public Land in Neoliberal Britain,* London: Verso.

Christophers, B. and B. Fine (2020) "The Value of Financialization and the Financialization of Value", in P. Mader, D. Mertens and N. van der Zwan (eds) *International Handbook of Financialization*, London: Routledge, pp. 19–30.

Cornwall, A. and D. Eade (eds) (2010) *Deconstructing Development Discourse: Buzzwords and Fuzzwords*, Oxfam and Rugby: Practical Action Publishing.

CRESC (2009) *An Alternative Report on UK Banking Reform*, jointly authored by a working group of practitioners and academics based at the ESRC Centre for Research on Socio Cultural Change, University of Manchester, Available from: http://www.cresc .ac.uk/publications/documents/AlternativereportonbankingV2.pdf.

Davis, L. (2017) "Financialization and Investment: A Survey of the Empirical Literature", *Journal of Economic Surveys*, vol 31, no 5, pp. 1332–358.

Davis, A. and C. Walsh (2016). "The Role of the State in the Financialisation of the UK Economy", *Political Studies*, vol 64, no 3, pp. 666–82.

Eaton, Charlie Jacob Habinek, Adam Goldstein, Cyrus Dioun, Daniela García Santibáñez Godoy, Robert Osley-Thomas. *Socio-Economic Review*, Volume 14, Issue 3, July 2016, Pages 507–535, https://doi.org/10.1093/ser/mwv030.

Epstein, G. (2005) "Introduction: Financialization and the World Economy", in G. Epstein (ed.) *Financialization and the World Economy*, Cheltenham: Edward Elgar, pp. 3–16.

Fasianos, A., D. Guevara and C. Pierros (2018) "Have We Been Here Before?: Phases of Financialization within the Twentieth Century in the US", *Review of Keynesian Economics*, vol 6, no 1, pp. 34–61.

Fastenrath, F., M. Schwan and C. Trampusch (2017) "Where States and Markets Meet: The Financialisation of Sovereign Debt Management", *New Political Economy*, vol 22, no 3, pp. 273–293.

Fine, B. (1985/6) "Banking Capital and the Theory of Interest", *Science and Society*, Winter, vol XLIX, pp. 387–413.

Fine, B. (1988) "From Capital in Production to Capital in Exchange", *Science and Society*, vol 52, no 3, pp. 326–37.

Fine, B. (2010a) "Locating Financialisation", *Historical Materialism*, vol 18, no 2, pp. 97–116.

Fine, B. (2010b) *Theories of Social Capital: Researchers Behaving Badly*, London: Pluto Press.

Fine, B. (2012) "Neo-Liberalism in Retrospect? – It's Financialisation, Stupid", in K-S. Chang, B. Fine and L. Weiss (eds.) *Developmental Politics in Transition: The Neoliberal Era and Beyond,* Basingstoke: Palgrave MacMillan, pp. 51–69.

Fine, B. (2014) "Financialisation from a Marxist Perspective", *International Journal of Political Economy*, vol 42, no 4, pp. 47–66.

Fine, B. (2016) "Across Developmental State and Social Compacting: The Peculiar Case of South Africa", ISER Working Paper No. 2016/1, Grahamstown: Institute of Social and Economic Research, Rhodes University, https://www.ru.ac.za/media/rhode suniversity/content/iser/documents/ISER_Working_Paper_No._2016.01.pdf.

Fine, B. (2017) "Neither Equilibrium as Such nor as Abstraction: Debating Fred Moseley's Transformation", *International Journal of Political Economy*, vol 46, no 1, pp. 22–28.

Fine, B. (2018) "N Things You Need to Know about Finnwhat", Workshop on Financialisation in Emerging Capitalist Economies, Cambridge, December 13/14, 2018, rough draft available from author.

Fine, B. (2019) "Post-Apartheid South Africa: It's Neoliberalism, Stupid!", in *Race, Class and the Post-Apartheid Democratic State*, co-edited with John Reynolds and Robert van Niekerk, Pietermaritzburg: University of KwaZulu-Natal Press, pp. 75–95.

Fine, B. (2020) "Financialisation and Development", new entry for fourth revised edition of the *Companion to Development Studies*, London: Routledge, forthcoming.

Fine, B., G. Gimm and H. Jeon (2010) "Value is as Value Does: Twixt Knowledge and the World Economy", *Capital and Class,* Special Issue, no 100, pp. 69–83.

Fine, B. and L. Harris, with K. O'Donnell and M. Prevezer (1985) *The Peculiarities of the British Economy*, London: Lawrence and Wishart.

Fine, B., A. Petropoulos and H. Sato (2005) "Beyond Brenner's Investment Overhang Hypothesis: The Case of the Steel Industry", *New Political Economy*, vol 10, no 1, pp. 43–64.

Fine, B. and G. Pollen (2018) "The Developmental State Paradigm in the Age of Financialisation", in M. Hyland and R. Munck (eds.), *Handbook on Development and Social Change*, Cheltenham: Edward Elgar, pp. 211–27.

Fine, B. and Z. Rustomjee (1997) *The Political Economy of South Africa: From Minerals-Energy Complex to Industrialisation,* with, London: Hurst, and Johannesburg: Wits University Press.

Fine, B. and A. Saad-Filho (2016a) *Marx's 'Capital',* London: Pluto, sixth edition.

Fine, B. and A. Saad-Filho (2016b) "Thirteen Things You Need to Know about Neoliberalism", *Critical Sociology,* vol 43, no 4–5, pp. 685–706.

Fine, B. and A. Saad-Filho (2018) "Marx 200: The Abiding Relevance of the Labour Theory of Value", *Review of Political Economy,* vol 30, no 3, pp. 339–354.

Fine, B. and A. Saad-Filho (2019) "Economic Policies for the Many Not the Few: Assessing the Economic Strategy of the Labour Party", *Theory and Struggle,* vol 120, pp. 76–88.

Gabor, D. and S. Brooks (2017) "The Digital Revolution in Financial Inclusion: International Development in the Fintech Era", *New Political Economy,* vol 22, no 4, pp. 423–36.

Haberly, D. and D. Wójcik (2016) "Earth Incorporated: Centralization and Variegation in the Global Company Network", *Economic Geography,* vol 93, no 3, pp. 241–266.

Hanlon, G. and S. Harney (2019) "Standardization, Disequilibrium, and Crisis: The Division of Labour and Financialization", *Human Relations,* DOI: 10.1177/0018726719884608.

Happer, C. (2017) "Financialisation, Media and Social Change", *New Political Economy,* vol 22, no 4, pp. 437–449, reproduced in Bayliss et al. (eds.) (2018).

Kaltenbrunner, A. (2018) "Financialised Internationalisation and Structural Hierarchies: A Mixed-method Study of Exchange Rate Determination in Emerging Economies", *Cambridge Journal of Economics,* vol 42, no 5, pp. 1315–1341.

Kaltenbrunner, A. and J. Panceira (2018) "Subordinated Financial Integration and Financialisation in Emerging Capitalist Economies: The Brazilian Experience", *New Political Economy,* vol 23, no 3, pp. 290–313.

Karwowski, E., M. Shabani and E. Stockhammer (2016) "Financialisation in Emerging Economies: A Systematic Overview and Comparison with Anglo-Saxon Economies", Post Keynesian Economics Study Group, Working Paper, no 1619, December, http://www.postkeynesian.net/downloads/working-papers/PKWP1619.pdf.

Karwowski, E. and E. Stockhammer (2016) "Financialisation in Emerging Economies: A Systematic Overview and Comparison with Anglo-Saxon Economies", Post Keynesian Economics Study Group, Working Paper, no 1616, August, http://www.postkeynesian.net/downloads/working-papers/PKWP1616.pdf.

Lagna, A. (2016) "Derivatives and the Financialisation of the Italian State", *New Political Economy,* vol 21, no 2, pp. 167–186.

Lai, K. and J. Daniels (2015) "Banking on Finance in Singapore: The State-led Financialization of Banking Firms", GPN Working Paper Series, July, National University of Singapore, http://gpn.nus.edu.sg/file/Karen%20Lai_GPN2015_002.pdf.

Lapavitsas, C. (2013) *Profiting without Producing: How Finance Exploits Us All*, London: Verso.

Mader, P. (2018) "Contesting Financial Inclusion", *Development and Change*, vol 49, no 2, pp. 46–483.

Mader, P., D. Mertens and N. van der Zwan (eds.) (2020) *International Handbook of Financialization*, London: Routledge.

Masso, M. (2019) "The Effects of Government Debt Market Financialization: The Case of Spain", *Competition and Change*, vol 23, no 1, pp. 166–186.

Mazzucato, M. (2018) *The Value of Everything: Making and Taking in the Global Economy*, Harmondsworth: Penguin.

Michell, J. and J. Toporowski (2014) "Critical Observations on Financialization and the Financial Process", *International Journal of Political Economy*, vol 42, no 4, pp. 67–82.

National Housing Federation (2017) "Public Expenditure on Housing: The Shift from Capital Spend to Housing Allowances. A European Trend?", http://s3-eu-west-1.amazonaws.com/pub.housing.org.uk/public_spending_housing_europe_uk_briefing.pdf.

Powell, J. (2018) *Towards a Marxist Theory of Financialised Capitalism*. University of Greenwich Business School, no GPERC62, https://gala.gre.ac.uk/id/eprint/20331/.

Santos, A. and N. Teles (eds) (2020) *Financialisation in the European Periphery: Work and Social Reproduction in Portugal*, Abingdon: Routledge.

Trampusch, C. (2019) "The Financialization of the State: Government Debt Management Reforms in New Zealand and Ireland", *Competition and Change*, vol 23, no 1, pp. 3–22.

Vitali, S., J. Glattfelder and S. Battiston (2011) "The Network of Global Corporate Control", Available from: http://arxiv.org/pdf/1107.5728v2.pdf.

Ward, C., G. Wijburg and J. van Loon (2018) "Neoliberal Europeanisation, Variegated Financialisation: Common but Divergent Economic Trajectories in the Netherlands, United Kingdom and Germany", *Tijdschrift voor Economische en Sociale Geografie*, vol 110, no 2, pp. 123–137.

Young, B. (2019) "A Macro-Level Account of Money and Credit to Explain Gendered Financialization", *New Political Economy*, vol 25, no 6, pp. 944–956.

CHAPTER 4

Value, Capital and Exploitation in Marx

Alfredo Saad-Filho

1 Introduction

This chapter outlines the key elements of Marx's theory of value and exploitation.[1] The theory of value provides the foundation for Marx's critique of capitalism, and it substantiates his claim that capitalism is an exploitative, contradictory and historically limited mode of production. Important elements of Marx's theory include his explanation of the value form and the price form, why wage workers are exploited, the sources of social conflict, the necessity of technical progress and the growing use of machinery in production, the determinants of wages, prices and distribution, and the role of finance in capitalism. The theory of value is important for another reason too: it provides the logical framework of Marx's approach to political economy. The articulation of *all* analytical as well as empirical applications of Marx's analysis with his theory of value is what gives Marxist political economy its analytical integrity, explanatory power and scope to influence transformative political activity.

From this point of view, the theory of value is a theory of *class, class relations* and *exploitation* in capitalism. In turn, capitalism is understood as a mode of production, social reproduction, and exploitation, distinguished by five closely related elements: first, the social form of the property relations, that is structured by the capitalist class monopoly of the means of production and, therefore, the separation between the workers and the means of production. Second, the social form of labor, which is wage labor imposed by means of the dispossession of the working class, the commodification of labor power and the generalization of the wage relation. Third, the mode of labor control, that is based on the capitalist right to manage the performance of work. Fourth, the social form of the products of labor, as commodities and, fifth, the goal of social production, which is the capture of profits.

This chapter includes this introduction and eight substantive sections. Section 2 examines the concept of commodity in Marx and its relationship

---

1 For overviews of Marxian value theory at different levels of difficulty, see Bottomore (1991), Callinicos (2014), Fine and Saad-Filho (2013, 2016), Harvey (2010), Heinrich (2012), Howard and King (1989, 1991), Saad-Filho (2002, 2019) and Weeks (2010).

with, on the one hand, money and, on the other hand, capitalism. Section 3 reviews the concept of labor within Marx's theory of value. Section 4 traces the essential categories within the capitalist mode of production and section 5 reviews the form of labor typical of capitalism, wage labor. The sixth section focuses on the form of exploitation that distinguishes capitalism, through the extraction of surplus value. The seventh outlines the meaning and significance of competition within the reproduction of capital(ism) and the relationship between capitalist production and the use of machinery. The eighth looks into the typically capitalist form of production: mass production (both in terms of the outputs and the use of labor). Section 9 concludes.

2   Commodities

In capitalist societies the products of labor and, more generally, the goods and services needed for social reproduction, typically take the form of commodities. Commodities are goods and services produced for sale, rather than consumption by their own producers. Commodities have two common features. On the one hand, they are *use values*: they have useful characteristics from a social point of view,[2] that is, they are useful for others, making them potentially saleable. The nature of the demand for them, whether it derives from physiological need, social convention, fancy or vice is irrelevant. What matters is that commodities must be socially useful on a consistent basis.

On the other hand, commodities have *exchange value*: they can, in principle, be exchanged for other commodities (through money, see below) in specific ratios. For example, one laptop may be equivalent to one weekend break on the seaside, two bicycles, four pairs of shoes, six pairs of trousers, three hundred postage stamps and so on. Exchange value shows that, in spite of their distinct use values, commodities are equivalent to one another at least in respect to one of their features, which allows them to be compared quantitatively.

In a commodity economy, where goods and services are produced for sale, money fulfils two roles. First, it simplifies the vast number of bilateral exchange ratios between these commodities. In practice, only the exchange value of commodities in terms of money (their price) is needed, as this is sufficient to establish (indirectly) the equivalence ratios between all commodities. Second, commodity exchanges are usually mediated by money. In general,

---

2   Idiosyncratic items which are non-reproducible and tend to be demanded only by eccentric individuals may or may not be commodities; it depends on their production and their role in social reproduction. These marginal items are not considered in what follows.

no one produces all the goods and services that they may want to consume. Rather, each member of a commodity society generally specializes in the production of one good or service – say, carrots, shoes, hairdressing, sewing, or singing – and exchanges it for the multitude of commodities that they want to consume. These exchanges are not direct (barter), as if farmers offered their carrots to passers-by in exchange for cinema tickets, shoes, songs, and automobiles. Instead, the farmers sell their produce to supermarkets or wholesalers in return for money and armed with notes, coins, or a bank card, they purchase what they wish to consume.

3   Labor

The double nature of commodities, as use values with exchange value, has implications for labor. On the one hand, commodity-producing labor is *concrete*, producing specific use values such as carrots, clothes, movies and so on. On the other hand, as was shown above, when goods are produced for exchange (and have exchange value) they have a relationship of equivalence to one another. In this case Marx highlights, for the first time – and this is one of his claims to fame – that labor is also *abstract* (general). Just like the commodities themselves, commodity-producing labor is both general and specific at the same time.

Concrete labor, producing these use values, exists in all societies because people always and everywhere need to produce and consume use values for their own reproduction and for the reproduction of their societies. In contrast, abstract labor is historically specific; it exists only where commodities are produced and exchanged.

Marx stresses that abstract labor has two distinct aspects – qualitative and quantitative – that should be analyzed separately. First, abstract labor derives from the relationship of equivalence between commodities. Even though it is historically contingent, abstract labor has real existence; it is not merely a construct of the mind. A visit to the local supermarket, for example, shows that the buyer's labor *really* is equivalent to the labors that have produced thousands of different goods, some of them nearby and others halfway around the globe. All commodity-producing labors are equivalent as abstract labor because commodities are made for exchange. Their equivalence appears through the convertibility between money and each commodity, represented by their price. In this sense, any purchase realizes the equivalence between the buyer's own labor – say, as a farmer, or a singer – and the labor of the producers of carrots, laptops, or any other commodity. The ability of money to purchase any commodity shows that money represents abstract labor, and, for this reason, Marx called money the *general equivalent* of commodities.

Second, the relative stability of the exchange values shows that there is a quantitative relationship between the abstract labors necessary to produce each type of commodity. However, this relationship is indirect (see below). In his *Inquiry into the Nature and Causes of the Wealth of Nations*, first published in 1776, Adam Smith claimed that in 'early and rude' societies goods exchanged directly in proportion to the labor time necessary to produce them. For example, if 'it usually costs twice the labour to kill a beaver which it does to kill a deer, one beaver should naturally exchange for or be worth two deer' (Smith 1991, p.41). However, Smith believed that this simple pricing rule breaks down when tools and machines are used in production. The reason is that, in addition to the workers, the owners of the 'stock' also have a legitimate claim to the value of the product.

Marx disagrees with Smith, for two reasons. On the one hand, 'simple' or 'direct' exchange (in proportion to socially necessary labor) is not typical of any human society; this is simply a construct of Smith's mind. In contrast, Marx is trying to identify the actual drivers of exchange and the social structures that explain the reproduction of really existing economies: Marx's thought experiments are driven by the attempt to explain material structures of social reproduction, rather than following flighty ideas, fancy, inventions or analytical 'convenience'. On the other hand, and even more importantly for the purposes of this chapter, although commodity exchanges reveal the quantitative relations of equivalence between different types of labor, these relationships are mediated and transformed at each level of abstraction of the analysis. In Marx's approach, concepts are transformed and gain richness and increasing capacity to represent the concrete reality as the analysis advances. In other words, whereas Smith abandons his own 'labor theory of value' at the first hurdle, Marx develops his own value analysis rigorously and systematically into a cogent explanation of commodity prices under capitalism (see below and, for details, see Saad-Filho 2002 and 2019, Part 1).

4   Capitalism

Commodities have been produced for thousands of years. However, in non-capitalist societies commodity production is generally marginal and most goods and services are produced for direct consumption by the household or for non-market exchange, e.g., tribute, taxes, or exchanges between friends and family. It is different in capitalist societies. *The first defining feature of capitalism is the generalization of the production of commodities.* Under capitalism, most goods and services are produced for sale, most workers are employed in the production of commodities and commodities are systematically traded in complex markets, where firms and households regularly purchase commodities as production inputs and as final goods and services.

The second is the production of commodities for profit. In capitalist society, commodity owners typically do not merely seek to make a living; they are there to make profits, that is, to increase the value of the resources they have advanced at the start of the process of production. For this reason, in capitalism decisions about the level and composition of the aggregate output, the level and structure of employment and so on and, consequently, the living standards of society, depend on the profitability of enterprise.

The third is wage labor. Like commodity production and money, wage labor first appeared thousands of years ago. However, before capitalism wage labor was always limited and other forms of labor were predominant. For example, co-operation within small social groups, slavery in the great empires of antiquity, serfdom under feudalism and independent production for subsistence or exchange in all types of society. Wage labor has become the typical mode of labor only recently; three or four hundred years ago in England and even more recently elsewhere, especially in the Global South.

In conclusion, capital is a totality engaged in self-expansion through the employment of wage labor for the production of commodities for profit. This implies that capital exists primarily at the level of society as a whole, that is, capital is primarily *capital in general*, existing at the level of *class*, and its reproduction is mediated by the market-led allocation of labor and its products. In other words, capital is a social relation of exploitation defined by the ability of the capitalist class to compel the working class to produce more than it consumes or controls and, correspondingly, by the capitalist command of the surplus (which includes the investment funds). In these circumstances, the products of labor generally take the form of values and economic exploitation is based on the extraction of surplus value.

This class interpretation of Marx's value theory aims to explain systematically the process of production of the material conditions of social reproduction in capitalist societies. The theory of value is, necessarily, dynamic and it is incompatible with the notion of 'equilibrium', that is a key organizing principle in neoclassical (mainstream or orthodox) economics. Instead, Marx's value theory focuses on the identification of systemic forces and tendencies and their interaction with the inevitable countertendencies, leading to complex outcomes in historical time. Finally, this approach recognizes the limits of abstract analysis and the need to incorporate historically specific material, whether reflecting broad outcomes, such as the stages of capitalism, or more concrete aspects such as country-specific relations between industry and finance or the balance of class or other forces.

Capital in general is represented by the general circuit of capital, M-C-M′, where M is the money advanced to buy commodities (means of production, or physical inputs and labor power), C, for production and, later, the sale of the output for more money M′. The difference M′ − M is the surplus value. The circuit represents the essence of capital: valorization through the production of commodities by wage labor. In this circuit, capital shifts between different forms (money, productive and commodity capital), as it moves between the spheres of exchange, production and, eventually, exchange again. Although this movement is critical for the process of valorization, profit is due to the surplus labor performed in production only (see below). In contrast, interest-bearing capital (IBC), whose form is M-M′, that is, money that becomes more money, does not produce profit, any more than money left inside a mattress begets more money simply by lying there. The expansion of IBC is due to transfers from productive capital, for example through fees, commissions, and interest payments (see Fine and Saad-Filho 2016, ch.12). However, profit is not the only thing that capital produces; at the social level, the outcome of the circuit is the expanded reproduction of capital itself. In this sense, 'Accumulation of capital is [...] multiplication of the proletariat' (Marx 1976, p.764; see also p.724 and Marx 1978, pp.428–430).

Value analysis implies that the working class is exploited because they work for longer than what is necessary to produce the commodities that this class consumes or controls (this principle is clear at the level of class, but it cannot be applied directly at the level of individual workers, who generally contribute only to a fragment of the processes of production and exchange and consume a wide variety of goods and services whose value cannot be directly measured against their efforts). Marx calls necessities the goods appropriated by the working class. They are produced by necessary labor and their value is the value of labor power. In contrast, the capitalists appropriate the surplus, which is produced by surplus labor and whose value is the surplus value. The latter is the part of the social value product appropriated by the capitalists or, alternatively, the difference between the value produced by the working class and the value of labor power (which, therefore, is also defined at the level of class, rather than in terms of averaged out consumption baskets; see below).

The existence of necessities and the surplus, and the division of the social labor time into necessary and surplus labor, are consequences of exploitation in any mode of production. However, the concepts of value of labor power and surplus value and their manifestation as wages and profits, are typical of capitalism because in this mode of production – for the first time – exploitation is mediated by value relations and the commodity form, instead of being grounded on overtly political and interpersonal relations as is the case, for example, in slave or feudal modes of production.

Finally, Marx highlights that, with all else constant, the rate of exploitation can increase for four main reasons. First, if more hours are worked. Second, if labor intensity increases. Third, if more productive workers (better skilled, faster, or more efficient in other ways) are employed. Fourth, if productivity increases in the sectors producing necessities, with a constant real wage, in which case the nominal wage can decline while the workers would still be able to purchase the same quantity of goods (by implication, more would be available for the capitalists).

Marx calls the first three cases the production of absolute surplus value, while the third produces relative surplus value. In brief, absolute surplus value involves the expenditure of more labor, whether in the same working day or in a longer day, with given wages. This form of exploitation was especially important in early capitalism, when the working day was stretched to twelve, fourteen or even sixteen hours. More recently, absolute surplus value has often been extracted through the lengthening of the working week and the infiltration of work into leisure time, at least for certain sectors of the workforce (work often extends into the weekend and holidays and the general availability of mobile phones and portable computers allows the employees to be permanently on duty). Moreover, the workers are frequently compelled to raise their productivity through more intense labor (e.g., faster production lines or reduced breaks) or coerced into acquiring new skills in their 'free' time (e.g., attending conferences and training programs). However, the extraction of absolute surplus value is limited because it is impossible to increase the working day or the intensity of labor indefinitely and because the workers learn to resist against these forms of exploitation.

In contrast, the introduction of new technology and new machines allows more inputs to be worked up into outputs in a given labor time; in other words, they reduce the quantity of labor necessary to produce each unit of the output. When productivity rises faster than wages across the economy, the share of surplus value in the total value-added increases and the workers' share declines. This is what Marx calls relative surplus value. Relative surplus value is more flexible than absolute surplus value and it has become the most important form of exploitation under modern capitalism, because productivity growth can outstrip wage increases for long periods.

5   Wage Labor

Historically, wage labor expands, and capitalist development takes off, when the peasants, artisans and the self-employed lose control of and direct access to, the means of production (land, tools, machines and so on), or as non-capitalist forms of production become unable to provide for their subsistence. It follows that the notion that the wage contract is the outcome of a free bargain between equals is both partial and misleading. Even though the workers are free to apply for one job rather than another, or to leave the labor market entirely, they are almost always in a weak bargaining position when facing their prospective employers. The wage workers need money to attend to the pressing needs of their household, including subsistence needs, mortgage, rent and debt service and suffer great uncertainty about the future, with severe penalties if caught short. These are some of the sticks with which capitalist society forces the workers to sign up 'freely' to the labor contract, 'spontaneously' turn up for work as and when required and 'voluntarily' satisfy the expectations of their line managers.

The wage relation implies that the workers' capacity to work, that Marx calls their labor power, has become a commodity. The use value of labor power is its capacity to produce other use values (clothes, food, laptops and so on). Its exchange value is represented by the wage rate. In this sense, labor power is a commodity like any other and the wage workers are commodity sellers.

Marx stresses the need to distinguish between *labor* and *labor power*. Labor power is the potential to produce things, while labor is its use, that is, the act of transforming given natural and social conditions into a planned output. When capitalists hire workers, they purchase the workers' labor power for a specific length of time. Once this transaction has been completed the workers' time belongs to the capitalists, who wish to extract from them as much labor as possible within the terms of the contract. The workers, in turn, tend to resist abuse by the capitalist and they may limit the intensity of labor unilaterally or reject arbitrary changes in the production norms. In sum, the purchase of labor power does not guarantee that a given quantity of labor is forthcoming, or that a certain quantity of value will be produced. The outcome depends upon persuasion and conflict in the shop floor, farm, or office.

This conclusion implies that there is an irreducible uncertainty in the translation from the purchase of labor power into the creation of value, in contrast, say, with the predictable depreciation of a tool, a machine or even a horse. This has important implications for Marx's theory of value. First, it shows that class conflict is inescapably at the core of capitalist production. Capitalists must press the workers to produce more, while the workers, by virtue of their humanity, will always resist. Second, the profitability of enterprise is fundamentally uncertain, and this is not so much for Keynesian reasons centred on expectations and effective demand (which are true enough, but analytically secondary), but because the outcome of conflict between capitalists and workers both within the production line and in society at large is always uncertain. Third, it suggests that in capitalism the workers are always *poor*, not because they tend to be paid below the value of labor power, or because absolute poverty must ultimately grind them down, but because the workers are unavoidably dependent upon capital for their employment and, consequently, for their access to necessities.

6   Value and Surplus Value

The capitalists combine the means of production, generally purchased from other capitalists, with the labor of wage workers in order to produce commodities for sale at a profit. The circuit of industrial capital captures the essential aspects of factory production, farm labor, office work and other forms of capitalist production:

$$M - C <^{MP}_{LP} \ldots P \ldots C' - M'$$

The circuit starts when the capitalist advances money (M) to purchase two types of commodities (C), means of production (MP) and labor power (LP). During production (... P ...) the workers transform the means of production into new commodities (C'), that are sold for more money (M'). It was shown above that the difference between M' and M is the surplus value. Surplus value is the source of industrial and commercial profit and other forms of profit, for example, interest and rent.

Marx stresses that surplus value cannot arise purely out of exchange. Although some can profit from the sale of commodities above their value (unequal exchange), for example, unscrupulous traders and speculators, this is not possible for every seller for two reasons. First, the sellers are also buyers. If every seller surcharged his customers by 10 per cent, say, their gains would be lost to their own suppliers, and no one would profit from this exercise. Therefore, although some can become rich by robbing or outwitting others, this is not possible for society as a whole (in other words, cheating transfers value, but it does not create new value); consequently, unequal exchanges cannot provide a general explanation of profit. Second, competition tends to increase supply in any sector offering exceptional profits, eventually eliminating the advantages of individual luck or cunning. Therefore, surplus value (or profit in general) must be explained for society as a whole, or at the level of *class*, rather than relying on individual merit or acumen.

A general explanation of surplus value and profits must, then, be based on equal exchanges at value. Inspection of the circuit of industrial capital shows that surplus value is the difference between the value of the output, C' and the value of the inputs, MP and LP. Since this difference cannot be due to unequal exchange, the value increment must derive from the process of production. More specifically, for Marx, surplus value derives from the consumption of a commodity whose *use value* is to *create new value*.

The means of production are, by definition, converted into the output (e.g., leather, plastic, glue, thread, and so on physically become a new shoe); this transmogrification creates a new use value, but not new value, as the value of the inputs is simply transferred to the output – if the transformation of materials created value by itself, humans could wait for nature to make them all rich. Sadly (or not), nature is not capitalist. Marx insists that value is neither a product of nature, nor a substance embodied in the commodities. Instead, value is a social relation between commodity producers that appears as a relationship between things (specifically, commodity values appear through their prices, that is, the relationship between goods and money, as was shown above). Goods and services possess value only under certain social and historical circumstances. The value relation develops fully only in capitalism, in tandem with the production of commodities, the use of money, the diffusion of wage labor and the generalisation of market-related property rights; that is, under capitalism, value incorporates all the most important economic relationships. In doing this, value relations regulate economic activity, influence the structure of output and employment and set limits to social welfare.

If value is a social relation typical of commodity societies, its source (and the origin of surplus value) must be the performance of commodity-producing labor (the productive consumption of the commodity labor power) rather than the metamorphosis of things. As was mentioned above, when a capitalist hires a worker to produce shoes, their labor transforms the inputs into the output. Because the inputs are physically blended into the output, their value is simultaneously transferred, and it becomes part of the value of the output. In addition to the transfer of the value of the inputs, labor simultaneously adds new value to the product. In other words, while the means of production contribute value because of the labor time necessary *elsewhere* to produce them as commodities, newly performed labor contributes *new value* to the output.

It follows that the value of the output is equal to the value of the inputs (MP) plus the value added by the workers during production. Since the value of the means of production is merely transferred, production is profitable only if the value added exceeds the wage costs: in other words, surplus value is the difference between the value added by the workers and the value of labor power. Consequently, *the wage workers are exploited as a class because they work for longer than the time it takes to produce the goods that they command or control.* In the rest of the time, the workers are exploited – they produce value for the capitalists. For example, if the goods necessary to reproduce the working class can be produced in four hours, but the working day is eight hours, the workers work 'for themselves' half the time and in the other half they work 'for the capitalists': the rate of exploitation (the ratio between what Marx calls 'surplus labor time' and 'necessary labor time') is 100 per cent.

7   Competition and Mechanisation

Competition plays an essential role in capitalism. Marx distinguishes between two types of competition: between capitals in the same sector (producing commodities with the same use value) and between capitals in different sectors (producing commodities with distinct use values). Capitals in the same sector compete for profits primarily through the introduction of cost-cutting technical innovations. If an innovating firm can produce at a lower cost than its competitors and they sell identical commodities at the same price, the more productive firm reaps a higher profit rate and it can increase its market share, invest more and, potentially, destroy its rivals. Competition between capitals producing identical use values with distinct technologies leads to the differentiation of the profit rates; this type of competition explains the tendency towards continuous technical progress in capitalism, which is absent in pre-capitalist societies; it also raises the possibility of monopoly and crises of disproportion and overproduction.

Mechanization is the most important aspect of competition within sectors. At the level of individual (many) capitals, mechanization maximizes the gains from co-operation, reduces unit costs, increases the value-productivity of labor, allows increasingly sophisticated goods to be produced with higher investment and raises the profit rate of the innovating capitals. This tends to reduce the scope for competition by independent producers and their ability to survive except as wage workers or as dependent contractors. In turn, within each firm, mechanization socializes production because it imposes production norms that reduce the scope for worker control over the expenditure of their labor power.[3] At the level of capital in general, mechanisation facilitates the extraction of relative surplus value.

In turn, mechanization can, potentially, give the workers greater control over their job conditions and reduce the drudgery associated with difficult or repetitive tasks, but this would surrender control of production to the working class, which capitalists will not willingly do. In other words, although capitalism and productivity growth are inseparable (because of competition within each sector), this relationship is not straightforward for two reasons. First, firms do not select the technologies that are most productive of use values but those that are most profitable, and these criteria may lead to distinct outcomes. Second, the imperative of social control in the production line and in society may introduce further biases in the choice of technology.

Competition between capitals in different sectors is different: it produces a tendency towards the equalisation of profit rates across the (international) economy. This type of competition explains the structures and processes associated with competitive markets, including supply shifts and capital migration. For example, faced with high profits in the (Swiss) pharmaceutical sector and low profits in the (US) steel industry, capitals may decide to invest in another sector and/or country, increasing supply in the former (which eventually lowers pharmaceuticals prices and profit rates), decreasing supply in the latter (which eventually raises steel prices and profit rates), migrate from the latter to the former, or pursue a combination of strategies. What these alternatives have in common is that they create a tendency towards the equalization of profit rates across the economy, whether national or global. Inter-sectoral competition and the tendency towards the equalization of profit rates are enormously facilitated by finance.

When it is considered across these two levels, capitalist competition does not lead either to monopoly or to equalization of profit rates. Quite the contrary; what Marx's analysis reveals is not inexorable outcomes, but complex processes which must be examined in their specific context. The future is always open, and Marx studiously avoids making predictions; he only identifies conflicting

---

3 'An automated labour process is [...] a labour process of a completely social scope, social in the terms of a science and a technology resting on the logic of appropriation peculiar to commodity value. The subjectivity of the individual labour-power, the mental, sensorial and nervous functions of an individual while at work, has been replaced by the electronics of automation [...] Automation amounts to the socialisation of the human labour-power which, in certain aspects, it surpasses in its scope of capability, range of action, its speed, reliability and precision, though only in a restricted and set specialisation [...] The worker is not freed from labour by the machine, but his labour is emptied of content' (Sohn-Rethel 1978, p.176).

forces and their drivers. More specifically, attempts to 'add up' the impact of competition within and between sectors are analytically illegitimate, because of their distinct levels of abstraction: competition within sectors is relatively more abstract and analytically more important, than competition between sectors, for two reasons. First, profit must be produced before it can be distributed and equalized, in which case analysis of technologies, methods of production and work practices should precede the study of market strategies. Second, although migration can raise the profit rate of individual capitals, changes in the profitability of capital as a whole are contingent upon technical progress.

8   Mass Production

Pre-capitalist production is characterized by small scale and fragmentation. In contrast, in developed capitalist economies, firms produce a wide range of goods and services in large quantities.[4] Underlying the variety of models, colors, types and commodities available for sale, there is a highly developed system of production, including finance, accounting, design, planning, logistics, hiring, training and managing the workforce, manufacturing, marketing, transport, distribution and other activities. These aspects of capitalist production are managed meticulously and professionally, often by large organizations, both within and across the chains of activities connecting production and consumption. Inevitably, mass production necessitates the employment of masses of workers.

Even when individual firms are small, downsize, or spin-off independent companies, capitalist production processes tend to become increasingly integrated vertically into systems of provision that employ large numbers of workers in order to produce food, clothes, autos, TV shows and other commodities. Within each system of provision, the labor of individual workers exists and can be analyzed, only as part of the whole. This labor is performed according to the rhythm dictated by technology, management, machinery, competition, and the demands of finance, limited by collective resistance on the shop floor and in society at large.

Two important implications follow from mass production. First, mass production and collective work increase the productivity of labor. The added

---

4 'Capitalist production only really begins [...] when each individual capital simultaneously employs a comparatively large number of workers and when, as a result, the labour-process is carried on an extensive scale and yields relatively large quantities of products [...] This is true both historically and conceptually' (Marx 1976, p.439).

power of collective (co-operative) work is created by capital, by virtue of its command of large groups of workers, and it is appropriated directly by the capitalist.[5] Second, the organization, integration and mechanization of production averages out the labor of wage workers directly in production:

> each worker, or group of workers, prepares the raw material for another worker or group of workers. The result of the labour of the one is the starting-point for the labour of the other [...] [T]he direct mutual interdependence of the different pieces of work and therefore of the workers, compels each one of them to spend on his work no more than the necessary time. This creates a continuity, a uniformity, a regularity, order and even an intensity of labour, quite different from that found in an independent handicraft or even in simple co-operation [...] In manufacture [...] the provision of a given quantity of the product in a given period of labour is a technical law of the process of production itself.
>
> MARX 1976, pp.464–465

Consequently,

> The labor objectified in value is labor of an average social quality, it is an expression of average labor-power [...] The law of valorization therefore comes fully into its own for the individual producer only when he produces as a capitalist and employs a number of workers simultaneously, i.e. when from the outset he sets in motion labor of a socially average character.
>
> MARX 1976, pp.440–441

Co-operation under centralized management in the shop floor averages out labor employed by capital already in the process of production, which creates the collective worker, as a typical consequence of capitalist production:

---

5   [A]ny co-operation and combination of labour in production generates a combined, social productivity of labour which exceeds the sum of individual, isolated productivities [...] Thus, in capitalism, the productive forces of social labour – collective unity in co-operation, combination in the division of labour, the uses of the forces of nature and the sciences – appear as productive forces of capital, the mediator [...] [C]apital secures [...] the productive power of socially combined labour, which appears as a productive power inherent in capital' (Lebowitz 1992, pp.67, 69, emphasis omitted).

The collective worker, formed out of the combination of a number of specialized workers, is the item of machinery specifically characteristic of the manufacturing period.

MARX 1976, p.468

In general, then, capitalist production is collective production, whether it is carried out in distinct locations or under the control of small firms, industrial and financial conglomerates, or transnational corporations. The unmediated socialization of production under capitalism transforms not only the process of labor into a collective process but it transforms, also, the formation of value; this is no longer an individual process that is averaged out at the point of sale of each individual commodity, as is the case under simple commodity production. In advanced capitalism, where production is mechanized and labor is collective and managed centrally within the production unit, value is created in production; in turn, the production process itself imposes social discipline through the planned integration and equalization of labor on the shop floor, the articulation of the processes of production and, at a further remove, by the regulation of the process of extraction of surplus value by financial market institutions and processes, with relatively low rates of exploitation attracting swift punishment in the form of divestment, declining share prices or the imposition of limits to the existing credit lines.

9   The Human Implications of Capitalism

The interpretation of Marx's theory of value outlined in this chapter can be summarized as follows. Marx's theory starts from the principle that human societies reproduce themselves, interact with one another and change over time through the performance of labor. Labor and its products are always socially divided, and, under capitalism, these processes and their outcomes are determined by the monopoly of the means of production by the class of capitalists, the commodification of labor power and the commodity form of the products of labor. In these circumstances, the products of labor generally take the value form and economic exploitation is based on the extraction of surplus value. Hence, the capital relation includes the monopoly of the means of production, wage labor and the continuous reproduction of two large and mutually conditioning social classes: capitalists and workers. When analyzed from this angle, the theory of value is a theory of class, class relations and exploitation. The concept of value is essential because it expresses the relations of exploitation under capitalism and allows them to be explained despite the misleading appearances created by the predominance of voluntary market exchanges.

This approach to Marx's political economy implies that value theory is not essentially a theory of the 'separation' of commodity producers, commodity exchange ratios, labor embodied in products or the allocation of labor in the economy. Quite the contrary, a class interpretation of Marx's theory of value highlights the social form of the property relations (the means of production are owned by the class of capitalists), the social form of labor (wage labor), the mode of labor control (capitalists hire and manage the expenditure of labor power), the social form of the products of labor and of goods and services more generally (commodities) and the objective of social production (profit rather than, say, need, exchange, tribute, consumption or investment).

In doing this, Marx's value theory can help us to overcome the fragmentation of the experience of exploitation in capitalism and it can show that capitalist production necessarily involves social conflicts both in production and in distribution. It can also inform action to end this system of production, not only as the implication of consistent theoretical work but, especially and much more urgently, in order to articulate the possibility of human freedom and even of biological survival given the rapid environmental degradation promoted by modern capitalism.

In sharp contrast with the Marxist approach, mainstream economic theory defines capital as an ensemble of things, including means of production, money, financial assets and, more recently, even human knowledge and community relations (named human capital and social capital, respectively). This is incorrect. These objects, assets and human attributes have existed as long as humans have been on Earth, while capital and capitalism are relatively recent. It is misleading to extend the concept of capital where it does not belong, as if it were valid universally or throughout history. For example, a horse, hammer or one million dollars may or may not be capital; that depends on the context in which they are used. If they are engaged in production for profit through the direct or indirect employment of wage labor, they are capital; otherwise, they are simply animals, tools or banknotes.

Like value, capital is a social relation that appears as things. However, while value is a general relationship between producers and sellers of commodities, capital is a social relation of exploitation. This relationship includes two classes, defined by their ownership, control, and use of the means of production: the capitalists, who own the means of production, buy labor power, and command the product of labor and the wage workers, who sell their labor power and operate the means of production without owning them. The relationship between these two classes is the basis for the social division of labor and the production and distribution of commodities.

Competition and exploitation through the extraction of surplus value render capitalism uniquely able to develop technology and the forces of production. This is the main reason why Marx admires the progressive features of capitalism. However, capitalism is also the most destructive mode of production in history. The profit motive is blind, and it can be overwhelming. It has led to astonishing discoveries and unsurpassed improvements in living standards. But capitalism has also led to widespread destruction and degradation of the environment and of human lives. Profit-seeking has led to slavery, mass murder and genocide (for example, against the native populations of the Belgian Congo and the United States, in South Africa under apartheid and in colonial and inter-imperialist wars, most clearly in World War I), the brutal exploitation of the workers (in 19th Century Britain, 20th Century Brazil and 21st Century China) and the uncontrolled destruction of the environment (in the USA, Europe, India, Indonesia and elsewhere), with long-term global implications.

Capitalism both generates and condones the mass unemployment of workers, machinery and land in spite of the prevalence of unsatisfied wants and it tolerates poverty even though the means to abolish it are readily available. Capitalism extends the human life span, but often empties life of meaning. It supports unparalleled achievements in human education and culture while, simultaneously, fostering idiocy, greed, mendacity, sexual and racial discrimination and other forms of human degradation. Paradoxically, the accumulation of material wealth often impoverishes human existence.

These contradictory effects of capitalism are inseparable. It is impossible to pick and choose the appealing features of the 'market economies' and discard those that we find distasteful. Private property of the means of production and market competition *necessarily* give rise to the wage relation, exploitation through the extraction of surplus value and they facilitate crises, war and other negative features of capitalism. This places a strict limit on the possibility of social, political and economic reforms.

Limitations such as these led Marx to conclude that capitalism can – and should – be overthrown and it should be replaced by another social system, that he called communism. For Marx, communism opens the possibility of realization of the potential of the vast majority through the elimination of the irrationalities and human costs of capitalism, including systemic inequality, material deprivation, destructive competition, greed and economic exploitation. This task remains to be achieved.

References

Bottomore, Tom (ed.). 1991. *A Dictionary of Marxist Thought*. Oxford: Basil Blackwell.

Callinicos, Alex. 2014. *Deciphering Capital: Marx's Capital and Its Destiny*. London: Bookmarks.

Fine, Ben and Saad-Filho, Alfredo. 2013. *The Elgar Companion to Marxist Economics*. Aldershot: Edward Elgar.

Fine, Ben and Saad-Filho, Alfredo. 2016. *Marx's Capital*, 6th ed. London: Pluto Press.

Harvey, David. 2010. *A Companion to Marx's Capital*. London: Verso.

Heinrich, Michael. 2012. *An Introduction to the Three Volumes of Karl Marx's Capital*. New York: Monthly Review Press.

Howard, Michael and King, John. 1989, 1991. *A History of Marxian Economics*, 2 Vols. Princeton: Princeton University Press.

Lebowitz, Michael (1992) *Beyond Capital, Marx's Political Economy of the Working Class*, London: Macmillan.

Marx, Karl. 1976. *Capital*, Volume 1. Harmondsworth: Penguin.

Marx, Karl. 1978. *Capital*, Volume 2. Harmondsworth: Penguin.

Saad-Filho, Alfredo. 2002. *The Value of Marx: Political Economy for Contemporary Capitalism*. London: Routledge.

Saad-Filho, Alfredo. 2019. *Value and Crisis*. Leiden: Brill.

Smith, Adam. 1991. *Inquiry into the Nature and Causes of the Wealth of Nations*. London: Everyman.

Sohn-Rethel, Alfred. 1978. *Intellectual and Manual Labour: A Critique of Epistemology*, London: Macmillan.

Weeks, John. 2010. *Capital, Exploitation and Crises*. London: Routledge.

CHAPTER 5

Social Oppression, Class Relation, and Capitalist Accumulation

Raju J Das

The dominant approach to social oppression is that of identity politics. The latter is generally informed not only by liberalism but also by post-structuralism that has been popularized by the likes of Foucault, and Laclau and Mouffe, and that rejects materialism, objectivity, systemic thinking, and socialism.[1] Armed with these ideas, identity politics sees the main division in society as the one between those who are (perceived to be) culturally privileged and those who are not, and not between classes. Lack of respect/recognition for certain groups is said to be the major cause of oppression.

Much identity politics is based on the concept of intersectionality.[2] Crenshaw (1989) developed the metaphor of an intersection of roads which denote the different axes of oppression. There is a matrix of oppression in which race, gender, sexual orientation, 'class-prejudice', etc. are all important, and they all interact, compounding the effects of the individual axis of oppression. The intersectionality approach is useful in that it sees the axes of oppression as inter-related. But it is problematic on various grounds. For one, the whole matter of oppression is often seen as based on how people think. For example, bell hooks (Gloria Watkins) (1989:175) says that there exist 'interlocking systems of domination' (or 'a politic of domination'), which share 'the ideological ground' in the sense of 'a belief in domination and a belief in notions of superior and inferior'. She *disagrees* that capitalism underlies the systems of oppression.

Intersectionalism cannot explain the nature of the surface on which different roads intersect, and without which no roads can exist. The roads of single oppressions (e.g. race, gender, etc.) that are said to intersect are built on a sandy

---

1   For them, the political is autonomous of the economic, and non-class relations are autonomous of class relations (see Wood, 1990).

2   There is a large amount of literature on the identity politics approach, including intersectionality. Its basic ideas are well known and need not be reviewed. On the Marxist examination of intersectionality, see *Science and Society*, 2018; Cassell, 2017; and Smith, 2008.

surface of subjectivity ('I think I am x and I am different from y, so I am that').[3] The main problem of identity politics, in terms of causality, is that it is 'class-deprived'.[4] *This* is the identity of identity politics. To the extent that class is mentioned at all, it appears in ways that show the poverty of thinking in identity politics, including intersectionalism.

Firstly, class is seen as class*ism* – i.e., in the sense of cultural-social prejudice against the working-class people (or 'the poor'). For bell hooks (original name, Gloria Watkins) (1989:175), capitalism is simply a *manifestation* of something deeper, which is merely cultural (or cultural-political). Followers of identity politics are indeed like the 'valiant fellow [who] had the idea that [people] were drowned in water only because they were possessed with the idea of gravity' (Marx 1845a). Secondly, class is seen in terms of oppression: (Marx's) class is inherently masculinist, Eurocentric, etc. So, the working class is automatically seen as (oppressive) white (straight) males (Di Stefano, 1991).[5] Thirdly, when the material dimension of class receives any attention, this is done in merely distributivist – gradational – sense of some people having less income, etc. than others.[6] Fourthly, the gradational view of economic problems such as low income is combined with an oppression framework such that: the economic problems are mainly seen as experienced by those who are socially oppressed (e.g. black women), i.e. as 'problems of the disproportionately poor' (Gimenez, 2018: 105), and not as experienced by the property-less as such. Oppression (cultural domination), and not class/capitalism, is then the main reason why some groups suffer. Fifthly, the identity politics approach gives class/capitalism no causal primacy over relations of oppression, treating both at the same level of analysis.[7] Green

---

3 The identity politics approach has no objective view about society: there are only '*situated knowledges* and for clearly identifiable subordinate groups, subjugated knowledges', as Patricia Collins (1990: 234) says approvingly.

4 Any view/action that ignores class relation serves to support the ruling class, so it *is* a class-view. By 'class-deprived' (or classlessness) of identity politics, I am referring to the ways in which it, more or less, ignores a) the impact of the objective class relation on oppression, and b) struggles of the property-less against the ruling class and its state.

5 Michele Barrett (1980: 125) says: 'it is evident that for Marx the typical wage-labourer is male'.

6 In some feminist circles, the material aspects of women's oppression *are* examined, but the mistaken emphasis is on the *empirical* relation between men and women, and not underlying class-mechanisms. Anne Pollert (1996) rightly says that while male dominance is almost ubiquitous, 'men's [unequal] relationship to women does not contain a mutually defining economic relationship in the same way as the relations of capitalism to wage labour' (p. 654).

7 According to the Black feminist version of intersectionality that Brewer (2018) endorses, one that does have an anti-capitalist moment, 'In the movement for social transformation we simply cannot articulate race, class, gender in reductionist terms but must move with a critical understanding of the deep interrelationality of social forces for fundamental social change'. This approach, explored in details in Brewer (1999), equates intersectionality to

(2006: 607) says: 'From their very origins, class relations are gendered, racialized, sexualized, just as gender is classed, racialized and sexualized and race is sexualized, classed and gendered'.

Finally, the de-emphasis on class leads to a problematic political proposal: the politics of idealism or cultural politics, or, the politics of recognition. Sonia Kruks (2001:85) says: in identity politics, 'what is demanded is respect for oneself as different'. It makes a demand 'for autonomy or for rights and recognitions' (Lancaster, 2017). Any distributivist politics takes the form of diversity politics – demanding employment for blacks and white women, etc., and not for *all* property-less people. Such a proposal does nothing to challenge accumulation under class relations that ultimately determines the total amount of employment opportunity in a country as a whole.

Given its near-aversion to class, which is central to Marxism, identity politics mistakenly claims that Marx/Marxism is race- and color-blind. As Sherry Wolf (2009:201) reports, Marxism is also accused of 'erotophobia', 'meaning presumably that Marxists are antisex'.[8] In any case, Marxism is the biggest 'other' of identity politics thinkers/activists. Tom Brass (2017:82) says: 'Marxism is emphatically not the same as identity politics – the two positions are in fact dialectically opposite and incompatible'.

In this chapter, I insist on the *primacy* of class relations (and class politics), but in a way that takes social oppression no less seriously than identity politics does. An alternative approach to society informed by Marx that explains the problems and issues in modern society in terms of the class relations of capitalism must take oppression seriously, both intellectually and politically. Therefore, I discuss how oppression is played out on the surface of class, as an objective set of social relations, and how class mechanisms explain oppression (and inform anti-oppression politics). However, unlike much discussion on oppression in and outside Marxism, not only do I not accept intersectionality but also do I not treat gender-inequality, racism, heteronormativity, religious discrimination, casteism, etc., separately.[9] I discuss these different forms of

---

inter-relationship, treating class and non-class relations as equally important, in terms of knowing the world and changing it.

8   One does not need to read Kollontai to know that given its materialist worldview, Marx/Marxism can be anything but antisex! (See Marx, 1844a; Engels, 1883; Engels, 1886).

9   The caste system oppresses 700–800 million people in India only. There is caste-like discrimination against the so-called 'untouchables' in Japan as well. Yet, caste is hardly mentioned in the identity politics literature, and curiously, indeed, in Western Marxism. Some even argue that caste, which is discrimination based on birth, is to be seen at par with race (Pinto, 2001). Of course, Hindu-nationalists playing the dangerous identity politics of religion deny the importance of caste oppression within Hindu society.

oppression in terms of what is *common* to them, and in their relation to class/capitalism.

The chapter has four sections. In section 1, I introduce two broad categories in Marx's thinking about oppression. In sections 2–3, I deal with what I consider the Marxist approach to oppression, including how Marx actually examined it, at the level of class and then capitalism, respectively. In the concluding section (section 4), I draw some theoretical and political implications of my arguments.

1   The Dialectical Marx and (the Fact of) Social Oppression

Marx's own contribution to the understanding of social oppression falls in two categories. Firstly, he has written, albeit sporadically and not always adequately, about oppression based on race, nationality, caste, religion, and gender. Secondly, and more importantly, his general theoretical writings (which are philosophical and social-theoretic as well as scientific) are such that they can be 'applied' to the study of oppression and to anti-oppression politics. Many of his specific writings on oppression have contemporary relevance precisely because they are informed by his general theoretical work.

1.1   *Marx and the Material Reality of Oppression*
The specific writings on oppression by Marx as 'a poor male white European' are a proof against the identity politics' fetishism of personal experience as the main/sole cause of our knowledge and action. Marx was not in India when the sepoy (troops) mutiny happened as a revolt against the British rule in the mid-1850s, nor did he experience or directly observe racist-capitalist slavery in the US and elsewhere. Yet, he writes against colonialism and slavery from the standpoint of the colonized and the slaves, and he inspires contemporary Marxists to take an anti-colonial and anti-racist stance. One might add that Marx hardly had the experience of being exploited as a worker, but he is the best theorist of exploitation. Marx says: 'nobody had written so much on money and had so little [of it]' (quoted in Eagleton, 2011:171).

Marx indeed draws attention to the facts of oppression in its various forms during his own time. As Anderson (2016: 3) says: 'Marx's proletariat was not only white and European, but also encompassed Black labor in America, as well as the Irish, not considered "white" at the time by the dominant cultures of Britain and North America'. Marx (1977:915) draws attention to 'the extirpation, enslavement and entombment in mines of the aboriginal population'. He writes about the oppression of women, including of the non-working-class background (Brown, 2012). Marx (1845b) laments that 'the general position of women in modern society is inhuman'. He disparagingly talks about the bourgeois family in which 'wife and children are the slaves of the husband' and are thus the first form of property. Marx (1844a) says that 'The direct, natural, and necessary relation of person to person is the *relation of man* to *woman*' and that 'From this relationship one can therefore judge man's whole level of development.'

Marx is also concerned about religious discrimination (including that against Catholics). He is concerned about the 'narrow forms of nationalism', that 'retreated into religious identities' (Anderson, 2016:241). Marx is concerned that people thought that "Mohammedanism could not exist in civilized states" (quoted in Anderson, 2016: 46). His remarks are important given rampant Islamophobia in the world as a part of the global turn to the right and to religious nationalisms (e.g., Hindu nationalism in India).

1.2   Marx's General Writings with Relevance for Understanding Oppression

Marx has produced wide-ranging general ideas in the realm of philosophy and social theory. These ideas help us see the weaknesses of identity politics some of which are discussed earlier and are relevant to a better understanding of oppression. These include the following (for details, see Das, 2017: chapter 5):

1.   the nature of a 'thing' depends on its relations to other 'things', producing a *totality/system* of many *relations/processes*, which has its internal *contradictions* that drive *change*.

2.   understanding the multiple determinations of the complex concrete requires *abstraction*, which involves slicing the reality into its components parts for analysis, seeing everything in terms of its *form and content*, and then putting these components back together;

3.   there is a *materiality* about all human beings in the sense that they have certain material needs, which is why they share some common traits with the natural world and with one another, but they are also thinking beings;

4.   *historically* developing *material conditions*, including how people earn their livelihood, shape *consciousness* and *politics*, which, in turn, shape the material conditions that have a degree of primacy.

Identity politics over-emphasizes thinking ('cultural identity') and politics (cultural politics of identity). But human beings, whether priests, popes, peddlers of ideas or politicians, cannot live on ideas or politics, although the latter are important. To paraphrase a long and famous footnote in *Capital 1* (Marx, 1977:176), it is the mode in which people gain their livelihood that explains why politics and ideas shape life. More dialectically, the material world and ideas about it exist in a system in which the former shapes the latter more than is shaped by the latter. So, oppression cannot exist merely in the mind independently of objective conditions, even if oppression does have a discursive aspect. Nor can politics merely be politics of identity. Politics is ultimately the politics of material conflict between classes (and class-fractions) (Marx and Engels, 1978:54). Marx would counter the identity politics' stress on the individual: Marx (1845c) says that 'the human essence is no abstraction inherent in each single individual' and that 'it is the ensemble of the social relations.' And when one stresses humanity's material conditions and their contradiction-ridden social relations, one cannot but think about the class character of society seriously. Marx would argue that: class as a relation, and oppression as a relation, coexist and form a system, in which class has primacy (as explained below).[10]

2   Marxism and the Explanation of Social Oppression: Class-Mechanisms

Marx's philosophical ideas and historical materialism inform his general theoretical ideas. These ideas include his work on political economy of class and capitalism and inform his understanding of oppression.

The distinction between content and form is crucial to Marx's (1977:125) thinking: e.g. wealth vs its commodity form. Following this idea, one can say that common to racism, sexism, casteism, etc., is the *content* of oppression (I am dealing with the social oppression of the exploited). Racism, etc. are its different *forms*. I would then argue that Marx's general writings allow us to view the content of social oppression as having at least five inter-related aspects, even if he himself does not view oppression like this. These are: a) inferiorization/devaluation and b) political-social subjugation, which produce/enable c) separation between the oppressed and the non-oppressed, and all of these mechanisms (a, b and c) in turn causing d) super-exploitation (subjection to above-average amount of exploitation), and e) consequent separation from the things that an average person needs in life. If all these different aspects are to be 'reduced' to one thing, it would be 'tyranny', in Marx's language, i.e., an attack on the democratic rights of the oppressed groups in

---

10   Brown (2012) has done extensive and admirable work on Marx's thinking about women. But I disagree with her strongly when she says that in relation to gender and class, 'Marx's theory of society ... does not fundamentally privilege either' (p.219). For me, Marx's dialectical method (which Brown favourably refers to) does not license a view that all things in the world are equally important.

a class society; this is also the language of Lenin (1901). All socially oppressed groups are treated as sub-human: they are treated as those who hold less than one unit of labor power and less than one unit of citizenship. If a black and a white, or if a white man and a white woman, can do a job equally, then deliberately denying the job to the black or to the white woman, is a violation of their democratic right. Oppression – seen as the violation of democratic right – is expressed as physical violence, denial of autonomy, symbolic humiliation, under-representation in well-paid jobs, and over-exploitation.[11]

The facts of oppression can only be explained in terms of how the effects of the *universal* mechanisms of class relations interact with particular actual/perceived traits/experiences of socio-culturally oppressed groups, *within* a class society. Such a framework can be built on the basis of Marx and on the basis of the work of Marxists since Marx who have sought to rectify his silences and develop his ideas.

Class is a universal process in the last 10,000 years of the 200,000-old history of the human species. Just like oppression, class has common mechanisms across class societies. Then class mechanisms take the capitalistic form (discussed in the next section). Class is a process whereby property is controlled by a small minority that extracts surplus labor from the majority. Marx (1977: 344), who did not write systematically about class, provides the following insight in *Capital Vol 1*:

> Wherever a part of society possesses the monopoly of the means of production, the labourer, free or not free, must add to the labour-time necessary for his own maintenance an extra labour-time in order to produce the means of subsistence for the owners of the means of production ...

Due to a rise in productivity, when society is able to produce more than what it needs for its immediate needs, there is a surplus (in the 'technical' sense). This surplus becomes a 'surplus' in the social sense when a small class, which has little direct role in producing the surplus, appropriates it from the majority (surplus producers). When society's property as well as the social surplus are controlled by a minority, a socially produced scarcity for many results.[12]

---

11   Oppression of women from non-capitalist toiling classes, as an oppressed group, is expressed as: rape, domestic violence, lack of control over reproductive capacity, sex trafficking, over-representation in low-paid work, and over-exploitation.

12   There can be scarcity due to the lack of development of productive forces relative to natural conditions too.

The dual separation – from property and from surplus – is not given, however. The continued reproduction and the degree of separation are a matter of class struggle. The majority must be *constantly* stopped from not only having significant access to the surplus but also from taking significant control over property. To achieve this separation and to increase surplus, various mechanisms are put in place, including repression of direct producers by the state and the use of ideologies that concern the *entire* society to justify exploitation. Another mechanism is the oppression of specific groups: tyranny (as explained above).

Social production – production of means of production and of subsistence under definite class relations – sets limit within which various mechanisms of oppression are played out, including, for example, men's control over women' labor, and upper castes' control over the labor of lower castes. In *German Ideology*, Marx (1845a) emphasizes division of labor in class-societies, an important aspect of which is the sexual division of labor. To the extent that certain biological traits of women make them responsible for childbearing and for much of child-rearing,[13] women tend to be less responsible for social production and for production of social surplus than men, so a material basis is created for women's labor to be *seen as* inferior or somehow less important. Apart from the division of labor, also relevant is the private property. As Engels (1884) argues: the monogamous family 'is based on the supremacy of the man, the express purpose being to produce children of undisputed paternity; such paternity is demanded because these children are later to come into their father's property as his natural heirs'. Given women's role in the physical and moral reproduction of the species and therefore of the future direct producer (of surplus) as economically efficient and morally suitable (as obedient people) and given their role in the transmission of property to the male heirs, it is important, from the ruling class standpoint, that women's labor and life be controlled. Inferiorization is a tool to control this important aspect of human life (as is coercion and violence): if women's labor was actually *not* important, there would be *no* need to control it.

Consider caste-based oppression. Like gender-based oppression, it is deeply connected to private property, reproducing class relations (Bandyopadhyaya, 2002; Namboodiripad, 1981; Patnaik, 2016; Ranadive, 1982). According to Marx,

---

13 Child-rearing includes both physical and moral – educational – aspects. These aspects involve women teaching, for example, the values of class society to the children (e.g. respect of private property and laws; rugged individualism, etc.). Indeed, 'raising children for their future entry into the labor market is not like raising calves and lambs for the livestock market. The reproduction of human labor power has not only a biological but also a social, i.e. ideological character', so one cannot 'treat mothers as only doing good for their children' (Workers Vanguard, 2015).

with social division of labor (the division of social labor into different occupations), the different groups specializing in different kinds of labor formed caste occupations. Marx (1859) says: 'legislation may perpetuate land ownership in certain families, or allocate labor as a hereditary privilege, thus consolidating it into a caste system', which is a system of oppression based on birth. Singh (2014) argues that caste hierarchy was originally grounded in a monopoly of land rights and political power supported by religious (and secular) ideas. Building on Marx, Ranganayakamma (2004) says: 'Generally speaking, all the upper castes ... possess land, capital and money' and 'perform a particular kind or kinds of labour which possess 'higher' exchange value'. They also 'have hegemony and engage in social organization and administration'. And 'generally speaking, ... the lower castes ... do not have properties even as means of livelihood. They live as laborers and servants. They are subjected to the hegemony and ruling of the upper castes, and live in dire poverty and social inferiority'. They also 'perform labor with 'low' exchange value' (ibid.).

Marx, interestingly, thinks that gender-oppression and caste-oppression are connected via their relation to private property, which is the basis of class relation. In pre-capitalist societies, women had some control over property. This is why men tried to take that control away. This struggle over property had a caste-dimension, as shown in Marx's discussion on suttee in India (a practice where a woman sets herself to fire following her husband's death):

> The beastliness of the Brahmins [the highest caste] reaches its height in the "Suttee". ... [The] suttee is simply religious murder, in part to bring the inheritance into the hands of the ... Brahmins for the religious ceremonies for the deceased husband and in part through Brahmin legislation to transfer the inheritance of the widow to the closest in the gens, the nearer family of the husband.
>
> quoted in ANDERSON, 2016:206

3   Marxism and the Explanation of Social Oppression: The Fundamental Role of Capitalism

Marx (1857) says, 'Some determinations belong to all epochs, others only to a few'. Class mechanisms are more universal than those of capitalism as a form of class relations. So, we need to move from class-mechanisms of oppression to capitalist mechanisms of oppression. One has to approach the relation between capitalism and oppression from the vantagepoint of capital-labor, capital-capital, and labor-labor relation and at different levels (i.e., capitalism and capitalist social formation). The objective exploitative class relations of capitalism (=capital-labor relations) are reproduced through the logic of capitalist competition (=capital-capital relations), and the logic of the separation of direct producers (labor-labor relations).

Capitalism is generalized commodity production, where the logic of accumulation of capital and exploitation of labor dominates. Marx famously analyzes capitalist production and exchange on the basis of his formula for the capital circuit: M-C (LP and MP)-P-C$^\Delta$-M$^\Delta$. Social oppression is connected to each component of the capitalist circuit and to its various consequences and aspects.

From one vantage point, capitalism is indifferent to oppression. Capitalism – where all inputs are, more or less, in their commodity forms and are assumed to be paid for at their value – is indifferent to the social identity of people it exploits and to whom it sells things. For capital, *all* potential workers represent one unit of the commodity labor power, and one unit of the producer of value and surplus value. To paraphrase Lenin (1914): 'it makes no difference to the hired hand' whether he (or she) is exploited chiefly by the white male capitalists rather than the black female bourgeoisie. As a contemporary Marxist, Eagleton (2011:213; 2003: 19) says: capitalism is characterized by 'relative indifference to gender, ethnicity, social pedigree and so on when it comes to who it can exploit or to whom it can peddle its wares'. Or, in the words of another scholar, 'Capital is by nature neither patriarchal nor 'white" (Tomba, 2015:82). Besides, and especially, with respect to women and children, to the extent that machinery dispenses with muscular power, 'Differences of age and sex have no social validity any more for the working class. They are merely instruments of labor which cost more or less, according to age and sex' (Marx and Engels, 1848).

Capitalism's indifference to social difference is only relative, however. To exploit all workers more, 'it utilises existing differences, and sometimes it promotes new ones, in order to create new differentials of surplus-value' in a competitive market environment (Tomba, 2015: 82). Eagleton says: the actual histories of capitalism and oppression are 'tightly intertwined in practice'. In Marx's capital circuit, capitalists exploit workers. But at a concrete level, it is the women workers, the aboriginal workers, the racialized workers, the *Dalit* (ex-untouchables in India's caste-system) workers – and not women, aboriginal people, racial and ethnic minorities as such – that are exploited, and it is they who suffer the most. This is because of the concrete ways in which capitalist class relations make use of race, gender, caste, etc. in order to keep the class of direct producers politically divided and disciplined and justify their super-exploitation. No one eats gender or race (see Fields, 1990). They exist for an objective reason.

The objectively-existing exploitative class relations of capitalist society (=capital-labor relations; capital-capital relations, and labor-labor relations) transform the existing divisions among human beings (some are biologically men and others are women; some have a darker skin than others) into relations of oppression and/or modify/intensify already-existing (pre-capitalist) forms of oppression based on these differences. It is possible to relate oppression to the different aspects of capitalism, especially, on the basis of the capital circuit.

3.1 Money and Its Social Power

The relation between capital and labor is partly a relation of exchange, and money is crucial to exchange. The social power of money is related to oppression. In identity politics, perception of someone lacking certain qualities (e.g., ability, good health, etc.) – social production of inferiority – is an element of oppression. But anyone who has a lot of money cannot generally be made to feel inferior, even if they lack certain physical and mental abilities. Consider these lines from Marx (1844b) on 'The power of money':

> I, according to my individual characteristics, am lame, but money furnishes me with twenty-four feet. Therefore I am not lame. ... I am brainless, but money is the real brain of all things and how then should its possessor be brainless?

Those who lack certain abilities *and* money (e.g., a poor disabled person) can, generally, be made to feel inferior at the societal level and be discriminated against. When some people lack money to meet their needs, this creates conditions for others to be disrespectful of them, and if they *are* already oppressed (e.g., Dalits or black women), they can face more humiliation. I return to this below.

3.2 Value of Labor Power, Unfree Labor, and Competition in the Labor Market

In the capital circuit, capital buys labor power as a commodity. It has value like all commodities. The value of labor power is the value of the means of subsistence necessary for the normal maintenance of the laborer and for the laborer's substitutes (i.e., children) (Marx, 1977:274–275). Many of the things/ services that a worker consumes are bought. Some are not. Getting a haircut at a saloon is paid for, but processing food, often done by women at home, is not. Women perform certain roles that are to some extent biologically conditioned (e.g., childbearing and child-rearing). So, they spend much time in the domestic sphere, the sphere where use-values and consumption dominate as opposed to the sites of production and exchange in their capitalist form outside of the home. The work involved in producing weapons of destruction is considered productive, but domestic work that nourishes life is not, as it does not directly produce surplus value, 'no matter how enormous an achievement the sacrifices and energy spent' (Luxemburg, 2014:241). This fact – greater importance attached to 'productive work' – contributes to the devaluation of domestic work, and thus of the work of women at home.

While the sphere of production and that of consumption (reproduction) inter-connect, ultimately it is the former that dominates. The subordination of women exists dominantly because of the way in which capitalist class relations (e.g., absence of a living-wage and universal socialized childcare, and absence of full employment causing competition for jobs between men and women) are articulated with the gendered organization of physical and social reproduction in the family environment (Gimenez, 2018).[14] She specifically argues that:

> capitalism produces and reproduces unemployment and insecurity in a context of universalized commodity production, where working class consumption depends on the prior sale of labor power, [so] the family form of the mode of reproduction emerges as an alternative source of economic survival for working-class people. Women's unpaid domestic labor stretches wages and salaries, thus enhancing the quality of life for the men whose earnings support them and ensuring their own and their children's well-being in the process. But this alternative has a price: economic and social inequality outside the home, and economic dependence and oppression within the home (pp. 13–14).

In a nuclear family where the male breadwinner is a wage worker and his spouse performs unpaid work at home, there is 'a hierarchical relationship' in which the men who command the wage also command the women, and 'thus mediate those women's relationship with capital' (Cleaver, 2019: 214). Lenin (1913) says: 'Millions upon millions of women in such families live (or, rather, exist) as "domestic slaves", striving to feed and clothe their family on pennies,

---

14   Gimenez (2018) says that: sex differentiation and sex-stratification contribute to 'women's over-representation in low-paid, low-skilled jobs', and their dependence 'on a gainfully employed husband or partner' which in turn contribute to the subordination/oppression of *'working class women'*, and the latter, in a society where the majority of the population are workers, appears 'as the oppression of *women in general'* (ibid.:12; italics added).

at the cost of desperate daily effort and "saving" on everything – except their own labor'. Capitalism benefits from workers' privatized reproduction which does not directly cost anything to capital, as women perform a large amount of reproductive work which is not commodified and which is not directly paid for by the employer.[15] Besides, to the extent that women do produce surplus value as workers, there is an issue: their role in biological reproduction (childbearing and child-nurturing) prevents them from being average workers (Vogel, 2013).[16] So even as workers in social production they are devalued. As well, because the nuclear family and its values are crucial for capitalism (they allow the physical-moral reproduction of the future working class), 'LGBT people are oppressed because their sexual and gender identities challenge the traditional family upon which capitalism continues to depend' (Wolf, 2009: 11).

Some workers experience a degree of physical and mental impairment or disability, and are subjected to discrimination (see Slorach, 2011). One explanation for this is the fact of the 'employers wishing to avoid paying the additional costs of hiring a disabled worker, whether in the form of workstation adaptations, interpreters, readers, environmental modifications or liability insurance'. In other words, 'Disability discrimination [which is the other side of able-ism] is a distinct but complex form of oppression, based on the (negligibly to substantially) greater expense to capital of the labor power of impaired people'.[17]

---

15   'There is a direct connection between lower value of labour [power] of women in general all over the world, and of non-white women in particular, and the profit margin' (Bannerji, 1995: 31).

16   'Women belonging to the subordinate class have ... a special role with respect to the generational replacement of labour power', and this fact 'lies at the root of their oppression in class-society' (Vogel, 2013: 150). 'Child-bearing threatens to diminish the contribution [that these women] can make as a direct producer and as a participant in necessary labour', because 'Pregnancy and lactation involve ... several months of somewhat reduced capacity to work', both for capital directly and also at home (p. 151). Besides, a part of the surplus value is used to support the women during these months. The ruling class encourages male supremacy within the exploited class in order to stabilize the reproduction of labour power (p. 153; 189). This argument has some validity, but its importance is diminished to the extent that women of working class (and petty producing) background in the South are forced to work, at home and/or outside, during their pregnancy and almost immediately after delivery, as they and their poor families have little choice. Besides, it is not necessary that surplus value – rather than the value of labor power itself – is used to look after women during maternity.

17   I agree with Slorach (2011) that: 'Capitalism in general does not scapegoat disabled people in order to divide and rule in the way it does with other forms of oppression. Such discrimination plays a less central ideological role than that of homophobia, women's oppression or racism'.

The greater expense that Slorach mentions is only one issue though. Related to this is an additional factor. In Marx's value theory, 'The labour objectified in value [of commodities] is labour of an average social quality, it is an expression of average labour-power' (Marx, 1977:440). This means that an impaired/disabled worker's labor does not count *as average labor*, which is the stuff of value. Impaired workers as bearers of below-average labor power must experience certain adverse material conditions: they are not employed or are under-employed, and when employed, they may not receive the average wage, thus reducing their income. These material conditions, produced by a prior discrimination rooted in the law of value operating under the capitalist class relation, reinforces discrimination via the social power money.[18]

Marx's theoretical assumption is that owners of labor power – workers – are free to work for whoever they wish to. But, in reality, the nominal freedom of labor to enter *and* exit the labor contract is taken away, producing unfree labor as a part of capital seeking to discipline labor (Brass, 2011). Marx's theoretical assumption is also that wages cover the value of labor power. But Marx does recognize that in actual cases, millions do not receive the value of labor power.[19] Inferiorization of certain groups (e.g., lowest castes; certain races), i.e., their oppression, is used to justify the imposition of unfreedom on black and Dalit workers, and to make their wages fall below the value of labor power. In some areas of India, workers from aboriginal areas are seen as people with simple needs and as primitive (Das, 2020: chapter 6). Not only are they often deployed as unfree labor but also are their wages below the cost of their subsistence.

Marx actually discusses oppression in relation to unfreedom and low wages in way that does not naturalize what are social relations. He says that a machine or a sum of money or so many pounds of gold are not necessarily capital, but they become capital when capital-labor relations and competition among capitalists exist. Similarly: 'A Negro is a Negro. Only under certain conditions does he become a slave' (Marx, 1847a). Slavery itself is color-blind and religion-blind. It serves capitalism by making available cheap labor. Racial oppression does not cause, but it justifies and intensifies, the super-exploitation of the

---

18 As Slorach (2011) rightly says: 'wealthy disabled people can afford to pay for goods and services to compensate for the effects of oppression, in the same way that rich women employ nannies or cleaners.'

19 'Individual workers, indeed, millions of workers, do not receive enough to be able to exist and to propagate themselves; but the wages of the whole working class adjust themselves ... to this minimum' (Marx, 1947b).

racialized. Social oppression allows capitalists to use labor and means of production (e.g., mines in aboriginal areas) in quantities not otherwise available
and/or obtain them at below their value.

Given that workers are separated from property, even if there were no
social-cultural differences in a capitalist society, they would still compete
for employment and for work at higher wages. Such competition (as a part
of labor-labor relation) exists because of their objective class position: i.e.,
their separation from property and from the control over the workplace. And
given that wages fall below the value of labor power, a part of the value of
labor power is socialized in the form of government welfare ('social wage'), for
which there is competition as well. The normal economic competition among
workers undermines their bargaining power and limits the potentially positive impact of increased investment on living conditions. And when there is
competition in a context where workers do have different identities, economic
competition among workers for work and better wages takes the specific form
of competition among workers with different identities, which is expressed as
antagonism based on socio-cultural differences. Such competition intensifies
normal economic competition. So economic competition among workers is
transformed into the competition between, for example, white workers and
black workers. Any potential unity among them as workers is further undermined. About the England of his time, Marx (1870) says this, which is relevant
to our times:

> Every industrial and commercial centre in England now possesses a
> working class divided into two *hostile* camps, English proletarians and
> Irish proletarians. The ordinary English worker hates the Irish worker as
> a competitor who lowers his standard of life.

> This antagonism is the secret of the impotence of the English working
> class, despite its organisation. It is the secret by which the capitalist class
> maintains its power. And the latter is quite aware of this.

So, capital seeks to keep alive such antagonism – relations of oppression
among workers. Marx (1870) says: 'workers' antagonism is artificially kept alive
and intensified ... by all the means at the disposal of the ruling classes', including 'the press, the pulpit, the comic papers [etc.]'. Thus, as an aspect of capitalist class society, competition among workers is manifested in the form of racism, etc.: some exploited groups come to oppress – exclude – other exploited
groups. That is why, Marx (1977:414) says: 'Labour in a white skin cannot eman-
cipate itself where it is branded in a black skin'. The real enemy of black or

Dalit or female workers are not white or upper-caste or male workers. The capitalist class and its state are the real enemy.

Far from seeing the capitalist class as the enemy, sections of the working-class identify themselves with the capitalist class, on the basis of national and/or racial etc. identity. So white workers identify themselves with white capitalists rather than with black workers. Marx (1870) notices that:

> In relation to the Irish worker he [the English worker] regards himself as a member of the *ruling* nation and consequently he becomes a tool of the English aristocrats and capitalists against Ireland, thus strengthening their domination *over himself*.

Often capital 'artificially' creates cross-class unity (capital-labor unity) at the national scale. Consider how the failure to deal with the coronavirus crisis leads bourgeois politicians to manufacture national chauvinism (America First attitude) and national hatred ('Chinese virus'). Consider how in India, Hindu workers are united with Hindu capitalists and with Hindu bourgeois politicians against Muslims, how upper-caste workers and peasants unite with upper-caste landlords/capitalists instead of solidarizing with lower-caste workers and peasants, and how Dalit citizens (workers and petty-producers) support Dalit politicians of bourgeois-landlord parties against socialistic politicians. This cross-class unity is a definite sign of false consciousness. It is false because it is out of line with workers' objective interests. It may offer a psychological compensation to the workers of the non-oppressor status, for their exploitation. False consciousness has the same effect as the antagonism within the working class. Bakan (2008:252) says:

> The sense of privilege cultivated among one section of workers over another may or may not be accompanied by material benefit ... Maintaining that sense of superiority is part of how oppression operates in capitalist society, and part of the contested terrain in the battle for ruling-class hegemony.

While false consciousness as a reason for oppression is real, identity politics rejects the very notion of it.

3.3   *Twin Methods of Exploitation of Labor, General Law of Accumulation, and Crisis*

Given the coercive law of competition, individual capitalists are driven to raise the level of exploitation of workers above the average. There are two major methods of increasing exploitation assuming that labor-power is paid at its value. One of them is the prolongation of the working day (another method is making workers produce more every hour with the help of technology). Socially oppressed people, more than others, can be made to work longer hours for a given wage. In the capitalist workplaces, labor is performed under strict capitalist control, so no more labor time or inputs are wasted than what is socially necessary. Workers are alienated from the process of production. Where workers lack control over their work, the gender and the ethnic/racial divide is used to reinforce the despotic control exercised by managers/supervisors, etc. This despotic control can be extremely harsh with respect to women, as shown by studies on labor process in factories and call centers and in export processing zones of the Global South.

In capitalist society, capitalist exploitation, as the primary form of exploitation, coexists with secondary capitalist exploitation, which is outside of the sphere of production. This occurs, Marx says in *Capital* vol 3, when, for example: 'the working class is swindled' by the retail dealer, who sells them means of subsistence, and by usurious capital (Marx, 1981: 745). In fact, as the *Communist Manifesto* notes, 'No sooner is the exploitation of the labourer' in the workplace comes to an end and 'he receives his wages in cash, than he is set upon by the other portions of the bourgeoisie, the landlord, the shopkeeper, the pawnbroker, etc.' (Marx and Engels, 1848). Now, to the extent that a large part of reproductive work falls on the shoulder of proletarian women, and that food and other necessaries have to be bought (and they have often to be bought on credit), it is often the women who come into contact with the secondary exploiters – i.e., retailers, pawnshops, merchants, money-lenders, etc., and this is especially the case in rural areas of the Global South. There are numerous cases of women – and male workers from the oppressed status – being insulted and harassed by these secondary exploiters.

Let us move from capitalist exploitation and competition to capitalism's general law of accumulation, as Marx (1977: chapter 25) calls it. In capitalism, the relation between accumulation and workers' living conditions itself depends on the competition among workers and their bargaining power. When investment $(c + v)$ expands, with c/v remaining more or less constant, labor market can tighten, so wages can rise. This process benefits all workers (although some identity groups might benefit more than other groups partly because some groups are more likely to remain in employment than other groups). But as soon as the rise in wages adversely affects the normal rate of accumulation, capital can expand the reserve army by mechanization (increasing the ratio of investment in c to that in v). This process increases competition for work and puts a stop to the rise in wage. As a result, the whole working class loses, although, once again, some identity groups might lose more than others. And the whole working class loses more than it would if there was no competition between socially oppressed and non-oppressed groups, and if consequently they were able to put pressure on employers for a higher wage. This is especially the case when capital creates a reserve army, not just through mechanization, etc. but through carefully planned immigration (see Foster et al. 2011). And the latter mechanism means that the reserve army has workers from different races, religious beliefs and nationalities. This fact potentially contributes to the political division within the working class in the absence of an effective multi-racial workers' organization. Their lack of unity means everyone gets lower wages than they otherwise would, even if the oppressed get lower wages than others. Sections of the racialized reserve army (e.g., Hispanic immigrants in the US) fall into working poverty, so they depend on welfare. This is seen by politically backward groups of the 'native' working class as competition for welfare, prompting them to engage in racism, and also supplying ammunition for right-wing bourgeois politicians.

For Marx, the most fundamental law of political economy pertains to the tendency for the average rate of profit to fall causing an economic crisis.[20] The rate of profit tends to fall because the investment in machines and raw materials, etc. relative to that in wages rises faster than the rate of exploitation (see Roberts and Carchedi, 2018). A countertendency is to increase the rate of exploitation. One way of doing this is super-exploitation, including via depressing wages below the value of labor power. Super-exploitation can be justified better if it involves oppressed groups, which are already social constructed as being worthy of less.

By using its militarily powerful state, capitalism of advanced countries externalizes its crisis and seeks to maintain global competitiveness: it finds markets abroad and it uses the cheapened labor and natural resources of less developed countries to decrease the cost of production. Capitalism takes the form of imperialism which 'means high monopoly profits for a handful of very rich countries' (Lenin, 1916). Imperialism in turn makes it economically possible to bribe the upper strata of the proletariat in imperialist nations. This fosters opportunism which is expressed in nationalist consciousness of workers in imperialist countries: the bribed workers, like the English workers Marx talks about, identify themselves with their national exploiting class rather than with the workers in the less developed countries. It is also the case that exploitation

---

20   The basis of this law is laid in *Capital 1* (chapter 25), although Marx develops it famously in *Capital 3*.

and social oppression of large segments of the working class in imperialist countries result in working class anger there. So imperialist war or aggression is deployed as a fix because such aggression produces a false psychological unity between workers and capitalists of imperialist countries on the basis of nationalism (including in its race-based form). One can generalize the process by saying that where-ever there is working class anger against the system for its failure to meet its needs, the ruling class and its state stoke nationalist sentiments against other nations. This is identity politics of the capitalist class.

The permanently crisis-prone late capitalism is vulnerable to fascism. Fascism is also a form of capitalist class identity politics. Social oppression is often intensified – especially against immigrants, religious minorities, etc. – as a part of an agenda that is a reaction to the capitalist crisis/slowdown. This agenda is conducted to not only divide the majority (the toilers) who can/do fight against capitalism and its political parties, but also divert their attention from the failures of capitalism and its state to meet their needs, making them falsely believe that their miseries are not because of capitalism and its state, but because of people with certain identities (e.g. Muslims, immigrants, etc.).[21] There is a real 'need' of the ruling class to use identity politics whether it is based on religion or race. Trotsky (1933) wrote about the connection between race and fascism (national socialism):

> In order to raise it above history, the nation is given the support of the race. History is viewed as the emanation of the race. ... In order to create the religion of pure German blood, Hitler was obliged to borrow at second hand the ideas of racism from [others]. ... On the plane of politics, racism is a vapid and bombastic variety of chauvinism in alliance with phrenology.

Capitalism not only creates objective conditions for fascism. By producing a vast reserve army, including lumpen-proletarian elements and economically sinking petty-bourgeois strata, and injecting a dose of identity politics into them, capitalism creates an agency that enacts the fascistic project: Hindu lumpen elements against Muslims (in India) and white lumpen elements against immigrants (in many Western countries) are infamous examples.[22]

---

21   The oppression of Muslims is one of the several aspects of the deepening fascistic tendencies in India. This topic is explored in detail in my newly released book (Das, 2020).

22   There are two caveats to be noted. A given degree of social oppression may not benefit all capitalists equally. For example, capitalists producing armaments and means of production may turn to fascism which oppresses minorities much more than those who produce the means of consumption (Mandel, 1995:114). Besides, while social oppression (e.g.

4   Conclusions and Political Implications

The socially oppressed sections of the working class (and small-scale producers) suffer more than socially-culturally dominant sections in capitalist societies. This, however, does not mean that, as the identity politics approach says,
the major division in society is between blacks and whites, upper castes and
lower castes, Hindus and Muslims, men and women, and homosexuals and
heterosexuals, and so on. The identity politics approach, given its rejection of
the importance of class as an objective relation, can only superficially understand oppression. This is why Marx's class approach is so relevant. The major
division in society *is* the class division. In Marxism, informed as it is by the philosophy of dialectics and materialism, class relations have primacy over social
oppression (see Wallis, 2015).

The dominant form of class relation now is capitalism. Marx's capital circuit, M-C-MΔ, is a useful analytical tool for exploring the link between capitalism and oppression. The totality of capitalist class relations feeds into, and
is reproduced through, intra-class divisions. If everyone has well-paid employment, there would be little reason for competition among workers, and for discrimination and oppression. Capitalism, and the state that defends it, are the
obstacles to such a situation. But many workers see, and they are encouraged
to see, sections of the exploited as the problem. This is false consciousness, but
this helps reproduce capitalism.

It is not class relation as such, but the effects of how that relation works
that shape, and are shaped by, race, gender and caste, etc. (and in this interaction, race, etc. are already colored by class).[23] Capital-labor relation is a totality
with a) an economic dimension which includes exploitation of the worker, and
class differentiation among commodity-producers, and b) an extra-economic
dimension, which includes coercive dispossession and social oppression ('tyranny' or the attack on democratic rights of oppressed groups), a totality within
which the economic dimension is the dominant element. Given capitalist
relation, surplus value will be appropriated irrespective of the racial or gender
status of the worker. But how much surplus value is extracted, and how and

---

Hindus' discrimination against Muslims) serves capitalism, the degree of oppression in
any given place could be more than what is functional to capitalism as such (too many
sectarian riots may undermine the business climate). There is no one-to-one relation
here, therefore.

23   At the level of everyday life, 'My gender, "race" and class are not separate persona or
persons – they make and re-present all of me in and to the world that I live in', says a
Canadian Marxist, Bannerji (1995:12).

with how much opposition in a given place, could be shaped by the cultural identities of the workers. Class and oppression belong to two different levels of analysis: oppression belongs to a more concrete level than class does.[24] So it is false to believe that class is constituted by oppression.

An iota of theoretical and political advantage does not accrue by diluting the primacy of class, i.e., by questioning Marx and Marxism which sees society 'from the viewpoint of the formation of the waged proletariat' versus seeing society 'from the viewpoint of kitchens and bedrooms in which labor power is daily and generationally reproduced' (Federici, 2017: 93; cf. Belkhir, 2001; Gottfried, 1998; Pincus et al. 2008). Most exploited workers tend to be women, blacks, and low castes, etc., but that does not mean that these extra-economic identities are the main reason for their (super-)exploitation. An iota of advantage does not accrue either by women treating men as the main enemy or by blacks and Dalits treating the whites and upper castes respectively as their main enemy (see Zetkin, 2015). Yet, a Marxism that is not sensitive to oppression is an impoverished version of Marxism (see Mojab, 2015). For Marxism, class is the dominant relation and cleavage, but class is not the only thing that matters.

The foregoing analysis with its underlying view of Marxism has specific political implications. It is clear that: in a society where there is no competition for well-paid work, where everyone gets adequate compensation for their work, where there is no ruling class which needs to divide and subjugate director producers by encouraging one group to oppress another, and so on, the material-political basis for oppression will be significantly gone, even if the ideas that justify oppression will not disappear immediately. But no matter how intense exploitation is and how savage oppression is, the new society will not automatically come. Men and women have to politically fight for such society.

For Marx, all politics is ultimately a struggle against class relations. He advocates for workers to fight for concessions from the property-owners and from the state, which benefit all workers and which benefit socially oppressed groups such as women. Marx famously said if it was Marxist to oppose these struggles for reforms, he was not a Marxist. Lenin agrees. For him, the Marxist-socialist is 'the tribune of the people, who is able to react to every manifestation of tyranny and oppression, no matter where it appears, no matter what stratum or class of the people it affects' (Lenin, 1901). This means that people's

---

24   With respect to class and gender, Anne Pollert (1996: 643) writes: 'The two sets of relationships – class and gender – are of a different analytical order'.

struggle should be in workplaces and communities, i.e., where-ever there is
tyranny. With respect to women's oppression, for example, Marx's approach
is absolutely unequivocal: 'Social progress may be measured precisely by
the social position of the fair sex' (Marx, 1868). And, for his greatest disciple,
Vladimir Lenin (1920), 'The proletariat cannot achieve complete freedom,
unless it achieves complete freedom for women'.

A part of the multipronged fight for a society that is democratic in every
sphere and that is beyond the rule of capital, is the need to educate common
people about the democratic rights of oppressed groups. Marxism does not
treat individual proletarians as saints when it comes to, for example, gender
rights. In an interview, Lenin said:

> So few men – even among the proletariat – realise how much effort and
> trouble they could save women, even quite do away with, if they were to
> lend a hand in 'women's work'. But no, that is contrary to the 'rights and
> dignity of a man'. ... [Therefore,] our political work ... embraces a great
> deal of educational work among men ... We must root out the old 'master'
> idea to its last and smallest root.
>
> LENIN in ZETKIN, 1920

Given how overarching capitalism is, the struggle for reforms, including in
the area of oppression and state's own biases against minorities (see Gordon,
2007), has serious limitations, however. As we have seen, as soon as improvements in the conditions of workers, whether men or women, White or Blacks,
interferes with the normal rate of accumulation profit, capital's economic logic
(e.g. the production of the reserve army) will counter it (Marx, 1977:771).[25]
Any serious threat to the control over property will be fought against politically: that is the basic role of the state. But it is the state in which the identity
politics people have what Lenin (1917) calls 'an unreasoning trust'. Therefore,
revolutionary overthrow of capitalism and its state and the establishment of
a new society is necessary. This society will have two aspects: it will benefit
humankind as a whole, and it will eliminate the suffering of the oppressed
groups, making it possible for them to enjoy full democratic rights in economic
and extra-economic spheres (Marx and Engels, 1848). The only means of doing
this – i.e., abolishing class and oppression – 'is political domination of the
proletariat' (Marx, 1871).

---

25   Although Marx did not argue this, but one could say: if social oppression helps capital
      increase its rate of profit and if successful struggle against oppression lowers the rate of
      profit, then there will be limits to the reduction in oppression in capitalist societies.

References

Anderson, K. 2016. *Marx at the Margins: On Nationalism, Ethnicity, and Non-Western Societies,* Chicago: University of Chicago Press.

Bakan, A. 2008. 'Marxism and Antiracism: Rethinking the Politics of Difference.' *Rethinking Marxism* 20, no. 2: 238–56.

Bandyopadhyaya, J. 2002. 'Class Struggle and Caste Oppression: Integral Strategy of the Left', *The Marxist*, Vol. 18: 3–4.

Bannerji, H. 1995. *Thinking through: Essays on Feminism, Marxism and Anti-racism.* Toronto: Women's Press.

Barrett, M. 1980. *Women's oppression today: Problems in Marxist feminist analysis.* London: Verso.

Belkhir, J. 2001. 'Marxism without Apologies: Integrating Race, Gender and Class; A Working Class Approach'. *Race, Gender and Class* 8, no. 2: 142–171.

Brass, T. 2011. *Labour Regime Change in the Twenty-First Century.* Leiden: Brill.

Brass, T. 2017. *Labour Markets, Identities, Controversies: Reviews and Essays, 1982–2016.* Leiden: Brill.

Brewer, R. 2018. 'Radical black feminism and the simultaneity of oppression'. *Monthly Review Online.* Retrieved from: https://mronline.org/2018/11/27/radical-black-feminism-and-the-simultaneity-of-oppression/.

Brewer, R. 1999. 'Theorizing Race, Class and Gender: The New Scholarship of Black Feminist Intellectuals and Black Women's Labor'. *Race, Gender and Class* 6 (2): 29–47.

Brown, H. 2012. *Marx on Gender and the Family: A Critical Study.* Chicago: Haymarket.

Cassell, J. 2017. 'Marxism vs intersectionality'. *Fightback: The Marxist voice of labour and youth.* Retrieved from: http://marxist.ca/e/marxism-vs-intersectionality.

Cleaver, H. 2019. *33 Lessons on Capital : Reading Marx Politically.* London: Pluto.

Crenshaw, K. 1989. 'Demarginalizing the Intersection of Race and Sex: A Black Feminist Critique of Antidiscrimination Doctrine, Feminist Theory and Antiracist Politics,' University of Chicago Legal Forum: Vol. 1989: Iss. 1, Article 8. Available at: http://chicagounbound.uchicago.edu/uclf/vol1989/iss1/8.

Collins, P. 1990. Black feminist thought in the matrix of domination: Knowledge, consciousness, and the politics of empowerment. Boston: Unwin Hyman.

Das, R. 2017. *Marxist Class Theory for a Skeptical World.* Leiden: Brill.

Das, R. 2020. *Critical Reflections on Economy and Politics in India: A Class Theory Perspective.* Leiden: Brill.

Di Stefano, C. 1991. *Configurations of Masculinity.* Ithaca: Cornell University Press.

Eagleton, T. 2003. *After Theory.* London: Penguin.

Eagleton, T. 2011. *Why Marx Was Right?* New Haven: Yale University.

Engels, F. 1883. Speech at the grave of Karl Marx. *Marxists.org.* Retrieved from: https://www.marxists.org/archive/marx/works/1883/death/burial.htm.

Engels, F. 1884. Origins of the family, private property, and the state. *Marxists.org*. Retrieved from: https://www.marxists.org/archive/marx/works/1884/origin-family/cho2d.htm.

Engels, F. 1886. Ludwig Feuerbach and the end of classical German philosophy. *Marxists.org*. Retrieved from: https://www.marxists.org/archive/marx/works/1886/ludwig-feuerbach/cho1.htm.

Federici, S. 2017. 'Capital and Gender'. In I. Schmidt and C. Fanelli. Eds. *Reading Capital Today*. London. Pluto Press.

Fields, B. 1990. 'Race and Ideology in the United States of America', *New Left Review*, Issue 181.

Foster, J., McChesney, R., and Jonna, R. 2011. 'The Global Reserve Army of Labour and the New Imperialism'. *Monthly Review* 63, no. 7: 64–64.

Gimenez, M. 2018. *Marx, Women, and Capitalist Social Reproduction: Marxist Feminist Essays*. Leiden: Brill.

Gordon, T. 2007. 'Towards an Anti-racist Marxist State Theory: A Canadian Case Study'. *Capital & Class*, no. 91, 1–30.

Gottfried, H. 1998. 'Beyond Patriarchy? Theorizing Gender and Class'. *Sociology* 32, no. 3: 451–468.

hooks, bell 1989. *Talking Back: Thinking Feminist, Thinking Black*. Boston: South End Press.

Kruks, S. 2001. *Retrieving Experience: Subjectivity and Recognition in Feminist Politics*. Ithaca: Cornell University Press.

Lancaster, R. 2017. 'Identity politics can only get us so far'. *Jacobin*. Retrieved from: https://www.jacobinmag.com/2017/08/identity-politics-gay-rights-neoliberalism-stonewall-feminism-race.

Lenin, V. 1901. What is to be done. *Marxists.org*. Retrieved from: https://www.marxists.org/archive/lenin/works/1901/witbd/iii.htm.

Lenin, V. 1913. Capitalism and female labour. *Marxists.org*. Retrieved from: https://www.marxists.org/archive/lenin/works/1913/apr/27.htm.

Lenin, V. 1914. The right of nations to self-determination. *Marxists.org*. Retrieved from: https://www.marxists.org/archive/lenin/works/1914/self-det/cho5.htm.

Lenin, V. 1916. Imperialism, the highest stage of capitalism. *Marxists.org*. Retrieved from: https://www.marxists.org/archive/lenin/works/1916/imp-hsc/cho8.htm.

Lenin, V. 1917. The tasks of the proletariat in our revolution. *Marxists.org*. Retrieved from: https://www.marxists.org/archive/lenin/works/1917/tasks/cho4.htm.

Lenin, V. 1920. To the working women. *Marxists.org*. Retrieved from: https://www.marxists.org/archive/lenin/works/1920/feb/21.htm.

Luxemburg, R. 2014. *The Rosa Luxemburg Reader*. Edited by Peter Hudis and Kevin Anderson. New York: Monthly Review Press.

Mandel, E. 1995. *Trotsky as an Alternative*. London: Verso.

Marx, K. 1844a. Private property and communism. *Marxists.org*. Retrieved from: https://www.marxists.org/archive/marx/works/1844/manuscripts/comm.htm.

Marx, K. 1844b. The power of money (from his economic and philosophic manuscripts of 1844). *Marxists.org*. Retrieved from: https://www.marxists.org/archive/marx/works/1844/manuscripts/power.htm.

Marx, K. 1845a. German ideology. *Marxists.org*. Retrieved from: https://www.marxists.org/archive/marx/works/1845/german-ideology/ch01.htm.

Marx, K. 1845b. The holy family. *Marxists.org*. Retrieved from: https://www.marxists.org/archive/marx/works/1845/holy-family/ch08_6.htm.

Marx, K. 1845c. Theses on Feuerbach. *Marxists.org*. Retrieved from: https://www.marxists.org/archive/marx/works/1845/theses/theses.htm.

Marx, K. 1847a. Wage labour and capital. *Marxists.org*. Retrieved from: https://www.marxists.org/archive/marx/works/1847/wage-labour/ch05.htm.

Marx, K. 1847b. Wage labour and capital. *Marxists.org*. Retrieved from: https://www.marxists.org/archive/marx/works/1847/wage-labour/ch04.htm.

Marx, K. 1857. Grundrisse – Introduction. *Marxists.org*. Retrieved from: https://www.marxists.org/archive/marx/works/1857/grundrisse/ch01.htm.

Marx, K. 1859. Introduction to a contribution to the Critique of Political Economy. *Marxists.org*. Retrieved from: https://www.marxists.org/archive/marx/works/1859/critique-pol-economy/appx1.htm.

Marx, K. 1868. Letter to Kugelmann. *Marxists.org*. Retrieved from: https://www.marxists.org/archive/marx/works/1868/letters/68_12_12-abs.htm.

Marx, K. 1871. Apropos of Working-Class Political Action. Retrieved from: https://www.marxists.org/archive/marx/works/1871/09/21.htm.

Marx, K. 1977. *Capital volume 1*. New York: Vintage.

Marx, K. 1981. *Capital volume 3*. New York: Vintage.

Marx, K and Engels, F. 1848 The communist manifesto. *Marxists.org*. Retrieved from: https://www.marxists.org/archive/marx/works/1848/communist-manifesto/ch01.htm.

Marx, K and Engels, F. 1978. *German Ideology*. Ed. C. Arthur. New York: International Publishers.

Mojab, S. 2015. *Marxism and Feminism*. London: Zed.

Namboodiripad, E. 1981. 'Once Again on Castes and Classes', *Social Scientist* Vol. 9, No. 12.

Patnaik, P. 2016. 'On Marxism and the Caste Question', *People's Democracy*. Retrieved from: https://peoplesdemocracy.in/2016/0403_pd/marxism-and-caste-question.

Pincus, F., and Sokoloff, N. 2008. Does 'Classism' Help Us to Understand Class Oppression. *Race, Gender and Class* 15, no. 1–2: 9–23.

Pinto, A. 2001. 'UN Conference against Racism: Is Caste Race?', *Economic and Political Weekly*, Vol. 36:3030: 2817–2820.

Pollert, A. 1996. 'Gender and Class Revisited; Or, the Poverty of 'Patriarchy''. *Sociology –
The Journal of the British Sociological Association* 30, no. 4: 639–659.

Ranadive, R. 1982. *Caste, Class and Property Relations*. Calcutta: National Book Agency.

Ranganayakamma, 2004. Marx on caste. Retrieved from: http://www.ranganayaka
mma.org/Marx%20on%20Caste.htm .

Roberts, M. and Carchedi, G. 2018. *World in Crisis: A Global Analysis of Marx's Law of
Profitability*. Chicago: Haymarket.

Science and Society. 2018. Symposium on Intersectionality. *Science and Society* 82, No.
2, 248–291.

Singh, H. 2014. *Recasting Caste: From the Sacred to the Profane*. Delhi: Sage.

Slorach, R. 2011. 'Disability and Marxism'. *International Socialism Journal*. Retrieved
from: https://isj.org.uk/marxism-and-disability/.

Smith, S. 2008. 'Marxism and identity politics'. *Socialistworker.org*. Retrieved from:
https://socialistworker.org/2008/07/11/marxism-and-identity-politics.

Tomba, M. 2015. 'Marx's Temporal Bridges and Other Pathways'. *Historical Materialism*
23, No. 4, 75–91.

Trotsky, L. 1933. What is national socialism. *Marxists.org*. Retrieved from: https://www
.marxists.org/archive/trotsky/germany/1933/330610.htm.

Vogel, L. 2013. *Marxism and the Oppression of Women*. Leiden: Brill.

Wallis, V. 2015. 'Intersectionality's Binding Agent: The Political Primacy of Class', *New
Political Science*, vol. 37:4, 604–19.

Wolf, S. 2009. *Sexuality and Socialism*. Chicago: Haymarket.

Wood, E. 1990. *The Retreat from Class*. London: Verso.

Workers Vanguard. 2015. 'The Marxist approach to women's liberation'. https://www
.icl-fi.org/english/wv/1068/communism.html.

Zetkin, C. 1920. Lenin on the women's question. *Marxists.org*. Retrieved from: https://
www.marxists.org/archive/zetkin/1920/lenin/zetkin1.htm.

Zetkin, C. 2015. *Selected Writings*. Chicago: Haymarket.

CHAPTER 6

The Power of Money

Penelope Ciancanelli

As capital, the role of money as a means of domination is established without much theoretical ado. All those with nothing else to sell can sell the disposition over their capacity to work to a money owner.

GANSSMAN, 1988: 307–308

∴

1 Introduction

Marx's writings on money are distinctive and original in their presupposition that money is no less real or consequential than the tangible forces of production. He is equally unusual in finding their common denominator in value, the distinctive social form taken by human effort once under the direction of capitalist enterprises. Within writings that are directly concerned with Marx on money, it is possible to identify important differences in method, especially in the attention paid to the ontological presuppositions that undergird Marx's own writings.

It is widely accepted that throughout all his work Marx relied on a method of immanent critique. This sets his work apart from the methodological proclivities which have shaped academic disciplines like Economics, the discipline in which many Marxist writers on money have their roots. Indeed, Marx's own methodological proclivities have been displaced, ignored, or reshaped by the academic disciplines in which contemporary Marxist thinkers are likely to be situated. Thus one finds a difference between those thinkers who focus on Marx's ideas on money's functions, that is those who claim, "money is what money does" (by implication, indicating that the boundary between money and credit is blurred, see Graziani, 1997) and those who claim that money does what money is (money as a fetish, see Lange, 2019a; Postone, 1993)

Following this distinction between function and social essence, the discussion in this chapter is organized as a contrast between the ideas developed around what money does versus those developed around a focus on what money is. The former works are concerned with the functions of money and feature in work and debate within the fields of Economics and Sociology (see Graziani, 1997). The latter is concerned with money as a fetish, with its political and social-psychological powers and is a feature of work developed within the complementary but distinct perspective of Critical Theory (see Postone, 1993; within Anthropology, see Taussig, 2010).

The aim of this chapter is to develop and discuss the central conclusions Marx drew in regard to the question of what money does and what money is, drawing attention to his view that one of the significant powers of money lies in Economists' widespread belief that money per se 'doesn't matter', that money per se has no 'real' economic substance but is a veil over the operations of the 'real economy.' This idea of the neutrality of money was asserted by many political economists cited by Marx in his critique of political economy, and continues to be asserted to this day by status-equivalent Economists. Both then (and now), those who Marx would have called bourgeois political economists declare that money per se is neutral, a device to overcomes the inconvenience of barter.

In this chapter I also argue that while Marx may (or may not) have produced a theory of money per se, his voluminous writings on the subject (published, unpublished, finished, and fragmented) do provide a richly detailed record of what he thought money was and what he thought were money's power in securing the hegemony of capitalism. His central idea is that money is "the most adequate form of value under capitalism" precisely because it provokes, embeds, and reinforces domination (rather than solidarity) in nearly all social-relational spheres. Last, but not least, I argue he identifies the money-fetish as the greatest barrier to emancipation because it instantiates impersonal domination as a feature of social life.

While attention to what money does (the functions it serves that secure its place in economic activity, widely understood) continues to be important, the major existential upheavals that mark the 21st Century (climate change, famine, and unprecedented global migration) suggest the need for greater attention to what money is and to how its 'fetish' quality limits the political imaginary of many contemporary progressive movements.

One caveat seems in order. The aim of the chapter is to provide an introduction and commentary on what Marx and Marxists think about money. However, it is impossible to do justice in this brief chapter to the extensive, century long Anglophone efforts to interpret and represent Marx's views on money. One indicator of the sheer volume of extant work is given in the over 20-pages-long Wikipedia entry which provides an outline history of the main schools of thought and debates over the past 150 years (Wikipedia, 2020). The Wiki source reveals the range and detail of these debates, including the copious writing on the subject by Marx himself – a great deal of which is now accessible via open-source websites and in translation into English.

This listing also provides an extensive bibliography of the hundreds of scholarly publications which have been circulating since de Brunhoff's 1976 work inspired the most recent revival of interest in the subject of money amongst Marxist scholars. Some of this thinking can be found in *Marx's Theory of Money: Modern Appraisals*, an edited volume of work by contemporary specialists (Moseley, 2005), including an essay by de Brunhoff herself, in which she follows up on contested elements in her 1976 exposition.

The discussion of these ideas is set out in three main sections. Section 2 provides a thumbnail sketch of what is generally accepted as Marx's views on the functions served by money in the capitalist system, followed by some points disputing the contemporary relevance of Marx's theory of money. Section 3 considers Marx's writings on money as a *fetish* and the method he devised to see though it, to identify material social relations at work. The concluding section considers the consequence of each emphasis on the political imagination, arguing for renewed attention to immanent critique as a tool to illuminate precisely those dimensions of human agency which the money fetish cannot suborn.

2   Money Is What Money Does: The Economic Powers of Money

> Money does not arise by convention any more than the state did.
> MARX, 1990: 165

What follows is an overview of the main economic functions Marx attributed to money, drawing on both his own writings on the subject as well as the available extensive secondary sources. This is followed by a brief discussion of the disputed relevance of Marx's views given the character of the global monetary system in the 21st century.

2.1   *Economic Functions (Powers) of Money*

Marx drew attention to three functions which money must serve in a capitalist society: measure of value, medium of exchange, and money as money – that is, as a store of value and a means of hoarding that value. These are set out in Ch 1–3 of Vol.1 of *Capital* (Marx, 1977) and this source is the basis of the summary that follows; commentaries are referenced, and each function is discussed in turn.

2.1.1   Measure of Value

Marx began his exposition with what he regarded as the first purpose of money – measuring the value of something (Ivanova, 2020: 140). Indeed, de Brunhoff's iteration of this idea relies on a widely accepted version of the labor theory of value such that the value of gold (itself a produced commodity) establishes a benchmark of labor value, and this property is used in exchanging all other commodities (de Brunhoff, 1976: 26).

Marx added that in providing a measure of value, money also created the possibility of evolving into a standard of price. The labor value of money could be expected to vary according to production technologies. The standard of price, however, would be a servant of institutional arrangements (particularly those of the state) and any social conventions which might arise over time as exchange and trade ebbed and flowed. Thus, for example, it might be the case that a given amount of a precious metal (say an ounce of gold) might come to serve as the conventional unit of measurement, thereby enabling comparison of the (gold) price of goods – however much the (labor) value of gold itself might fluctuate or vary across different transaction spaces.

Thus, commodities are said to enter a market with a price and (gold) money with a value; the possibility of deviations of price from value is regarded as inherent in the price form itself, being subject to the behavior of individuals in actually existing markets (de Brunhoff, 1976: 27). In addition, price itself is not to be regarded as an abstraction of what is immanent in commodity circulation but as a concrete, social phenomenon which can itself be the object of study (Lange, 2019a). In this way the abstracted (labor) value of gold is variably and flexibly linked to the (variable) price (in terms of gold) for which a commodity is bought or sold.

Once established by custom, practice and legal convention, money seamlessly provides a unit measure of value within a transaction space where it simultaneously provides a standard of price and a unit of account for record-keeping purposes. As such, the latter enabled the emergence and widespread dissemination of such essential mercantile and banking technologies as double-entry bookkeeping, the calculation *ex post,* of profit and loss, as well as *ex ante* forecasts to support investment decisions.

2.1.2   Medium of Circulation

The second main function Marx attributes to money is acting as a *medium of circulation* – that is, money is the medium through which capital circulates so that it can grow, i.e., circulation facilitates the accumulation of more capital. This function lends itself to representation as 'circuits' of capital and Marx used these to portray the dizzying variety of successive value transformations in which money is an 'intermediate' moment, whereby this activity had the sole purpose of accumulating more value at the end of the circulation period than was put into motion at its beginning (Marx's M-C-M' formulation).

In this function, money is a servant of the circulation of value, and this implies gold per se may never need make its appearance. Or, if it does, then it will do so only intermittently. Even if it is used at the beginning of an enterprise or venture, within the transaction space of circulation, money as such inevitably gives way to other forms of value. Greasing the wheels of complex value transformations might be agreements between counterparties which in turn may (or may not) be settled in gold. Indeed, at a systems level, as de Brunhoff observes, "... the quantity of gold that actually circulates depends on ... prices and the volume and speed of transactions" (1976:31).

In this sense, the medium of circulation only needs to become money per se when money is surplus to a capitalist's circulation requirements and, in aggregate, to the totality of all money in circulation. To this one can add the observation that logic dictates there are two distinct pathways from which such a surplus of money can arise. There may be a surfeit of money on the purchase side, or a deficit of money on the sale side (Ivanova, 2020). By implication, one may give rise to the other, ruptures in circulation may occur at any time and scale, and these may in turn build into a crisis when both buying and selling grinds to a halt.

2.1.3   Money as Money: Hoarding and Universal (Value) Equivalence

The third function Marx attributes to money is variously characterized as providing a store of value, as an instrument of hoarding, or money as money (e.g., the general (value) equivalent). If we start with hoarding, simply put, one can observe that not everyone who sells may wish to buy thus indicating a willingness to 'hoard' or hold money for a time – perhaps until better commercial opportunities present themselves. This function implies the separation of purchase and sale which in turn makes hoarding (savings) decisions an endemic source of disruption to the circuits of capital (and any related crisis) and thus, an essential feature of how capitalism works.

Additionally, as Ivanova (2020: 141) points out, Marx's ideas about money as a means of hoarding offer an instructive critique of quantity theories of money (popular at the time of Marx's writing, and now again in the 21st century where such ideas continue to dominate the thinking of most central bankers). Thus, instead of treating the supply of money as in the gift of the central bank (exogenous), hoarding itself can be seen as a regulator of the quantity of money in circulation – of greater or lesser importance, depending on the circumstance.

The recent COVID pandemic offers a vivid illustration of what happens to the "supply" of money when well-to-do households cease to have routine opportunities to spend, and when less well-to-do households cease to earn money and need to rely on money as a 'gift' of state policies. The former hoard, the latter are reduced to reliance on aid-in-kind (such as food banks) with any money they have going to pay the rent and utility bills. Thus, we observed how the pandemic cut through the most monetized societies in the world, revealing previously opaque differences in the extent of individuals' and households' dispossession and their reliance on money today in order to survive until tomorrow.

2.2   *Disputed Relevance*

Because Marx's relied on commodity (gold) money in his exposition of money's functions, it is argued this limits his theory's contemporary relevance. For example, in his theory, money, as a measure of value, appears to require a labor-value anchor, as is achieved via a link to gold. Or, in the idea of its function as a store of value (hoard) there is an implication that money requires a link to something of 'intrinsic value.' In other words, the argument goes, Marx has a commodity theory of money in which money, to be money, must be backed by something that is the product of labor (like gold) as set out by de Brunhoff (1976) and others. It is fair to ask whether such a conception of money is relevant in the post-gold-standard, a post Bretton Woods world characterized as it is by a post-communist 'global' transaction space in which capital has been accumulated using state issued 'fiat currencies' for over half a century?

In this regard, it is worth remembering that Marx argued that capitalism (as a specific political economy) was built on pre-existing forms of money (e.g., metals like gold and silver). Matters did not end there, however. Capitalism's growth into the dominant economic system of 19th Century Europe featured transaction spaces that were marked by periodic and frequent 'monetary' innovations (for example, paper bank notes issued in Scotland by Scottish commercial banks). Innovations were undertaken by state-actors, by hybrid state-capital actors such as central banks, and by the money-market men and finance capitalists of that era.

Transformative innovations continued well into the 20th century, with money's link to gold continuing to be a feature of international trade and cross-border payments. Subsequently, the post-World War II agreements included an international monetary agreement (Bretton Woods Accord) which ratified the continued linking of gold to the paper currencies issued by sovereign states. When this agreement ended, in the early 1970's, sovereign currencies' link to gold was severed. After a period of adjustment, various agreements were reached to recognize the fiat currencies issued by nations and to accept market determined measures of its value in foreign trade. National central banks were given expanded powers of oversight and ad-hoc supervisory bodies were formed to monitor the international activities of commercial banks. The banks themselves, however, would continue to be licensed at the nation-state level and continue to serve as the transmission belt for global payments and capital flows (Parboni, 1981).

Money and finance are once again objects of innovation, this time propelled by digital technologies. This type of innovation is referred to as "FinTech" and it is made up of a number of monetary/financial services including, *inter alia*, mobile/internet-based payment technologies, foreign exchange, money transfer technologies, novel 'value' storage technologies (blockchain) and most recently, central bank issuance of digital or e-currencies. By and large, FinTech is a direct competitor with banks for certain retail services (e.g., cross–border money transfers) but at the same time relies on the global intermediation structure these self-same banks are required by regulators to maintain (Auer, et al., 2020; Thakor, 2020).

Thus, one could argue that if money *is* what money *does* then the various new forms innovated (whether physical paper or digital) are not particularly relevant to Marx's theory of money. Would not the form that money takes mutate according to the mutating purposes required, within a historically specific transaction space, since its overriding purpose, according to Marx, is to provide capitalists with a form of value fully adequate to their aim of accumulation?

A second and related challenge concerns the boundary between money and credit. Returning to Marx's discussion of circulation, Graziani (1997) intervenes in this dispute by arguing that Marx's analysis of money as a circulating media (medium of exchange) is ultimately concerned with the broader concept of purchasing power, which would include both credit instruments (in modern parlance, "near money instruments" such as commercial paper) and money per se (cash or bank money). Thus, Graziani emphasizes that nothing prevents (or requires) capitalists to require payment in gold so long as other enterprises are content with other forms of payment which some may regard as credit.

Based on this reasoning, Marx's views on the boundary between money (as money) and credit appear to be more open ended that some might imagine (c.f. de Brunhoff, 2005). Underscoring that opinion is the fact that most of what Marx wrote about money consisted of notes and short entries that focused on capitalists' actual behavior in money markets, situations in which any boundary between money and credit could, as a practical matter, be negotiated (Graziani, 1997: 34).

This casts a different light on the question of whether money needs to be tethered to a commodity. Indeed, isn't it plausible that Marx's theory is not a commodity theory but some other kind of theory that sits outside of the Schumpeterian classification system de Brunhoff used in her 1976 book. His theory (if it is a theory) holds that gold is only money if money is gold. That is, the money-ness of gold lies not in its intrinsic or purportedly useful features. Rather the opposite direction of effect is at work: the requirements of money endow or find in gold's feature a useful 'technology' (Lange, 2019a; Heinrich, 2002).

3   Money Does What Money Is: Money as a Fetish

> Each individual holds social power in his pocket in the form of a thing. Rob the thing of its social power and you must give this power back immediately to the person over the person ... the ties must be organised as political, religious, etc., as long as the money-power is not yet the *nexus rerum et hominum*.
>
> MARX cited in GANSSMAN 1988: 31

If money does what money is, then, one must ask: "What is money?" In the previous section, we discussed the functions (precapitalist and capitalist) served by money. The functions themselves were developed by Marx on the basis of presuppositions that are often overlooked. As Lange (2019a) points out, for Marx, the political-ideological status of money as *fetish* was a presupposition of the functions that money has served. This implies that in any discussion of Marx's ideas on money, his assertions about its fetish quality warrant at least as much attention as is paid to its functions (Lange, 2019b).

This 'political consciousness' approach to the study of money in capitalism has been explored mainly in the ambit of Critical Theory and Philosophy rather than Economics and Sociology. The work of Postone (1993) is of particular importance as it reinvigorated Anglophone interest in a Frankfurt School reading of Marx's value theory (see also Heinrich, 2002 and Lange, 2020). In addition, there is work by continental monetary economists, such as Graziani (1997) who are better versed in the philosophical underpinnings of Marx's method. The first part of the discussion that follows establishes a definition of 'fetish' as used by Marx and then moves on to consider some of the fetish powers money exercised in capitalist society.

3.1   *What the Money Fetish Is*

At its core, a fetish entails the transfer of powers from an individual or society to a thing. According to Marx such a transfer was not illusory "... because the transferal of powers between commodities and human beings appear to those producers as what they really are: material relations between persons and social relations between thing (Marx, vol 1, p 84 cited in Boerin, 2018, p3)". To clarify the meaning of this point, Boerin restates it as follows:

> In other words the process of transferral is a thought form that has become objective, utterly real. The commodity-form and the value of abstracted labour it attracts are both products of thought *and* objective, imaginary and real, mysterious and concrete. As with the fetish, indeed with the idol of the religious believer, the gods may not be real but the transfer of powers to the object made, along with the resultant effect on the workers, is very real indeed.

According to Boerin (2018), Marx's writings reveal a life-long preoccupation with the idea of the fetish as a key to understanding capitalism. Ultimately, Marx came to regard the interpretive frame of "money-as-fetish" to be the central means by which domination was instantiated as the governing social relation of capitalist societies. Moreover, much of its functionality in the realm of capital accumulation appeared to depend on prior fetishization in the realms of ideology and political consciousness.

The question arises as to why Marx thinks he can 'see' the fetish character of money whereas bourgeois political economists and utopian thinkers like Proudhon, could not. All (including Marx himself) attributed this capacity to the methodological labors Marx undertook, what some refer to as his method of immanent critique. Indeed, Marx viewed his work on method as a requirement for developing a scientific understanding of capitalism. It was not a work of political economy but a critique of how others were doing political economy. He emphasized that "... all science would be superfluous if the form of appearance of things directly coincided with their essence ..." (Marx, 1993: 956). Thus, a science of society required suitable intellectual tools that would enable one to go beyond mere appearances, it needed methods of interrogating the empirical world that help establish the social relational nexus that animates how reality appears to us.

The power of the method Marx devised, according to Postone (1993), lies in its ability to account for the possibility of its own standpoint; thus, Marx's theory of money not only understands what it is talking about (the object of critique) but why it is talked about it in the way it is (his standard of critique). It "… entails a shift from the subject-object paradigm of classic epistemology to a social theory of consciousness" (Postone, 1993: 77).

This method of immanent critique and a social theory of consciousness is essential in overcoming the analytic blindness induced by fetishism (Lange, 2019a). It reveals the social relations through which money's 'appropriated' powers are secured. With the development of the fetish concept, Lange argues,

> Marx demonstrates that it (money) is the inverted and 'dazzling' expression of the social form of labour that … as fetish … obfuscates its constitutive content, in the specific social form that labour take, under the conditions of its confrontation with capital.
>
>   LANGE, 2020: 55–56

3.2   *What the Money Fetish Does*

According to Marx, once capitalism is hegemonic, money emerges as the most adequate form of value – what might be described by analogy as the 'software' which directs the laws of motion of the capitalist system. Thus, in addition to the functions that money may have served in the past, once capitalism is entrenched, money takes on a higher, more politically transformative purpose as the *nexus rerum et hominum.* Indeed, Marx regarded the latter as the key historical novelty of capitalism, its installation of a social order in which relations between people was mediated by things.

Put another way, one could say the first thing the money-fetish money does is bring into being a society integrated by money, that is by the disparate, monetized choices of atomized individuals. Commerce—the purchase and sale of goods and people's 'time' —is the obscured and contradictory (yet visible and unremarked upon) means whereby social coherence is achieved, rendering domination as impersonal as it is pervasive. Thus a social order is created behind the backs of individuals who will have little idea of the mechanisms' that brought it into being.

The social order thereby produced is not particularly orderly, from a financial-monetary perspective. Thus, the second thing the money-fetish does is present 'speculation' as investment thereby planting the seeds of recurring financial crises (sometimes referred to as bubbles in the popular press, sometimes as secular stagnation; these labels in effect normalize the fetish). These seeds are sown by interest bearing capital, in as much as debt is a condition of existence of capitalist firms. Thus, Marx singled it out, writing, "... the relations of capital assume their most external and most fetish like form in interest bearing capital" (Marx, Capital, vol 3, section 5: 388). The 'short-circuit' of capital associated with interest bearing capital (M-M') dispenses with any direct connection to human effort.

Over years of writing, Marx expanded the category of the fetish to include ever more items and then distilled all of them into three: capital-profit, land-rent, and labor-wages, labelling this the Trinity formula. He commented:

> In this economic trinity represented as the connection between the component parts of value and wealth in general and its sources, we have the complete mystification of the capitalist mode of production, the conversion of social relations into things ... It is an enchanted, perverted, topsy-turvy world, in which Monsieur Capital and Madame la Terre do their ghost-walking as social characters and at the same time directly as mere things
>
> MARX,1990: 817

The entire exposition of the Trinity Formula gestures toward the disputes within Christianity about the nature and substance of the Holy Trinity, that is, of the unity of God despite different forms of appearance as 'father', 'as son' (Jesus) and as the 'holy spirit' (sometimes translated as ghost). By inference, a link is made to debates amongst Christians regarding how best to worship God and those believers in Capitalism on how best to worship money.

A third, and possibly the greatest fetish power of money, is the insistence by mainstream Economists (in Marx's time and now) that money doesn't matter. The long reach of that belief is found in the consensus on that point amongst academic-scholars, central bankers, and pundits of every kind. This denial of money's powers finds an analogy in something Baudeliare wrote in 1864 that was reprised in the film *The Usual Suspects*. Thus, Baudelaire wrote:

> Satan ne se plaignit en aucune facon de la mauvaise reputation (sauve) ... le jour ou elle avait entendu un predicateur qui ... s'ecrere en chaire ...

n'oubliez jamais, que la plus belle des ruse du Diable est de vous persuade qu'il n'existe pas!

BAUDELAIRE, 1864

The greatest trick the Devil ever pulled was convincing the world he didn't exist.

The Usual Suspects, MCQUARRIE, 1995

Thus, one might say that the greatest trick monetary theories past and present have pulled is convincing the world that money is a mere device that overcomes the limitations of barter, a metaphoric veil on commercial exchange. Indeed, it is commonplace, in the age of global monetary flows, for leading figures to proclaim that money itself is nothing more than a facilitator of economic activity, rather than the beating heart of a system of exploitation.

Baudelaire's devil (unconventionally portrayed as a woman) is much less concerned about her bad reputation or the endless gossip about the devil incarnate. Much more worrying to her, and possibly to some central bankers today, is that someone will get on a pulpit and proclaim to all that money *does* matter because it disguises and distorts so much of the evil that is done by it, behind the backs of capital and labor alike. Thus, what sets Marx's writings on money apart is their insistence that money does matter, both in its economic guise as the initiator of accumulation (what it does) and in its political-ideological social substance (what it is).

One might ask what Marx found so useful in this concept? It is possible its usefulness lay in the fact that, at its core, the symbolic transfer of human agency to a fetish had no obvious limits; every aspect of human agency could be assigned to it and thereby be subsumed as one of its powers. Thus:

> If the fetish involves the shifting of the powers and values of human social interaction to the relations between objects, then the full realisation of that transfer will result in the complete elevation of those things and the complete abasement of human relations so much so that those relations simply disappear from the scene.
>
> BOERIN, 2018:4

In other words, to a decisive extent, money could turn into anything, a substitute for power, influence, commitment, replacing what Marx described as the brightly colored cohesive means of humanity with the silent force of economic relations (Ganssmann,1988:312).

4   What's at Stake: The Political Imaginaries for the 21st Century

> There is no royal road to science and only those who do not dread the
> fatiguing climb of its steep paths have a chance of gaining its luminous
> summits.
>
> MARX, 1977:104

The powers of money today are arguably far more extensive and unsettling
than when Marx began his political analytic project over 170 years ago. The first
indicator of this can be found in the historically unprecedented proportion of
the global population who depend on money for access to food and other necessaries to sustain life (Ciancanelli and Fasenfest, 2017: 42); the second indicator and closely linked to the first is the scale of international labor migration
and its financial twin, the money remitted to buy food and shelter for their
households of origin (Ciancanelli, 2022). The third and most vivid perhaps is
daily evidence of how a global pandemic short-circuited the monetary survival
strategies of billions of people worldwide.

It seems fair to say innovative ways to analyze that power are sorely needed
if only to construct political imaginaries that can address the existential challenge of climate change and the related dispossession and immiseration. The
discussion of Marx's theory of money has, thus far, given equal weight to what
money does (a focus on money's functions in capitalist commerce) and to what
money is (a focus on money as a fetish and the method of immanent critique).

Of the two, the idea of money as fetish, as an abstract, impersonal from of
domination, poses a fundamental challenge to those that understand domination as a feature of overt social relations of the state and capitalist firms.
Arguably, the challenge is greatest for those Marxist who have paid little attention to Marx's writings on money as a fetish and the related method of immanent critique, something that could be said to include not only some of the
traditional Marxist writings on money but also, ironically, work falling under
the rubric of the cultural turn. We consider first the view of money manifest
in progressive movements today (a solution) and contrast it with the view that
money (as fetish) is a problem to be overcome.

4.1   *Money as a Solution*
The money powers of the state are seen a politically strategic resource, enabling
poverty reduction and the use of the state powers to create a path to democratic
socialism. It was (and is) scrutiny of money's functions, innovations and technical changes affecting them that inevitably leads to some version of money

as a solution. For example, during the 1930's in the US, Marxists went along with the fiscal policies imagined by Keynes, implemented in the New Deal and today, many supporters of Democratic Socialist and left-leaning Democrats in the US support some version of essentially post-Keynesian ideas, such as universal basic income as both an ameliorative as well as creative pathway to even greater reform of the state.

In short, attention to money's technical features and functions have enabled electoral (and other) alliances which produced reforms that ameliorated the worst excesses of capitalism in some countries. Consequently, the vision of money as a solution has great ideological purchase in broad sections of society, even as the powers of their social democratic sponsors themselves have waned. Any trawl through the demands of contemporary progressive movements in Anglophone countries soon reveals persistent belief in money (government spending, fiscal policy, etc.) as a solution to the most pressing problems of the day. Amplifying this are books popularizing ideas around the unlimited spending power of governments and the better (capitalist) future that lies ahead, with more money allotted for those without enough.

Two problems with this are obvious. First, any redistribution of money doesn't subsequently and permanently redistribute the power to redistribute food, housing, and education. One particularly vivid example of this limitation is how initiatives to address climate change are routinely represented as job creation opportunities, with the rare serious, materialist critiques of consumption patterns side-lined or limited to small audience journals (see Huber, 2021). The second is a simple logic: one must admit there is something odd in the continuing insistence that the solution to capitalism lies in a making more money (and with it the ability for greater consumption of commodities) more available to more people to commodify yet even more areas of human life.

4.2   *Money Is the Problem*

Marxist studies of money that focus on it as a fetish establish money as the problem, in as much as it is the source of analytic blindness to the social relations underpinning economic activity. The central political implication is that the money-fetish constitutes a greater barrier to emancipation than direct and visible forms of domination. Far from being a strategic resource, money-fetish also blinds individuals to what contemporary forces of production make possible: freedom from the necessity of alienating labor. Thus:

> ... with advanced technological production, expenditure of direct human labour time no longer stands in any meaningful relation to the production of (material) wealth and this is a fundamental contradiction which

implies the value form becomes more and more anachronistic. For the first time in history, the possibility of freedom from drudgery is possible.

POSTONE,1993:197

We have reached a point where the production of essentials far outstrips the need; there is the awful spectacle of the daily burial of vast quantities of food in the wealthy nations because its suits the profit-maximization needs of different commercial participants in the global food supply chain. From this perspective, there is less and less reason to regard labor or the working class as providing the only perspective on capitalism and its limitations. Instead, there is every reason to consider the capacity to produce wealth a product of collective human knowledge, gained over centuries (Stoezler, 2004:278).

It seems fair to agree with Postone's diagnosis that the current crisis of environmental degradation and the hollowing out of working society challenge the triumphalism of both neo-liberalism and post-Marxism and demonstrate a continued need for a critical theory of capitalism which not only reappropriates Marx but rethinks its relevance to recent historical developments, including the vast increase in the wealth-creating capacity of the forces of production today (Postone, 2017:39–40).

We agree, at least in so far as his theory of money is concerned, there is a need to rethink as well as reappropriate Marx's ideas on money in ways that better link its function with its nature as a fetish. One starting point would be renewal of methodological curiosity, including more systematic interest in the method of immanent critique. Equally warranting rethinking and renewal is further study of the concept of fetish if only because it was not only central to Marx's theory of money but to his overall analysis of capitalism. Renewal should enable two essential prerequisites of progressive political imaginaries in the current circumstances of reactionary and authoritarian populism: an end to viewing money as the solution, and the beginning of efforts to identify social spaces and social processes in which money is less and less relevant.

In his own time, Marx regarded the way bourgeois economist talked about money as a useful rhetorical battleground for his own views on the subject. The method of immanent critique was the tool he used to disrupt taken-for-granted understandings and self-serving views of capitalism. Maybe the time is ripe for a similar tactic to be adopted, submitting money-doesn't-matter-proponents and pundits to the thorough going immanent critique they deserve.

References

Auer, R, G Cornelli and J Frost (2020) "Rise of the central bank digital currencies: drivers, approaches and technologies", BIS Working Papers, no 880, August.

Baudelaire, C (1864) "Le Joueur Généreux" *Le Figaro*, February 7 accessed on June 1, 2021, available at http://gallica.bnf.fr.

Boerin, R (2018) Religion and capitalism. *Culture Matters*, item 2738, Feb 19, accessed at https://culturematters.org.uk/index.php/culture/religion/item/2738.

Ciancanelli, P (2022) "Securitizing Migration: Finance and Household Reproduction" in Boris, et al., eds., *Global Labor Migration: New Directions*, Champaign: University of Illinois Press.

Ciancanelli, P and D Fasenfest (2017) "Monseiur Le Capital and Madam La Terre on the brink." P North and M S Cato, eds., *Towards Just and Sustainable Economies: Comparing Social and Solidarity Economy in the North and South*. Bristol: Policy Press, pp 37–55.

de Brunhoff, S (1976) *Marx on Money*, New York: Urizen Books.

de Brunhoff, S (2005) "Marx's Contribution to the Search for a Theory of Money" in F Moseley, ed., *Marx's Theory of Money: Modern Appraisals*. New York: Palgrave-MacMillan, pp. 209–221.

Ganssman, H (1988) Money – A symbolically generalised medium of communication? *Economy and Society*, 17: 3 (August): 285–316.

Graziani, A (1997) The Marxist Theory of Money. *International Journal of Political Economy*, 27: 2: 26–50.

Heinrich, M (2002) A Thing with Transcendental Qualities: Money as a Social Relationship in Capitalism. An Introduction to Marx's Notion of Money. *Iz3w*, no 258, Jan/Feb accessed on 9 April 2021 at http://oekonomiekritik.de.

Huber, M (2021) Rich People are Fueling Climate Catastrophe – but not mostly because of their consumption. *Jacobin*, May 2, accessed June 2021 at https://jacobinmag.com/2021/05/rich-people-climate-change-consumption.

Ivanova, M (2020) Marx's Theory of Money: A reappraisal in the light of unconventional monetary policy. *Review of Radical Political Economy*, 52: 1: 137–151.

Lange, E (2019a) The Proof is in the Pudding: On the Necessity of Presuppositions in Marx's Critical Method, in R Bellofiore, et al, eds, *Marx Inattuale, Consecutio Rerum*, Anno III, Numero 5, Roma: Edizioni Efesto, pp. 153–174.

Lange, E (2019b) The Transformation Problem as A Problem of Fetishism, *Filosofski Vestnick*, 40: 3: 51–70 accessed at www.zora.uzh.ch .

Lange, E (2020) Money versus Value, *Historical Materialism*, 28: 1: 51–84.

Marx, K (1977) *Capital*, Vol 1, fourth German edition, translated by Ben Fowkes. New York: First Vintage Books.

Marx, K (1990) *Grundrisse*, London: Penguin Press.

Marx, K (1993) *Capital: A Critique of Political Economy*, Volume 3, trans. By David Fernbach New York: Penguin Books.

McQuarrie, D (1995) *The Usual Suspects*. Script written for film of the same name. Available at http://www.screenplaydb.com/film/scripts/the_usual_suspects.pdf.

Moseley, F., ed. (2005) *Marx's Theory of Money: Modern Appraisals*. London: Palgrave MacMillan.

Parboni, R (1981) *The Dollar and Its Rivals*. London: New Left Books.

Postone, M (1993) *Time, Labour and Social Domination*. Cambridge: Cambridge University Press.

Postone, M (2017) The Current Crisis and the Anachronism of Value: A Marxian Reading, *Continental Thought and Theory*, 1: 4: 38–54.

Stoetzler, M (2004) Postone's Marx: A Theorist of modern Society, its Social Movement and its Imprisonment in Abstract Labour, *Historical Materialism*, 12: 3: 261–283.

Taussig, M (2010/1980) *The Devil and Commodity Fetishism in South America*, Chapel Hill: The University of North Carolina Press.

Thakor, A (2020) Finch and banking: What do we know? *Journal of Financial Intermediation*, 41: 1–14.

Wikipedia, (2020) Criticism if value-form, series on Marxian economics, accessed at https://en.wikipedia.org/wiki/Criticism_of_value-form.

CHAPTER 7

Great Replacement and/as the Industrial Reserve

Populism or Marxism?

Tom Brass

1   Introduction: The Last Taboo

If there is one process that rivals climate change for the label of an inconvenient truth, it is the current migration pattern from Third World and erstwhile Soviet bloc countries into the metropolitan capitalist nations of Europe. At present, however, there exists a worrying conflation that stems from on the one hand the rise up the western capitalist political agenda of the fact/role of the industrial reserve army of labor, and on the other a leftist approach to this development that is indistinguishable from populism. Accordingly, the result is an epistemological gulf between the increasing significance of surplus labor and an unwillingness on the part of the left generally to confront this issue in specifically Marxist – as distinct from the 'new' populist postmodern – terms.

Hence the importance of understanding and accounting for this gulf, and in particular what – if anything – differentiates Marxist from non-Marxist approaches to the issues involved.[1] As conceptualized both by its exponents and by those addressing its discourse, causes, and impact, the Great Replacement (hereafter GR) refers to a process of ethnic/national displacement, by an incoming population of an existing one, a supplanting effected by means of mass immigration from one country (or continent) to another. It is a transformation that is perceived to be total: not just confined to demography, therefore, but involving also a change in ethnic composition, in religion, in culture, in language, and in politics. In metropolitan capitalist nations, GR is deemed largely responsible for generating a populist backlash, at the center of which are disputes about national/ethnic identity and belonging.

Accordingly, examined here from a Marxist point of view is the way GR and its related issues/processes/outcomes are addressed in four recent analyses: that by Eric Kaufmann, Stephen Smith, Renaud Camus, and Bret Easton

---

1   The question mark at the end of the title signals the possibility of opposing viewpoints: on the one hand, that on the subject of surplus labour the GR and Marxism appear to share a common narrative; and on the other, that such an assumption is itself to be challenged.

Ellis.[2] Although there are significant differences between them in terms of approach, each attempts to explain the emergence and consolidation of all or particular aspects of the immigration/GR/populism combination, without considering in any detail the connection either to capitalist accumulation, to its neoliberal variant and the accompanying *laissez-faire* project, or to the formation, expansion and role of a global industrial reserve army of labor. Missing or downplayed, consequently, is a link between GR and ever more intense labor market competition, plus the kinds of non-class identity and struggle this has generated historically, a dynamic and its attendant conflict that continues into the present.

Approaches to GR in either positive or negative terms, tend to interpret it chiefly in Malthusian terms, and focus on the ethnic/national/cultural identity both of those inhabiting the host context and of the migrant. Marxism, by contrast, perceives the latter subject principally in economic terms, as part of the industrial reserve army. Whereas in the Malthusian variant the migrant features largely as a potential/actual consumer, for Marxism s/he appears mainly in the role of potential/actual worker. Implicitly or explicitly, therefore, GR theory adopts a Malthusian reading, linking immigration into metropolitan capitalist nations to population growth in the so-called Third World.[3]

Traced here, therefore, are the contrasting approaches of populism (GR, postmodernism) and Marxism to current migration patterns and their role within the accumulation project of modern capitalism. Different variants of GR discourse attribute European cultural erosion and de-authentication to immigration, a mobilizing ideology fueling the rise of populism, the 'other' of Marxism. In this discourse blame for this process is attached to the left, deemed responsible for promoting identity politics that privilege any and all forms of 'otherness'. It is argued, however, that what GR discourse perceives as the left is more accurately interpreted as a rival form of populism: the 'new'

---

2   It must be stressed that, with the exception of Camus, none of the others is a GR advocate. Hence the term GR exponent refers simply to those who address the issue without necessarily endorsing all its ideological, economic and political claims, a distinction that is absolutely crucial. See Kaufmann (2018), Camus (2018), Smith (2019), and Bret Easton Ellis (2019). Whereas the focus of Smith is principally on causes of migration from the sending context, that of Camus, Kaufmann, and Bret Easton Ellis is mainly on the debates/impact of this same process in the receiving context. Not considered here, however, are other analyses making the same case (Esman, 2010; Murray, 2018, 2019).

3   Although he disavows being a demographer, Smith (2019: 39, 45, 49–50) nevertheless focuses on population data/projection, and invokes Malthus. In keeping with this and responding to his own question 'Why is all this happening now?', Kaufmann (2018: 12) answers: 'Population change – demography – lies at the heart of the story'.

populist postmodernism. Unlike Marxism, both the cultural turn and GR itself misrecognize or downgrade the economic causes structuring their respective discourses. Because of its focus on class struggle, however, Marxism is able to explain migration in terms of the crucial economic role played by the industrial reserve army in capitalist production. Herein lies the continuing relevance – not to say political and economic importance – of Marxist theory.

The presentation which follows is divided into three main sections, the first of which examines the components of GR discourse. Blaming what is claimed to be the political left for promoting 'otherness' as empowerment, the next section considers cultural arguments and disagreements as to the responsibility for GR, and specifically how/why the 'new' populist postmodernism has empowered its discourse. Questioning the view that the left is complicit with GR, the final section looks at economic aspects of the immigration debate, with particular reference to Marxist theory about the industrial reserve army.

2   Components of GR Discourse

2.1   *White Fright, White Fight*
Denying that he is 'an alarmist Eurocentric', Smith (2019: 4, 131) examines 'Africa's importance as a reservoir of migrants' and maintains that over the next two generations one hundred million Africans 'are likely to cross the Mediterranean Sea,' warning that 'neither Europe nor Africa has yet taken the full measure of the challenge that lies ahead [since the] two continents are still unprepared for a migratory encounter of unprecedented magnitude.' In his opinion, therefore, Africa will soon become 'a departure hall' (Smith 2019: 132). Whereas historically the main pattern of migration has been an internal one, within Africa itself, now it has become largely an external process, with Europe as its objective. Currently the path followed begins with rural exodus to the cities, and from thence to Europe (Smith 2019: 118–19). The main reasons encountered inside Africa for this transformation, argues Smith, are a combination of rapid demographic growth, the youthfulness of the population, urbanization, development aid, and the entrenched political power at the grassroots of gerontocracy.

Ironically, therefore, one result of development aid has been a 'burgeoning middle class', the components of which will migrate in search of better paid employment in Europe (Smith 2019: 86).[4] According to Smith, therefore, migrants will consist of two categories: those belonging to the bourgeoisie,

---

4 In what he (Smith, 2019: 107) terms the development paradox, 'the countries of the North subsidize the counties of the South with development aid so that the poor can live better

who can afford to pay the passage, and will go in pursuit of improved lives and jobs; and – to a far less extent – the poor and/or unemployed, who hope to find any kind of work, well-paying or otherwise.[5] Accepting that such population movement is composed for the most part of economic migrants, Smith highlights an obvious difficulty: the jobs sought in Europe will be the ones that are automated, confronting migrants with no other prospect than joining the ranks of the unemployed in another country (Smith 2019: 15, 123, 149). He contrasts this bleak economic future with that of Europeans who migrated to the United States in the late nineteenth century, when there was a strong demand for labor-power in the host nation.

Challenging the view that the fundamental structural divide within Africa is the persistence of ethnic/tribal politics, Smith (2019: 69, 83, 91) maintains instead that the 'significant obstacle to democracy' is much rather the 'principle of seniority'. Arguing that 'the postcolonial state in Africa represents the pursuit of "gerontocracy" by other means', he insists that it is the latter (and not ethnicization/tribalization of politics) that not just undermines the democratic process, but by doing so blocks the prospects of African youth, who then turn towards Europe in order to realize their hopes. Among the pull factors are welfare provision, which enable migrants without a family support network to survive during the search for employment (Smith 2019: 145). That such labor market competition possesses negative implications for European workers is clear, since 'in traditionally wealthy countries of the North, the least qualified workers – increasingly exposed to international competition – have sunk into the "precariat" ' (Smith, 2019: 100–101). In this, Smith agrees with Camus, for whom the disadvantages affect not just those in the host nation but also the migrants themselves, since the attractions which the latter hope to find in the destination are rapidly dissipated by the very fact of migration itself.[6]

---

lives and – though this is rarely said so directly – stay where they are. By doing so, however, rich countries shoot themselves in the foot [because] development aid subsidizes migration.'

5   'Not everyone in Africa who wishes to migrate to Europe can simply pack up and head out,' observes Smith (2019: 103, 104), so it is 'a less indigent stratum of Africans – the continent's middle class – that migrates.'

6   This paradox is outlined by Camus (2018: 41) in the following way: 'Their real opinion of what French and European colonialism was about, Africans express it with their feet, as they run to France and to Europe to settle down here with the French and the Europeans ... They think they are rushing to paradise, at least by comparison. They are running into a wall of illusions, as what made Europe so desirable for them was ... the simple fact that they were not there. As soon as they are present in sufficient numbers, Europe is lost for Europeans, because they are being replaced, and lost for the Africans, because it becomes just another Africa, plagued with the same kinds of problems, be they religious, political ... For them the whole European

Unlike Smith, whose focus is principally on the sending context, and the causes there of outmigration, Camus (2018) explores the impact on the host nations in Europe. Lamenting what he regards as a process of de-authentication operating across the whole of European culture – affecting everything from language, music, and art, to food, images, and gestures – Camus assigns blame internally: not to migrants from Africa but rather to the political and ideological spread within Europe itself of the idea of equality, which has proscribed any/all criticism of immigration.[7] Cultural erosion is an effect of what he terms 'the dictatorship of the petty-bourgeoisie', or the consolidation of an inclusiveness 'whose limits more or less coincide with the world itself' and consequently 'knows practically no outside world' (Camus 2018: 111, 121–122). Exercising as a result an ideological hegemony (equality = deculturation = de-authentication) which it is impossible politically to challenge, the 'petite bourgeoisie is *par excellence* the class of replacement' (Camus 2018: 128).

Cultural erosion/de-authentication is also central to the investigation by Kaufmann (2018) into the dynamics of GR fears now circulating among the inhabitants of developed societies. Rightly linking immigration to the rise of populism, he nevertheless attributes the latter development simply to the numerical decline in western nations of populations constituting a hitherto dominant white ethnic group (= 'whiteshift'), insisting that populism is determined by 'concern over identity, not economic threat'.[8] As a framework for analyzing GR issues, however, problems with this kind of approach surface quickly; political differences in such contexts are explained in psychologistic terms, a difficulty that stems in part from a methodology based on attitudinal surveys. Thus, both supporters and opponents of immigration are categorized as belonging to distinct psychological types, since in his opinion 'all social systems work with the grain of some of our evolutionary psychology' (Kaufmann, 20, 295). Denying that they are informed by inequality, wealth, and power,

---

continent is like one of those fabled alchemical treatises where the text on each page vanishes as soon as the book is opened at it.'

7 Regarding this locus of blame, see Camus (2018: 88–89). On GR as a process of cultural de-authentication, see Camus (2018: 139, 146, 147). 'If there is no culture,' he observes (Camus,2018: 98), 'culture will be the name of whatever there is.' He continues (Camus,2018: 114): 'Equality between century-old local traditions and mores and imported ways of life and foreign traditions will let nothing standing, or worth standing, of any nation.'

8 Kaufmann (2018: 2, 4). Lest it be thought that 'other'-culture-as-disbarment is applied just by Europe to migrants from the Third World, it was also applied by colonies to immigrants from Europe (Lochore, 1951).

Brexit voting patterns are instead ascribed by him to 'psychological quirks' (Kaufmann, 196–7, 200).

Although Camus maintains that, conceptually, GR 'is of my own creation', much the same kind of approach was applied by the historian Tenney Frank at the start of the twentieth century to the study of ancient Rome.[9] His argument was that in no small way the decline of Rome was due to 'Orientalizing', a process he equated with the decline of 'native stock' (= Italian population) and its replacement with 'oriental stock' from Asia Minor or Syria. Unlike other concepts of the GR considered here, however, in the case of ancient Rome this change occurred as a result of internal dynamics: locals were not displaced by immigration, since in economic terms immigrants were not attracted to Rome. Instead, slaves acquired as a result of conquest or purchase eventually became freedmen, and – as citizens – increased in numbers.[10] To some degree, this approach was shared by A.H.M. Jones, when observing that 'a decline in public spirit in the later Roman Empire' was due to a corresponding decay of 'civic patriotism [whereby the] idea of public service waned'.[11]

This transformation, maintained Frank, underwrote the trend licensing political absolutism based on Emperor worship and deification. The latter accompanied the process whereby the Italian population, which represented liberty and law, was increasingly replaced by those from the East who 'had never known self-government'. That is to say, inhabitants who had helped put in place the politics and ideology of the Republic, based as these were on a democratic ideal, gave way over time to non-Italians who did not subscribe to the same processes/ideals, and consequently lacked a similar commitment to their continuation, preferring much rather – or at least not objecting to – the anti-democratic rule of an Emperor. An important aspect of this transformation was the change in religious belief, towards what Frank termed the 'emotional and mystical religions of the East' which privileged 'faith' and 'intuition'.[12] The difficulties with this and later variants of the 'white fright' GR discourse are not difficult to discern.

---

9   For this claim, see Camus (2019: 163).

10   The rise in non-Italian population was attributed by Frank (1920: 156–7) to a liberal manumission policy that conferred freedom and citizenship, whereby those who started out as slaves were able 'to merge into the citizen body of Rome'.

11   See Jones (1966: 369).

12   Frank (1920: 164) sums up this position in the following manner: 'Did Rome's capacity to govern fail because the people of iron will, indefatigable purpose, and prudent vision that had built the state bequeathed its government to men of softer fibre'.

2.2   *Demography, Culture, Civilization*

Upholding the view that political organization in Africa is an effect of generational power, Smith overlooks the fact that in many instances ethnic/tribal identity has been mobilized in a populist fashion, either from within (to secure electoral support or to lay claim to a better share of existing resources) or from without (to divide and rule, by focusing on non-class identities). In cases where 'old men rule,' therefore, and equate tribal/ethnic identity with that of the nation, this can be linked to imperialism, which installs and keeps in power those such as Mobutu in order to further its own economic and political interests. Although he decries the concept of migration as a form of 'revenge colonization' on the part of a 'resentful Africa', Smith nevertheless comes close to endorsing this very notion.[13] Hence the inference by him that where European workers experience a descent into the ranks of the 'precariat', they were lucky to have a decent standard of living in the first place, and should neither be surprised nor complain when as a result of globalization this is taken away from them (Smith 2019, 101). This is a politically reactionary argument, one that is heard frequently from some who see development as a zero-sum process. In this discourse those belonging to the European working class currently enduring a decline in living standards are perceived as undeserving victims, now that they are being replaced (both at home and abroad) by the Third World 'other', a politically more deserving case.[14]

The pejorative description by Smith of the post-1945 welfare provision enjoyed by working class in Europe as 'a well-cosseted exception in an otherwise more exposed world', suggests that he does indeed regard this as in some sense illegitimate, despite the fact that what there remains still of such provision ('a social safety net') has had to be fought for in the course of class struggles waged 'from below' throughout history (Smith 2019, 145). What is not mentioned in this variant of 'revenge colonization' discourse is to whose advantage it really is: namely, capitalists undertaking labor process restructuring, undermining any consciousness of class (and thus solidarity) by playing workers of different ethnic/national identities against each other. Where this 'divide-and-rule' strategy is combined with economic restructuring, the political outcome throughout Europe has been, unsurprisingly, the rise of populism. This is particularly relevant to the contrast Smith makes between two historically distinct migration flows. Whereas the 1880s migration to the

---

13   Smith (2019: 139). For an example, more broadly, of 'revenge colonization' discourse, see
        Mehta (2019).

14   This is because European workers are seen as complicit historically in the colonization by
        imperialism – and thus exploitation – of the Third World 'other'.

United States corresponded largely to a situation in which migrants were an addition to existing workers, and thus not in the main competitors with them, early twenty-first century migration to Europe by contrast is – and is perceived to be – informed by a different economic dynamic. Instead of simply labor-power added to the existing workforce, it is in many cases 'instead of' the latter. As such, it can be seen by those in employment, or hoping to enter this, as an unwarranted source of labor market competition, designed to drive down wages and working conditions.

A similar refusal to address economic determinants generally, and more especially those generated by accumulation, its dynamics and attendant forms of class struggle, means that Kaufmann must confine within capitalism any political remedies he suggests. Hence the anodyne nature of his political solutions to the issues raised by GR, along the lines of different attitudes towards immigration 'need to be respected', 'I set out a vision for a new centre, which entails accepting the legitimate cultural interests of reconstructed, open ethnic majorities. This can pave the way towards a more relaxed, rational political conversation,' and 'Conservative whites need to have a future and I believe most will accept an open form of white majority identity.'[15] His conclusion – that the 'appropriate policy response is ... a compromise between equity and efficiency' – underlines the extent to which Kaufmann (2018: 330) remains trapped within the epistemological and political limits imposed by capitalism, and thus an inability to resolve the contradictions it reproduces. Without, that is, addressing either what accumulation entails systemically, or its need to restructure the labor process by creating and then taking advantage of an industrial reserve army. Contrary to the claim by Kaufmann, that GR is an effect simply of demographic growth, throughout history population change has always occurred – and continues to do so – within specific contexts; what is happening now is not so much demographic growth *per se* as population *movement*. This is what has to be explained, in economic terms: that is, the systemic dynamic governing/preventing such movement, and with it the contradiction between workers who want to protect their wage levels, jobs, and living standards from yet more competition, and the need of capital to force down these same wage levels and conditions in order to compete (and even, perhaps, to survive). In short, the systemic contradiction which generates populism.

Equating culture with civilization, Camus – like so many others – uses the latter term in its restricted sense: that is, civilization without its economic and political dimensions, and their achievements. In keeping with this, he conflates

---

15   For these views, see Kaufmann (2018: 4, 27, 28).

'race' and 'people', concepts which for him 'are more or less exchangeable' (Camus 2018: 75). As with Kaufmann, this in turn takes Camus directly onto the theoretical terrain of populism, for which the words 'race' and 'people' are similarly interchangeable. What is interpreted by Camus as a process of *decul-turation* is much rather one of *re*-culturation, or a combination of extending cultural inclusiveness while at the same time forbidding Marxist political economy. This of course is a project that brings together neoliberalism (= the sacredness of individual economic choice), the 'new' populist postmodern-ism (= the sacredness of individual identity choice), and deregulated market capitalism. For this reason, the contention that everything is allowed is linked to – and indeed generates – the kindred argument that nobody may criticize any cultural/ideological position one chooses to take.[16] In turn, this licenses the empowerment of identity politics, which combines everything-is-allowed with no-criticism-is-permitted, since non-class identities (and their advocates) cease to be the object of critique. Hence the emergence – or re-emergence – of a politics linked to these identities, and the ensuing fusion of postmodernism and populism.

Mimicking postmodern support for the culture of the migrant 'other', and opposition to GR discourse, current historiography of ancient Rome reverses the earlier negative interpretation of Tenney Frank and recasts 'otherness' as positive. Accordingly, focus has shifted, both epistemologically and (thus) polit-ically: away from a discourse about locals-as-victims to one about migrants-as-culturally-empowered. The emphasis is no longer on the disadvantages to the (Italian) self, as argued long ago by Frank, but rather on the advantages of incorporation enjoyed by the (non-Italian) 'other'.[17] As in the case of so many other contexts, epochs, and issues, the historiography of ancient Rome has not escaped the desire by postmodern theory to find instances of culturally empowering 'otherness' involving identity politics. Noting that 'scholarly views of Roman imperialism and colonialism have altered considerably in the past few decades', another historian describes the result of this kind of reinterpreta-tion in the following manner: 'Rome the reflective, self-conscious power is out; Rome the self-assured maligner of other cultures is in' (Adler 2011, 1). It is not surprising, therefore, to encounter in a number of current analyses influenced

---

16   Among those who also make this case is Vargas Llosa (2015).

17   Although no mention is made of him by name, it is clear that Beard (2013:179) has Tenney Frank in mind when she makes the following dismissive observation: 'No writers today quite echo the strident complaints of early twentieth-century historians who ... lamented the dilution of true Italian stock with the foreign blood of freedman, whose origins often lay in the East.'

by postmodernism a positive reading of the very same processes understood as negative by exponents of GR.

This is itself part of a broader trend, away from materialist concepts positing the existence of an objective reality and towards an aporia, or the notion that historiography of ancient Rome is nothing more than literature.[18] Consistent with the latter approach is the privileging of culture at the expense of political economy, an epistemological break that moves the element of determination from the material base to superstructural phenomena. In what is an unmistakably Panglossian view, one such analysis – by an influential present-day historian of ancient society – perceives the extension of citizenship and the consequent increasing ethnic/national 'otherness' of Rome's population as a positive development, evidence simply of success, without asking too closely either about the political implications of this or about its impact on the labor market and working conditions.[19] That such a celebratory approach fails to engage analytically with political economy invites a riposte to criticism that those who invoke Roman history in order to draw parallels with contemporary developments do so without knowledge of the former.[20] Much rather, it could be said that those who apply to ancient society currently fashionable paradigms drawn from the present invariably do so without knowledge of the latter.[21]

---

18   On this point, see Lendon (2009), who observes that 'most contemporary writing in English about Latin historians slights these historians' concern for truth, [an] indifference to so important a part of what historians thought they were doing [that] constitutes a pervasive affliction in the scholarship ...'. Aporia is central to the 'new' populist postmodernism, since by questioning reality – *all* reality – it bolsters the view that nothing is (or ever can be) real, and consequently history is just competing opinions: epistemologically, no objective reality is possible, or indeed desirable.

19   Significantly, this positive interpretation (Beard, 2016: 330) regarding the 'widespread image of Rome as an open culture [which] made the Roman citizen body the most ethnically diverse that there ever was before the modern world' is itself structured by an idealized/benign view of slavery. The latter takes the form that no clear line separated the free from the unfree, and that slavery was anyway only a 'temporary status'. In short, the familiar revisionist trope to the effect the unfree were essentially no different from the free, a claim based on the observation that both worked together, alongside one another. Such a view overlooks a number of things. To begin with, substantial evidence confirms that in other contexts where free and unfree toiled together, differences did occur, in terms of hours worked, payment received, and control exercised. Moreover, unfreedom coincided largely with the productive life of a slave, and manumission occurred only when this ceased to be profitable.

20   For this criticism, see Gillett (2017).

21   Thus, for example, Beard (2013) invokes the term 'multicultural' in relation to ancient society, without considering whether such a modern concept has the same meaning in the historical period and context to which it is applied. For more on this, see Brass (2021).

3   The Causes of GR

3.1   *Who/What Is Responsible?*

If immigration results in cultural erosion/de-authentication, contributing thereby to GR, then how is it to be explained in terms of who or what is deemed to be ideologically and politically supportive of – and thus in an important sense responsible for – this process? With the exception of that by Smith, all the approaches examined here are clear about where to place the blame for the emergence and consolidation of GR: on the promotion by the left of identity politics, championing any/every anguished ethnic/national 'other' by means of a victim narrative.

Hence the focus of the approach to GR by Kaufmann (2018: 21) is on conflict from the 1960s onwards between 'white tribalism' and what he terms 'left-modernism'. The latter is defined by him as a combination of 'modernist anti-traditionalism' and 'cultural egalitarianism', a synthesis which he accepts 'meshed nicely with capitalism and globalization'. This 'left-modernist cosmopolitanism, which rejected both communism and fascism in favour of cultural radicalism and social democracy, emerged victorious from the war' (Kaufmann, 2018: 313). In terms of effect, the twofold political impact of 'left-modernism' was to move debate from 'tolerating to mandating diversity' which in turn banished discussion of immigration, 'keeping it off the political agenda' (Kaufmann, 2018: 22). Equated by Kaufmann with the 'cultural turn', 'multiculturalism', and the New Left, among the main characteristics he ascribes to 'left-modernism' are 'political correctness' and privileging 'subaltern ethnic narratives'.[22] Describing himself as a 'liberal and moderate egalitarian', he is nevertheless critical of 'the excesses of left-modernism': in particular, its exclusionary account together with support for subaltern ethnicity/'otherness' while at the same time decrying non-subaltern ethnic identity. As will be seen below, Kaufmann rather spoils his critique by insisting that all these characteristics are a specifically leftist vice, rather than what they in fact are: a conservative form of anti-capitalism that has a long history.

Like other approaches to GR, and especially that of Camus, Bret Easton Ellis resents having to apologize for being white, a sense of guilt inculcated in his view as a result of cultural democratization which encourages blandness and conformity.[23] Again like them, he attributes such developments to what he

---

22   On these points, see Kaufmann (2018: 298, 305–6, 321, 338, 341, 345).

23   According to Bret Easton Ellis (2019: 117–18), therefore, 'the logical endgame of the democratization of culture and the dreaded cult of inclusivity, which insists everybody has to live under the same umbrella of rules.'

regards as the political left, responsible in his opinion for the rise and consolidation of identity politics which on the one hand castigate those like him,
simply on the grounds of belonging to a privileged ethnicity, and on the other
favor all those categorized as ethnically/nationally 'other'. Again like other
approaches to GR, Bret Easton Ellis perceives the main attack on his identity
as coming from the younger generation in the same society, an age-group he
regards with contempt (millennials = 'Generation Wuss') for having in his
view succumbed unjustifiably to an all-embracing concept of victimhood, and
consequently being unable to engage critically with the world they inhabit.[24]
Unsurprisingly, in this discourse generational difference fuses with political
difference, and Bret Easton Ellis ends by blaming millennials on the left –
'social justice warriors' – for generating/reproducing/endorsing the social ills
to which he objects.[25]

Camus (2018) blames the left in similar terms, arguing that its promotion of
egalitarianism has culminated in an alliance between the left and 'high finance'
(= 'Davocracy', or the very rich, 'the great paymasters of the world, bankers
and giants of finance'), enabling the latter to justify as benign/progressive the
'great replacism' policy from which it benefits (Camus, 2018: 114ff, 134). This it
does by the creation of additional consumers – in the form of migrants – to
whom it can then sell commodities. Accordingly, to the right-wing trope of
'high finance' (code for 'Jewish' in this discourse) Camus adds the proponents
of anti-racism, seen by him as providing 'Davocracy' with protection against
the historical accusation that, because it has always been seen as rootless cosmopolitanism, finance has no loyalty to any nation. Hence the fusion of high
finance/money/power on the one hand, and on the other anti-racism/virtue/
righteousness is for him a combination of right and left ('traditional business
interests of the right' + 'traditional moral ideals of the left').[26]

---

24 Hence the view (Easton Ellis, 2019: 139–40, original emphasis) about the way in which the
    left always and uncritically accepts the way the 'other' defines itself: 'This widespread epi-
    demic of self-victimization – defining yourself in essence by way of a *bad* thing, a trauma
    that happened in the past that you've let *define* you ...'

25 'The high moral tone seized by the social justice warriors, and increasingly an unhinged
    Left', he maintains (Easton Ellis, 2019: 181, 184), 'is always out of scale with whatever
    they're actually indignant about [and] had begun to create an authoritarian language
    police ... we were entering into an authoritarian cultural moment fostered by the Left'.
    Much the same criticism of 'social justice warriors' is expressed by Kaufmann (2018: 304,
    340) and Camus.

26 'That unique combination, money and virtue (or the image thereof), power and righ-
    teousness, traditional business interests of the right and no less traditional moral ide-
    als of the left,' notes Camus (2018: 163), 'is in my opinion what makes replacism such a

Like Bret Easton Ellis and Kaufmann, therefore, Camus is strongly critical of the left, which he censures for combining with and providing a justification for the GR policies followed by neoliberalism.[27] An analogous connection – but with one important difference – is made by Houellebecq, who argues that responsibility for the rise and consolidation in France of Islam lies with the left: instead of depicting this development as evidence for the power of the left (as do Camus, Kaufmann and Bret Easton Ellis), however, Houellebecq regards it as an effect of the ideological weakness of socialism.[28] The critique of Camus is not confined to the left, but extends to include the State. Again like Houellebecq, therefore, Camus draws a historical parallel between collaboration with the German invasion of France by the Vichy regime in 1940s, and the inability or unwillingness of 'collaborationist circles' – 'a tiny minority (of radicals)' – to oppose/resist GR, for him an analogous process of occupation.[29] This equivalence, he explains, stems from a situation 'where the government of an invaded or occupied country, having admitted defeat, applies its best efforts to befriend the invader, usually with little success quite simply because the invader despises him ...'.[30]

3.2   *Rival Ethnicities, Rival Populisms*

Contrary to what Kaufmann claims is the case, his concept 'left-modernism' is neither left nor modern: all the defining characteristics he ascribes to it – 'mandated diversity', 'ethno-traditional nationalism', 'subaltern ethnic narratives', and 'political correctness' – are more accurately those which inform the discourse of the 'new' populist postmodernism.[31] The latter deprivileges concepts such as modernity, materialism, class, and even economic development,

---

formidable enemy, so formidable indeed that one often wonders if there is any point in trying to fight it ...'

27   See, for example, Camus (2018: 107).

28   See Houellebecq (2015) and also Brass (2017: Ch. 9).

29   In 'two recent occupations of France – the shorter German one in the 1940s and the longer African one of the past forty years,' argues Camus (2018: 58–59, original emphasis), 'the two collaborations serving the respective occupying forces are perfect look-alikes ... it soon became clear that as far as the term *collaboration* was concerned, it appeared to be decidedly legitimate and appropriate to refer to the successive French governments which, after the Vichy government during the previous occupation, constantly displayed a typical eagerness to anticipate and meet the occupants' wishes and whims half-way ...'

30   See Camus (2018: 63).

31   Conceptually, the 'new' populist postmodernism refers to a variety of discourses (post-development, the Subaltern Studies project, post-colonialism, everyday-forms-of-resistance, post-structuralism, multitudes, etc.) which have in common hostility towards the theoretical apparatus of Marxism.

all dismissed as illegitimate Enlightenment/Eurocentric forms of 'foundation-alism' inapplicable to an understanding – let alone empowerment – of 'other' cultural identity and agency, either in the so-called Third World or within met-ropolitan capitalism itself. Instead, 'new' populist postmodernist discourse re-essentializes historical (and in some instances pre-capitalist) forms of cultural and economic identity. It is opposed (or resistant) to state power supportive as much of *laissez-faire* accumulation as of socialist central planning and property.[32]

Again, contrary to the claim by Kaufmann, that the 'cultural left' pursues radical social transformation (as does Marxism, with its 'going beyond' capital-ism to socialism), the 'new' populist postmodernism advocates recuperating traditional non-class (= lost) grassroots institutions and authority structures, in much the same way as populism does. Culture wars that he rightly criticizes are no more than an attempt by populists to find a non-Marxist form of grassroots empowerment that does not pose a fundamental threat to existing property relations and wealth. As such, it is the mirror image of what Kaufmann labels 'white tribalism', invoking not just the same arguments concerning the need to empower 'those below' (but not in class terms), but also promoting claims to empowerment using different kinds of ethnic/national/'other' identity. The ideological role of the cultural turn is that it enables one to claim to be a partic-ipant in a struggle that is ostensibly radical (for example, objecting to statues of colonizers or Confederate soldiers), whereas it is actually a substitute for struggle, since the latter process is confined merely to acts of symbolic opposi-tion. This is misrecognized by Kaufmann (2018: 299), who maintains wrongly that 'left-modernism triumphed despite the retreat of socialism', whereas in fact it triumphed not despite but much rather *because* of this retreat.

Although the politically divisive aspect of identity politics traced by Kaufmann is also well captured by Bret Easton Ellis, because the latter – again like Kaufmann – mistakenly attributes its origin to the left, and blames the latter for its spread, he overlooks two crucial issues: the question of who/what benefits from this discourse, and the fact that identity politics (= the

---

32   As outlined elsewhere (Brass, 2000, 2014), in rural Latin America and India grassroots ethno-nationalism harks back to a mythical Golden Age informed by agrarian myth ideol-ogy, which – among other things – entails the restoration of pre- or non-capitalist hierar-chy/authority and its attendant institutions/practices, most of which are fundamentally anti-democratic and non-progressive (e.g., subordination of women, concentration of landownership, the presence of unfree production relations). To some degree, and under the label of 'gerontocracy', this is the same kind of problem as that raised by Smith with regard to Africa. In his latest publication, Houellebecq (2019) invokes and laments the demise of agrarian myth ideology in the French countryside.

cultural turn) is a characteristic not of Marxism but rather of the 'new' populist postmodernism.[33] Equating postmodern identity politics with Marxism is profoundly mistaken, since the two positions are epistemologically incompatible: because it deals principally with ethnic/national identity, the 'new' populist postmodernism tends especially in its post-colonial guise to attack not the rich and powerful owners/controllers of the means of production, distribution, and exchange – as does Marxism – but rather all those belonging to an erstwhile colonial/imperial power. In the recent past, and continuing into the present, therefore, postmodernism makes no distinction between the ruling class and its plebeian components in what were once colonizing nations. Consequently, struggle as interpreted by this kind of approach is mainly or only about national (or ethnic) empowerment on the part of countries and/or populations that were once colonies. As such, the 'new' populist postmodernism is a theory that is largely unconnected with the formation/consciousness/ agency of those whose identity is based on class: namely, struggle undertaken by workers that necessarily transcends national/ethnic boundaries.

For the 'new' populist postmodernism, therefore, class is at worst a Eurocentric concept inapplicable outside its geographical area, and at best an add-on, to be addressed and resolved (if at all) only when all other non-class identities have been empowered. In many cases, however, it is only the latter, not the former, that interest exponents of the 'cultural turn'. Splitting working class identity/consciousness/empowerment along ethnic/national lines is the project of capital, not of the left. Yet this is precisely what the 'new' populist postmodernism entails. In keeping with this epistemology are those who align themselves with the 'cultural turn' simply because it is against neoliberalism. Among those who regard populism as progressive, and consequently advocate what is conceptualized by them as 'left populism', is Chantal Mouffe (2018). This is a view that emerged from earlier post-Marxist theory, which championed multi-class alliances based on hegemony, with the object of achieving a politically non-specific form of radical democracy (= a return to a 'kinder'/ 'caring' capitalism). Not the least problematic aspect of building multi-class

---

33   'I was increasingly reminded by a certain faction', notes Easton Ellis (2019: 243, original emphasis) about what he regards as the Left, 'that we *should* be defining ourselves by our white identity because that was itself a real *problem*. Actually, this faction *demanded* it, without bothering to recognize that identity politics of any kind might be the worst idea in our culture right now, and certainly one that encourages the spread of alt-right and all-white organizations. Across the board, identity politics endorse the concept that people are essentially tribal, and our differences are irreconcilable ... This is the toxic dead-end of identity politics: it's a trap.'

alliances is that as soon as their object is achieved (the defeat of feudal proprietors), capitalist producers turn on their erstwhile allies (workers, poor peasants). Categorizing populist movements as the way forward politically, simply
because such mobilizations oppose *laissez-faire* accumulation, overlooks the
fact that their bourgeois components are just as – if not even more strongly –
hostile to any form of socialism.

4 Economic Aspects of the Populism/Immigration Debate

4.1 *Political Economy and/as Great Replacement*

The economic background to the rise of immigration and populism, one that
GR analyses tend to avoid or downplay, is clear. An effect of labor's stronger
position in the immediate post-1945 era was that hours worked fell and industrial conflict increased. Class struggle 'from below' in metropolitan capitalist
nations – the results of which were full employment, higher wages, and the
welfare state – led in turn to class struggle 'from above', in the form of the new
international division of labor. From the 1960s onwards, therefore, the Green
Revolution drove peasants off the land and made them available to capital as
workers, thereby enabling the outsourcing/downsizing of capitalist production.
This was compounded in the late 1980s by the provision of additional sources
of cheap and available labor-power nearer Europe, from countries previously
part of the USSR and now members of the EU. Whereas development theory
deploying the 'precariat' concept worries about the inability of temporary and
low-paid labor-power to reproduce itself economically, this does not arise as
long as capital can draw on an industrial reserve army that is global. Hence the
need to preserve the well-being of its workers is no longer a major concern.

Like their cultural equivalents, economic arguments about the GR/immigra-
tion/populism connection, divide into two: between those who, because they
support capitalism, perceive an expanding industrial reserve army as positive,
since it contributes to economic growth, and those critics of accumulation
who regard the same process as negative.[34] On the one hand, therefore, are

---

34   Broadly speaking, where negative discourse is concerned, the overlap between cultural
      and economic theory can be illustrated in the following way:

Theory	Discourse	Process	Cause	Beneficiary	Victim
Marxist	economic	Industrial reserve army	Over-accumulation	employer	worker
Anti-/Non-Marxist	culture	Great Replacement	Over-population	'other' identity	self

the early pro-market liberal theorists and later neoclassical economists who endorse the market, and are supportive of the historical project of capitalism. On the other are Marxists opposed to the impact of the industrial reserve army on the solidarity, consciousness and struggles of the working class.

From the mid-eighteenth century to the mid-nineteenth, liberal political economists in France, such as Dunoyer and Turgot, formulated a *laissez-faire* project in defense of 'pure' capitalism, leading to neo-classical economic theory and culminating in present-day neoliberalism. At its center was the economic argument that, like any other kind of trade involving the circulation of commodities, the free movement of labor could – and, indeed, should – operate not just at the national level of a nation (= within a country) but also amongst nations (= between countries), thus paving the way for the globalization of the capitalist system.[35] By advocating the principle of a free labor market, one that was not confined to workers of a particular nationality but extended also to include foreigners coming to or residing within the nation concerned, therefore, liberal political economy established the rationale underwriting the formation and operation – on a world scale, eventually – of what Marxism, its main theoretical opponent, came to regard as the industrial reserve army of labor.

Where immigration is concerned, current support for an open-door policy combined with opposition to any criticism of it, extends from international financial institutions (the World Bank, the International Monetary Fund), via national business organizations and *laissez-faire* think-tanks, to NGOs and academia. This support divides into two distinct kinds of defense: arguments that are based either on culture (as outlined above) or economics – and sometimes both. More recently, therefore, academic supporters of the neoliberal project have argued that, as labor-power is the main commodity those in developing nations have to sell, its appearance unprotected by minimum wage or other legislation in deregulated global markets – whether at home or abroad – is justified politically and necessary to the well-functioning of the capitalist

---

A Similar overlap informs cultural/economic theory taking a positive approach:

Theory	Discourse	Process	Cause	Beneficiary	Victim
neoliberal	economic	empowerment	(economic) choice	society	none
postmodern	culture	empowerment	(identity) choice	subject	none

35   For additional details about the post-1789 emergence of this liberal economic discourse, see Brass (2019: Chapter 4).

system.[36] Thus, for example, Bhagwati champions the use of child labor, which in much of the Third World is unfree, since it enables producers who employ it to undercut and outcompete those who do not.[37] Moreover, he justifies this by claiming that 'diversity of labor practices and standards is widespread and reflects ... diversity of cultural values', maintaining that such relational forms are no more than culturally-specific kinds of national 'otherness' (see Bhagwati 1995, 28). In all but name, such endorsements of *laissez-faire* approaches to the labor market, combining economic and cultural discourse, amount to a positive view of the cost-effective dynamics informing GR theory.

In a sense, it could be argued that the focus of Marxist theory is and has always been on the process of replacement, great or otherwise: of feudalism by capitalism and of the latter by socialism. Such an historical process involves economic, political, and ideological changes that correspond to the totality of a transformation as perceived by GR. For Marxism, therefore, systemic transition – from feudalism to capitalism, and from the latter to socialism – could be seen as entailing a great replacement, particularly since as in the case of GR it is accompanied by social conflict. An important difference, however, exists; whereas change as interpreted by GR is demographic and structured by the empowerment/disempowerment of different ethnic/national categories and identities, that of Marxism by contrast entails a struggle culminating in the replacement not of one ethnicity or nationality by another but rather of one class by another. Thus, for Marxism the post-1980s process of capitalist restructuring corresponds to a double replacement: initially, production was outsourced to third world countries, where labor-power was cheap; now, however, labor-power from the same (and other) contexts is being insourced to metropolitan capitalist nations, in the form of immigration into Europe.[38]

---

36   Some economists who are not neoliberals also support open door immigration, simply on the grounds that it contributes to efficient and cost-effective national growth. Maintaining that 'immigrants bring dynamism' because they are 'entrepreneurial', and that 'immigration is an opportunity', Portes (2016: 176–79) insists that 'free markets should mean free movement'. Again, no mention is made by this kind of approach, either of the association between migration and increases in the industrial reserve army, or of the link between the latter combination and the political and ideological rise of populism.

37   This is but one aspect of the ongoing case made by him and other neoclassical economists (Bhagwati, 1993, 2007; Bhagwati and Panagariya, 2013a, 2013b) against 'State interference' with free trade.

38   The position of Marxist theory on nationalism, and its difference from that of the varieties of non-Marxism considered here, is best summed up by Lenin (1964: 35, original emphasis): 'Combat all national oppression? Yes, of course! Fight *for* any kind of national development, *for* "national culture" in general – Of course not.'

It is significant, therefore, that the approaches considered here which examine GR discourse either fail to mention the role of the industrial reserve army, or note this briefly and in passing, without naming it as such. Thus accumulation, both as creator of surplus labor and as necessitating this resource, escapes observation and condemnation. Only far into his analysis does Smith hints at a possible connection between cost-cutting, immigration and surplus labor, but says nothing about who benefits (capital) and what in systemic terms currently generates such a development.[39] Unmentioned, therefore, is the necessity of the industrial reserve so as to enhance competitiveness and profitability in a global context where failure to do this on the part of corporations risks going out of business. Avoiding mention of capitalism and class struggle, like the other approaches considered here, Camus maintains that what causes GR is too complex a process to comprehend, let alone oppose.[40]

Nevertheless, Camus (2018) recognizes the difficulty for his argument about a desire for additional consumers rather than workers as the dynamic informing GR, given that immigrants have little money with which to consume, and filling poorly paid jobs is not going to give them much spending power anyway. Accordingly, he shifts the focus onto public spending (schools, health, etc.), arguing this kind of state expenditure to meet their needs will amount to the increased consumption sought (Camus, 2018: 153–54). The problem with this is that the capitalist state is following the opposite path: using the availability of cheap immigrant labor-power not to build up but rather to run down public spending generally, and welfare provision in particular. Coming from contexts where social benefits and/or state expenditure are absent or negligible, neoliberalism counts with the fact that new workers will not miss these resources when absent or largely unavailable. In any case, were such workers to demand better provision and resources, they, too, would quickly be replaced by yet more recent additions to the labor market. So the connection between public spending and consumption linked to immigration is not made. The old argument, a Marxist one, about the cheapness of labor-power – not its capacity to

---

39 Smith (2019: 148). Like him and Camus, Kaufmann (2018: 208) also recognizes that immigration exercises a downward pressure on wages/conditions of those already in work, but like them omits to connect this to the presence/role of the industrial reserve army.

40 Outlining both the causes and thus the possibility of impeding GR, Camus (2018: 165) observes: 'I would rather think of some enormous, bizarre and complex processes, so intricate that no one can understand perfectly how they work and why, and no one can master and stop them once they are started.' Elsewhere – in a 2016 interview – he has stated that 'I have very little interest in determining who is responsible for our fatal situation [= GR], except for general statements about it.'

consume – necessary to restore or enhance competitiveness and profitability at the center of the accumulation process, still holds.

4.2   *Marxism and the Industrial Reserve*

Apart from GR exponents, opponents of the neoliberal project fall into two categories: those who to some degree share the assumptions of neoliberals themselves, and Marxists who reject its epistemology. Among the former are those who subscribe to a moral discourse and criticize accumulation for not caring sufficiently about its workforce. Thus, for example, Davis – much influenced by Jan Breman – insists analogously that 'there is no official scenario for the reincorporation of this vast mass of surplus labor into the mainstream of the world economy.'[41] To present it in this fashion, however, is in effect to agree with the way supporters of capitalism interpret the process: namely, as a residual population lacking any economic role or prospects. In this discourse of despair, therefore, surplus labor appears as some form of accidental or 'natural' occurrence, regrettable but unavoidable. The solution espoused by those adhering to a moral discourse is to advocate a return to a 'caring'/'kinder' capitalism that eschews the highly exploitative market regime of neoliberalism. Such an approach departs from that of Marxism, which regards the industrial reserve as neither accidental nor 'natural', but rather as outcome of an increasingly acute form of class struggle between capital and labor, a situation in which the enlargement of potential/actual workers has been engineered politically, economically and ideologically. In short, a conflict in which surplus labor is itself a non-accidental creation of the accumulation process, in the furtherance of which it discharges a crucial economic role.

Appearances to the contrary notwithstanding, therefore, Marxism departs substantially from all earlier and/or later arguments supportive of or opposed to immigration. That is, from economic theory which endorses neoliberal globalization; from approaches to GR theory informed either by (non-economic) cultural determinants or by Malthusian assumptions; and from Malthus himself, for whom population growth was defined as a general phenomenon linked epistemologically and politically to the food supply. Unlike them all, Marxist theory deploys the concept of the industrial reserve army of labor, which is based on the growth not of population *per se* but rather on its economic

---

41   See Davis (2006: 199) who, because he was writing before the upsurge in migration towards metropolitan capitalist nations, maintains incorrectly that (Davis, 2006: 200–201): 'With a literal "great wall" of high-tech border enforcement blocking large-scale migration to the rich countries, only the slum remains as a fully franchised solution to the problem of warehousing this century's surplus humanity.'

implications: the impact of under- or unemployed plebeian elements both on the labor market and thus on class formation and struggle.[42] Hence the centrality to the accumulation process of the industrial reserve army is (and always has been) key to Marxist theory, not just about the reproduction and development of the capitalist system, but also about the possibility (or otherwise) of struggle leading to a socialist transition.[43] Merely by its presence, let alone by its expansion, the industrial reserve permitted employers not just to keep wages down – thereby depressing payment below the value produced by labor-power – but also avoid having to improve work conditions. According to Marx himself, therefore, the reserve army comes into its own once the early stage of capitalism – that generally associated with primitive accumulation – has been left behind (Marx 1976, 784–85).

The threat an increasing reserve army posed not just to hard-won wage levels and employment conditions but also to the protection of these gains – by means of solidarity among and capacity of an existing workforce to organize – was such that Marx gave serious consideration to opposing further immigration.[44] In ways that anticipate current argument about withdrawal from EU membership so as to stem competition from the industrial reserve army, a century and a half ago Marx advocated severing the link with Ireland precisely in order to prevent migrants from competing with and undercutting English workers.[45] He insisted that working class emancipation in England depended ultimately on Ireland following its own path of capitalist development, and to this end international solidarity would take the form of support from English

---

42   Despite almost recognizing the presence and economic role of the industrial reserve, Camus (2018: 116, 139, 153, 173) nevertheless omits to do so, not least because he cannot bring himself to blame the capitalist system *per se* – as distinct from its financial/foreign variants (= 'Davocracy') – for creating and reproducing surplus labour.

43   See not just Marx (1968: 257; 1969: 17, 477, 554, 557, 559–61; 1972: 350) but also Trotsky (1940), Luxemburg (2013), Dobb (1955: 215–225), and Glyn (2006). Along with other Marxists, Lenin (1963: 179, original emphasis) regarded the industrial reserve army as the *sine qua non* of capitalism, 'which could neither exist nor develop without it.' Accordingly, for him the industrial reserve 'being an inevitable result of capitalist accumulation, is at the same time *an indispensable component part of the capitalist machine.*' This, he goes on to argue, is the opposite of the view held by populists ('romanticists'), who saw the presence of surplus labour as an extraneous aspect ('a mistake') of the accumulation process.

44   Among those who recognized this was Engels (Marx and Engels, 1934: 496–7).

45   For details, see Marx and Engels (1934: 289–90). Observing that '[t]he average English worker hates the Irish working man as a competitor who lowers his wage and his standard of life', Marx (Collins and Abramsky, 1965: 170) argued that the Irish Question was central to the interests of the labour movement in England, adding that 'to forward the social revolution in England ... the decisive blow must be struck in Ireland'.

workers for Irish equivalents in their struggle for economic and political independence, as distinct from migrating to where this had already occurred. Not the least of the many ironies arising in the course of current debate about Brexit is that, advocating a no-deal approach has not prevented those on the political right continuing to promote the necessity of yet more immigration so as to enhance competitiveness of capitalist producers in the UK.[46] This of course is precisely what those belonging to the working class who voted to leave were against.

When Marxists depart from the strategy of opposing more labor market competition, and endorse not a class and internationalist approach but much rather one based on national/ethnic identity, history teaches a sharp lesson. In the case of late nineteenth and early twentieth century Austria, therefore, a burgeoning industrial reserve army had a deleterious impact on the solidarity of a working class differentiated in terms of ethnicity/nationality.[47] When capitalists turned to Czech migrants so as to displace unionized German workers, fueling thereby the rise of nationalism (much like GR theory nowadays), the response on the part of Austrian Social Democracy and trade unions was to advocate organizational separatism reflecting this national/ethnic 'otherness'. The result was that not only did proletarian institutions and politics split along ethnic/nationalist lines, but labor market competition between Czech migrants and German workers, together with the intense economic rivalry to which it gave rise, laid the ground for the emergence and consolidation during the 1920s and 1930s of the far right in Austria and Germany.

---

46 Following the leave vote in the 2016 referendum, the desire of employers for continued access to a reserve army composed of immigrant workers has been a constant refrain. See '[Conservative Home Secretary] Rudd promises door will be kept open to EU workers after Brexit', *Financial Times* (London), 27 July 2018; 'CBI wants new rules to keep open pipeline of EU workers after Brexit', *The Guardian* (London), 10 August 2018; 'Farmers say visa scheme will not solve shortage of staff after EU departure', *The Guardian* (London), 7 September 2018; 'Business anger at "elitist" plan to axe visas for lower-paid', *The Guardian* (London), 19 September 2018; 'Fear of skills shortages prompts business to plan moves abroad', *Financial Times* (London), 29–30 September 2018; 'Immigration waiver allows cheap labour to build windfarm', *The Guardian* (London), 22 October 2018; 'Ease entry rules for Indians to win deals after Brexit, say MPs', *The Guardian* (London), 24 June 2019; 'International graduates to be offered two-year work visas', *The Guardian* (London), 11 September 2019; 'Visa climbdown allows overseas students to stay for longer', *The Times* (London), 11 September 2019; 'Foreign students to get longer visas', *The Telegraph* (London), 11 September 2019.

47 See Brass (2019: Chapter 3).

5   Conclusion

Where the structure and development of the capitalist labor regime is concerned, the current relevance of Marxist theory is simply put: not only does
it force us to confront the burgeoning role in the accumulation process of an
industrial reserve army that is now global in scope, but it also (and consequently) enables us to deploy a materialist approach to this issue. It thereby
arms the left in its struggle against the attempt by resurgent populisms (GR,
postmodernism) to interpret the same issue in purely cultural terms, as a conflict between those possessing non-class identities (nationalism, ethnicity).

Ostensibly, there is an overlap between GR discourse and Marxism in that
conceptually each deals with systemic totality, its mode of transformation, and
its effects. However, unlike Marxism, GR discourse examined here focuses on
demographic aspects, as embodied in large-scale migration to metropolitan
capitalist nations, and the rise there of populism. The latter, such analyses of GR
maintain, is a political response to non-economic issues such as cultural ero-
sion/de-authentication and population displacement. This externally-driven
dynamic is blamed in turn on the complicity of internal advocacy: that of the
political left, deemed culpable for GR on account of the ideological support it
extends to any/all forms of 'otherness'. Such an approach, it is argued here, is
problematic for two reasons in particular: what GR regards as the political left
is itself much rather a rival form of populism, and consequently the misrecog-
nition of the economic issues structuring both GR and a resurgent populism.

As framed in these two narratives, for and against GR, it appears at times
as if the struggle is simply over rival claims to victimhood – who is the more
oppressed and disadvantaged, and thus more worthy of support. Insofar as it
privileges cultural identity as empowering, therefore, postmodern theory is
complicit with the kind of nationalist ideology informing populism. The latter
feeds off *laissez-faire* accumulation where economic crisis – generating both
an expanding industrial reserve army of migrant labor and also more intense
competition between capitalists themselves and between workers seeking
employment results inexorably in political crisis. To the postmodern argument
emphasizing the cultural identity of the migrant-as-'other'-nationality, therefore, populism counterposes an argument similarly emphasizing cultural identity, only this time the nationality of the non-migrant worker.

In the discourses opposed to and supportive of GR, hostility towards anti-
racism licenses as a reaction an endorsement of another ethnic/national
identity. As recognized by some GR analyses, anti-racism is itself transformed
thereby into a narrative sustaining nationality/ethnicity, albeit of an 'other'
kind, to the extent that it becomes in turn a defense of such identities. Pushed

to its logical conclusion, it becomes in effect a form of what might be termed pro-'otherness'. Ideologically, white identity is itself counteracted by an analogous form of difference; politically, therefore, one kind of populism confronts another variant of the same kind of discourse. The difficulty is, and remains, that the analyses examined here misattribute this transformation: it is regarded as emanating from – and thus an ideology belonging to – the left, whereas it more correctly has to be placed at the other end of the political spectrum. This difficulty possesses as a corollary the unwillingness of many on the left to engage with GR via the lens of political economy, rather than share with populism an approach the focus of which is only on culture.

Accordingly, much analysis purportedly from a leftist position simply attaches a label of racism to any/all GR argument, and – having refused to engage with it, and overlooking what Marxism has said about it – moves on to other things. Ironically, this is itself a mirror image of what exponents of the GR themselves do, which is to attach a label of mistaken/naïve leftist thinking to their political opponents, similarly overlooking what Marxism says about both the presence and the impact of the industrial reserve army. In short, about this particular issue neither approach is correct: leftist dismissal of GR argument ignores an economic dimension that GR itself overlooks or demotes, while the blame that GR attributes to the left should more accurately be attached to the 'new' populist postmodernism.

Rather than an indictment of Marxism, therefore, the kind of view held by the GR analyses considered here is more accurately a critique of the 'new' populist postmodernism. It is the latter, *not* the former, which – like GR itself – privileges ethnic/national (= non-class) 'otherness', to the extent that its theory by inference legitimizes the *laissez-faire* position of 'high finance' regarding the desirability of the free movement of labor. By contrast, the argument here is simple: whether owners of the means of production bring additional potential/actual workers into the labor process of metropolitan capitalist nations, or instead employs them in outsourced enterprises where they already are, in their own countries, the economic function and outcome of the industrial reserve army is in all cases the same. In whatever the context, surplus labor is available to replace those in employment who may ask for – let alone organize in pursuit of – higher wages and better working conditions.

Hence the current relevance of Marxism lies precisely in its championing of a materialist (= class struggle) approach to the capitalist labor regime, in the shape of the fact/role of the industrial reserve army, as against the non-class identities privileged by the discourse of rival populisms (GR, postmodernism). Continuing to misunderstand or misinterpret this crucial distinction, together with its implication for the kind of struggle taking place in today's capitalism, is something the left does at its peril.

References

Adler, E. 2011. *Valorizing the Barbarians: Enemy Speeches in Roman Historiography.* Austin, TX: University of Texas Press.

Beard, M. 2013. *Confronting the Classics.* London: Profile Books.

Beard, M. 2016. *SPQR: A History of Ancient Rome.* London: Profile Books.

Bhagwati, J. 1993. *India in Transition: Freeing the Economy.* Oxford: Clarendon Press.

Bhagwati, J. 1995. *Free Trade, "Fairness" and the New Protectionism.* London: Institute for Economic Affairs.

Bhagwati, J. 2007. *In Defense of Globalisation.* Oxford: Oxford University Press.

Bhagwati, J. and A. Panagariya. 2013a. *India's Tryst with Destiny.* London: HarperCollins.

Bhagwati, J. and A. Panagariya. 2013b. *Why Growth Matters.* New York: Public Affairs.

Brass, T. 2000. *Peasants, Populism, Postmodernism.* London: Frank Cass.

Brass, T. 2014. *Class, Culture and the Agrarian Myth.* Leiden: Brill.

Brass, T. 2017. *Labour Markets, Identities, Controversies.* Leiden: Brill.

Brass, T. 2019. *Revolution and Its Alternatives.* Leiden: Brill.

Brass, T. 2021, Marxism Missing, Missing Marxism. Leiden: Brill.

Camus, R. 2018. *You Will Not Replace Us!* Plieux: Chez l'auteur.

Collins, H. and C. Abramsky. 1965. *Karl Marx and the British Labour Movement.* London: Macmillan & Co. Ltd.

Davis, M. 2006. *Planet of Slums.* London: Verso.

Dobb, M. 1955. *On Economic Theory and Socialism.* London: Routledge & Kegan Paul.

Easton Ellis, Bret. 2019. *White.* London: Picador.

Esman, A. 2010. *Radical State.* Santa Barbara, CA: Praeger.

Frank, T. 1920. *An Economic History of Rome.* Baltimore, MA: The Johns Hopkins Press.

Gillett, A. 2017. The fall of Rome and the retreat of European multiculturalism: A historical trope as a discourse of authority in public debate. *Cogent: Arts & Humanities,* 4:1, DOI:10.1080/23311983.2017.1390915.

Glyn, A. 2006. *Capitalism Unleashed.* Oxford: Oxford University Press.

Houellebecq, M. 2015. *Submission.* London: William Heinemann.

Houellebecq, M. 2019. *Serotonin.* London: William Heinemann.

Jones, A.H.M. 1966. *The Decline of the Ancient World.* London: Longmans Green & Co. Ltd.

Kaufmann, E., 2018, *Whiteshift: Populism, Immigration and the Future of White Majorities,* London: Allen Lane, Penguin Random House.

Lendon, J.E. 2009. Historians without history: Against Roman historiography. In Andrew Feldherr (ed.), *Cambridge Companion to Roman Historians,* Cambridge: Cambridge University Press, pp. 41–61.

Lenin, V.I. 1963. A Characterization of Economic Romanticism [1897]. *Collected Works,* 2: 129–265. Moscow: Foreign Languages Publishing House.

Lenin, V.I. 1964. Critical Remarks on the National Question [1913]. *Collected Works*, 20: 17–51. Moscow: Progress Publishers.

Lochore, R.A. 1951. *From Europe to New Zealand*. Wellington, NZ: A.H. & A.W. Reed.

Luxemburg, R. 2013. *Complete Works – Volume I* (Economic Writings 1), London: Verso.

Marx, K. 1968. *Theories of Surplus Value: Part I*. London: Lawrence & Wishart.

Marx, K. 1969. *Theories of Surplus Value: Part II*. London: Lawrence & Wishart.

Marx, K. 1972. *Theories of Surplus Value: Part III*. London: Lawrence & Wishart.

Marx, K. 1976. *Capital – Volume I*. Harmondsworth: Penguin Books.

Marx, K. and F. Engels. 1934. *Correspondence 1846–1895*. London: Martin Lawrence Ltd.

Mehta, S. 2019. *This Land is Our Land: An Immigrant's Manifesto*. London: Jonathan Cape.

Mouffe, C. 2018. *For a Left Populism*. London: Verso.

Murray, D. 2018. *The Strange Death of Europe: Immigration, Identity, Islam*. London: Bloomsbury.

Murray, D. 2019. *The Madness of Crowds: Gender, Race and Identity*. London: Bloomsbury.

Portes, J. 2016. *Capitalism: 50 Ideas You Really Need to Know*. London: Quercus Books.

Smith, S. 2019. *The Scramble for Europe: Young Africa on Its Way to the Old Continent*. Cambridge: Polity.

Trotsky, L. 1940. *The Living Thoughts of Karl Marx, Based on Capital: A Critique of Political Economy*. London: Cassell and Company, Ltd.

Vargas Llosa, M. 2015. *Notes on the Death of Culture*. London: Faber and Faber.

PART 2

Marx and a Changing Society

∴

CHAPTER 8

Emancipatory Thought in Latin America

The Enduring Legacy of Carlos Marx

Ricardo A. Dello Buono and José Bell Lara

When Karl Marx was developing his early thought, Latin American republics were busily engaged in nation building. Much of South and Central America had won their independence from European colonialism in the immediately preceding three decades, leaving the young republics rife with intra-elite struggles and political instability as the general rule. As many observers have pointed out, Marx devoted relatively little attention to the post-independence struggles of Latin America during period of neo-colonial oligarchic consolidation.

One notable exception was in an essay commissioned by a US encyclopedia in 1857 where Marx offered a generally unflattering review of Bolívar, disputing the label of liberator and likening him to an authoritarian Bonapartist. In a letter to Engels written the following year, Marx reflected on the essay, reiterating his dislike of Bolívar while indicating that the publisher had complained about the partisan optic exhibited in the encyclopedia entry (Marx 1857). Marx's dismissive treatment and journalistic accounts of Bolivar's thwarted vision for the Americas has been treated critically by various scholars (e.g., Draper 1968; Aricó 2015). Some critics have presented this as evidence supporting a larger pattern of Marx's "eurocentrism" (e.g., Munck 1984). Others assert that Marx simply did not focus his attention in a serious way on the region as he did on other colonial dramas such as the Irish Question. Engel's himself subsequently indicated in a letter to a colleague that Marx's brief encyclopedia piece on Bolivar's military campaigns should be dismissed as work was done for hire (Engels 1938). However this lacuna is interpreted, it is quite clear that the social conditions of Latin America did not neatly resemble the realities and class struggles of Europe in which Marx was more deeply immersed. The application of Marx's critical insights to the Bolivarian era would largely fall to other Marxian thinkers and would later enjoy a resurgence with the outbreak of the revolutionary Bolivarian movement in Venezuela under the Fifth Republic led by Hugo Chavez.

Even if Marx was not a fan of the rise and fall of Bolivar's eccentric leadership and his home grown brand of Latin American nationalism, the former did not hesitate to denounce the dynamics of slavery where actively employed in the Americas nor the long reach of European imperialism. In 1861, Marx expressed his revulsion over European imperialist designs on Mexico, viewing it as "one of the most monstrous enterprises ever chronicled in the annals of international history" (Marx 1861). The anti-imperialist elements of Marx's thought assured that his theoretical influence would eventually inspire movements and intellectual development in Latin America just as it did throughout the world. Indeed, it is difficult to over-estimate the influence that Marx eventually wielded in Latin America.

The two regional points of Marx's initial influence in the region were centered in Mexico and Argentina. As the Paris Commune of 1871 shook Europe, it certainly did not go unnoticed in Latin America. Some of the survivors of its collapse became exiled to Buenos Aires, yielding the formation of a chapter of the International Workingmen's Association and carrying with them Marx's influence that contrasted with the anarchist inclinations more typical of European immigrants of that era (Tarcus 2007). By the latter 1870s, excerpts of Marx's writings were being published by workers' periodicals in Mexico, including *El Socialista* that several years later published an edition of *The Communist Manifesto* with ten thousand copies placed into circulation (Carr 1983: 280). Even as familiarity with the views of Marx grew, his ideas generally remained in the minority among the radical circles across the region that were more attracted to the anarchist, nationalistic and social democratic currents of the period. This largely remained true up until the Russian Bolshevik Revolution of 1917 and the subsequent formation in 1919 of the COMINTERM.

The rapid growth of Soviet influence and formation of Communist Parties worldwide was the prime mechanism for disseminating the views of Marx by the 1920's. Just as Lenin's influence was projecting the practical application of Soviet vanguard Marxism in the post-WWI era, the twists and turns of early 20th century events would also inspire creative Marxist theorists such as Lukács and Gramsci in Europe. In this same period, Latin America like other regions in the global periphery would produce its own share of creative thinkers who were interpreting the legacy of Marx. In Peru, one of the most original Marxist thinkers of the period could be found in the work of José Carlos Mariátegui.

1   The Birth of Latin American Marxism

Mariátegui grappled with some of the particular dynamics of the Andean sub-region that would inform his creative interpretation of Marxian concepts. While he first encountered Marxist thought during the several years (1919–1923) he spent in Italy, he identified with the rejection of dogmatic interpretations of Marx, and this has led many to consider him the "Latin American Gramsci" (Gonzales 2019: 7–8). When Mariátegui returned to Peru, his zeal was dedicated to uniting the disparate currents of revolutionary fervor in the complex and highly fragmented political setting of his Andean homeland. He sought to form a "united front" of the left that could contest the legacy of colonialism and the deepening contradictions of a highly dependent form of neocolonial, dependent capitalism (Becker 2020). Importantly, Mariátegui founded the journal *Amauta* to provide a forum of debate across the left and like in so many other national settings, this journal propitiated the development of domestic currents of Marxist thought.

While some of Mariátegui's work resembles Gramsci's linking of politics and culture, his work contemplated the huge cultural divide between indigenous and creole Peru. Some of his most famous work dealt with reconciling "The Indian Question" and indigenous demands for land with the broader worker's struggle for a higher standard of living and popular self-determination, seeing them as a complex array of national currents that could unite under the banner of eradicating class exploitation. Eerily similar to Gramsci, Mariátegui suffered from physical ailments as a child, including an amputated leg in his case that confined him to a wheelchair and led to complications that culminated in an early death just prior to his thirty-sixth birthday.

Mariátegui's comprehension of the heterogeneous social conditions of Peru under an emerging dependent capitalism being fueled by mineral and raw material exports and stunted under the domination of a landed oligarchy was exceptional. This led him to advance the cause of mass militancy or a popular "multitude" galvanized by a collective mystique of revolutionary fervor towards a new order in which land and dignity in work could be symbolized by "bread and beauty" enjoyed by all (De Castro 2020). He spoke of making revolution through creative forms of mobilization in which "myths" were not employed to romanticize but rather to serve as culturally sensitive tools of anti-capitalist praxis capable of consolidating a multi-sectoral united front against the established order. This further implied that revolutionary myths as a catalyst for fervor must necessarily vary from one historical and cultural setting to another (Gárate Sánchez 2018). Mariátegui's final work, *Defense of Marxism* published after his death stressed the power of the Marxist approach, as earlier illustrated by Lenin, but in this case precisely by rejecting the COMINTERM formula for national revolution and instead focusing on an analysis of the historically constituted social relations of Peruvian reality and on discovering the most adequate strategy for revolution in Peru.

This meant confronting a national bourgeoisie that was weak in global terms, unable to assert national needs in the face of growing dependency. It would be the task of a working class that was small and unevenly organized, with a massive cultural distance that separated it from an impoverished indigenous peasant majority dominated by a quasi-feudal landowning class, all alongside of a fragmented and differentiated set of creole intermediate classes struggling for material and cultural advancement. For Mariátegui, the dialectical method of Marx demanded a structural grasp of the whole, with adequate weight to multiple subjectivities that were formed out of the objective conditions of neocolonial capitalism and imperialist extractivism. At the same time, his work stressed the ultimate goal of another possible world that could surpass the insufficiencies and shortcomings encountered by the Stalinist Soviet era.

In sum, Mariátegui was a pivotal figure in spreading the influence of Marx. He developed a distinctly Latin American school of Marxist thought that would influence revolutionary upsurges of later decades in the region. In his words, socialism in Latin America was to be "neither a copy nor a tracing, but a heroic creation" (Allen 2018). His application of Marxist ideas to the women's struggle anticipated a trend of socialist feminism, just as his writing on the "Indian Question" would influence later critical theorists of race and ethnicity in the region, suggesting an early school of Marxist intersectionality that shaped later political movements well beyond Peru itself.

2   Marx and Latin American Anti-imperialism

Marx fell short of a comprehensive, structural analysis of the colonial problem (Bell Lara 1970). His ambitious and unfinished analysis in *Capital* focused like a laser on the structural dynamic of capitalist social relations and its tendencies towards concentration and centralization that wrought an immiserating exploitation upon the laboring classes. He was certainly well acquainted with the imperial designs that sought the gold and silver of the Americas, with its campaigns of banditry, conquest, extermination, and enslavement, and he was acutely aware of how this fueled capitalist expansion. In short, Marx was clear on how the colonial powers converted their exploits into capital that catalyzed the consolidation of capitalism in Europe.

Marx therefore had no crude illusion that some kind of mechanical evolution of primitive production to slavery to feudalism to capitalism was going to be repeated in the Americas. Rather, the rising American republics were destined to be incorporated into the core development of capital. At the same time, Marx saw in Ireland, the contradictory role which anticolonial struggle could assume in the development of capitalism, where strength in the former could serve to weaken the latter. Equally clear was how the colonial consolidation over Ireland obstructed the emerald isle's own possibilities for expansive capitalist development.

It is of course now clear that the anti-imperialist struggle produced its own distinguished history in the Americas following the death of Marx. In this regard, "late colonialism" in Cuba spawned a variety of radical movements that would emerge out of its struggle for independence from Spain. When Marx died in 1883, Cuban independence leader José Martí spoke at the legendary memorial meeting at New York's Cooper Union, referring to Marx as "a man driven by a burning desire to do good" who "saw in everyone what he carried in himself: rebellion, highest ideals, struggle" (Friends of Jose Martí 1982). This was just eight years before Martí would pen his essay *Our America* written in the tradition of Bolivar and other patriots of Latin American independence, clamoring for Latin American self-determination while denouncing the last foothold of the Spanish in the Caribbean and the rising expansionist aims of the United States. Just four years later, he gave his life in combat fighting the Spanish on Cuban soil.

A much less well-known Cuban was Marx's own son-in-law, Paul Lafargue, who was born in Santiago de Cuba to a French father that owned a Cuban coffee plantation. Lafargue at a young age migrated to France where he eventually became radicalized, joining the French Section of the First International in London where he met and became close to Marx and his circle of allies. He later married Laura Marx, Marx's second daughter and helped to popularized Marx's work in France, translating a significant portion of *Capital* into French. It was to Lafargue that Marx wrote his famous assessment about French Marxism of the time, calling it a "peculiar formation," leading him to consequently exclaim that "If anything is certain, it is that I am not a Marxist" (See Lafargue 1890).

The foundation of the Cuban Republic in mid-1902 led various anarchist and socialist activists to begin to visualize the contours of a liberation from a rising, neo-colonial elite. With the US Platt Amendment keeping a tight grip over a nominally independent Republic turned US "protectorate," radical opposition circles, particularly in the University, emerged by the 1920's including Cuba's own Communist Party with its legendary militants such as Julio Antonio Mella (1903–29). Despite his short life, Mella stood out for his intense activism and acute comprehension of the Cuban reality.

Mella founded the Cuban University Student Federation (FEU) and sought to link the student movement to workers struggles. To that end, he also helped create the Jose Martí Popular University that was dedicated to education of Cuban workers. Mella was a prolific writer who stressed the importance of Marti's anti-imperialist thought and linked it to the challenges facing popular struggles. Having participated in the activities of the Mexican Communist Party, Mella was one of the founders of the first Cuban Communist Party as well as the Anti-imperialist League of the Americas. While forced into exile into Mexico during the Machado Dictatorship in Cuba, he continued his revolutionary activities there and was assassinated in Mexico City at the age of 26 while walking with his Italian companion, the revolutionary photographer Tina Modotti.

The original Cuban Communist Party of Mella renamed itself the Popular Socialist Party and participated in electoral campaigns at different points and won some posts up until 1952 when the Batista Dictatorship outlawed it. Communist parties that were established throughout Latin America were fundamentally tied to the Third Communist International. These parties played an important role in promoting the classic works of Marx, Engels and Lenin, often through their own publishing houses. For a variety of geopolitical reasons, these parties did not always rush to embrace every revolutionary upsurge as in the case of Cuba.

It was in 1953 that Fidel Castro Ruz, a former law student who became radicalized in the struggle against Batista, attempted to lead an uprising by attacking the Moncada provincial army garrison in Santiago de Cuba. While unsuccessful in capturing the garrison and achieving its other immediate objectives, the operation sparked a rebellious spirit across the island and marked the beginning of a people's armed struggle against Batista's tyranny. Fidel Castro was tried, convicted and imprisoned along with his brother Raul and other survivors of the rebel assault. When Fidel and Raul Castro were released in 1955 under a general amnesty, he went into exile to Mexico where he regrouped forces with the slogan "in 1956, we will be free or martyrs."

Fidel and Raul launched the famous Granma expedition that very year along with others, including the Argentine revolutionary Ernesto Che Guevara who had arrived to Mexico from Guatemala following a US sponsored military coup. Che who had already studied Marx was embittered at the US intervention in Guatemala which led to the overthrow of the progressive Arbenz government. He was now convinced that armed struggle was the sole path to socialism. After the expedition to Cuba landed and were confronted by Battista's forces, Che, Fidel, and Raul along with other survivors took to the Sierra Maestra mountains and successfully mobilized the Cuban peasantry into a rebel army, the July 26th Movement, that engaged and would ultimately defeat the Batista Regime on New Year's Day 1959. The pro-Soviet Popular Socialist Party only supported the July 26th Movement in the final period of insurrection as Moscow generally had viewed it as "adventurism" in a country where conditions were not yet ripe for a socialist revolution.

The revolutionary triumph in Cuba was a sea change in Latin America. On 2 December 1961, an already enormously popular Fidel Castro declared to the world in a studio broadcast that he was a Marxist-Leninist (Castro 1961). On that occasion, he announced that the July 26th Movement would fuse with the Popular Socialist Party and the Revolutionary Directorate, and that the three would together form a unified Marxist-Leninist Vanguard Party that emerged as the Cuban Communist Party (PCC). Marxism in Cuba would become a dynamic force in promoting a far-reaching reorganization of Cuban society with socialist principles. Fidel Castro proved to be a master tactician who would guide Cuba through unprecedented perils as the Cuban revolutionary project was consolidated and deepened.

The influence of Che Guevara helped to promote the role of mass organizations during the early period of Cuban socialism. Che's Marxism promoted the formation of a Communist "new man" that worked to create revolutionary ethics of selfless service to the masses. He favored the development of moral incentives to encourage the formation of socialist social relations. At the same time, Che was unhappy that unrelenting US hostility after the unsuccessful, counterrevolutionary mercenary invasion at the Bay of Pigs followed by the Cuban missile crisis was bringing Cuba ever closer to Moscow and an over-assimilation of the Soviet Model as a survival strategy.

Che made no attempt to conceal that he was something less than sympathetic to the Soviet model. His revolutionary thought did not hesitate to speak out against the menace of bureaucratism, of ossified ideologies and elements that he saw as inconsistent with radical transformation. Che, the Marxist, felt comfortable in critiquing Marx himself:

"We Latin Americans don't have to be in agreement with his [Marx's] interpretation of Bolívar, or his and Engel's analysis of the Mexicans as seated in certain theory about race or nationality that today are no longer acceptable. But these great figures, discoverers of luminous truths, live on in spite of these small shortcomings and in fact, just serve to show that they were human, that they could err even as we remain clearly aware of the tremendous heights achieved by these gigantic thinkers".
GUEVARA 1968

After Che's departure from Cuba in 1965 to embark on an internationalist mission to support revolutions throughout Africa and Latin America, he was captured and executed in Bolivia in 1967.

The intersecting revolutionary thought of Fidel Castro and Che Guevara flourished in Cuba and reverberated throughout Latin America. An effervescent air of radical thought would spawn numerous periodicals with a Marxist orientation. In Cuba itself, one exemplary publication was the journal *Pensamiento Crítico* (Critical Thought).[1] A group of Cuban intellectuals began a project in 1966 to discuss and explore the revolutionary potential of Marxist thought for socialist construction in accordance to Cuba's condition as a rebellious Latin American nation. The journal's editors included Cuban thinkers such as Fernando Martínez Heredia, Jose Bell Lara and Aurelio Alonso Tejada who together broke boundaries with creative, critical reflection and became widely read throughout Latin America, in Universities across Mexico, Peru, Venezuela, Argentina, Chile and including by revolutionary leaders such as the Sandinistas of Nicaragua and other Central American revolutionaries operating in their countries clandestinely (Amador de Jesús 2002).

The journal was eventually shut down in 1971, seen as "deviating" from the Party line of the time where Cuba entered a period of cultural and ideological over-assimilation into the Soviet bloc that lasted several years. This notwithstanding, five of its six contributing editors remained revolutionaries and continued to work in Cuba (Solar Cabrales 2017).[2] By the mid-1980s, Cuba recognized the missteps and moved towards a period of "Rectification" in which the Party attempted to undo the over-assimilation of the Soviet social framework and reach back to the authentic revolutionary values of the 1960s.

If Soviet influence was far reaching through its allied Communist Parties and affiliated trade unions and intellectual circles worldwide, the political influence of the Cuban revolution soon reached similar proportions across Latin America, with some considerable but not complete overlap. For example, most Trotskyist parties and their affiliated movements and thinkers likewise remained enthusiastic supporters of Cuban revolutionary thought, regardless of their break with the USSR which it viewed as Stalinist. Armed guerrillas in Colombia embraced the Cuban example and in Peru, the non-Maoist currents of the revolutionary left strongly identified with Cuban socialism. In general terms, the Cuban revolution inspired radicalization throughout the hemisphere and beyond, building on the frustrated sectors of reformism that even when successful were habitually met with sabotage by a systematic US interventionism locked into its paranoid Cold War doctrine.

In this period, even the Catholic Church which at the time remained largely unchallenged as the dominant spiritual force in the region felt the shock waves of radicalization as Liberation Theology arose, first in Brazil and Peru,

---

1   http://www.filosofia.org/rev/pch/portadas.htm
2   Jesús Días abandoned Cuba and relocated to Spain.

and soon began to spread like wildfire through Central America. Beginning with The Second Vatican Council of the mid-1960s, reforms in traditionalist Catholic doctrine opened the ideological doors for priests serving in oppressed communities. In Colombia, Fr. Camilo Torres Restrepo was actively working on reconciling revolutionary Marxism and Catholic theology. In 1960, Torres teamed up with Orlando Fals Borda to form the Department of Sociology at the National University of Colombia. Fals whose familiarity with Marxian theory led him to develop the influential and activist sociological approach known as Participatory Action Research (IAP in Spanish). Fals stressed the need for commitment to social justice and to building understanding through praxis in research, rejection of elite or hegemonic narratives and receptivity to counter-narratives by oppressed communities actively engaged in resistance.

Fals and Torres mutually influenced each other and actively linking up student radicalization to the broader social struggles of Colombia (Robles Lomeli and Rappaport 2018). In 1965, Torres formed the "United Front of the People," openly appealing to Christians to make common cause with Communists, and for students to link up with workers and the growing number of peasants fleeing violence and arriving to the city. Facing persecution from the government as a subversive and growing pressure from the church hierarchy, he reached out to the ELN guerrilla group (National Liberation Army of Colombia) and in an open letter declared that he would now embrace armed struggle. Torres was killed in combat in 1966 while Fals who rejected armed struggle was nevertheless detained in 1979 for a short time along with his wife, both accused of subversion.

The Latin American encounter of Marx and Christianity quickly mushroomed. The Peruvian Catholic theologian Gustavo Gutiérrez published his *A Theology of Liberation* in 1971 that would galvanize an entire generation of Catholic social activists (Gutierrez 1988). At the same time, it intensified opposition from more conservative quarters in Rome over the growing Marxist overtones of the movement. The assimilation of Marxist ideas into Christian visions of social justice opened new terrains of potential influence and political mobilization. This dovetailed with the critical pedagogy being developed by Paulo Freire, the Brazilian educator who was forced into the exile by the military dictatorship installed in his country after the 1964 military coup. After detention by the military, Freire embarked on an international career that brought him to Chile where he worked with poor rural communities in a radicalizing environment marked by the growing protest and demands for agrarian reform. In 1968, he published his *Pedagogy of the Oppressed* that articulated his Christian socialist approach in what became an entire school of critical pedagogical thought destined to gain worldwide attention.

Even while armed struggle for socialism gained currency throughout the 1960s, the fall of Camilo Torres and Che Guevara led many leftist parties to doubt the prospects for successfully repeating a Cuban-style armed insurrection. Mass mobilizations in this period also pointed to the possibility of an electoral path to radical change, particularly in nations where democratic institutionality was strong, such as in Colombia, Venezuela and Chile. The litmus test for this ultimately arose in Chile.

3   The Chilean Road to Socialism

The Socialist Workers Party of Chile was formed in 1912 with Marxist inspiration in the Chilean labor movement. With the Soviet triumph of 1917, the Chilean socialists formed bonds of solidarity and cooperation with Russia that led to their decision to adhere to the principles of the Third International in 1922 and renaming of the party as the Communist Party of Chile. The party became a formal member of the Third International in 1928 (Barnard 2017). Like many of the other communist parties of the region, the Chilean Communist Party published and distributed the ideas of Marx and Lenin. It likewise shared a history of severe political repression during some periods and modest electoral success in others, often forced to participate under an alternative name.

The electoral victory of the Popular Unity government in Chile led by Salvador Allende brought the party into national power as part of a coalition government. Allende's Socialist Party in electoral alliance with the Chilean Communist Party and disaffected elements of more moderate political parties gradually accumulated force, overcame their differences and won the presidency in 1970. Allende admired the Cuban Revolution but saw a peaceful road to socialism for Chile. For his part, Fidel Castro enthusiastically endorsed Allende's concept of multiple paths to building socialism, including by electoral means, and was received in a tumultuous visit to Chile following Allende's victory that buoyed an ascendant Left in the Americas. The Chilean Revolution opened the decade of the 1970s with an effervescent atmosphere of hope for a new day.

As a whole generation of radicals now entered into the Chilean popular government, the ensuing cultural revolution vastly expanded access to Marxist works. Prior to the Popular Unity Government, the ZigZag Publishing House in Chile was one of the largest publishers in Latin America. Its radicalized workers launched a strike against the owners, demanding its nationalization by the Popular Unity government, which was implemented in 1971, leading to the creation of the Quimantú National Publishing House (Memoria Chilena 2018).

Quimantú sponsored a host of progressive journals and a broad array of books that included many classic Marxist texts, sold in popular, inexpensive formats in Chile and around the region.

At the same time, an independent newspaper *Punto Final* which had been formed in the year leading up to the Allende victory offered a new medium of communication for Chileans to read Marxian analyses of day-to-day events. Contributors included Chilean Communist Party members, adherents of the previously underground armed group the Revolutionary Left Movement (MIR) and Socialist Party members whose differing views on building socialism could be openly aired in public. At the same time, *Punto Final* featured advances and developments of the left throughout the hemisphere, with the Cuban Revolution featuring prominently. The short-lived socialist experiment in Chile offered a space for applying Marxist ideas to the complex class struggle that both produced and soon threatened the stability of the revolutionary government. Ultimately, the Allende government was brought down in the violent, US sponsored military coup of September 11, 1973 that unleashed a wave of repression. The newspaper *Punto Final* was literally burned down under direct orders from Augusto Pinochet's military junta, while virtually all of the newspaper's editorial team was either murdered, detained, or exiled along with an entire generation of accumulated aspirations. The state publishing house Quimantú was disbanded by the military government, its books publicly burned and its machinery used to start up a pro-Dictatorship Publisher that ultimately failed ten years, forcing a liquidation of its assets. Chile under military rule would become a new laboratory at gunpoint for US economists to test out extreme forms of privatization and structural adjustment in what would later become recognizable in its final form as neoliberalism.

The diaspora of Chilean Marxists became legendary in the region. The overarching set of lessons seemed clear. The peaceful road to socialism was now being thought of as an illusory objective under US imperialism and the surviving Chilean revolutionaries carried the message to the rest of the hemisphere, namely, that the military apparatus must be completely transformed for any radical reorganization of society. This lesson was not lost in Central America where the stage was set for a new wave of leftist insurgencies. Armed revolts were breaking out in Guatemala, El Salvador and Nicaragua as landed oligarchies unleashed systematic repression against peasantries mobilizing for their survival. The Sandinista Front for National Liberation (FSLN) managed to bring down the longstanding dictatorship of the Somoza dynasty in 1979, creating another wave of hope for Latin America. The FSLN was composed of three underground Marxist organizations, each of which had their own revolutionary strategy based on a distinct, strategic understanding of the Nicaraguan class struggle.

The revolutionary triumph of the FSLN's armed struggle that continued until the destruction of the dictatorship's national guard was complete. This removed any threat of domestic military destabilization such as that which brought down Allende in Chile and Arbenz in Guatemala, both of which were Cold War interventions orchestrated by Washington. Unlike in Cuba, however, the USSR made it clear at the outset that it would not come to the military defense of Nicaragua nor could it count on abundant economic assistance. This led the FSLN to abandon the option of a rapid socialist transformation in favor of a revolutionary mixed economy that would seek to keep its private sector intact but constrained under popular hegemony, along with political pluralism and international non-alignment as its declared principles. The unique circumstances of the Nicaraguan revolution transformed it into another emblematic experiment where Marxists throughout the region evaluated its potential and possibilities.

Working in favor of Nicaragua's revolutionary transformation was an independent thinktank CRIES (Regional Coordinator of Economic and Social Investigations) directed by Xabier Gorostiaga, S.J., an activist Jesuit priest from the Spanish Basque Country, thus preserving a direct channel of influence for liberation theology in the Nicaraguan Revolution that it earned in the preceding years of struggle. Gorostiaga first visited Latin America in 1958 where he lived during the final six months of the Batista Dictatorship and the first year of the Cuban revolution. As he moved on to experience other Latin American countries, he was deeply impressed by the Cuban people's revolutionary struggle and deplored the reactionary position taken by the church in the face of social needs that demanded deep, structural changes (Gorostiaga 2003). The Jesuit Central American University likewise actively allied with the government while four Jesuit Priests held high positions in the revolutionary state. CRIES was dedicated not only to supporting the revolutionary changes taking place in Nicaragua but brought analysts from Chile, Cuba, and elsewhere to promote progressive structural changes and popular forms of integration across the region.

Another European Christian activist that made Latin America his home was Franz Josef Hinkelammert, a German theologian and radical economist who founded the Ecumenical Department of Research in Costa Rica. Hinkelammert employed dialectical critique to Latin American development theory, powered by a Christian-humanist system of ethics and commitment to social justice. His commitment to a socialist path made him a great friend of Cuba and his critique of the "global tyranny of capital" had been influential worldwide.

At the same time, the growing Central American solidarity movement in the US helped strengthen a rebirth of US leftist currents. Even before the 1979 revolutionary triumph, Nicaragua enjoyed strong solidarity from activists around the world, including the United States, and the solidarity movement soon grew to include the rest of Central America, particularly Guatemala and El Salvador where insurgencies were now being met by strong counterinsurgency efforts directed from Washington. As the US-sponsored counterrevolution in Nicaragua gained force during the 1980s, the circumstances aroused strong support from the Latin American left which in some cases resulted in moderate Latin American governments challenging US interventionism. While some Marxist elements were critical of the Nicaraguan revolution for abandoning an explicitly socialist strategy of transformation, the spirit of anti-interventionism coupled with strong Cuban support helped galvanize a rebirth of anti-imperialist currents earlier seen during the Viet Nam era, favoring new engagements with Marxist ideas.

The concerted effort of the Reagan Administration to covertly fund counterrevolutionary forces in Nicaragua, even if in violation of its own laws, to dramatically increase military aid to El Salvador, and to utilize Israel as a proxy to funnel military aid to Guatemala long since prohibited by the US Congress amounted to a full-court press against the Central American Revolution. The 1980 electoral defeat of the Democratic Socialist government of Michael Manley in 1980 and the collapse of the Marxist New Jewel Revolutionary Movement in Granada, hastened by a U.S. military invasion of the island in 1983, largely succeeded to quell Marxist influence in the English-speaking Caribbean. The subsequent militarization of Central America created the conditions of a military stalemate in El Salvador while in Guatemala, the Guatemalan National Revolutionary Unity (URNG) proved incapable of sustaining any major military offensives. The extremely costly counterrevolutionary war of an impoverished Nicaragua effectively produced tremendous austerity and succeeded in blocking Sandinista efforts at further revolutionary transformation. When the Sandinistas finally prevailed against the armed counterrevolution and held their second round of elections in 1990 in a war-weary nation, they lost by several percentage points and handed over power to the conservative opposition (Dello Buono and Chamorro 1990). As if this were not traumatic enough for the global left, the political defeat of the FSLN was soon joined by the collapse of the Soviet Union at the following year's end.

The combined effect of the collapse of the Soviet Union, the Sandinista electoral defeat, and the economic crisis of Cuban socialism effectively placed the ideological points of reference of the Latin American Left in total disarray. The prospects of a Central America-wide revolution quickly evaporated, and the remaining guerrilla movements opted for disarmament under peace negotiations, first in El Salvador in 1992 and later in Guatemala in 1996. With only few notable exceptions such as the FARC in Colombia, formerly armed movements found themselves attempting under adverse conditions to form their own political parties and return to the fold of electoral politics.

Cuba, the only consolidated socialist country in the hemisphere, had now abruptly lost all of its former major trading and cooperation partners, with Washington seizing the opportunity to tighten its economic blockade of the island. Cuban socialism entered into the greatest economic crisis of its history, with the severity of the crisis having a braking effect on its process of social transformation, forcing it to adopt emergency economic measures designed to ensure its survival. New debates on the island focused on establishing alternative means of viability, including a return to the once thriving tourist industry that had been largely abandoned by the revolution.

The post-Soviet era in the region coincided with the rise of neoliberalism peddled by the so-called "Washington Consensus," touting the benefits of unbridled economic deregulation and the transnationalization of regional economic flows. This neo-liberalization of dependent capitalism imposed complex changes in the regional structures of national decision-making. The privatization and financial transnationalization of primary commodity production intensified the de-nationalization of economic rents so strategic to the prior era of state-directed development. High unemployment and intense pressure to make existing labor regimes more flexible dealt severe blows to the region's trade unions. The crippling of the social spending base of national states, coupled with surging rates of poverty and social exclusion, conspired to produce a crisis of legitimacy shared by various political party regimes in power across the region. The pressure was most acute upon political parties whose electoral strength was based in the representation and defense of the interests of those sectors being most adversely affected by neoliberal policies.

Western intellectuals wasted no time in imagining the advent of a "final" and historic triumph of liberal capitalism best symbolized by Francis Fukuyama's 1992 essay on the "End of History." But not all went completely to script. The initial stirrings neoliberal crisis could be seen in the *Caracazo* in 1989 when the neoliberal policies of Carlos Andrés Pérez sparked an urban uprising in Caracas. The violent suppression of the rebellion led to hundreds of fatalities at the hands of the Venezuelan armed forces, many discovered later in mass graves. The *Caracazo* marked history in another sense since it inspired a dissident movement of cadres within the Venezuelan Armed Forces known as the Revolutionary Bolivarian Movement-200 (MBR-200). The MBR-200 denounced the use of military force to suppress the *Caracazo* and their subsequent organizing culminated in 1992 with an attempted coup which quickly unraveled, led by Hugo Chávez who was forced to surrender to authorities.

In Mexico, meanwhile, a dramatic event took place on New Year's Day in 1994, the day that the North American Free Trade Agreement (NAFTA) was slated to take effect. From a clandestine base in Chiapas, the Zapatista Front for National Liberation (EZLN) declared a people's war on the neoliberal government of Carlos Salinas de Gortari. The Zapatistas captured the imagination of social movements worldwide in a context where it was thought that armed struggle had permanently evaporated. The insurrection actually marked the beginning of a resurgence of continental-wide movements in opposition to neoliberal free trade agreements (FTAs) sponsored by Washington.

As an organization rooted in the poorest and southernmost state of the country, the EZLN called attention to the increasing social exclusion and growing poverty that accompanied the neoliberal transformation of Mexico. With its fiery, anti-imperialist discourse and timely appearance with the launching of NAFTA, the Zapatistas shook the Mexican authorities as soon as it grasped the extent to which it was organized among the largely indigenous population of Chiapas. This movement grabbed the attention of Marxists throughout the region. Particularly evident in the speeches by "sub-commandant Marcos" was that the Zapatista movement was anti-verticalist from its inception. The EZLN stressed the importance of community base organization in contrast to a traditional focus on the capture of state power. For that reason, it indefinitely suspended armed struggle as a strategy shortly after the initial insurrection upon reaching an accord with the Mexican government to recognize the autonomy of indigenous communities. What has especially distinguished the Zapatista revolutionary vision from the outset was its unified, anti-capitalist analysis of ecological and socio-economic issues along with its effective utilization of alternative media.

The lesson was not lost on transnational global justice activists to Mexico's North who likewise began to develop new slogans and distinctive forms of protest, harnessing new communications technologies to construct increasingly more complex networks and alternative media access. The 1999 protests against the World Trade Organization (WTO) in Seattle marked an early consolidation of popular resistance, cultivating a growing "alter-globalization" movement.

4   **Latin America Revisits Bolivar**

If the violent events of 1989 in Venezuela amounted to a wakeup call for the neoliberal model, the failed 1992 military coup of Commander Hugo Chávez was only a temporary setback. After Chávez was released two years later in the face of strong public sympathy, the Fifth Republican Movement (MVR) he led staged a remarkable political comeback with his electoral victory of 1989. Once elected, he launched the Bolivarian Revolution with the successful establishment of a Constitutional Assembly that was approved by popular referendum and was followed by the 1999 Constitution that proclaimed the Bolivarian Republic of Venezuela. Initially, the Chávez government was not explicitly anti-capitalist but socially oriented towards combating poverty and social exclusion via the construction of a more inclusive democracy and the recovery and expansion of the state's capacity to strategically intervene in the economy (Figueroa, 2007: 207–8). This challenged the neoliberal model and sought to reorient Venezuela's development model to better serve popular interests.

During the time Chávez was imprisoned following the 1992 attempted Coup, he reported having time to read some Marxist works. One such work that he made specific mention of was *Beyond Capital* by the Hungarian Marxist István Mészáros (Sader 2013). Chávez referred to Mészáros as the "Pathfinder" in charting the transition to socialism at a 2001 award ceremony in Caracas (Foster 2014). In 2012 during the final months of his life, then-President Chávez referred back to this book, arguing for a full socialist political transformation in order to render the Bolivarian Revolution irreversible and he urged his ministers to study Mészáros' analysis.

Washington viewed with alarm the steadily warming relations between Caracas and Havana. High oil prices beginning in 2003 brought in unprecedented oil revenues that allowed Venezuela to repay its debts with the International Monetary Fund (IMF) and World Bank. Soon, the Chávez government turned to help other South American countries pay off their debts, allowing them to get released from financial conditionalities. Oil supply at preferential prices was also used to strengthen relations with other countries and to support new, alternative regional integration projects, beginning with Cuba and extending into other Caribbean nations (De la Barra and Dello Buono 2009). U.S. dependence on imported oil made it potentially costly to overtly threaten Venezuela, allowing Chávez to leverage the situation and deepen the revolutionary content of his programs, openly declaring Venezuela's commitment to developing a 21st Century socialist alternative to neoliberal capitalism.

By attempting simultaneously to transform the circumstances and transform the capacities of the popular sectors, the Bolivarian revolution aimed to build its own path to development as an alternative to neoliberal capitalism. Following the re-election of President Chávez in 2006, he considered it an urgent task for 2007 to legally create a local, regional and national confederation of communal councils: "We need to start dismantling the old bourgeois state and move towards the communal state, a socialist state, a Bolivarian state, a revolutionary state." Predictably, opposition forces branded the communal councils as simply a way for Chávez to reward his supporters.

The Bolivarian Revolution of Venezuela ultimately created a different vision for development, for the structuring of the state and a way of developing socialism. Revolutionary strategy was informed by the formation of a Marxist thinktank in Caracas, the Miranda International Center (CIM), whose researchers assisted in implementing transformational policies. One head researcher in the CIM was Marta Harnecker, a renowned writer whose 1969 work *Elementary Concepts of Historical Materialism* circulated far and wide in the region with 70 editions that helped form generations of leftists throughout Latin America. Harnecker did her university study in Chile before doing her graduate study in Paris with Paul Ricoeur and Louis Althusser. She returned to Chile and taught political economy at the university of Chile while editing the publication *Chile Today*.

The military coup against Allende in 1973 forced Harnecker into exile in Cuba where she lived for decades until she relocated to Venezuela to serve as a policy advisor to Hugo Chávez when she joined the Miranda International Center (CIM) in Caracas. Her Canadian partner, noted Marxist Michael Lebowitz, likewise produced important theoretical works about accomplishing a transition to socialism under 21st Century conditions. Like Chile and Cuba before it, Venezuela would need to struggle in the face of a whole panorama of punitive policies instigated by Washington, particularly after the global price of oil began to sharply decline off its earlier peak highs.

5   The Movement towards Socialism in Bolivia

Revolutionary Venezuela soon found an ally in Bolivia following the election of Evo Morales and the Movement to Socialism (MAS) political party. Morales was an indigenous syndicalist active in the Bolivian *Cocaleros* (legal coca leaf producers). Like the Zapatistas, Morales was generally averse to any participation in establishment politics but instead focused on movement building. As successive governments turned to privatization and neoliberal orthodoxy, however, the MAS leadership correctly perceived that the conditions were present for significant electoral victories that could further challenge the Bolivian power structure.

Hence, the formation of the "political instrument," i.e., the formal registration as a political party of a grouping known as the Assembly for the Sovereignty of the Peoples (ASP). Initially failing to gain official recognition, the indigenous ASP organizers joined the United Left (IU), a coalition of leftist parties headed by the Communist Party of Bolivia (PCB). In 1997, Morales formed the Political Instrument for the Sovereignty of the Peoples (IPSP) and in successive elections, he and other IPSP organizers began to achieve legislative representation. In 1999, the group revived a former political party known as the Movement to Socialism (MAS) and became a fully recognized electoral party. The MAS was a new formula for a political party, riding on a social movement as its political instrument. After a series of nationwide protests, the leadership role of this social movement catapulted Morales and the MAS to national prominence, with Morales eventually capturing the national presidency with his 2005 electoral victory.

MAS followed the Venezuelan strategy of first focusing on a rewriting of the Bolivian Constitution. Once it entered into force in 2009, it established the Plurinational State of Bolivia, supporting important structural reforms such as the nationalization of hydrocarbons and other radical changes taken in accordance with popular interests of the historically excluded majority. The MAS government faced deeply entrenched political elites, backed by Washington, that sought to utilize every possible legal and illegal means imaginable to halt the revolutionary process. Much to the dismay of the most militant fractions of his political base, Morales had to walk a tightrope of appeasing sectors of the oligarchy while delivering benefits to the popular sectors in a kind of "Andean capitalism" that would seek to limit transnational exploitation (De la Barra and Dello Buono 2009). Strong increases in the international prices of basic resources, especially hydrocarbons and minerals, resulted in substantial revenues for government coffers thanks to the reforms enacted by the MAS government. This allowed the MAS government to sustain increased social spending and a robust development of new, badly needed public programs.

At the international level, Bolivia's moves to renationalize its energy resources inspired the ire of transnationals which had greatly profited from its privatization. Evo Morales expressed strong support for the creation of new ties of regional integration and benefited from increased cooperation and development assistance from Venezuela and Cuba. At the same time, Morales promoted the indigenous concept of "*Vivir Bien*" (Living Well) in which development takes on a more egalitarian and ecologically sustainable character (Solón 2018). This amounted to an indigenous peoples encounter with Marxism, ultimately making decisive contributions to the reformulation of an emancipatory strategy of ecologically sustainable, bio-cultural development under popular hegemony (Weyer 2017).

One of the most prominent Marxist intellectuals to surface in Bolivia's MAS was Morales' Vice-President, Álvaro García Linera. García Linera did his university studies in Mexico City in the 1980s and was active in the Central American solidarity movement. During that period, he grew particularly interested in the indigenous Mayan role in Guatemala, the only other country in Latin America that like Bolivia had a majority indigenous population. When he returned to Bolivia, he firmly resolved to reconcile Marxian revolutionary concepts with the growing indigenous militancy of the Andes. This led him to join the Tupac Katari Guerrilla Army (EGTK) that espoused class struggle and ethnic self-determination, leading to his capture and imprisonment from 1992–97. After release, he emerged as a highly visible professor of sociology in La Paz at the public university and was a founding member of *Comuna*, a forum for radical thought (Farthing 2010). Garcia Linera was as comfortable with Marx and Lenin as he was with Gramsci and Bourdieu (Musto 2019), and his political alliance with Evo Morales helped transform Bolivia into the plurinational state that it remains today. As he stated in his 2014 speech to the São Paulo Forum, a regional gathering of leftist parties:

> Every revolution in the world, since the days of Marx, has always had one quality: it always comes in waves ... There is the moment of social rise, the moment of the heroic community, the moment of full sacrifice, of retreat and slight social decline, the moment of meeting necessity. Every revolutionary and every revolutionary party must learn how to move in both directions, at both moments, and soon another flow and ebb, and every revolutionary and every revolutionary party must learn to conduct and manage these two collective action logics ... This is a long-term struggle that will last decades, and we must be prepared for moments of confrontation and of management, of ideological and spiritual radiation, and for the moments of meeting necessity ... We, the revolutionary forces, are here not to manage a good form of capitalism, but to ride capitalism toward its transformation and negation, toward a socialist, communitarian society.
>
> GARCIA LINERA 2014

6   Conclusion

The Uruguayan writer Eduardo Galeano once wrote that "in 1492, America Discovered Capitalism." The open veins of a region that would eventually emerge from colonialism only to become plagued by imperialism ultimately provided fertile ground for the assimilation, further development, and deployment of the ideas of Marx. Clearly, the yearning for self-determination and the struggle for unfettered development was present in the region well before the appearance of Marx's writings. Legendary independence fighters such as Miranda and Simón Bolívar lifted up a vision for a Grand Colombia and threw themselves into direct confrontation with Imperial Spain.

As discussed in this chapter, Marx was welcomed to the region, like elsewhere, as a voice for radical change. As the opus of Marx filtered into the Americas, most decisively on the wave of the Bolshevik victory of 1917 in Russia, it later reverberated in various institutions and resonated with many of the region's most iconic figures. In his famous work *Imperialism, the Highest Stage of Capitalism*, Vladimir Lenin endeavored to refute non-Marxian conceptions of imperialism while applying Marx's ideas to the context of World War I. Imperialism, backed by relentless interventionism as experienced throughout Latin America, ultimately vindicated many of Lenin's ideas. Not only was his writing on revolutionary strategy key to the organization of communist parties throughout the region, but his understanding of capital as an expansive world system would ultimately prove to be influential in the paradigmatic development of Marxist Dependency Theory.

Carlos Eduardo Martins (2020) chronicles how the Marxist view of dependency was originated in the 1960–1970s by the work of Theotonio Dos Santos, Ruy Mauro Marini, and others in their orbit. Martins suggests that the embryonic elements of this paradigm were also be found in the writings of Mariátegui as well as the US Marxist Paul Baran (1957), both of whom extended Marx's theory of value (Martins 2020: 222). Sotelo (2020) explains that Marxist dependency theory also grew out of and challenged the mainstream, structuralist version which originated in the Economic Commission for Latin America and the Caribbean (ECLAC) formed in 1948 and popularized in the 1950s by the Argentine economist Raúl Prebisch. As the structuralist paradigm began to fall into paradigmatic crisis in the early 1960s, the political shock waves from the Cuban Revolution impelled a radicalization of the paradigm. The very existence of Cuban socialism contradicted official Soviet development theory and its notion of "revolution by stages." As Marxian categories were creatively deployed, the theory of imperialism was grafted upon the particular regional characteristics of the Latin American reality, forming a more militant

and anti-capitalist branch of dependency theory that focused on systemic critique. It was this current of Marxist thought that gained considerable regional
currency and would come to influence a whole generation of Latin American
activists and leaders.

Latin America's own dramatic events would continue to fuel Marxian
thought and enrich its critical, transformative potential. Che Guevara's
encounter with Marx was punctuated by US imperialism's interruption of
Guatemala's democracy, producing a legacy of internationalism and participation in armed popular struggles that reshaped the Americas. In many ways, it
was revolutionary Cuba that most fully embodied the regional call to transform
capitalism and to construct socialism. It was this experience that positioned
Latin America for additional revolutionary upheavals since that time such as
Chile in the early 1970s, Nicaragua in the 1980s, and of Venezuela, Uruguay,
Bolivia and Ecuador as the region made its entry into the 21st century. In every
instance, these emancipatory projects have had to confront the forces of interventionism, destabilization, and militarism on the part of the United States
(De la Barra and Dello Buono 2009).

Marx set forth the outlines of a post-capitalist future and the most advanced
agents of popular struggle in the region have set their sights on transforming
it into a reality. Yet, revolutionary Latin American thinkers like Che and others
in Cuba and elsewhere have struggled against what amounted to be a transient
stagnation in the Marxism of their era. Global accumulation by capital has
never been a smooth, linear and entirely predictable process. Just as those in
the driver's seat of global capital have responded to periodic crises with erratic
lurches from one strategy to another, the social stability and systemic viability
of countries on the receiving end has been shaken by periodic waves of social
unrest. Social movements have persistently mobilized to confront the failure
of neoliberal capitalism to provide for sustainable improvements in the living standards of the poorest and laboring sectors of Latin American nations.
For that reason, popular resistance continues, even as it unfolds in an uneven
manner and its most recent upsurges have focused on forming broad opposition fronts against neoliberal policies.

In some cases, resistance has dovetailed with successful electoral strategies of anti-neoliberal candidates from non-traditional, leftist political parties.
The potential to respond more decisively with an alternative, popular model
of development capable of carrying the region towards emancipation from its
dependent capitalism remains incipient and incompletely realized to date. New
social actors acting in concert with traditional leftist organizations and indigenous movements have defended national sovereignties while bringing about
some of the most important progressive and far-reaching political changes

achieved so far. The brakes being slammed on privatization in many countries
and demands for greater social spending have exacerbated the contradictions
of the region. The sharpening of class struggle helped place re-nationalization
back on the national agenda of countries that have broken with the neoliberal
model such as in Bolivarian Venezuela and Plurinational Bolivia. These were
ideas present in *The Communist Manifesto* of the mid-19th century and continue
to form part of the development struggles of today.

Socialist movements throughout the region have taken Marx as their inspiration and Marxian concepts as tools for social transformation. Socialist Cuba
marked the first break with capitalist hegemony and the history of Latin
American revolutionary struggles since 1959 continues to be written. As stated
at the outset, it is difficult to over-estimate the impact that Marx has had on
these popular upsurges. We have amply treated how his writings inspired nov-
elists and journalists, researchers and movement activists, priests and educa-
tors, reformers and revolutionaries of the Americas. Emancipation is not possible without a transformative vision. Marx provided that vision and it continues
to resonate far and wide throughout the region. It is certain to say that for Latin
America, Marx matters.

References

Allen, Nicolas. 2018. "Mariátegui's Heroic Socialism: An Interview with Michael Löwy."
    Jacobin   https://www.jacobinmag.com/2018/12/jose-carlos-mariategui-seven-inter
    pretive-essays-peru-marxism-revolutionary-myth.
Amador de Jesus, Jose 2002. "Being Transparent: An Interview with Fernando Martinez-
    Heredia." *Journal of the International Institute*, Vol. 9, Issue 3, Spring/Summer. http://
    hdl.handle.net/2027/spo.4750978.0009.305.
Aricó, José. 2015. *Marx and Latin America*, Translated by David Broder. Chicago:
    Haymarket Books [1982. *Marx y America Latina*. Mexico: Alianza Editorial Mexicana].
Baran, Paul. 1957. *The Political Economy of Underdevelopment*. New York: Monthly
    Review Press.
Barnard, Andrew. 2017. *El Partido Comunista de Chile, 1922–1947*. Ariadna Ediciones,
    Santiago, Chile.
Becker, Marc. 2020. "The Life of José Carlos Mariátegui – Review," *Monthly Review* 71(9)
    February.
Bell Lara, Jose. 1970. "Marx y el Colonialismo." *Pensamiento Crítico*, 37.
Carr, Barry. 1983. "Marxism and Anarchism in the Formation of the Mexican
    Communist Party, 1910–19." *The Hispanic American Historical Review*, Vol. 63, No. 2
    (May): 277–305.

Castro, Fidel. 1961 "Fidel Castro Speaks on Marxism-Leninism," December 2, 1961. http://www.walterlippmann.com/fc-12-02-1961.html.

De Castro, J.E. 2020. *Bread and Beauty: The Cultural Politics of José Carlos Mariátegui.* Leiden, The Netherlands: Brill.

De la Barra, X. and Dello Buono, R.A. 2009. *Latin America after the Neoliberal Debacle: Another Region Is Possible.* Lanham, Maryland: Rowman & Littlefield.

Chamorro Z, A. and Dello Buono, R.A. 1990. The Political Economy of the Sandinista Electoral Defeat. *Critical Sociology,* Vol. 17, No. 2: 93–101.

Draper, Hal. 1968. "Karl Marx and Simon Bolívar: A Note on Authoritarian Leadership in a National-Liberation Movement." *New Politics,* Vol. VII, No.1 Winter: 64–77.

Engels, Friedrich. 1938. "Engels to Schlüter," Marx-Engels Correspondence [1891] in *Science and Society,* Volume II, Number 3.

Farthing, Linda. 2010. "Controlling State Power: An Interview with Vice President Álvaro García Linera." *Latin American Perspectives,* Vol. 37(4): 30–33.

Figueroa, Víctor M. 2007. "Venezuela's Chávez: An alternative for democracy in Latin America?" In *Imperialism, Neoliberalism and Social Struggles in Latin America,* Brill Academic Publishers, pp. 195–219.

Foster, John Bellamy. 2014. "Mészáros and the Critique of the Capital System," *Monthly Review* 66(7). https://monthlyreview.org/2014/12/01/meszaros-and-the-critique-of -the-capital-system/#fn1.

Friends of José Martí 1982 "Opinion" *New York Times,* September 6. https://www.nyti mes.com/1982/09/06/opinion/l-friends-of-jose-marti-127576.html.

Gárate Sánchez, Luis. 2018. *El Mito Persistente: Los comunistas en el Perú del siglo XXI.* Lima: Ruta Pedagógica Editora S.A.C.

García Linera, Álvaro. 2014. "Speech by Vice President of State Álvaro García Linera at the Opening Ceremony of the 20th Meeting of the São Paulo Forum." September 15. https://forodesaopaulo.org/speech-by-vice-president-of-state-alvaro-garcia-linera -at-the-opening-ceremony-of-the-20th-meeting-of-the-sao-paulo-forum/.

Gonzales, Mike. 2019. *In the Red Corner: The Marxism of José Carlos Mariátegui.* Chicago: Haymarket Books.

Gorostiaga, Xabier. 2003. "The Legacy of a Life Intensely Lived." *Envío* 267 (October).

Guevara, Ernesto Che. 1968. "Notas para el estudio de la ideología de la Revolución cubana," *Pensamiento Crítico,* No. 14 (March).

Gutiérrez, Gustavo. 1988. A Theology of Liberation. Maryknoll: Orbis Books. [1971. Teología de la Liberación, Perspectivas (Editorial Universitaria, CEP, Lima, Perú, 1971].

Lafargue, Paul. 1890. "Reminiscences of Marx." Lafargue Internet Archive https://www .marxists.org/archive/lafargue/index.htm.

Martins, C.E. 2020. *Dependency, Neoliberalism and Globalization in Latin America.* Leiden, The Netherlands: Brill.

Marx, Karl. 1857. "Bolivar y Ponte." *The New American Cyclopaedia*, Vol. III. Edited by George Ripley and Charles A. Dana, New York, D. Appleton and Co. https://www .marxists.org/archive/marx/works/1858/01/bolivar.htm.

Marx, Karl. 1861. "The Intervention in Mexico." *New-York Daily Tribune*, November 23, 1861. https://www.marxists.org/archive/marx/works/1861/11/23.htm.

Memoria Chilena. 2018. "Editora Nacional Quimantú (1971–1973)" http://www.mem oriachilena.gob.cl/602/w3-article-3362.html.

Munck, Ronaldo. 1984. "Marx and Latin America." *Bulletin of Latin American Research*, Vol. 3, No. 1 (Jan., 1984), pp. 141–146.

Musto, Marcello. 2019. "Bolivian Vice President Álvaro García Linera on Marx and Indigenous Politics." *Truthout* November. https://truthout.org/articles/bolivian-vice-president-alvaro-garcia-linera-on-marx-and-indigenous-politics/.

Robles Lomeli, J. D. and Rappaport, J. 2018. "Imagining Latin American Social Science from the Global South: Orlando Fals Borda and Participatory Action Research." *Latin American Research Review*, 53(3), 597–612. DOI: http://doi.org/10.25222/larr.164.

Sader, Emir. 2013. "Chávez, a Reader of Mészáros." *Monthly Review*, Mar 11, 2013. https:// mronline.org/2013/03/11/sader110313-html.

Solar Cabrales, Frank Josué. 2017. "Cuba: critical thought in the socialist transition." In Defense of Marxism. *Monthly Review*. https://mronline.org/2017/07/11/cuba-criti cal-thought-in-the-socialist-transition/.

Solón, Pablo. 2018. "Vivir Bien: Old Cosmovisions and New Paradigms," *Great Transition Initiative: Toward a Transformative Vision and Praxis* (February). http://greattransit ion.org/publication/vivir-bien/.

Sotelo Valencia, Adrián. 2020. *United States in a World in Crisis: The Geopolitics of Precarious Work and Super-exploitation*. Leiden, The Netherlands: Brill.

Tarcus, Tarcus. 2007. *Marx en la Argentina: Sus primeros lectores obreros, intelectuales y científicos*. Buenos Aires: Siglo Veintiuno Editores.

Weyer, Frédérique. 2017. "Implementing 'Vivir Bien': Results and Lessons from the Biocultura Programme, Bolivia," *Revue internationale de politique de développement*, 9(1): 128–137.

CHAPTER 9

Marx, the Commons and Democratic Eco-socialism

Vishwas Satgar

1   Introduction

Human and non-human life face a perilous existential crisis. COVID 19 has been merely one of many crises bringing into focus the society-nature relationship. In this regard, the notion of the commons is apposite, both as a social-scientific category, part of transdisciplinary thinking, and as part of lived planetary experience. How we think and engage the commons from a radical and critical perspective also means reckoning with Marx. However, Marx's thought has been layered by interpretations by his followers and the historical experiences of 'socialism'. With the global defeat of the Left and over three decades of relentless commodification, precarity, inequality and environmental destruction, re-finding Marx's own thought has become crucial. Marx is not surpassed as providing one the most trenchant, systematic and compelling critiques of capitalism. However, with ecological crises – pollution, global warming, extractivism, species extinction and resource constraints – looming large, the relevance of Marx's thought to these challenges has become a terrain of intellectual combat but also of renewal. At stake has been Marx's conception of ecology. Central to the perspective of this chapter is a reading of Marx as a thinker on the commons. This is not to argue that Marx was the first thinker on the commons. Instead, it is suggested that Marx had a conception of the commons that was central to his philosophical outlook, that his critique of capitalism was also a critique of the destruction of the commons, and this has implications for how we think about eco-socialism. It just might be that Marx had a richer understanding of the commons than assumed and which provides the basis for a theory of the commons.

This chapter has four objectives. First, to highlight the extent of the ecocidal destruction of the commons. The large-scale loss of human and non-human life is immense since the advent of proto capitalism, about 500 years ago. Enclosures of the commons have been central to this process in the global north and south. However, this has been about more than expropriation and the transformation of life enabling systems into private property. Such a process has also been about obliterating the conditions that sustain life. Private capitalist property is anti-ecological. Today we are living through the last great dispossession of the natural commons, including the Earth system, as capital seeks to reduce all of nature to natural capital. This foreground assists in thinking with Marx about the significance of the commons. However, this is not as straightforward as it seems because Marx's thought is contradictory and has lent itself to being Anthropocentric and anti-ecological. Thus, the second objective of this chapter is to highlight how the 'Promethean Marx' came about. This has to do with the canonization of scientific socialism as productivist socialism and the neglect of the naturalist basis of Marx's thought. It is argued that this is the Marx and Marxism that has to be rejected in the 21st Century. This casts a long shadow which hinders an ecological appreciation of Marx.

The third objective of this chapter is to highlight the central role of commons thinking in Marx's work. This is not about a search for a definition of the commons but rather an attempt re-read aspects of Marx's work to identify space for the commons in his thought. Such a reading spans the ecological premises of Marx's thought, key categories in his critique of capitalism, which can be extended into emancipatory ecological critique and serve as a basis for the defense of the commons, and a reading of his approach to non-capitalist societies, to the commons and to *commoning* as a practice of reproducing the commons. This reading of Marx is also about establishing whether there is potential in Marx's thought for a theory of the commons, a Marxist ecological theory of the commons. The fourth objective of this chapter is to think through the implications of Marx's approach to the commons for contemporary class and anti-oppression struggles, particularly climate justice struggles. Climate change brings the question of the natural commons front and center. Carbon capitalism's use of fossil fuels has ruptured the earth system and imperils all life. How this is engaged with as part of elaborating a democratic eco-socialist project in South Africa is elaborated, as part of assessing the proximity of Marx's approach to the commons in contemporary struggles to defend the commons.

2   The Last Great Dispossession of the Commons

According to De Angelis (2019:124) the commons refers to 'social systems formed by three basic interconnected elements: 1) a commonwealth, that is, a set of resources held in common and governed by 2) a community of commoners who also 3) engage in the praxis of commoning, or doing in common, which reproduces their lives in common and that of their commonwealth'. While this definition of the commons is extremely useful, it lacks a systems understanding of what it classifies as 'resources'. The concept of resources is laden with instrumentalist reason and a reductionist approach to nature as a 'thing'. Instead, the historical experience of the commons has been about life enabling socio-ecological systems, entangling human and non-human relations, ranging from land (including soils), water (oceans and freshwater systems), biodiversity (including plants, insects, trees and animals), labor, energy and more recently the cybersphere and the earth system. The commons have been about defending and reproducing life. With the emergence of capitalism, and its transition from feudalism to capitalism, numerous enclosures where imposed which reduced the commons to private property relations and subsumed such systems as part of capitalist accumulation. Karl Polanyi in the *Great Transformation* (1944) provides important insights into how land and labor were transformed into fictitious commodities through enclosures. Colonial expansion further extended enclosures into dominated peripheries. In this regard Rosa Luxemburg's classic text, *The Accumulation of Capital – A Contribution to the Economic Theory of Imperialism* (2002) highlights how the expansion of capital from the centers to the non-capitalist peripheries is premised on the destruction of the 'natural economy'. As life enabling systems the commons has supported pre-capitalist forms of life, culture and interstitial processes of socio-ecological reproduction.

Over the past one hundred fifty years of carbon capitalism and imperialism, the ecocidal logic of industrial capitalism and its dominated peripheries have continued to impact negatively on the commons. From the middle of the twentieth century earth scientists refer to this process as the 'Great Acceleration' which has increased the enclosures of life enabling systems (Will Steffen et al, 2015: 849–853). Industrial scale capitalist societies increased growth, car use, fast food, tourism and other resource intensive practices. This pattern of industrial scale dispossession has fueled the expansion of carbon capitalism and together with the most recent wave of globalization (late 1970s to the present), based on intensifying the conversion of nature into private property, there have been ecocidal consequences on life enabling socio-ecological systems. Several studies confirm this including the most recent report by the International Panel of Bio-diversity and Eco-system Services. The key highlights of this study underline the following:[1]

– Three-quarters of the land-based environment and about 66% of the marine environment have been significantly altered by human actions. On average

---

1   See https://www.ipbes.net/news/Media-Release-Global-Assessment

these trends have been less severe or avoided in areas held or managed by
Indigenous Peoples and Local Communities.
- More than a third of the world's land surface and nearly 75% of freshwater
  resources are now devoted to crop or livestock production.
- The value of agricultural crop production has increased by about 300% since
  1970, raw timber harvest has risen by 45% and approximately 60 billion tons
  of renewable and non-renewable resources are now extracted globally every
  year – having nearly doubled since 1980.
- Land degradation has reduced the productivity of 23% of the global land
  surface, up to US$577 billion in annual global crops are at risk from polli-
  nator loss and 100–300 million people are at increased risk of floods and
  hurricanes because of loss of coastal habitats and protection.
- In 2015, 33% of marine fish stocks were being harvested at unsustainable
  levels; 60% were maximally sustainably fished, with just 7% harvested at
  levels lower than what can be sustainably fished.
- Urban areas have more than doubled since 1992.
- Plastic pollution has increased tenfold since 1980, 300–400 million tons of
  heavy metals, solvents, toxic sludge and other wastes from industrial facil-
  ities are dumped annually into the world's waters, and fertilizers entering
  coastal ecosystems have produced more than 400 ocean 'dead zones', total-
  ing more than 245,000 km2 (591–595) – a combined area greater than that
  of the United Kingdom.

In this context, the recent United Nations Environmental Program report is
appropriately titled: *Making Peace with Nature* (2021).[2] However, the pattern
of dispossession and ecocide (the large-scale destruction of human and non-
human nature), underpinning these realities, has to be understood as the last
great dispossession of the commons. This antagonism with nature threatens
everything. Land use patterns, topsoil depletion, water privatization, bio-diversity loss, oil peak, precariatized labor, increasing corporate and state control of
the cyber commons and the rupture in the earth system due to worsening corporate induced planetary heating are where the battle lines of the last great dispossession of the commons are being drawn. The commons has been part of the
ecological sub-stratum of capitalism enabling socio-ecological reproduction of
countries and planetary civilization. Commoning practices and patterns have
emerged to resist such ecocidal practices and even opt out of capitalist logics,
informed by socio-ecological and cultural contexts. These counter-hegemonic
practices include indigenous peoples defense of forests, water and land, food
sovereignty, democratically owned public goods, socially owned renewable

2   Full report available here: https://www.unep.org/resources/making-peace-nature

energy, climate justice approaches to deep just transitions and cyber commoning (peer-to peer learning, Wikipedia, open-source systems). It is in this context
we have to ask the question: what does Marx's thought offer radical social theory and praxis today? Given how high the ecological stakes are, including for the
future of human and non-human life, is Marx's Marxism up the to challenge of
overcoming ecological catastrophe and informing a more emancipatory historical trajectory based on the commons and the practice of commoning?

3   Marx the 'Promethean'?

The anti-ecological Marx or Marx the 'Promethean' is a powerful critique of
Marx's Marxism. Such a critique resides within and outside Marxism. There
is a lot to wrestle with in these critical engagements and in trying to situate
Marx in relation to commons. These critiques speak to an imaginary in dominant streams of Marxism that emerged in the 20th Century, and which still
has a powerful hold on the Left imagination. In summary Marx is considered
a 'Promethean' for the following reasons: (i) belief in the linear development
of industrial capitalism and its technologies as the basis for progress. His theory of historical materialism also gave primacy to economic reductionism
and ultimately the 'forces of production'; (ii) he disagreed with Malthus on
the universality of population growth as providing limits to capitalism. While
Marx was correct in this position, he tended to foreground intentional and
agentic human action as the basis to overcome such socially constituted limits.[3] Ultimately capitalist or socialist modernization did not face any natural
limits. (iii) this relates to Marx wanting human domination over nature, as a
measure of self-realization, and ultimately a rational organizing of production as the means to ensure needs are met. It is a view that Marx is essentially
Anthropocentric, and nature is an object to be exploited by humans. Marx's
corpus is vast, unfinished, contradictory and there is evidence in his work that
these positions exist and lend support to these critiques.

Moreover, several other crucial factors entrenched this strand of productivist Marxism. In the 20th Century, 'actually existing socialist societies',
social democratic societies and revolutionary nationalist ones were shaped

---

3   Engel's articulated this conception of rationally organizing society to overcome natural limits also in his *Outlines of a Critique of Political Economy* ([1981] 1977). He believed that the
'productive power at mankind's disposal is immeasurable. The productivity of the soil can be
increased *ad infinitum* by the application of capital, labour and science ... Capital increases
daily; labour power grows with population; and day by day science increasingly makes the
forces of nature subject to man'.

by this approach and reading of Marxism. Stalin's forced march industrialization (despite being informed by Engel's approach to dialectic materialism
as applying to nature), China's post-Mao embrace of market reforms, technocratic managerialism in welfare states and corrupt nationalist ruling classes in
the global south all contributed negative environmental impacts. Chernobyl
was the world's worst nuclear disaster, pollution in Chinese cities is beyond
basic standards of clean air quality, most Western welfare states were carbon
democracies with extensive human consumption footprints and most peripheral ruling classes have opened their economies to extractivist practices and
mono-industrial farming systems. In a sense proving the anti-ecological thrust
of growth obsessed, industrial and productivist Marxism.

In the Western Marxist tradition, there was a backlash to Engel's version of
dialectical materialism as applicable to both nature and society; the 'dialectics
of nature' were considered anachronistic (Foster, 2008). However, this rejection went even further and even rejected the naturalist aspect of Marx's thinking. As a result, and despite the critical approach to Marx, Marx's ecology was
not part of Western Marxist theorizing for most of the 20th Century. The rise of
modern environmentalism further entrenched the 'green critique' of Marx and
Marxism in general. Marx's ontology of work, commitments to linear industrial progress and Anthropocentric intellectual orientation were all regarded as
anti-ecological. The bogey of the Promethean Marx was born. Finally, many of
Marx's crucial writings and works were not published when these productivist
strands of Marxism took root. Marx's *Economic and Philosophical Notebooks*
(1932), the *Grundrisse* (1939), *Ethnological Notebooks* (1974) and his *Scientific
and Natural Notebooks* (part of the *Marx-Engels-Gesamtausgabe* or MEGA project which has been in the making for several decades in the 20th Century)
were all published much later and only engaged with after these projects were
shaping the imaginary of many on the planet.

4   Towards a Marxist Ecological Theory of the Commons

Marx is not perfect, and neither is there a true Marx that has all the answers.
Marx's development as a radical thinker evolved and he was constantly
attempting to think with the intellectual raw materials of his time to ground
his historical materialist method and critique of capitalism. Thus when thinking about Marx's work as a whole, the Promethean Marx is contradicted by an
ecological Marx, with a strong naturalist basis to his thinking. Such a Marx was
always present but becomes pronounced at different moments in his corpus.
The ecological Marx expands the *political economy critique of capitalism* to an

emancipatory ecology critique and as the basis for *defending the commons*. Such a critique is also a decolonial critique, recognizing that colonialism had deleterious consequences and Euro-America is not the universal civilizational standard, we all have to inhabit, to achieve socialism. What follows is an attempt to foreground Marx's ecology as the basis to develop a Marxist theory of the commons. Three tasks are performed: (i) highlighting the ecological premises of Marx's Marxism; (ii) foregrounding several categories, in Marx's thought, that provide resources of emancipatory ecological critique of capitalism and the defense of the commons and (iii) providing an interpretation of Marx on the transition beyond capitalism that emphasizes the commons and commoning.

4.1   *The Ecological Premises of Marx's Marxism*

Callenbach provides a useful definition and insight into what ecology is all about. He says:

> Actually, the science of ecology studies all interactions among living beings and their environment, whether we humans are involved or not. Air and even some rocks that function as parts of life's cycles are included too. Ecology is a study of patterns, networks, balances and cycles rather than the straightforward causes and effects studied in physics and chemistry. The goal of ecology is to understand the functioning of whole living systems, not simply to break them down into component parts of analysis (1999:34).

While Marx did not invent modern ecology, there are important ecological premises to his thought. Moreover, Marx was also a pioneering systems thinker in how he understood the totality of capitalism, including nature. The re-reading and retrieval of the ecological premises of Marx's thought has produced a rich body of work. Since the end of the 1990s till the present there has been a revisiting of the classical foundations of Marx's thought and an attempt to reconstruct Marx's Marxism from the standpoint of Marx's conception of ecology. This has been about reading Marx afresh, informed by the full corpus of his work, while clearly specifying where and how the thread of nature features in his thought. This research agenda has come a long way and has been extremely fruitful in bringing to light Marx's ecology.[4]

---

4   Such works includes Bellamy Fosters *Marx's Ecology- Materialism and Nature* (2000), Paul Burkett's *Marxism and Ecological Economics- Toward a Red-Green Political Economy* (2006) and *Marx and Nature – A Red and Green Perspective* (2014), and more recently Kohei Saito's

Deriving from this Marxist ecological reconstruction are four crucial ecological premises in Marx's thought that place Marx on the terrain of understanding the commons as life enabling socio-ecological systems. The first ecological premise in Marx's thought recognizes that *humans are dependent on nature*. This is a theme central to the basis for the elaboration of historical materialism in the *German Ideology*. In this regard, it is stated as follows:

> The first premise of all human history is, of course, the existence of living human individuals. Thus, the first fact to be established is the physical organization of these individuals and their consequent relation to the rest of nature. Of course, we cannot here go either into the actual physical nature of man, or into the natural conditions in which man finds himself – geological, oro-hydrological, climatic and so on.
>
> MARX and ENGELS, 1998:37

The point about this premise is that the dependence of humans on nature is an empirical reality that needs to be studied and confirmed; there is a natural history bound up with a human history. While modes of production and divisions of labor become more complex, it does not mean that the natural conditions of production and the dependence of nature disappears. A second crucial ecological premise in Marx's thought relates to *humans being part of nature*. In the more Hegelian inspired *Economic and Philosophical Notebooks* Marx states:

> Nature is man's inorganic body – nature, that is, insofar as it is not itself human body. Man lives on nature – means that nature is his body, with which he must remain in continuous interchange if he is not to die. That man's physical and spiritual life is linked to nature means simply that nature is linked to itself, for man is a part of nature.
>
> MARX, 1981: 67

As part of nature and in a dependent, symbiotic relationship with nature, the human is more than just a social being but a socio-ecological being. The socio-ecological nature of the human is also contingent and historical. This links also to a third ecological premise in Marx which recognizes *nature is also as a source of wealth together with labor*. In *Capital* (1976, 1981 and 1981), Marx's labor centered ontology is further elaborated with an emphasis on the labor theory of value,

---

Karl Marx's Eco-socialism – Capital, Nature, and the Unfinished Critique of Political Economy (2017).

which is crucial to demonstrate exploitation through the extraction of surplus value. However, within productivist and anthropocentric Marxism this occludes any relationship with nature. All the ecological premises of Marx's thought are thrown out of the window. However, Marx reminds the German working class about the wealth creation role of labor and nature in his *Critique of the Gotha Program*. He states:

> Labour is not the source of all wealth. *Nature* is just as much the source of use values (and it is surely of such that material wealth consists!) as labour, which itself is only the manifestation of a force of nature, human labour power.
>
> MARX, 1996:8

The final ecological premise of Marx's thought relates to *human impacts on nature and limits*. In Saito's (2017) ecological reading of Marx, particularly the *Scientific and Natural Notebooks,* he provides extremely novel insights about Marx's deep concerns with impacts of capitalist agriculture on nature and deforestation. Marx was concerned with depletion of the fertility of soils, the 'robbery from the soil', and extensive destruction of forests. Marx began to acknowledge and recognize natural limits to capitalist accumulation. This was also central to his conception of the metabolic rift with nature, involving the flow of energy and matter but mediated by labor relations, which has been elaborated into metabolic rift theory by John Bellamy Foster and others.

4.2   Marx's Critique of Capitalism and the Defense of the Commons

With Marx having solid ecological premises to his Marxism, his political economy critique of capitalism can be situated and shifted towards emancipatory ecological critique of capitalism. Such critique recognizes natural and social relations are contradictory and mutually constitutive on a planetary scale, but are nonetheless constrained by our dependence on, our imbrication in nature and the limits of nature. A society, a capitalist system, built on the endless and total destruction of nature, will not survive. In this regard, four important categories in Marx's critique of capitalism provides a bridge to such an emancipatory ecological critique and most importantly to locating the commons, both its enclosure/destruction and life enabling role, as central to how we understand capitalism.

The first category is *primitive accumulation*. While Marx observed the process of primitive accumulation firsthand, as a young journalist, when he wrote about the *Theft of Woods*, this was not understood as part of the larger process of the making of capitalism. Yet as Linebaugh (2014:43–62) points out, Marx's writings (five articles) in 1842–43 for the *Rheinische Zeitung*, were related to a particular phase of development of capitalism in Germany but also the struggles around agrarian relations. More specifically, it would seem these writings and actual insights of the class struggle, related to peasants stealing wood from forests, where also about a shift from an inadequate study of crime to the study of political economy. In *Capital* Marx provides a detailed analysis of how enclosures of the commons were established, in different phases, to separate the peasantry from the means of production in Britain. Moreover, in *Part 8* of *Capital*, Marx explores primitive accumulation as forming the basis for the origins of capitalism and providing the pre-conditions for the development of this mode of production. Central to this study is an analysis of colonialism which highlights the role of slavery, racism, brute force and the appropriation of land. However, while Marx is trying to situate the making of capitalism in the peripheries, he is also showing how a racialized colonial subjectivity, the making of wage labor and land enclosures are crucial in this process. Primitive accumulation as a category central to the critique of capitalism then and now assists with the emancipatory ecology critique of capitalism to highlight the mass scale destruction of human and non-human nature, that is, ecocide. Thus, a more appropriate phrasing and appreciation of these contemporary processes would be *accumulation through ecocide*.

The second crucial category is *alienation*. This is central to Marx's critique of capitalism both in the *Philosophical and Economic Notebooks* and *Capital*. For Marx alienation is centered on four aspects for labor: (i) from the products of labor – this refers to labor being part of the product produced resulting in objectification and then such products being separated from the worker; (ii) in the division of labor the worker is a commodity, their labor is external to themselves, it is forced and is dehumanizing; (iii) as species being alienated from nature and herself. The universal human is now reduced to utilizing her individual self to ensure her physical existence; and (iv) estrangement from human to human. Marx's conception of alienation has a strong hint of Anthropocentricism, in parts, in how he understands the superiority of humans to animals. However, read and interpreted from the standpoint of the ecological premises to his thought, the human as a manifestation of nature engaged in exploitative work and separated from natural relations is in a state of alienation. Capitalism ensures the alienated human is not part of the natural commons. But underlying this labor centered ontology and conception of alienation is the role of property relations. It is the creation of labor as property, and through labor the creation of property, Marx places at the heart of alienation. Workers and ultimately humanity- in -nature is part of the struggle for de-alienation at the point of production. More concretely, this means traditions of worker control and resistance have to embrace an emancipatory ecological consciousness and ultimately a crucial role for the commons. Put more sharply, an ecologically conscious working class and subaltern should be at the frontlines of defending and advancing the commons to ensure de-alienation.

The third category that emancipatory ecology can draw on from Marx's political economy is the notion of *use value* to both deepen the critique of capitalism and defend the commons. In *Capital* labor and nature are use values, to meet human need. However, with capitalism labor and nature are commodified; labor sells labor power for a wage, nature such as land produces rent. Labor as a commodity is exploited and generates surplus value; the worker is constantly forced to supersede necessary labor time (the wage) and ensure an increasing role for surplus labor time (unpaid labor). At the same time, capital uses the use value of labor and nature to produce more commodities as exchange values. Commodities as exchange values also have use value to them, but mediated by labor and the labor process, produce surplus value for capital. For emancipatory ecology, the defense of the natural commons, including labor, is about defending use values. This is central to class and anti-oppression struggles.

The fourth crucial category is *social reproduction*, both in its broad social sense and as it relates to abode of the household and care labor. Production and social reproduction are two sides of the same coin in how life and society is reproduced. Marx in *Capital* understood that the socially necessary labor time was also about reproducing the worker and her dependents. Exploited, low wage and precariatized workers thus struggle to reproduce themselves and their families. However, it was Marxist feminists in the 1960s and 1970s that went further than this and recognized women's care labor as a use value, was unpaid but was also not inherently gendered.[5] Today social reproduction theory is making a return and Marxist feminist theorizing is locating the production/ reproduction contradiction within periodized regimes of reproduction. Nancy Fraser's (2017) work on reproductive regimes from (i) liberal capitalism; (ii) state managed capitalism and (iii) financialized capitalism provides a framing to bring in the commons and the ecological premises of Marx's Marxism. Put more sharply, socio-ecological human beings have been organized into socio-ecological regimes of reproduction. How these regimes destroy the commons and oppress women are crucial for analysis and ongoing struggles.

---

5   See Vogel (2013) and Gottfried (2015)

4.3   Non-Capitalist Societies, the Commons and Commoning

In the *Communist Manifesto* (*Marx and Engels, 2002*) there are two problems
that loom large in Marx's thought. First, there is a strong Eurocentric message
about the progressiveness of capital and capitalism, ending primitive societies.
Moreover, the world historic advance of capital produces its 'grave digger,' the
working class, in its wake. This is an epistemological Eurocentrism which continues in Marx's thought into the mid 1850s. However, according to Anderson
(2010), there is an epistemological rupture in Marx who leaves behind this
Eurocentric moment; Marx moves beyond linearity in his understanding of
history. This requires Marx to break with a Hegelianized and theological understanding of world history. Moreover, a recognition that non-capitalist societies
have their own histories, differentiated ownership systems and hence their
own modalities for the transition beyond pre-capitalism. The West's transition
from feudalism to capitalism was not a universal process. Finally, instead of
colonialism and the world market bringing about progress and the development of the forces of production it had deleterious consequences. Besides his
insights in *Capital* about the brutality and racialized basis of primitive accumulation, Marx's writing on race, ethnicity, class and colonialism in relation
to slavery in America and British colonial control of Ireland are apposite. This
is the decolonial Marx recognizing that history was much contingent, open
and subject to multi-linearity with a variegated processes of transition from
feudalism to capitalism and from capitalism and beyond. This becomes even
more stark in his political writings after the *Communist Manifesto,* and which
also have profound implications for how we think about the commons and
commoning in non-capitalist societies.

   However, to appreciate the shift to multi-linearity we have to return to the
second problem raised by the Communist *Manifesto* in Marx's thought. This
relates to the issue of abolishing bourgeoise property. The part of the manifesto dealing with measures to be taken by the working class and Communists
is explicitly state centric. An instrumentalized conception of the state is
at work and a working class led state merely has to wield the instrumental
power of the state and take over key forms of bourgeoise property. Centralized
state control is needed to be exercised over key instruments of production
such as credit, communication, transport and factories. However, informed
by his non-Eurocentric approach to history, Marx departs from this state centric approach to property relations, and which converges more with affirming a role for the commons and commoning in advancing beyond capitalism.
This comes through in his support for cooperatives in his *Inaugural Address*
to the First International, support for the Russian commune in his exchange
with Vera Zasulitch and in the *Preface to the Russian edition of the Communist*

Manifesto, embrace of the Paris Commune as a new form of organizing working class power (also through cooperatives) in the *Civil War in France* and firm
support in the *Critique of the Gotha Program* for the 'common' or socialized
ownership of the means of production. In short, while Marx did not blueprint
a post-capitalist society, he recognized free and associated labor came into
existence through collective inherited property forms, socialized interstitial
property forms and more decentered and participatory forms of democracy
as crucial for a post capitalist society. These are all institutional forms consistent with the commons and commoning to ensure life enabling systems
bring about all rounded human development. However, this thread in Marx's
thought is a consistent one and goes back to his search for an anti-dote to the
alienation and estrangement that comes with private property relations. In the
1844 *Philosophical and Economic Manuscripts,* he resolves this problem, in general terms, in this way:

> This material, immediately perceptible private property is the material
> perceptible expression of estranged human life. Its movement – pro-
> duction and consumption – is the perceptible revelation of the move-
> ment of all production up till now i.e. the realization or the reality of
> man. Religion, family, state, law, morality, science, art, etc. are only par-
> ticular modes of production, and fall under its general law. The positive
> transcendence of private property as the appropriation of human life,
> is therefore the positive transcendence of all estrangement – that is to
> say, the return of man from religion, family, state etc., to his human, i.e.,
> social, existence (1981:91).

5   The Deep Just Transition and Democratic Eco-socialism

The ecological side of Marx's thought is certainly anti-Promethean. The ecological premises of his thought, his critique of capitalism as emancipatory ecological critique and his understanding of non-capitalist modes of existence as
part of the transition beyond capitalism are consistent with affirming the commons and commoning practices. Today in the contemporary world, socialism
is being rethought from the standpoint of an ecological Marx, lessons learned
from the mistakes of historical and state centric productivist socialisms and
at the frontlines of struggles to defend the commons. One of the most important struggles in this regard is the climate justice struggle, which is entering a
third cycle of resistance in the midst of COVID 19. Climate Justice forces are

intensifying the struggle to give definition and content to the notion of the deep, systemic and just transition. More sharply, 'system change, not climate change'.

While capital is increasingly waking up to the realities of worsening climate crisis, the hegemonic influence of carbon capital over the multi-lateral climate negotiations, during the past three decades, has brought the world to the brink of irreversible disaster. In 2018, climate scientists raised the alarm bell the loudest with the 1.5C IPCC report which argues we have the current decade to prevent a 1.5C planetary overshoot. The world is now at 417 parts per million (ppm) carbon concentration. According to Earth scientists we are in a danger zone far from the safe boundary of 350ppm, in which several dangerous tipping points and feedback loops can kick in.[6] This carbon capitalist rupturing in the Earth system is propelling the planet towards a hot house earth, which will make it unlivable. Our planetary commons, including the Earth System, is being turned against human and non-human life. The last great dispossession of the natural commons threatens everything.

In this life and death struggle, the defense of the natural commons takes on a salience and meaning, that brings it to the fore in climate justice struggles on a planetary scale. The deep, just and systemic transition is nothing short of realizing a Democratic Eco-socialist project to preserve human and non-human life. In the South African context this is expressed in the struggle to advance a Climate Justice Charter.[7] There are four striking aspects about the charter that affirm its Democratic Eco-socialist orientation. First, it envisages a decolonial approach to knowledge and to resisting capitalism. It explicitly rejects capitalist ideologic underpinnings of productivism, extractivism and technotopia. Instead, it affirms a critical embrace of knowledge (including Earth science, global emancipatory ecology and indigenous knowledge), local history and culture as the basis to inform a delinking approach to the deep just transition. In other words, the charter affirms the importance of multi-linear approaches to transition beyond capitalism and it is certainly not about reproducing the Euro-American standard of 'civilization'.

Second, it contains fourteen systemic alternatives (including democratic just transition plans, food sovereignty, solidarity economy, socially owned renewable energy, water commoning, zero waste and natural climate solutions) which are all about democratizing life enabling systems. In other words,

---

6   These insights are contained in an interview with Earth scientist, Will Steffen, available here: https://www.tandfonline.com/doi/full/10.1080/14747731.2021.1940070

7   The Climate Justice Charter is endorsed by over 260 organisations and is available here: https://www.safsc.org.za/climate-justice-charter/

it affirms eco-centric modes of living that place the commons and common-ing central to the deep just transition. Third, it is premised on a constitutive understanding of power. Power is organized, made and institutionalized from below. Thus, the charter envisages democratic systemic reforms pre-figured in local spaces but scaled up and pursued beyond. In other words, the working class (urban and rural), grassroots women and the most vulnerable must lead deep just transitions and ensure systemic alternatives are deepened over time through mass power. Fourth, this in turn ensures the South African state is remade as a climate justice state, and is people driven to create enabling con-ditions for democratic systemic reforms, to build new capabilities, to redirect resources and to renew radical Pan-Africanism. The charter does not envisage a state centric transition beyond carbon capitalism.

6 Conclusion

Marx's Marxism is a crucial resource in the 21st Century to confront the last great dispossession of the commons and the ecocidal logic of carbon capital-ism. Marx has crucial ecological underpinnings to his thought that embraces the commons. Moreover, his political economy critique of capitalism pro-vides crucial resources of critique for an emancipatory ecology that stands in defense of the commons, as part of frontline struggles. These categories also assist with studying the commons and elaborating its significance as part of the transition beyond capitalism. In this regard the decolonial Marx (or non-Eurocentric) and ecological Marx meet. The commons and commoning are certainly part of a multi-linear and context specific approach to the transition beyond capitalism. Such an approach challenges narrow state centric concep-tions of socialism but also enriches how the deep and just transition to demo-cratic eco-socialism can come about from below.

In South Africa this is certainly what the Climate Justice Charter is all about. Rooted in a context in which a history of race, class and gender oppression looms large and which has continued under a black majority government, sys-tems transformation and redistribution are conjoined, as the climate crisis is addressed. This simply means inequality, unemployment and all other socio-ecological reproduction contradictions have to be addressed in a manner that also socializes property relations, at a higher level, through the commons and commoning. This brings us on to intellectual ground occupied by the ecologi-cal and the non-Eurocentric Marx.

Far from being implicated in the last great dispossession of the commons, Marx stands against it and provides resources to develop a Marxist theory of the commons. It is up to us to clarify this and assert it. This chapter makes a start and a contribution in this regard. From here, we must continue deepening how 21st Century Marxists think and act as commoners in the struggle to defend life enabling commons systems.

References

Anderson, K. 2010. *Marx at the Margins*. Chicago: University of Chicago Press.

Burkett, P. 2006. *Marxism and Ecological Economics- Toward a Red-Green Political Economy*. Leiden: Brill.

Burkett, P. 2014. *Marx and Nature – A Red and Green Perspective*. Chicago: Haymarket Books.

Callenbach, E. 1999. *Ecology – A Pocket Guide*. India: Universities Press.

De Angelis, M. 2019. 'Commons.' In *Pluriverse -A Post-Development Dictionary*, edited by Ashish Kothari, Ariel Salleh, Arturo Escobar, Federico Demaria and Alberto Acosta. India: Tulika Books.

Engels, F. 1981 [1959]. *Outlines of a Critique of Political Economy*. USSR: Progress Publishers.

Foster, B. 2008. 'The Dialectics of Nature and Marxist Ecology' In *Dialectics for the New Century*, edited by Bertell Ollman and Tony Smith. New York: Palgrave Macmillan.

Foster, B. 2000. *Marx's Ecology- Materialism and Nature*. New York: Monthly Review Press.

Fraser, N. 2017. 'Crisis of Care? On the Social-Reproductive Contradictions of Contemporary Capitalism' In *Social Reproduction Theory* edited by Tithi Bhattacharya. London: Pluto Press.

Gottfried, H. 2015. *The Reproductive Bargain – Deciphering the Enigma of Japanese Capitalism*. Leiden: Brill.

IPBES (2019): Summary for policymakers of the global assessment report on biodiversity and ecosystem services of the Intergovernmental Science-Policy Platform on Biodiversity and Ecosystem Services. S. Díaz, J. Settele, E. S. Brondízio E.S., H. T. Ngo, M. Guèze, J. Agard, A. Arneth, P. Balvanera, K. A. Brauman, S. H. M. Butchart, K. M. A. Chan, L. A. Garibaldi, K. Ichii, J. Liu, S. M. Subramanian, G. F. Midgley, P. Miloslavich, Z. Molnár, D. Obura, A. Pfaff, S. Polasky, A. Purvis, J. Razzaque, B. Reyers, R. Roy Chowdhury, Y. J. Shin, I. J. Visseren-Hamakers, K. J. Willis, and C. N. Zayas (eds.). IPBES secretariat, Bonn, Germany. 56 pages. https://doi.org/10.5281/zenodo.3553579 .

Linebaugh, P. 2014. *Stop, Thief! The Commons, Enclosures and Resistance*. Oakland: PM Press.

Luxemburg, R. 2003 [1913]. 'The Accumulation of Capital – A Contribution to the Economic Theory of Imperialism' London and New York: Routledge.

Marx, K. 1976 [1867]. *Capital: A Critique of Political Economy, Volume One.* England: Penguin Group.

Marx, K. 1978 [1885]. *Capital: A Critique of Political Economy, Volume Two.* England: Penguin Group.

Marx, K. 1981 [1894]. *Capital: A Critique of Political Economy, Volume Three.* England: Penguin Group.

Marx, K. 1981 [1959]. *Economic and Philosophic Manuscripts of 1844.* USSR: Progress Publishers.

Marx, K. 1996. [1875] *Critique of the Gotha Programme.* Beijing: Foreign Language Press.

Marx, K. and Friedrich Engels, (1998) *The German Ideology.* New York: Prometheus Books.

Marx, K. and Friedrich Engels (2002 [1888]) *The Communist Manifesto.* London: Penguin Books.

Polanyi, Karl (1944 [2001]), *The Great Transformation: The Political and Economic Origins of our Time,* Boston: Beacon Press.

Saito, K. 2017. *Karl Marx's Eco-socialism – Capital, Nature, and the Unfinished Critique of Political Economy.* New York: Monthly Review Press.

Steffen, W., Broadgate, W., Deutsch, L., Gaffney, O., Ludwig, C., (2015). The trajectory of the Anthropocene: The Great Acceleration. *The Anthropocene Review* 2, 81–98.

Vogel, L. (2013 [1983]). *Marxism and the Oppression of Women – Toward a Unitary Theory.* Chicago: Haymarket Books.

CHAPTER 10

Marx Matters, in Theory and Practice

Reflections from the Corporate Mapping Project

William K. Carroll

Marx matters, not only to our interpretations of the world of late capitalism, but to our efforts to change it. Marx's substantive analysis of capitalism as a way of life that has at its core class exploitation, alienation and endless growth on a finite planet is a resource for all movements aspiring to human thriving and ecological sanity. But his insistence on the dialectical relation between critical theory and practice challenges Marxists to go beyond theorizing, to 'prove the truth – i.e., the reality and power, the this-sidedness' of critical theory in practice (Marx 1845).

Since 2015, I have co-led a research and public-engagement partnership inquiring into the power and influence of Canada's fossil-fuel sector. With co-director Shannon Daub (Director of the Canadian Centre for Policy Alternatives, British Columbia) and a team of a hundred or so fellow researchers, policy analysts and community advisors active in progressive movements, we have mapped the various social relations that enable this industry to thrive at a time when carbon emissions pose an urgent existential challenge for humanity.[1] These relations constitute a *regime of obstruction*, with a distinctive political-economic architecture. Building on hegemonic structures installed during successive eras of organized capitalism and neoliberal capitalism, this regime is constituted through modalities of power that protect revenue streams issuing from carbon extraction, processing and transport while bolstering popular support for an accumulation strategy in which fossil capital figures as a leading fraction. The regime incorporates a panoply of hegemonic practices at different scales, reaching into civil and political society, and into Indigenous communities whose land claims and worldviews challenge state mandated property rights.

---

1 A recent study projects that carbon pollution already in the atmosphere will drive global temperatures to approximately 2.3 degrees of warming since pre-industrial times, well past the 2.0 threshold considered a point of no return. However, if the world were to achieve net zero carbon emissions soon, breaching that threshold could be substantially delayed, creating time to adapt or find technological solutions. See Zhou et al (2021).

This chapter presents our Corporate Mapping Project (CMP) as an exemplar of how Marxism can inform scholarship and political practice, within a wide-ranging, praxiological intervention.

1   Setting the Context for the Corporate Mapping Project

Anderson (1976: 42) has recounted how, from the 1920s onward, Western Marxism emerged as the 'product of defeat'. The failure of socialist revolution to spread beyond Russia and the Stalinization of Communist Parties meant that Western Marxism, 'produced in situations of political isolation and despair,' would carry as its hallmark 'the rupture of political unity between Marxist theory and mass practice' (ibid:55). This 'structural divorce of theory and practice' also meant 'a seclusion of theorists in universities' (ibid:92), a problem recognized more recently by observers of contemporary academic feminism and other putatively radical perspectives (Fraser 2013; Eisenstein 2016). Although Western Marxism reached crucial insights on the psycho-cultural mechanisms that sustain advanced capitalism as a way of life, these achievements often issued from positions of political detachment. However, successive waves of movement formation have also rekindled a dialectic of theory and practice, exemplified in radical pedagogy (Mayo 2020), Institutional Ethnography (Smith 2005) and Participatory Action Research (Hall 1979), all of which find their lineages, broadly speaking, in the new left (Carroll 2004). In our current setting, alternative policy groups like the Transnational Institute and Focus on the Global South develop strategies and networks for transformative change, in dialogue with social movements (Carroll 2016), while political organizations like the Progressive International and Democracy in Europe Movement 2025 (DiEM25) strive to re-connect theory and practice in addressing the power of capital transnationally. The Corporate Mapping Project has been one such praxiological initiative, designed to be laser-focused on a key existential issue facing humanity.

The causal relations between consumption of fossil fuels, emission of greenhouse gases into the atmosphere and global temperature increase have been understood for decades, not least by mega-polluters like ExxonMobil, whose scientists' findings from as early as 1977 were repressed in the pursuit of profit (Banerjee, Song and Hasemyer 2015). James Hansen drew these causal connections unequivocally in June 1988, before a US Senate committee (see Shabecoff 1988). In the three ensuing decades, global warming became a climate emergency. Not only did rising carbon emissions from the burning of fossil fuels enhance the greenhouse effect, knock-on effects, amplified by feedback loops, have brought extreme weather (droughts, heat waves, hurricanes, floods, and cyclones), sea-level rise and ocean acidification, losses in biodiversity, and the spread of diseases once confined to the tropics (United Nations Framework Convention on Climate Change 2007: 8–9).

Crisis, as James O'Connor understood, is a time of intense contingency; of danger and opportunity; of social struggle; 'a time for decision; a time when what individuals actually do counts for something' (1987: 3). Interleafed with the ongoing crisis of neoliberalism – a slow-motion train wreck playing out since the global financial crisis of 2008 – and the dramatic dampening of accumulation due to the global pandemic, the climate crisis is a clarifying moment. It raises the real prospect of corporate-driven ecocide (Whyte 2020). The Corporate Mapping Project (CMP) has sought to mobilize the insights of historical materialism and kindred critical perspectives as cognitive/political resources in understanding and responding to the crisis. With the theory/practice dialectic top of mind, the project has delivered a critical analysis of fossil capital's regime of obstruction while helping to build a broad alliance for climate justice in our struggle against corporate power, which is also a race against time.

It is not surprising that Canada has been the CMP's base of operations and research focal point. A recent ranking of 61 countries on Climate Change Performance placed Canada 58th (Burck et al. 2020). In 2013, when the project first took shape, Canada had gained notoriety as a major climate laggard under reactionary management. Already in 2006 Stephen Harper had, in his first speech abroad as Prime Minister, announced his plan to make Canada a 'global energy powerhouse' (Taber 2006). This vision was soon matched by policy initiatives to rapidly expand the tar sands in Alberta (Harper's home province), to build pipelines to transport diluted bitumen, and to withdraw (in 2011) from the Kyoto climate accord. By 2015, McCormack and Workman could observe that Alberta had become 'the new centre for capital accumulation in Canada and thus an important source of employment and income,' (2015: 42) and, we might add, foreign exchange for a Canadian state concerned about trade deficits. Enormous fixed-capital investments in bitumen mining and pipelines pushed Alberta ahead of Ontario as a locus for the country's capital stock (ibid: 32–3).

Yet the collapse of oil prices in 2014, due mainly to an oil glut and a price war launched by OPEC against US shale oil, portended trouble for the extractivist business model. Bitumen's high costs of production and the low quality of the product (highly polluting, costly to refine) brought a flood of red ink to Canada's oil patch. A second collapse in 2020 was triggered by the COVID-19 pandemic, but it also reflected increasing investor skepticism about the future of bitumen in the global energy mix.[2] A disinterested observer of all this would surely recommend sunsetting a failing industry. Yet the exact opposite occurred: a sell-out strategy designed to valorize carbon assets by pushing them in volume to market while they still held value. Five big Canadian banks led the world in directing $73 billion in financing to the tar sands between 2016 and 2019 (Kirsch et al. 2020: 36; Gutstein 2021) while state managers doubled down on subsidies for industry. As of 2018, Canada led the G7 in support for fossil-fuel companies (Cox 2018). Later moves only deepened that commitment through direct government investment in pipeline projects, solidifying a scenario of carbon lock-in, against the grain of a slow but undeniable global energy transition.[3]

My previous work had prepared and positioned me for leadership in the CMP. Beginning in the 1980s, I had developed a two-track research program. The first followed the path broken by 'power structure' analysis in the 1970s, as new left sociologists mapped elite networks of corporate directors and executives, offering a window on the social organization of monopoly capital (Domhoff 1980). The second track took up a Gramscian framing of social movements as potential carriers of counter-hegemony and worked with movement organizations in examining their political projects, networks and strategies. Each of these had a Canadian focus initially but expanded to a global field by the 2000s. By that time, I was, on the one hand, mapping the elite networks of the transnational capitalist class while also, in a more participatory-research initiative, studying 'transnational alternative policy groups' like progressive think tanks whose projects and networks extend beyond national political theaters.

The first track highlighted the power bloc in which leading capitalists and associated organic intellectuals (highly placed corporate lawyers, consultants, academics and politicians) form a 'corporate community' (Domhoff 2009), competing for shares of surplus value yet united at a strategic level via business councils, industry lobbies, neoliberal think tanks and the like (Carroll 2010a, 2010b). The second track explored the praxis of organic intellectuals of the left: the dialogical relations they cultivate with movements and the 'modes of

---

2 On April 22, 2021, the Western Canadian Select oil price index fell to -$41.13, but soon recovered to $30/barrel (down from $77.93 US in 2011 https://www.aer.ca/providing-information/data-and-reports/statistical-reports/st98/prices-and-capital-expenditure/crude-oil-prices/western-canadian-select), where it hovered throughout the rest of the year https://oilprice.com/oil-price-charts/block/49)

3 The federal government purchased the TransMountain Expansion pipeline project in 2018 when its corporate owner threatened to walk away from the project's dubious profit prospects; the Alberta government gifted TC Energy in 2020 with a $1.5 billion investment in the now-defunct KXL project, to increase the odds of its being completed.

cognitive praxis' they employ in 'striving to produce transformative knowledge concomitantly with knowledge-based transformation' (Carroll 2016: 4). The in-depth interviews I conducted with scores of activist-intellectuals impressed upon me their pragmatic appreciation of the theory/practice dialectic, often missing from academic Marxism. As Hilary Wainwright of the Transnational Institute put it,

> how do you maintain a radical critique and develop it in a way that reaches the kinds of popular forces through which it can have an impact? A radical critique that doesn't reach the people, who can actually realize its goals, is fairly useless.
>
> quoted in CARROLL 2016: 115

My work with left policy groups focused on those with a transnational remit but included a parallel study of the Canadian Centre for Policy Alternatives (CCPA) (Carroll and Huxtable 2014), whose Vancouver office would become the key community-based partner within the CMP. My ties to the CCPA (where I had been a research associate for many years) proved instrumental in launching the Corporate Mapping Project, as did my skill set as a critical sociologist focused on the social organization of corporate power and the counter-hegemonic potentialities of social movements. However, from the start, the project has been a collaborative, collective effort.

2   Designing and Launching a Praxis-Oriented Project

In October 2013 CCPA-BC Director Seth Klein invited me to propose a partnership of university- and community-based researchers to expose the power structures holding in place Canada's outsized fossil-fuel sector. As Canada's leading progressive policy outfit (with extensive links to activist communities as well as left academics[4]) the CCPA had hosted a highly productive Climate Justice Project since 2007 and understood the need to ground its ideas and interventions in a robust critique of corporate power. CCPA-BC Associate Director Shannon Daub, whose sharp strategic mind and extensive involvement with progressive movements enable her to move fluidly across the

---

4 See Carroll and Huxtable (2014). The CCPA-BC currently lists 69 research associates, 35 of them based in academe and others based in unions and community groups, or freelance. https://www.policyalternatives.ca/offices/bc/about/research-associates

intersecting problem-spaces of class, gender, colonialism and ecology, would co-direct the project, with core responsibility for knowledge mobilization.

The design of the project was partly dictated by its main funder, Canada's Social Sciences and Humanities Research Council (SSHRC). Its Partnership program was designed under the conservative Harper regime (2006–2015) to torque academe toward business interests (who would 'partner' with universities in various endeavors suiting corporate needs, with SSHRC providing matching funds). In practice, the program evolved to allow partnering with non-profits and in-kind contributions from the latter. This enabled us to create a partnership of six Canadian universities (with University of Victoria as host institution) and four civil-society organizations: two progressive policy groups (CCPA and Alberta-based Parkland Institute), Unifor (Canada's largest industrial union) and the Public Accountability Initiative (PAI, a US-based NGO that runs LittleSis.org, an online database of the US corporate and political elite). Launched in the fall of 2015, the CMP included in its roster a core team of 24 university-based researchers and 12 community-based researchers and policy analysts. Members of the core team were entitled to receive funds from a $2.5 million budget from SSHRC; partner organizations committed approximately $1.5 million in matching cash and in-kind contributions. But our team extended beyond that core to 48 'collaborators', most of them active in environmental, Indigenous, labor, independent-media and other groups who could provide advice while participating in CMP initiatives. We thereby leveraged the extensive movement connections of our civil society partners and began in the autumn of 2015 to build a 'community of practice'[5] via several meetings with activist collaborators in Western Canadian cities. At these gatherings we introduced the project and asked participants what their needs for knowledge were and how the knowledge we would produce could inform effective movement practice. A few months into this seven-year partnership (2015–2022), we had assembled a network of researchers, progressive policy analysts and activists sharing a deep concern about corporate power, fossil capital and the climate crisis.

Concurrently, we began to roll out a four-stream program of research and knowledge mobilization (Figure 10.1), which had been written into our 2014 proposal to SSHRC. The first stream would investigate the structure and dynamics

---

5 A community of practice is 'formed by people who engage in a process of collective learning in a shared domain of human endeavor.' As Wenger-Trayner and Wenger-Trayner (2015) go on to note, 'members of a community of practice are practitioners. They develop a shared repertoire of resources: experiences, stories, tools, ways of addressing recurring problems – in short a shared practice. This takes time and sustained interaction.'

of Canada's fossil-capital sector, its various linkages to regional, national and transnational capitalist structures and agencies, its extractive logic of accumulation by dispossession and the business strategies carbon-extractive corporations use in the current era of decreasing fossil-fuel prices and the increasing risk (to fossil-capital investors) of stranded assets. The second stream would focus on the hegemonic moment, the struggle for hearts and minds – the networks and discourses reaching into state and civil society, through which fossil capital strives to secure popular consent and to coopt, disorganize or marginalize dissenting perspectives. Significantly, this stream would also research the reach of corporate power into Indigenous communities whose land claims and collectivist traditions often stand in the way of oil and gas infrastructure (and who have suffered the worst environmental and health impacts from carbon extraction, as part of ongoing colonization). The third stream would consider power wielded and conflict managed along fossil-capital commodity chains, from extraction through pipelines and processing, to finished products. This stream would map the corridors of corporate power as well as the flashpoints of resistance (where power is visibly contested and the flow of value resisted or disrupted) and emergent forms of counter-power, some of which point to alternative energy futures.

In the project's fourth stream, the knowledge developed in the first three would be mobilized. Our models for this most praxiological component were twofold. From Michael Burawoy, we adopted a framing of the project as *public sociology*. Burawoy has advocated public sociology as a break from both elite parochialism (academics writing exclusively for academics) and servility to established power (sociologists conducting policy research for moneyed clients). In contrast, public sociology addresses publics, beyond academe, in ways that contribute to discussions integral to democratic process. Burawoy further distinguished two forms of public sociology: traditional (sociologists addressing mass publics monologically, as in a newspaper op-ed) and organic, 'in which the sociologist works in close connection with a visible, thick, active, local and often counter-public.' (2005: 7). Although the CMP would practice traditional public sociology (our left think tank partners have many connections to mainstream media, and strong capacity for op-eds and media releases), our emphasis has been on the organic. Indeed, a focus of stream 4, as shown in Figure 10.1, has been to build an information-rich website (including not only our research reports and commentaries, but an interactive database enabling activists, journalists and concerned citizens to create their own mappings of corporate power), and to train activists in monitoring and researching corporate power.

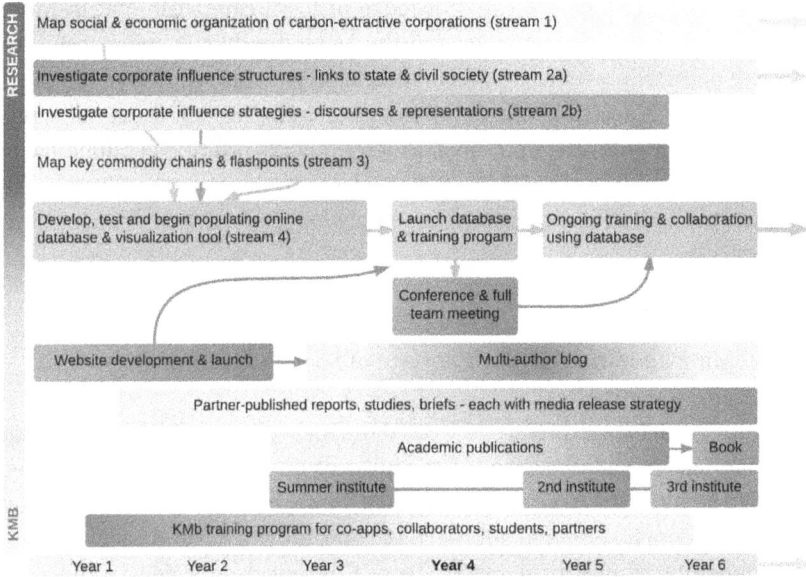

FIGURE 10.1 CMP overview and timeline
Note: KMB=knowledge mobilization
SOURCE: CARROLL AND DAUB (2014). GRAPHIC BY SHANNON DAUB

As a complementary praxiological component, the project embraced the spirit of Participatory Action Research (PAR). Budd Hall (1979) describes PAR as a three-pronged initiative: a method of research involving participation of the community, a dialogical educational process, and a means of taking action for change. PAR is a way to democratize knowledge, and to erode the boundaries between knowledge and action, researchers and actors. From the start, the CMP was embedded in activist and progressive-policy communities, and we pursued extensive popular education through a variety of initiatives (some of them diagrammed in the lower half of Figure 10.1). Our research agenda thus implied a social-change agenda, through

– exposing and problematizing corporate power in its multiple modalities, to various publics,
– providing evidence-based ammunition to allies in progressive movements, and
– offering policy analysis and feasible alternatives based in climate justice.

In this way, the project was designed to foster a change-oriented community of practice, including researchers, activists, progressive policy wonks in and around the state, academics and journalists. At the core of our mission, we endeavored to produce critical knowledge of fossil capitalism and to mobilize that knowledge among allies and the general public in order to inform effective political practice. This was reflected in the composition of our steering committee (consisting of five protagonists in the two left think tanks plus myself) and our publishing protocol, which explicitly prioritized public-facing publications over professional journal articles (without in any way precluding the latter), to counteract the strong tendency for academics to write for other academics.[6]

3   Marx and Gramsci in the Service of Social Engagement

These design elements directly addressed the theory/practice schism in historical materialism while incorporating resources from related critical perspectives and traditions. From an open Marxist vantage, our project incorporated a number of praxis-oriented approaches, some of which had developed quite independently of historical materialism. Conceived as a developing community of practice, the project would, as organic public sociology, connect researchers (academic and community-based) with activists and progressive policy analysts, while reaching beyond progressive communities to engage the general public. It would create dialogical and participatory initiatives, bridging the divide between research and action. In producing and mobilizing critical knowledge of fossil capital, the project would endeavor to shift the balance of forces within what one core team member termed a first world petro-state (Adkin 2016). The struggle was not simply one of the people versus capital and the state; indeed, many of 'the people' were strongly aligned with the hegemonic bloc. Not only oil-field workers in Alberta, but sections of Indigenous leadership and mainstream environmentalism were committed to working with industry. Decades of neoliberal globalization had bequeathed a political landscape characterized by a highly variegated and largely disorganized working class, a weak social-democratic left (and nothing beyond zombie corpuscles to the left of that) and a well-organized capitalist class controlling the lion's share of material and cultural production. Yet the sharpening social and ecological contradictions of settler-colonial capitalism had also inspired vibrant

---

6   At the time of writing (March 2021), our website contains 31 in-depth research reports and 108 shorter reports and commentaries, all written in accessible prose (https://www.corporate mapping.ca/). In an interim tallying of the impact of our online publications in the spring of 2018, we found that they were cited in mainstream and online news media over 230 times and viewed over 42,000 times.

political countercurrents for Indigenous resurgence and environmental sanity while opening sections of the labor movement to the need for a just transition from fossil capitalism. These forces comprised our socio-political constituency.

Within the CMP, Marxism was from the start a core perspective, but was rarely named as such, and was always in dialogue with anti-colonial, feminist and heterodox-economic (particularly left-Keynesian and Polanyian) approaches. Our 'Open' Marxism[7] took up historical materialism 'as a family of approaches rather than a single unified system' (Sum and Jessop 2014: 10) – a cognitive-strategic resource open to insights from other critical perspectives, in constructing a transformative historical bloc. Our approach was consistent with Harvey's (2011: 253) observation that 'the whole field of political action has undergone a radical transformation since the mid-1970s'. The transformations have included the rise of politically oriented NGOs, the development of new anarchist, autonomist and grassroots organizations, the growth of diverse struggles against accumulation by dispossession, the flourishing of emancipatory movements around identity politics, and tentative moves to reinvent the labor left within unions and parties (ibid 253–59). In the circumstances, 'it becomes imperative to envision alliances between a range of social forces' (ibid: 138), as in the tentative convergence of the strands of liberal-left, Marxist and autonomist environmentalism that Reitan and Gibson (2012) detected in their case study of the COP15 climate meeting in Copenhagen.

On the theory side of the dialectic, as our research program was rolling out in the project's first year, I devised a basic framework that could orient much of our work, incorporating insights (borrowed from O'Connor 1973 and others) on accumulation and hegemony as primary forms of corporate power. The framework identified two dialectically constituted faces of contemporary corporate power – the economic and the political-cultural. Following Urry (1981), I schematized these as a distinctive architecture comprised of three overlapping fields: state, civil society and economy (see Figure 10.2). As Gramsci observed, 'the state intervenes at every moment of economic life, which is a continuous web of transfers of property' (2007: 10); hence, these are not separate spheres.

---

7 According to Watcharabon Buddharaks (2018:62), open Marxism 'demands 'openness' in both empirical research in political economy, and more crucially openness of the Marxist categories themselves.' The differences between open Marxist and heterodox economics are not trivial, as O'Kane (2020) has shown. Heterodox approaches downplay class struggle and capitalism's inherent crisis dependencies and tend to view the state as a neutral arbiter whose policies can be reshaped to serve the public interest. Yet, from a strategic perspective, in a context in which the revolutionary left is non-existent as a political force, there can be no denying the need for an alliance politics that draws on the resources of left social democracy in a war of position constituted by a series of nonreformist reforms.

In Gramsci's thinking 'there is a generative understanding of "civil society" not as a separate sphere in opposition to the "state" but as an element in dialectical unity with "political society" ' (Bieler and Morton 2018: 14).

At the centre of the framework was the idea that corporate power is wielded through a number of distinct modalities, calling attention to specific practices and relations. Among the economic modalities, operational power functions to appropriate surplus labor within the firm through a chain of command, but also flows along commodity chains. Strategic power, the power to set corporate strategies, involves control of the corporation, often through ownership of strategic share blocs and representation on the board of directors. Allocative power stems from control of the money-capital on which large corporations (and the economic future) depend. As for corporate power's hegemonic face, the framework emphasized the multifaceted roles that organic intellectuals play in organizing consent particularly within civil society and the state, through public relations and media, policy formation, lobbying, higher education, accounting and corporate law, etc. (Carroll and Shaw 2001). Such experts often serve on multiple corporate and other governance boards, solidifying the

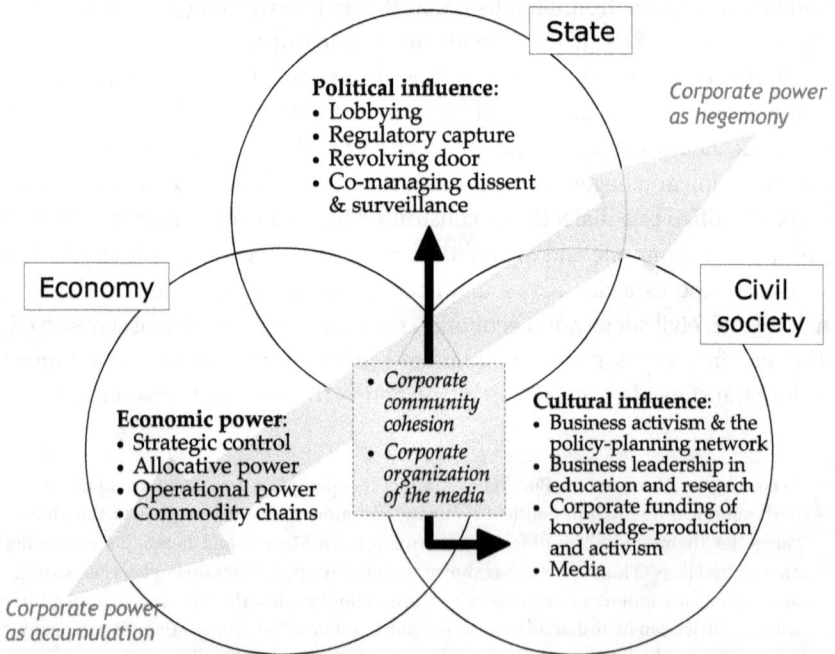

FIGURE 10.2 Modalities of corporate power
SOURCE: CARROLL AND SAPINSKI 2018:101

power bloc as an integrated elite, a corporate community capable of maintaining a moving consensus on political priorities.

As a complement to elite integration, the framework further identified the *reach* of corporate power into the public sphere. The routinized practices of business councils and industry groups, policy-planning organizations, lobbying, revolving doors between 'private' and 'public' sectors, selective funding of civil-society initiatives, business-friendly media, etc. shape the agendas, policies, discourses, institutions and values that add up to an entire way of life. Importantly, these persuasive powers are backed up by coercive force. Corporate power is sometimes directly engaged with the state in co-managing dissent and surveillance, as in the semi-annual closed-door meetings around threats to 'energy infrastructure', beginning in 2005, of Canadian federal ministries, police and intelligence agencies, and corporate representatives granted high-level security clearance (Lukacs and Groves 2013). When hegemony fails, coercive force becomes visible. Otherwise, it is exercised routinely, both as the rule of (property) law and the 'dull compulsion of economic relations' (Marx 1867, Chapter 28) which subject workers and communities to the discipline of capital.

This framework not only created space for many specific research initiatives; it pointed to the sites and social forces that can counter corporate power – to the prospects for building a counter-hegemonic bloc which JP Sapinski and I (2018) took up in the first CMP book. Its main body traces how each modality of power operates; its last chapter considers how each modality can be undone – how corporate power can be eroded and replaced with forms of power (power-with and power-to) that promote economic democracy. The same framework organizes the analysis in our collection of CMP studies (see Carroll 2021c).

4 Evolution of the Project

As the project evolved, we found many ways to make good on our praxiological commitments. This was perhaps most evident in our knowledge-mobilization initiatives. As partners deeply embedded in progressive movements, CCPA and Parkland, as well as PAI, enabled the project to connect with large networks of activists and progressives, and provided capacity for elaborate media strategies in launching reports – not only in media releases but also in training scholars in media relations. Our organic public sociology efforts included webinars, workshops, book launches and a 2018 conference on fossil fuel accountability (in partnership with Westcoast Environmental Law, Greenpeace, 350.org and SumofUs.org) which attracted high-profile activists and activist-scholars, placing them in dialogue with BC-based climate justice activists. As we built an information-rich website we took advantage of the convivial relations our community-based partners had with online progressive independent media, which has emerged as a new media ecosystem organized around 'coopetition' more than competition (Beers 2017). Many of the short pieces on our multi-author blog, featuring timely expert commentary by team members, were also disseminated as articles in the *National Observer, Tyee* and *Narwhal* (all of which have won awards for investigative journalism).

These activities helped solidify our community of practice, as did three summer institutes at the University of Victoria, which attracted scores of graduate students from across Canada to an intensive graduate-level course on 'corporate power, fossil capital, climate crisis', at which CMP team members – researchers and activists – headed up panel discussions. As Burawoy (2005) observed, one of sociology's most important publics is students. Our summer institutes have been venues for developing new cadres of climate-justice activists.

Last but not least, we uploaded our database on the fossil-capital elite and its ties to other corporations and civil-society organizations, to PAI's LittleSis website. This empowered community researchers and journalists to do their own analyses of the fossil-capital power bloc. As part of this work, we developed case studies of the key organizations within the regime of obstruction, the 'Fossil Power Top 50', reversing the cloying 'Fortune 500' celebrations of corporate power in the business press. The Top 50 conveyed the gist of our Gramscian analysis to a wide public, as we identified the 'emitters' (fossil-capital corporations), 'enablers' (financial institutions and captured regulators) and 'legitimators' (industry associations, think tanks, lobby groups, business councils and pro-oil advocacy groups) that sustain the regime of obstruction.[8] Launched in 2019, this participatory-research initiative was amplified in a series of workshops and webinars through which we have been training activists, journalists and concerned citizens in the use of LittleSis's interactive network-visualization tool, Oligrapher. A recent training webinar (February 17, 2021) attracted 200 participants.

On the research side of the project, we developed an *open* research program, evolving as its target evolved and hence flexible in responding to events in a changing conjuncture. In catapulting Canada to the 'energy superpower' level, massive investment in extractive operations would need to be matched

---

8   https://www.corporatemapping.ca/database/

by correspondingly massive investment in new pipelines. Blocking the latter could deter investment in the former. To counter the misinformation, pumped out by both industry and government, about the need for new pipelines CMP team member David Hughes, a prominent earth scientist, wrote a series of in-depth reports (e.g., Hughes 2018). These nontechnical, graphics-rich documents, complemented by shorter pieces and extensive media interviews, used scenarios based on Canada's commitments under the 2015 Paris agreement to establish that existing transportation infrastructure could handle the traffic. This provided evidence-based ammunition to Indigenous and environmental activists campaigning to block the construction of new pipelines. Other CMP team members explored how resistance to pipeline projects reveals power at work, thereby disrupting hegemony, as in Karena Shaw's study of flashpoints along the proposed TransMountain Expansion. This flashpoint (ongoing as I write this), where innovative direct actions have garnered extensive media coverage, 'has expanded many people's sense of what is possible, and what is desirable, as well as pointing to some of the blockages obstructing the needed transition' (2021: 412).

Some of the research output from our studies of the organization of fossil-capital power (including its financial enablement) within the economy, its reach into political and civil society, and grassroots resistance was compiled into *Regime of Obstruction*. In that volume we mapped a tightly knit, local network of Canada-based fossil-capital firms, linked through interlocking directorates into the broader national and global power structure largely via mediating relations involving the largest fossil-capital corporations and financial institutions (Carroll 2021a). Paralleling that structure of corporate-elite integration, we documented a pervasive pattern of fossil-capital reach into several domains of political life and civil society, forming a single, connected elite network centred in Alberta yet linked to the central Canadian corporate elite through hegemonic capitalist organizations, including major financial companies (Carroll et al. 2021). Apart from that 500-page volume (available free as a pdf at https://www.aupress.ca/books/120293-regime-of-obstruction/, reflecting our open-access policy), many of our deliverables have appeared in a wide range of professional social-science journals. For instance, Hudson and Bowness (2021:3) identified, in the loans, shareholdings and directorate interlocks linking the major financial and fossil-capital players, 'the enabling structure' for a power bloc enforcing 'what appears to be a unified, hegemonic, capitalist interest in the long-term maintenance of the fossil energy sector.' Typically, however, our research first appeared online, at our website and related platforms, as public-facing reports written in accessible prose, and released with robust media strategies to maximize political impact.

5   Emerging Strategies

As the 21st Century's second decade closed out, the evolving conjuncture and the shifting correlation of forces within it inspired new initiatives within our project. Already in 2015, the fossil-fuel divestment movement, inspired by the 1980s campaign against South African Apartheid and the contemporary campaign against Israeli apartheid, had gained momentum on some university campuses and with some municipal governments. As I write this chapter six years later, the movement (helped along by the souring profit prospects of fossil capital, Stankiewicz 2020) has become an important component of climate-justice activism. Given fossil capital's dependence on financing for massive fixed-capital investments, we began to realize that our commodity-chain analysis needed to commence one step before the circuit of industrial capital, M-C ... P ... C'-M'. Emilia Belliveau, James Rowe and Jessica Dempsey (2021) took the concept of 'flashpoints' beyond the site-bound concept inspired to some extent by Naomi Klein's (2014) analysis of 'blockadia' (which highlighted direct resistance to the building of new fossil-capital infrastructure). They developed an interpretation of divestment as a political intervention in the commodity chain, at the point of finance. Although anti-capitalist critics have sometimes dismissed divestment as a co-opted politics that produces no more than a shift in investment portfolios, Belliveau's et al interviews with divestment campaigners revealed strong anti-capitalist commitments, despite the movement's pragmatic external messaging. The latter may not inspire a storming of the ramparts but does open conversations challenging the legitimacy and economic viability of big carbon, while attracting new activists to climate justice. On this basis, Belliveau and her colleagues presented divestment as a non-reformist reform in André Gorz's (1967) sense – disturbing the capitalist status quo in ways that build popular power.

Our team also tracked the evolving strategies for organizing consent to continued carbon extraction. In their research on pipeline politics in northwestern British Columbia, Fiona MacPhail and Paul Bowles developed a typology of flashpoints that foregrounded the enabling conditions for effective coalition-formation and thus effective anti-pipeline campaigns (MacPhail and Bowles 2021b). Yet the coalition of Indigenous communities, ranchers, landowners, trade unionists and environmentalists that blocked the Northern Gateway tar sands pipeline project in 2015–2016 splintered two years later, as the fossil-capital bloc devised new strategies for legitimating a proposed natural-gas pipeline. The 'state-corporate nexus' recruited local mayors as well as Indigenous band councils through financial agreements and donations to local community projects, and reframed natural gas as a 'clean energy' 'transition fuel' that could substitute for coal in China and other destinations (MacPhail and Bowles 2021a). By winning a modicum of 'social license' in this way, fossil capital and its allies weakened the resistance, although protests and blockades have continued, along with repression from the Royal Canadian Mounted Police (Kwan 2021).

Alongside these developments, we tracked other emergent strategies and discourses from the side of fossil capital, in particular, 'new climate denialism' and the rise of 'extractive populism'. The former, first noted in a public-facing blog by Klein and Daub (2016) and mainly deployed from the top down, acknowledges fossil capital's central role in the climate crisis but denies the need to decarbonize energy systems at a pace commensurate with what we know from climate science. Informed by ecological modernization as a pathway to 'clean growth', new denialism trumpets market-based and technological fixes that leave corporate power intact while opening new fields for accumulation. Building on earlier formulations (in particular, Derber's 2010 distinction between 'stage 1' and 'stage 2' climate denialism), 'new denialism' became a way for us to track the shift in rhetoric that accompanies the transition to climate capitalism (discussed below). Daub et al. (2021: 235) case studies of new denialism in action led them to a multifaceted typology highlighting key discursive, strategic and policy contrasts between 'traditional' and 'new' denialism. As climate breakdown becomes more visible and as oppositional forces gain strength, New Denialism partially supplants traditional denialism as 'a strategic effort to proactively define the solutions to climate change in a manner that mitigates the threat of action, to protect not only the interests of producer industries and governments but also the larger economic regime' (ibid.: 238).

But only partially. In Canada, traditional denial increasingly finds expression in extractive populism, which has emerged as a response to the perceived threat of even the gently incremental policies favored by new denial proponents (Carroll, Daub and Gunster 2022). A research team headed by Shane Gunster identified extractive populism as an emergent discourse, sometimes promoted through astro-turf platforms like CAPP's energycitizens.ca, but often developing from the conservative grassroots (like Canadaaction.ca). They defined extractive populism as 'an emerging effort to position extractivism as under attack from elites, as an economic and political project that demands popular mobilization to defend, and as a democratic expression of the public will to fight for an industry that serves the common good' (Gunster et al. 2021: 196). Gunster et al. study of the narratives and tropes of online pro-industry populism revealed 'how the skillful but partial assemblage of factual raw material by these groups constructs a world view that is simultaneously compelling and pernicious ... transforming alienated workers and other pro-industry individuals into an engaged petro-public that can forcefully advocate for the sector in social media, everyday life, and the public sphere.' (ibid 218–19).

Clearly, new climate denialism and extractive populism tell different stories, to different publics. Yet within the regime of obstruction, the tensions between them are hardly a liability. In postmodern times of cultural fragmentation, such ideological diversification can mobilize a range of elite, mainstream and fringe constituencies, satisfying the basic hegemonic requirement to organize consent, without building a national consensus (Carroll 2006:12).

Our praxiological commitments also led to the creation of two research streams within the project. In 2017 we added a fifth stream employing investigative journalism methods to uncover cases of fossil capital interests taking precedence over environmental concerns and/or public health and safety. Journalism and social science have a complex and sometimes conflictual relationship (Gans 2018), but our public sociology mandate encouraged us to build upon their potential synergies. Our investigative-journalism stream, often involving collaboration of journalists and social scientists, has produced numerous high-profile feature stories exposing egregious cases of regulatory capture, each resulting in major risks to public health and safety and the environment (e.g. Cribb et al. 2017), as well as an award-winning documentary, Crude Power http://www.crudepower.jschool.ca/. Concurrently, CMP media researcher Robert Hackett and colleagues have documented the pro-fossil biases in Canada's highly concentrated mainstream media, exposing a strong tendency to treat 'Big Oil with kid gloves, and environmentalists and climate scientists with hostility' (Hackett and Araza 2021; Hackett and Adams 2018).

A year later, we designated a new research stream on Indigenous issues and perspectives, addressing a major omission in the original project design. Decolonization has been pivotal in many struggles against extractive capitalism. In Canada, the resurgence of Indigenous culture and politics, building unevenly across half a century in response to the assimilationist 1969 federal White Paper and further catalyzed by the Truth and Reconciliation Commission (whose final report in 2015 castigated the state for its cultural-genocidal 'residential school' system), has become a strong current opposing settler-colonial capitalism (Manuel and Derrickson 2016). This stream has documented the subaltern status that Indigenous oil patch workers occupy in a labor market coded by both gender and race (Alook et al. 2021), while reflecting on the ideological ambivalence many Indigenous people experience, as currents of resurgence mix with the allure of escaping state-managed chronic poverty via deeper integration into consumer capitalism (Atleo 2021). But it has also supported the articulation and presentation of Indigenous-led alternatives to fossil capital (e.g., Shaw et al. 2017).[9]

These various developments in the research program were all part of a shift in emphasis, already planned at proposal stage, from *exposing* to various publics the irrationalities and injustices of the regime of obstruction to *proposing* alternatives to that regime. With the latter, we would take up Gramsci's (1977:65) question: 'how can the present be welded to the future, so that while satisfying the urgent necessities of the one we may work effectively to create and "anticipate" the other?' For Gramsci, such prefigurative change encompasses a multifaceted war of position to create, within economy, civil society and state, both the nascent social forms and the collective agency for a post-capitalist formation – in short, a counter-hegemonic historical bloc. As our research into the regime analyzed its practices and relations at different scales – from everyday life to global scale – our conceptualization of an alternative historical bloc and its transformative project also took on a multi-scalar form (Carroll 2021b:477–81).

We found a serviceable encapsulation of this project in the concept of 'energy democracy'. This framing was introduced to academe from the climate-justice movement by Kunze and Becker (2014: 8) as a project 'capable of integrating energy and climate struggles,' grounded on the understanding that decisions that shape our lives should be made democratically and without regard to the principle of profit (cf. Szulecki 2018). Energy democracy portends a double power shift, from fossil power to renewables and from the power-over of corporate oligarchy to participatory democracy. This means localizing energy production, where feasible, and implementing complementary non-reformist reforms such as enhanced and free public transit, but it also invokes climate justice as global transformation, implying a shift toward democratic eco-socialism (including global resource management in the service of social justice, Candeias 2013: 19).

---

9 Since 2020 the CMP has been supporting Indigenous Climate Action's Decolonizing Climate Policy Project, whose two stages begin with an analysis and critique of recent federal climate plans, followed by the formulation of Indigenous-led climate policy, guided by an Advisory Council of Indigenous climate leaders tasked with gathering climate policy ideas from Indigenous peoples across Canada. See Indigenous Climate Action (2021). https://www.indigenousclimateaction.com/entries/advisory-council-announcement-for-decolonizing-climate-policy-project.

6   Energy Democracy as a 3-D Project

As a multi-scalar bundle of non-reformist reforms, inclining toward green democratic socialism, energy democracy contends with a regime of obstruction that is itself in transition toward climate capitalism. In Canada, the hybrid project of fossil and climate capitalism, evident in federal and provincial climate plans, conserves much of the fossil-capital bloc while managing a passive revolution toward clean growth.[10] The same transition is evident internationally, and symbolized in corporate rebranding, as colossal fossils like BP move to shift their image from Big Oil to Big Energy (Reguly 2021). The strategy is to enable valorization of existing fossil capital while market forces (incentivized by carbon taxes and cap-and-trade measures) and state-supported technological changes (from efficiency improvements to geoengineering) usher in a lower-carbon future, under a slightly reconstituted power bloc. This is a scheme for a molecular shift in the historical bloc, as fossil capital goes into managed decline while renewable-energy substitutes and associated workforces develop under the control of big capital. Although Green New Deal and Managed Decline initiatives are distinct from the carbon-pricing and geoengineering schemes that suit capital most directly, in themselves they do not break with the logic of climate capitalism (Eaton 2021). Green New Deal reforms emphasize the need for a just transition, but (like the original New Deal) operate largely within a demand-side framework that does not challenge capitalist control of the means of production. Managed Decline (sunsetting the production of fossil fuels) does attend to the supply side of the problem – the need to decarbonize the forces of production – but is equally silent on transforming the relations of production.

For the green left, this suggests, as a strategic path forward, pushing for energy democracy in both its local and global climate-justice versions, as circumstances permit, while pushing back against co-optative tendencies that might circumscribe the Green New Deal within purely redistributive reform and restrict Managed Decline to a technocratic wind-down, repressing issues of corporate power. Our diagnosis of the regime of obstruction recommends

---

10   As I write this, the latest iteration in this hybrid project is the Alberta–Canada Carbon Capture, Utilization and Storage (CCUS) Steering Committee, announced on 8 March 2021. In the words of Seamus O'Regan Jr., Canada's Minister of Natural Resources, 'Carbon capture technology creates jobs, lowers emissions and increases our competitiveness. It's how we get to net zero.' https://www.canada.ca/en/natural-resources-canada/news/2021/03/canada-and-alberta-launch-steering-committee-to-advance-ccus.html

the pursuit of an anti-passive revolution[11] that features what Vishwas Satgar terms a 'deep just transition'[12] and a democratically managed wind-down. Globally, and particularly in settler-capitalist states, this counter-hegemonic project must incorporate, besides decarbonization and democratization, a third 'D': decolonization. In Canada, as CMP researcher Emily Eaton has argued, 'There can be no justice in just transition without Indigenous leadership on climate change policy, without expanding the 0.2% land base[13] and economies of Indigenous Nations, nor without state recognition of Indigenous jurisdiction over their full territories' (2021: 9). This 'Three D' approach is at the centre of a public-facing book now in progress (Alook, Eaton et al. forthcoming), following on the heels of Seth Klein (2020), who reflected on the successes (and limits) of World War Two mobilization and offered a robust social-democratic policy framework for transitioning beyond carbon. These accessible products of the Corporate Mapping Project are praxiological contributions to shifting the balance of politico-cultural forces, within an ongoing war of position.

Indeed, through a Gramscian lens, one could view the Corporate Mapping Project as performing a dissection of hegemonic transition, from fossil capitalism to climate capitalism, dialectically joined with evidence-based contributions to building a counter-hegemonic historical bloc. But if, in the latter moment, 3-D energy democracy is a multi-scalar project, incorporating a range of non-reformist reforms within a war of position, our research also flags the need to widen the struggle beyond energy issues, to target the *enablers* and *legitimators* of fossil capital. Given the close, symbiotic relation within which financial institutions enable fossil capital, it is clear that robust energy democracy must bring the financial sector itself under democratic control. Much the same can be said about the need to undo hegemonic corporate power within communications media, key legitimators of the industry and of corporate

---

11   As Simon (1982:49) suggests, the appropriate strategic response to a passive revolution is an anti-passive revolution: a war of position that extends popular-democratic and class struggles 'so as to mobilize ever-wider sections of the population for democratic reforms.'

12   Much of the literature on just transition calls simply for retraining workers who are displaced as fossil fuels give way to renewables. In Satgar's view, a *deep* just transition entails much more. Such transformation must (1) address the multiple, systemic crises of capitalist civilization, (2) shift from capital's growth principle to a principle of sustaining life, for the present and for future generations and (3) give the transition a multilinearity, so that deep democratization occurs 'at different scales, locales and tempos, in workplaces, communities, civil society, on the internet (cyber democracy), and throughout the state and public sphere' (2018: 64–5).

13   The landmass occupied by Indigenous peoples in Canada has declined from 100% at the beginning of colonization to 0.2% today (Manuel 2017) – WKC.

capitalism generally: to 'remake media' along democratic lines (Hackett and Carroll 2006). The challenge is to articulate the social forces striving for 3-D energy democracy into an expansive and coherent bloc extending to other sectors of capital and the integral state. The struggle against fossil capital can leverage a wider struggle for green democratic socialism.

7   Conclusion

Marx matters, now more than ever. What matters in Marx, and in the rich Marxist tradition, is both the critical theorizing of capitalist modernity and the insistence on the dialectical unity of theory and practice, obliging Marxists to go beyond mere interpretations of our troubled world. The CMP's praxiological interventions have addressed the climate crisis in dialogue and solidarity with popular movements and currents opposing fossil capitalism and climate capitalism. The process has been one of co-learning, integrating the practical knowledge gained from struggle with theoretical knowledge from historical materialism and related formulations.

Perhaps the finest example of this can be seen on Indigenous issues, where ongoing colonization accords political priority to self-determination. CMP initiatives in this field have built ethico-political relations of allyship, supporting the resurgence of Indigeneity that is a crucial force both in land-based resistance to fossil capital and in the creation of post-carbon alternatives. As Algonquin Anishinaabe-kwe scholar Lynn Gehl (undated) notes, responsible allies 'understand that they are secondary to the Indigenous people that they are working with and that they seek to serve' (quoted in Bishop 2016: 98). Yet Gehl goes on to observe that sometimes allies are manipulated to serve the interests of entrenched leadership, rather than the needs of the people. Indeed, the colonial apparatus of the Canadian state, combined with capitalist intrusions onto Indigenous land, has given rise to a stratum of neo-colonial Indigenous leadership, creating 'deep political divisions between the grassroots and the Indigenous establishment' (Manuel 2017: 133–4).

Recognizing this reality, our project has engaged with the anti-colonial (and anti-extractivist) Indigenous current, to which we could be of service developing evidence-based knowledge that contributes to what Gramsci termed a process of intellectual and moral reformation (Robinson 2005). Importantly, the process has been reciprocal (Reed 2013). The strongly collectivist and ecological beliefs and practices of Indigenous communities, maintained over centuries of colonization, now provide vision and inspiration for non-Indigenous people. By the same token, Indigenous scholar-activists have turned to Marxism in their critiques of colonization (e.g., Coulthard 2014; Dunbar-Ortiz 2016). CMP Indigenous-focused initiatives have thus engaged in co-learning within a decolonizing framework and in facilitating the development of Indigenous-led alternatives to fossil capital. The left needs the communal vision and ethical sensibilities of Indigenous lifeways – encapsulated in *bien vivir* – but Indigenous peoples need Marxist analysis of capitalism and colonialism, as a resource for Indigenous resurgence and a counterweight to the lure of bourgeois modernization. Ultimately, in settler-capitalist formations, any serious movement toward socialism will require substantial Indigenous leadership in addressing the horrific legacy of ongoing colonization. But at the same time, Indigenous resurgence can only succeed as part of a broader historical bloc: 'without mass movements for structural transformation of the colonial/capitalist state, Indigenous self-determination cannot be realised' (Dunbar-Ortiz 2016: 86).

What emerges from our work within the CMP is an appreciation of Harvey's thesis that capitalism has co-evolved as 'a socio-ecological totality' (2011: 128) across several dialectically related 'activity spheres' – technologies and organizational forms, social relations, institutional and administrative arrangements, production and labor processes, relations to nature, social reproduction, and mental conceptions of the world (2011: 123). From this complex perspective on capitalist development, Harvey draws an important conclusion. If revolutionary anti-capitalism

> cannot move within, across and through the different spheres then it will ultimately go nowhere at all. Recognizing this, it becomes imperative to envision alliances between a whole range of social forces configured around the different spheres (2011: 138).

'The trick', Harvey continues, 'is to keep the political movement moving from one moment to another in mutually reinforcing ways' (2011: 229). The CMP has proceeded from one key sector of industrial capital in one country, inquiring into how other activity spheres are implicated, and thereby exploring, as much as possible, the full relationality of fossil capital and its opposition.[14]

Perhaps by implication, praxiological action research more generally can benefit from striving for a holistic approach within any project, identifying

---

14   Thomas Muhr and colleagues (2013:12ff) have applied this framework to left movements and regimes in the Latin American pink tides.

various points of inquiry and practical intervention – in economic, political and cultural fields, in addressing how a multi-scalar historical bloc can
be pulled together within a coherent, co-revolutionary project that keeps the
movement moving.

References

Adkin, Laurie E. (ed.) (2016) *First World Petro-Politics: The Political Ecology and Governance of Alberta*. Toronto: University of Toronto Press.

Alook, Angele, Emily Eaton, David Gray-Donald, Joel Laforest, Crystal Lameman and Bronwen Tucker (forthcoming) *Righting Relations: Winning a Just Transition in So-called Canada*. Toronto: Lorimer.

Anderson, Perry (1976) *Considerations on Western Marxism*. London: Verso 1976.

Banerjee, Neela, Lisa Song and David Hasemyer (2015) 'Exxon's own research confirmed fossil fuels' role in global warming decades ago.' *Inside Climate News* September 16, https://insideclimatenews.org/news/16092015/exxons-own-research-confirmed-fossil-fuels-role-in-global-warming/.

Beers, David (2017) 'A good news story about the news in British Columbia.' *The Conversation* 8 November, https://theconversation.com/a-good-news-story-about-the-news-in-british-columbia-87091 https://thetyee.ca/Mediacheck/2017/02/06/New-Canadian-Media-Ecosystem/.

Bieler, Andreas and Adam David Morton (2018) *Global Capitalism, Global War, Global Crisis*. Cambridge: Cambridge University Press.

Buddharaks, Watcharabon (2018) 'Big Society, Free Economy, and Strong State: Bonefeld's Open Marxism and the Critique of Political Economy.' *Journal of Social Sciences* 48 (1): 59–74.

Burawoy, Michael (2005) '2004 ASA Presidential Address: For Public Sociology.' *American Sociological Review* 70: 4–28.

Burck, Jan, Ursula Hagen, Christoph Bals, Niklas Hohne and Leonardo Nascimento (2020) *2021 Climate Change Performance Index Results*. Berlin: GermanWatch https://ccpi.org/download/the-climate-change-performance-index-2021/.

Candeias, Mario (2013) *Green Transformation: Competing Strategic Projects*. Translated by Alexander Gallas. Berlin: Rosa Luxemburg Foundation. http://www.rosalux-nyc.org/green-transformation.

Carroll, William K. (ed.) (2004) *Critical Strategies for Social Research*. Toronto: Canadian Scholars Press.

Carroll, William K. (2006) 'Hegemony, Counter-Hegemony, Anti-Hegemony'. *Socialist Studies* 2(2): 9–43.

Carroll, William K. (2010a) *Corporate Power in a Globalizing World*, revised edition. Toronto: Oxford University Press.

Carroll, William K. (2010b) *The Making of a Transnational Capitalist Class*. London: Zed Books.

Carroll, William K. (2016) *Expose, Oppose Propose: Alternative Policy Groups and the Struggle for Global Justice*. London: Zed Books.

Carroll, William K. (2021a) 'Canada's fossil-capital elite: A tangled web of corporate power.' Pp. 141–66 in William K. Carroll (ed.) *Regime of Obstruction*. Edmonton: AU Press.

Carroll, William K. (2021b) 'Conclusion: Prospects for energy democracy in the face of passive revolution.' Pp. 475–499 in William K. Carroll (ed.) *Regime of Obstruction*. Edmonton: AU Press.

Carroll, William K. (ed.) (2021c) *Regime of Obstruction: How Corporate Power Blocks Energy Democracy*. Edmonton: AU Press.

Carroll, William K. and Shannon Daub (2014) *Mapping the Power of the Carbon-Extractive Corporate Resource Sector*. Proposal to the Social Sciences and Humanities Research Council of Canada. Victoria: University of Victoria, October.

Carroll, William K., Shannon Daub and Shane Gunster (2022) 'Regime of Obstruction: Fossil capitalism and the many facets of climate denial in Canada.' In David Tindall, Mark C.J. Stoddard, and Riley E. Dunlap (eds.) *Handbook of Anti-Environmentalism*. Cheltenham: Edward Elgar, in press.

Carroll, William K. and David Huxtable (2014) 'Building Capacity for Alternative Knowledge: The Canadian Centre for Policy Alternatives.' *Canadian Review of Social Policy* 70: 93–111.

Carroll, William K. and Murray Shaw (2001) 'Consolidating a neoliberal policy bloc in Canada, 1976 to 1996.' *Canadian Public Policy* 27:195–217.

Carroll, William K. and J.P. Sapinski (2018) *Organizing the 1%: How Corporate Power Works*. Halifax: Fernwood Publishing.

Coulthard, Glen Sean (2014) *Red Skin, White Masks*. Minneapolis: University of Minnesota Press.

Cox, Sarah (2018) 'Canada leads G7 in oil and gas subsidies: new report.' *The Narwhal*, 4 June https://thenarwhal.ca/canada-leads-g7-in-oil-and-gas-subsidies-new-report/.

Cribb, R., S. Sonntag, P.W. Elliott and E. McSheffery (2017) 'That rotten stench in the air? It's the smell of deadly gas and secrecy.' Toronto *Star*, Oct. 1 https://www.thestar.com/news/canada/2017/10/01/that-rotten-stench-in-the-air-its-the-smell-of-deadly-gas-and-secrecy.html.

Daub, Shannon, Gwendolyn Blue, Lise Rajewicz, and Zoë Yunker (2021) 'Episodes in the New Climate Denialism.' Pp. 225–248 in William K. Carroll (ed.) *Regime of Obstruction*. Edmonton: AU Press.

Derber, Charles (2010) *Greed to Green*. London: Routledge.

Domhoff, G. William (ed.) (1980) *Power Structure Research*. Sage Publications, Beverly Hills (CA).

Domhoff, G. William (2009) *Who Rules America?* sixth edition. McGraw-Hill, New York.

Dunbar-Ortiz, Roxanne A. (2016) 'The relationship between Marxism and Indigenous struggles and implications of the theoretical framework for international Indigenous struggles.' *Historical Materialism* 24:76–91.

Eaton, Emily (2021) 'Approaches to energy transitions: Carbon pricing, managed decline, and/or green new deal?' *Geography Compass* 15(2):e12554. https://doi.org/10.1111/gec3.12554.

Eisenstein, Hester (2016) *Feminism Seduced: How Global Elites Use Women's Labor and Ideas to Exploit the World*. London: Routledge.

Fraser, Nancy (2013) *Fortunes of Feminism*. London: Verso.

Gans, Herbert J. (2018) 'Sociology and Journalism: A Comparative Analysis.' *Contemporary Sociology* 47(1):3–10.

Gehl, Lynn (undated) *Ally Bill of Responsibilities*. www.lynngehl.com.

Gramsci, Antonio (1977) *Selections from Political Writings, 1910–1920*. New York: International Publishers.

Gunster, Shane, Robert Neubauer, John Bermingham, and Alicia Massie (2021) '"Our Oil": Extractive Populism in Canadian Social Media.' Pp. 197–224 in in William K. Carroll (ed.) *Regime of Obstruction*. Edmonton: AU Press.

Gutstein, Donald (2021) *Fossilized Finance: How Canada's banks enable oil and gas production*. Corporate Mapping Project, April 29, https://www.corporatemapping.ca/fossilized-finance-how-canadas-banks-enable-oil-and-gas-production/.

Hackett, Robert A. and William K. Carroll (2006) *Remaking Media: The Struggle to Democratize Public Communication*. London: Routledge.

Hackett, Robert A. and Philippa R. Adams (2018) *Jobs vs the Environment? Mainstream and alternative media coverage of pipeline controversies*. Corporate Mapping Project, 19 December https://www.corporatemapping.ca/jobs-vs-environment/.

Hackett, Robert A. and Hanna Araza (2021) 'Petromedia: Postmedia and Big Oil.' *National Observer* April 29, https://www.nationalobserver.com/2021/04/29/opinion/petromedia-how-postmedia-gives-big-ink-big-oil.

Hall, Budd L (1979) 'Knowledge as a Commodity and Participatory Research.' *Prospects* 9(4):393–408.

Harvey, David (2011) *The Enigma of Capital*. New York: Oxford University Press.

Hudson, Mark and Evan Bowness (2021) 'Finance and fossil capital: A community divided?' *The Extractive Industries and Society* 8(1):383–394.

Hughes, David (2018) *Canada's Energy Outlook*. Corporate Mapping Project, 1 May https://www.corporatemapping.ca/energy-outlook/.

Indigenous Climate Action (2021) *Decolonizing Climate Policy in Canada: Report from Phase One*. 29 March, https://www.indigenousclimateaction.com/entries/new-ica -report-critique-of-federal-climate-policy-plans.

Kirsch, Alison et al. (2020) *Banking on Climate Change: Fossil Fuel Finance Report 2020*. San Francisco: Rainforest Action Network, 18 March https://www.ran.org/wp-cont ent/uploads/2020/03/Banking_on_Climate_Change__2020_vF.pdf.

Klein, Seth (2020) *A Good War: Mobilizing Canada for the Climate Emergency*. Vancouver: ECW Press.

Klein, Seth and Daub, Shannon. (2016) 'The new climate denialism: time for an inter-vention.' Corporate Mapping Project, 30 September https://www.corporatemapp ing.ca/the-new-climate-denialism-time-for-an-intervention/.

Kunze, C. and Becker, D. (2014) *Energy democracy in Europe. A survey and outlook*. Brussels: Rosa-Luxemburg-Stiftung https://www.rosalux.de/fileadmin/rls_uploads/ pdfs/sonst_publikationen/Energy-democracy-in-Europe.pdf.

Kwan, Braela (2021) 'For BC's two pipeline fights, it's Spring forward.' *The Tyee* 22 March, https://thetyee.ca/News/2021/03/22/BC-Two-Pipeline-Fights-Spring-Forward/.

Lukacs, Martin and Tim Groves (2013) 'Canadian spies met with energy firms, doc-uments reveal.' *Guardian* 9 October https://www.theguardian.com/environment/ 2013/oct/09/canadian-spies-met-energy-firms-documents.

MacPhail, Fiona, and Paul Bowles (2021a) 'Fractured alliance: state-corporate actions and fossil fuel resistance in northwest British Columbia, Canada.' *Journal of Political Ecology* (in press).

MacPhail, Fiona, and Paul Bowles (2021b) 'Toward a typology of fossil fuel flash-points: The potential for coalition building.' Pp. 425–48 in William K. Carroll (ed.) *Regime of Obstruction*. Edmonton: AU Press.

Manuel, Arthur and Ronald Derrickson (2016) *Unsettling Canada: A National Wake-Up Call*. Toronto: Between the Lines.

Manuel, Arthur (2017) *The Reconciliation Manifesto: Recovering the land, Rebuilding the Economy*. Toronto: Lorimer.

Marx, Karl (1845) 'Theses on Feurbach.' Marxist Internet Archive https://www.marxi sts.org/archive/marx/works/1845/theses/theses.htm.

Marx, Karl (1867) *Capital* volume 1, Chapter 28. Marxist Internet Archive https://www .marxists.org/archive/marx/works/1867-c1/ch28.htm.

Mayo, Peter (2020) 'Praxis in Paulo Freire's emancipatory politics.' *International Critical Thought*, 10:3, 454–472, DOI: 10.1080/21598282.2020.1846585.

McCormack, Geoffrey and Thom Workman (2015) *The Servant State: Overseeing Capital Accumulation in Canada*. Halifax: Fernwood Publishing.

Muhr, Thomas (ed.) (2013) *Counter-Globalization and Socialism in the 21st Century*. London: Routledge.

O'Conner, James (1973) *The Fiscal Crisis of the State*. New York: St. Martin's Press.

O'Connor, James (1987) *The Meaning of Crisis*. Oxford: Basil Blackwell.

O'Kane, Chris (2020) 'Capital, the state, and economic policy: Bringing Open Marxist critical political economy back into contemporary Heterodox Economics.' *Review of Radical Political Economics* 52: 684–692.

Reed, Jean-Pierre (2013) 'Theorist of subaltern subjectivity: Antonio Gramsci, popular beliefs, political passion, and reciprocal learning.' *Critical Sociology, 39*(4): 561–591. https://doi.org/10.1177/0896920512437391.

Reguly, Eric (2021) 'Message from the Norway wealth fund to oil sands companies: Clean up your act or suffer.' Toronto *Globe and Mail*, 26 February https://www.theglobe andmail.com/business/commentary/article-message-from-the-norway-wealth -fund-to-oil-sands-companies-clean-up/.

Reitan, Ruth and Shannon Gibson (2012) 'Climate change or social change? Environmental and leftist praxis and Participatory Action Research.' *Globalizations*, 9:3, 395–410.

Robinson, A. (2005) 'Toward intellectual transformation: The critique of common sense and the forgotten revolutionary project of Gramscian theory.' *Critical Review of International Social and Political Philosophy* 26(4): 469–481.

Satgar, Vishwas (2018) "The Climate Crisis and Systemic Alternatives." In *The Climate Crisis: South African and Global Democratic Eco-socialist Alternatives*, edited by Vishwas Satgar, 1–27. Johannesburg: Wits University Press.

Shabecoff, Philip (1988) 'Global Warming has begun, expert tells Senate.' *New York Times*, June 24, 1988. https://www.nytimes.com/1988/06/24/us/global-warming -has-begun-expert-tells-senate.html.

Shaw, Karena (2021) 'Flashpoints of possibility: What resistance reveals about path-ways toward energy transition.' Pp. 395–424 in William K. Carroll (ed.) *Regime of Obstruction*. Edmonton: AU Press.

Shaw, Karena, Dana Cook, Eryn Fitzgerald and Judith (Kekinusuqs) Sayers (2017) 'BC First Nations are poised to lead the renewable energy transition.' Corporate Mapping Project, 12 October https://www.corporatemapping.ca/bc-first-nations -are-poised-to-lead-the-renewable-energy-transition/.

Simon, Roger (1982) *Gramsci's Political Thought*. London: Lawrence and Wishart.

Smith, Dorothy E. (2005) *Institutional Ethnography. A Sociology for People*. Lanham MD: Altamira Press.

Stankiewicz, Kevin (2020) 'There's no more money to be made in oil and gas stocks, Jim Cramer says.' CNBC, 3 February, https://www.cnbc.com/2020/02/03/jim-cra mer-the-profit-in-oil-and-gas-stocks-is-drying-up.html.

Sum, Ngai-Ling and Bob Jessop (2014) *Towards a Cultural Political Economy: Putting Culture in its Place in Political Economy*. Cheltenham: Edward Elgar.

Szulecki, K. (2018) Conceptualizing energy democracy. *Environmental Politics*, 27(1), 21–41. https://doi.org/10.1080/09644016.2017.1387294.

Taber, Jane (2006) 'PM brands Canada an "energy superpower." ' Toronto *Globe and Mail*, 15 July https://www.theglobeandmail.com/news/world/pm-brands-canada -an-energy-superpower/article1105875/.

United Nations Framework Convention on Climate Change (2007) *Climate Change: Impacts, Vulnerabilities and Adaptation in Developing Countries*. Bonn: Climate Change Secretariat.

Urry, John (1981) *The Anatomy of Capitalist Societies*. New York: Macmillan.

Wenger-Trayner, Etienne and Beverley Wenger-Trayner (2018) 'Introduction to communities of practice.' https://wenger-trayner.com/introduction-to-communities -of-practice/.

Whyte, David (2020) *Ecocide: Kill the Corporation before It Kills Us*. Manchester: Manchester University Press.

Zhou, C., M.D. Zelinka, A.E. Dessler et al. (2021) 'Greater committed warming after accounting for the pattern effect.' *Nature Climate Change* 11:132–136 https://doi.org/ 10.1038/s41558-020-00955-x.

CHAPTER 11

The Capitalist Racial State and Black Lives in Struggle

Rose M. Brewer

> Given the extended or integral state of late capitalism, racialization as a part of bourgeois hegemonic strategy informs not only state policies but also institutions and activities of civil society, and in so doing suppresses the potential for expansive democracy by reinforcing racial hierarchy and authoritarian statism founded on national chauvinism.
>
> E. SAN JUAN, JR. 1989: 63

∵

1 Introduction: Dialectic of the Capitalist Racial State and Black Struggle

My mind stays on Ferguson, Baltimore, Minneapolis, and the hundreds of other cities that have risen up in rebellion in the US during the past 50 plus years. My mind stays on freedom. At the center of the rebellions is Black resistance against police violence, economic dispossession, and white supremacy. This rise-up is laser focused on state violence leveled at Black lives/communities. Whether Detroit in 1967 or Minneapolis in 2020 the Black clarion call is to stop killing us. There is the never-ending dance against the system of capitalist heteropatriarchal white supremacy. Black dispossession is centered given the capitalist racial state response. As E. San Juan, Jr. articulated more than 30 years ago, racialization is part of bourgeois hegemonic strategy, informing not only state policies but institutions and activities of civil society. This should give us pause in 2021, posing the questions of why and what is to be done through interrogation of the capitalist racial state. The US capitalist racial state builds power through racialized violence and exclusion to advance its economic interests and power (Lebowitz 1995) Capitalist interests are protected and solidified as the ruling class asserts its common prerogatives through state practice (Jessop 2013). The capitalist state works to legitimate through consent and if not consent, multiple mechanisms of threat, coercion, and violence. Yet this cannot be a singular assessment, certainly given theorizing beyond a state that only considers capital's needs and tendencies and not those of workers contends Lebowitz (1995). He goes on to say, "that in short, to consider the capitalist state, we need to situate it within the totality that is capitalism, we need to situate it within the totality that is capitalism as a whole, as the concentration of bourgeois society." Black Neo-Marxist feminists have mediated these conceptions of the capitalist racial state. As radical Black feminist geographer Ruth Wilson Gilmore contends, "the poverty that attaches to *race:* -as Immanuel Wallerstein exposes in "The Myrdal Legacy," racism is a necessary component, rather than a passing phase, of capitalism. The poverty that attaches to *gender*: women do two-thirds of the world's work for five percent of the income and one percent of the assets ..."

I contend that race and racial struggle under capitalism have always been at the center of capitalist state formation in the US. Given this, my argument unfolds thusly

1. The Kerner Commission as policy trope is threaded through as a partial case example of the machinations of the capitalist racial state.
2. Given the dialectic of the capitalist racial state and Black struggle, the argument draws upon a Black Marxist feminist articulation.
3. The historical underpinnings of the racial state and Black response and struggle against it are articulated as a key contradiction in the making of the capitalist racial state but has never transformed or completely dismantled it.
4. The centrality of capitalism and slavery in state construction are deeply intertwined. Black struggle continues as the core site of contest, resisting state violence into the 21st century.
5. The capitalist racial state must be contended with over the short and longer terms given its ongoing contradictions as a white supremacist, heteropatriarchal capitalist formation. The struggle continues in Minneapolis and beyond.

2   The Kerner Commission Redux: A Capitalist Racial State Consideration

In the wake of the urban rebellions of the l960s President Lyndon B. Johnson appointed an 11-member commission known as the Kerner Commission, established in 1967, to find out why (as it was put) the "riots" happened (Kerner

Report 2016. This response was rooted in the assumption that Black communities were responsible for the violence of the rebellion. State violence inculcated in the police was not scrutinized or interrogated. The key issue for the Commission was discovering who was involved, and what could be done. Apparently, Johnson's desire for a safe report exploded with the release of the Commission's findings (Gillion 2018). The Commission indicted white racism. But nothing was done to mitigate racial capitalism's violent impact on Black people. Lifting up this report provides some evidence of how the capitalist racial state responds to deeply rooted structural racism. It becomes one example in this interrogation of the racist capitalist state. As Gillon points out, the Commission, in the political terrain Johnson was maneuvering involved holding on to his liberal supporters and the southern conservatives (completely opposed the Commission). He needed them politically to win.

The Black radicals of the day indicted the structure of white supremacy and understood the sham of the Commission. Since the Brown v Board decision of 1954, little had changed for Black America. Brown did not, could not dismantle the system of capitalist exploitation or the Black internal colony that Black radicals in Detroit, L.A., Chicago, and other major cities lifted up.

These political realities run deep in the long durée of capitalist racial state formation in the US. The racial state manages Black rebellion largely by containment, cooptation, duplicity, or violent repression. George Bush lied about investing millions of dollars in Los Angeles after the 1992 uprising following the Rodney King verdict. The capitalist racial state would not allow LA's full reconstitution. The exoneration of the white cops responsible for the near fatal beating of King was true to form for the racial state. The dynamics of the capitalist state are exemplified whether at the level of Commissions such as Kerner, jury decisions as in the case of the all-white jury verdict in the Rodney King case or the FBI labeling and targeting Black Lives Matter activists as Black Identity Extremists (The Brennan Center for Justice 2020; see also Levin 2017).

These racial state responses set the context for understanding why the capitalist racial state is not held accountable. Even as the racial state gloms on to the justice narrative in the case of the recent indictment and guilty verdict of Dereck Chauvin in the George Floyd murder in Minneapolis on May 25, 2020, the fundamental underpinnings of state violence remain unaddressed. Weak police reform efforts such as George Floyd Act are not passed and languish in Congress currently. The chapter places these capitalist state responses in the context of its historical and current formation. Today's Black uprisings in the US are placed in the logic of the capitalist racial state and the dialectical interplay of Black fight back and struggle in this dynamic. The argument is made that the racial state is recalibrated in the context of Black struggle and resistance even though it has not been dismantled and transformed into a new social order. The struggle continues.

3   The Capitalist Racial State: A Black Marxist Feminist Lens

Who tells the story of how the capitalist racial state unfolds? How the story is told, and the precursor social dynamics, are key. A Black Marxist feminist lens is critical to the story craft of interrogating the capitalist racial state. The scholarship of political economist Rhonda Williams (1995) sets the stage . William's work is too little known. She died prematurely just as she was developing a neo-Marxist foundation of political economy rooted in a radical queer Black feminist articulation. She explained her position thusly: "gender, race and class as critical to class struggle and foundational to articulating the racial capitalist state". She asserts,

> Feminists continue to theorize the gendering of race and class in capitalist social formations. The experience and meaning of race and class within families, workplaces, kinship systems, workplaces, kinship systems, migratory communities, settler colonies, unions, clubs, and political movements is deeply gendered. To paraphrase Stuart Hall, if race is the modality in which class is lived, it is a gendered and multivalent modality as well.
>
> WILLIAMS 1993: 35

Relatedly radical Black feminist geographer Ruth Wilson Gilmore contends

> The poverty that attaches to *race* -as Immanuel Wallerstein exposes in "The Myrdal Legacy," racism is a necessary component, rather than a passing phase, of capitalism. The poverty that attaches to *gender*: According to the United Nations International Labor Organisation, women do two-thirds of the world's work for five percent of the income and one percent of the assets; since we know the poorest among us are people of color, these data quantify racism and sexism on a. global scale. The race/gender excess of these dead women is expendable enough for the LAPD to refuse to state categorically whether or not the murders have ceased ... War is the enemy of the poor. (1993: 34)

If we start from where we're at, and organize in and for work, conceived in the fullness of our imaginative powers, we might push and pull the current tendency of crisis away from a national resolution in fascism: terrorism, imprisonment, deportation, sterilization, state supervised death. All of these are features of everyday elements of life in California, in Arkansas, in Texas, New York, you name it. This is where we're at; where are we headed. (1993: 35)

I would say Minneapolis, MN.

4   Making the US Capitalist Racial State

Howard Winant and Michel Omi rightfully point out in their often-cited work on racial formation that race is a central organizing principle of American society (1994). Anthony Marx (2002) goes on to argue that state policies were built upon ideologies of racism but also but articulated through a deeply rooted class divide. State decisions aligned in a way that created as well as responded to racial divisions. As critical race theorists such as Crenshaw, et al. (1995) have argued, the creation of unjust laws was central to building the racial state and the US social order. White elites organized to legitimate the order once slavery was inculcated in the English colonies by the 17th century. Through law the owning class made slavery permanent in the English colonies for progeny of enslaved African women. This meant slavery in perpetuity. White settlerism and genocidal wars targeted Native Americans, and for those born of African women permanent bondage. The Naturalization Act of 1790 embedded whiteness into the law giving naturalized citizenship only to free white males with property. In the interest of national unity, wealth creation and racial bonding, the structuring of the racial state was well under way. Certainly, racism deflected attention away from class inequalities deeply evident among what would become the white population. Mills (1997) would call it the racial contract. This contract excluded Blacks from citizenship full humanity and rights. It would be the catalyst for Black resistance into the current period.

This racial contract was underwritten in blood and violently maintained. Indeed, it is difficult to understand today without interrogating the longer durée of anti-Blackness written into the US capitalist racial state, the constitution and state laws. While race is an idea that has no real biological meaning, it is socially powerful. This social creation was crucial to crafting a society that defined African peoples as inferior and as nonhuman. These conceptions were used to justify the exploitation of Black labor and the buying and selling of Black bodies. The reproductive and productive labor of Black enslaved women was fundamental to the expropriation for accumulation and building US racial capitalism. Racism was solidified in the context of enslavement – at least its legal parameters. It would take the racial science of the 19th century to fully refine the idea of inferior and superior races. This assumption and practice of racial hierarchy would set the parameters of racism in US society and structure the capitalist racial state for centuries. Racism, colonialism, patriarchy, and capitalism work in deep relationality with in structuring the capitalist racial state. This is the fundamental theorization of radical Black feminism.

The expansion of European colonialism into what became the Americas catalyzed the process. The Caribbean – Haiti, Jamaica, Cuba and South American Brazil were the initial sites of this wretched trade in humans (Williams 2021). Its stock and trade were the labor-intensive crop of sugar. African labor and indigenous lands would be the source for its production and the tremendous profits slavery would yield, building capitalism (Eric Williams). From the 15th century to the 19th this expropriation of Black labor would be the great engine of Europe's wealth. British Europe would colonize North America, and the colonies would ultimately become the site of a burgeoning slave trade (Cox 1948). The wealth of Europe was built on indigenous land, Black bodies and labor in the production of tobacco, rice, indigo and, of course, cotton.

It is clear that, over time, Africans would move in the English colonies of North America from being something akin to being free of slavery to a highly stigmatized permanent servitude to full scale enslavement for Africans. Charles Mills (1997) rightly points out that political doctrines framing this nation were, in fact, a particular kind of contract, not liberty and justice and freedom for all, just for some. He calls this the racial contract that underpins US society. It is rooted in the ideology of white supremacy. Structurally, it is a system in which all whites would have guarantees of citizenship –life, liberty, and the pursuit of happiness, though divided by class and Blackness would become the great signifier of inferiority.

5 Slavery: State Policies and Early Racial Thinking

State policies which encoded racism emerged out of another pressing demand: how was white unity to be established especially in the wake of tensions about slavery, not fully embraced by all the colonists? State configuration involved incorporation of racist policy and practice as well as using race as the practical glue for nation building, reshaped class divides through the increasing solidification of whiteness. Indeed, by the establishment of the new nation in the 18th century it was clear that Blackness was heavily stigmatized, othered and unprotected. Nonetheless, the story is more complicated and racial thinking was constructed over time rather than immediately in deep conflict and interplay with religion and class. Nonetheless the ongoing dynamic of Black resistance played out in a number of ways. There were numerous slave rebellions (Aptheker 1937.).

The ongoing rebellions and resistance of the enslaved Africans was persistent. Quite notable was Maroonage. Beginning in the late 17th century fled plantations in the southern American colonies and joined with the newly formed Seminole Confederacy in Spanish-colonized Florida (Gil 2014). Africans made common call with them, fought with the Seminole Confederacy against the slave holders, destabilizing and complicating enslavement in the English Colonies. Indeed, Maroon communities of Africans in the Americas who fled to the hills or swamps rather than live in slavery are documented facts (Hines, Hines and Harrold 2018). Later, organized Black communities often embodied the nationalist spirit of being self-defined and autonomous in the antebellum period (Cha Jua, 2000). Cha Jua's research also gives sustained attention to the frequently overlooked Black town movement in the north.

Nonetheless the white settlerism continued as did the solidification of the racial state. The earliest white settlers of the eastern colonies were stratified by religion and social position. The important distinctions were religious (Christians versus heathens) and position (masters versus dependents of various kinds –women, children, servants – who were required to obey their master). Nonetheless, the narrative of Black inferiority would intensify, heavily rooted in the idea that physical differences, especially skin color, marked Africans as inferior and as slaves. This ideology was deeply connected to the profitability of the institution that would ultimately shape every aspect of Black and white life in the nation – slavery, encoded in racial capitalism (Bush 1999).

Reproductive labor and forced reproduction were critical components of capitalist exploitation. Sexual exploitation, of course, was a continuing legacy of Black women's lives under enslavement and in the post-slave period. As W.E. B. DuBois sorrowfully notes in his *Souls of Black Folk* (1990), he could forgive the South much but not the horror of the system they inflicted on African women. Angela Davis (1971) would refine this analysis in her seminal article, "The Role of Black woman in the Community of Slaves." In this piece she powerfully argues that rape and assault on Black enslaved women was calculated to instill fear into the entire slave community. White male patriarchal power to dominate women was deployed strategically and violently against Black women. In *Women, Race, and Class* (1981), Davis articulates the Marxist feminist underpinnings of Black women's dual exploitation: productive and social reproductive. African enslaved women resisted and were central to sustaining enslaved communities as attacks intensified on the community of slaves.

The ban against slavery passed in 1807, and the transatlantic traffic slowed to a trickle, although slaves were still imported illegally (Hines, Hines, Harrold, 2018). The production of cotton would infuse new life into the trade. Cotton became the great engine of wealth accumulation in the US and in Europe. The cotton gin and British textile manufacturing created an insatiable demand for cotton and further catalyzed the inter-relationality among state practice, economic exploitation, and racism.

Indeed, the central tension of new nation building centered on the question of slavery. In 1787, the Northwest Ordinance banned slavery in the Northwest Territories (Hines, Hines, Harrold, 2018). But in the next century state policy shifted toward the slave owners. The 1820 Missouri Compromise let Missouri become a slave state but permanently outlawed slavery north of the latitude 36 degrees and 30. In the Compromise of 1850, California became a free state, but Utah and New Mexico were allowed to write their constitutions as either slave or free states, Similarly, in 1854, the Kansas-Nebraska Act let Kansas and Nebraska decide whether to be slave or free states (Hines, Hines, and Harrold).

Thus, from the 15th century to the 19th the expropriation of Black labor would be the great engine of Europe's wealth. The British would enter into this buying and selling of human beings to build its North America colonies. These colonies would ultimately become the site of a burgeoning slave trade that would make merchants and slaveholders rich. The wealth of what would become the United States was built on the violent seizure of Indigenous peoples' lands and the stolen labor of enslaved Africans. The very bodies of African men and women were commodified and the enslaved were rendered less than human. Banks, shipbuilding, shackle making, slavery was the engine of the entire economy making the United States economically poised for Empire. This is the logic of racial capitalism deeply intertwined in the formation of the capitalist racial state from the beginning into the current period (Robinson 1983)

6   Capitalist Racial State Formation and Black Struggle: The Current Period

The Black rebellions of the late 1960s, were at the center of the Kerner Commission investigation. The leading Black radicals understood quite clearly that dispossession in Detroit in 1967 and 100s of cities nationally was about who had power (Carmichael and Toure 1992). The issues of Black self-determination, political resistance and power were front and center in the Black rebellions. It is notable that by 1967, Black liberation was rooted in a liberatory rhetoric that extended beyond the mantra of racial equality, Civil Rights mantra of the years before. Even Dr. King in his 1967 speech on Vietnam named the ills as war, militarism, and racism. Of course, these ideas could not, would not be heard by Kerner Commissioners. The internationalism of these frames, indeed, touched at what was most sensitive to President Lyndon Johnson at the time, his war in Vietnam. This extended Black resistance beyond national boundaries tied the Black freedom movement to struggles for decolonization and imperialism in the Third World. Having said that, it's really not surprising that this analysis of Black internationalism was given short shrift, would not be heard. Indeed, the two Black members of the Commission, Roy Wilkins, Head of the NAACP and Senator Edward Brooks, US senator from Massachusetts were not supporters of Black Power (Gillion 2018).

By 1967, the central theoretical framework beginning to shape Black insurgent political thought was the idea of an internal colony. Black people in the U.S. were part of an internal colony. This paralleled the colonial status of the global Third World. Of course, this analysis gained no traction given the members making up the Commission. Indeed, it was out the question for President Lyndon B. Johnson who along with J. Edgar Hoover, Director of the FBI floated conspiracy theories about who was really behind the "riots". The idea that the rebellions were instigated by outside agitators was not missing from the explanations given by some members of the Kerner Commission (Shellow, 2018).

The Kerner Commission could name white racism at core to the uprisings but was not willing to name and undo the capitalist racial state. The report was shelved. Moreover, the shelved document did not articulate o articulate the relationship Between white racism and the economic foundations of US racial state. There was articulation of the race/gender dynamic of the racial state even though the organizing of the National Welfare Rights Organization. It was founded in 1966 led by Mrs. Johnnie Tillmon and other mainly Black poor women demanding economic, gender and racial justice. The systems of race and class were foundational to their argument. Tillmon and the National Welfare Rights organization understood and articulated an integrated/intersectional analysis of Black exploitation (Shilevitz, 2018; Collins 1990) This economic reality, cross cut by race, class, and gender, fractures the idea of black inequality, unmediated by race, sexuality, gender, and class. The complexity of this situation was missed in the Kerner Report.

Gender matters publicly and is being articulated more visibly and substantively in analyses of Black life in the US and the structuration of the racial state in today's Black uprisings. The gender dynamic is not simply female but across genders, expressed most poignantly in a class fact: the convergence of poverty and its entanglement with race and gender is a simultaneous nexus. Ruth Gilmore articulated this point in her interrogation cited earlier.

Relatedly, the Black Panther Party, the most revolutionary expression of Black resistance during the late 1960s, articulated a revolutionary Black nationalism, the Marxist-Maoism leveled as against Imperialism, capitalism, and white supremacy. Panther Elaine Brown asserts the fight was also against patriarchy. Just as their cultural nationalist counterparts, revolutionary nationalists began with traditional gender notions, some so harsh that women left the party (Brown 1992). Elaine Brown, in fact, was one of the few women in leadership at the highest level of the party.

7   21st Century Race Craft, Whiteness, and the Patriarchal Capitalist Racial State

Beyond the internal dynamics of class, the political economy of racialized gender is key to understanding 21st Century capitalist racial state formation. American state and economy have given way to changed labor markets and opportunity structures for Blacks within the US. The internationalization of the labor force, the robotizing, computerizing and technology changes generally, have profound consequences for the US Black population. Black displacement was already in full swing in the context of the first rebellions in Harlem and later in Watts in the mid-sixties and certainly by the Detroit rebellion in 1967 (Georgakas and Surkin 1998). The Kerner Commission elided these complex economic dynamics. Indeed, the Civil Rights model did not capture the nasty race/class/gender dynamics at play in the large urban ghettos of northern cities nor in smaller Midwestern cities like Minneapolis. Below the surface of the states professed "liberalism" resides the full capitalist state dynamics of Minnesota. These would be revealed during the George Floyd rebellion. Indeed, fewer and fewer workers are needed for the everyday operation of late capitalism.

White supremacy remains foundational to the capitalist racial state (Bush 1999). It most caustic form has reemerged in right wing nationalism. As Harris (1993 contends, whites have been able to convert whiteness into property, whiteness as property. Indeed, the deeply rooted power of historic white supremacy was not simply based in institutional structures that excluded. Although it is quite true that education, the economy, housing, and the polity have been key sites of racial exclusivity, giving preference to whites. But whiteness ideologically anchors the capitalist racial state in the US has a cultural base that disperses and deploys whiteness in consciousness, expectations, and status markers which are exceedingly difficult to dislodge. Race, gender and class, sexuality, whiteness and class positioning, are deeply imbricated with one with the other.

Coming full circle, J. San Juan (2002) articulates racism as part of a totality wherein the bourgeoisie constructs its domination via "the production of subjects, inscribed in racist discourse and institutional domination." This is hardly the world of economic parity imagined in the wake of the Kerner Commission assertion of two societies/ one black/ one white, that must be attended to. The economic decline in many urban Black communities has been exacerbated by the dismantling of the social wage in the form of social supports to working Americans and, of course, mass incarceration. New state practices support high levels of military spending, a minimalist role for government social spending – shifting this onto the states – and increasing support for the corporate sector through tax breaks, subsidies, and bailouts. White nationalism and right reaction in the wake of Trumpism is on the rise and deadly dangerous.

Thus, the Kerner Report was a limited tool for deep level change, and political economic realities constrained what is possible under such efforts given a racialized- capitalist state order. At the center of the current morass today is the relentless push to privatize under the ideology of fiscal austerity, under the practice of financialization. Indeed, at the heart of the austerity claim is the push for the erasure of the racial inequality reference, and replacement of it with a post-racial rhetoric of equality, which is empty on the ground. It's in this context we connect to 2020 the murder of George Floyd and global uprise.

8   Capitalist Racial State Minnesota: The Murder of George Floyd

The radical impulses which inform this era of struggle are drawn from the long durée of revolutionary Black political resistance for self-determination and social transformation – enduring tropes. I insert myself in this history, living in Minneapolis, MN in the context of the murder of George Floyd and the uprisings that occurred in its wake. It is a capitalist racial state structured in the protection of property and capital. Policing is shaped by these structural realities. We have been in resistance against state violence for a long time in Minneapolis, long before George Floyd.

9   And Now, George Floyd, May 25 2020

There is a long history of police violence in the Cities of Minneapolis and St. Paul. The Minneapolis story has been documented. In terms of the broader history of Minnesota, war and militarism are foundational to its establishment as a state in 1858. From the white settler colonialism that initiated the

state with the removal of the Dakota people into the current period structured on the legacies and ongoing practices of white supremacism and protection of the property, policing is shaped by these systemic realities. They
are woven into the very fiber of police violence against Black communities in
Minneapolis.

In the last 30 years multiple police killings by the Minneapolis police are on
the record, as is other so-called collateral damage to Black lives. The MPD150
Report (2020) offers the following information:

– There is the killing of Tycel Nelson in 1990, a young black teenager shot and
  killed by Minneapolis police.
– There is the 1990 "Raid Gone Wrong:" It resulted in the deaths of Lillian
  Weiss and Lloyd Smalley in a no-knock drug raid by the Minneapolis Police
  SWAT team.
– And the more recent murders of Terrance Franklin in 2013, Jamar Clark in
  2015, Philando Castile in 2016 (which occurred outside of Minneapolis in
  the St. Paul suburb of Falcon Heights).

And then there is the political economic context of the city. On May 30, 2020,
five days into the Floyd rebellion the Washington Post ran an article (Ingraham,
2020) with this headline: "Racial Inequality in Minneapolis is among the worst
in the Nation." In the body of the article were these statistics:

> Median Black family income in Minneapolis was $36,000 in 2018 accord-
> ing to US Census data. While median white family income was $83,000.
> Black families earned only 44% of white income. This is a $47,000 dispar-
> ity or gap. The numbers are damning. While Minnesota in 2018 had some
> of the lowest white poverty rates in the country, it had one of the worst
> Black poverty rates. While Black Minnesotans make up 6% of the state
> population, in 2018 32 percent of the Black population lived in poverty.
> The national Black number was 26%.
>
> INGRAHAM, 2020

Over the past few years, attention has been drawn to these "disparities" especially given the multiple police murders in the last 5 years in Minneapolis, St.
Paul and suburbs. Yet the economic order in which racism is rooted in the state
is not deeply interrogated and has long been in place. The state and the city
are economically capitalist. It is a capitalist racial state. The state was founded
on white settler colonialism built on the removal, genocide, and land expropriation of the Dakota people from their ancestral home. The logic of inferior and superior peoples, white supremacy continues. The ideology, while not
always visible, operates into the current period. It is structured in the ongoing

practices of racial exclusion and economic dispossession. It is expressed in the protection of capital's property and policing built in these structural realities.

Historian Christopher Lehman in his recent book, *Slavery's Reach* (2018), unearths this invisibility of the early features of Minnesota's racialized political economic history. Lehman points out that "investment wealth poured into Minnesota territory from the northeastern US." Lehman argues that the money made in banking and industries grew because of the labor of enslaved Africans, investment in slave labor and in Black bodies by which slavers bought land in Minnesota.

Sociologist Joe Feagin's articulation of the national logic of slavery and racialized capital is relevant here:

> Without slave labor it seems likely that there would have been no successful textile industry and without the cotton textile industry ... it is unclear how or when the United States would have become a major industrial power. There was not a New England merchant of any prominence who was not then directly or indirectly involved in the trade.
>
> cited in the *Color of Wealth*, LUI 2006

Let me rearticulate Feagin's observations in the context of Minnesota, again drawing on Lehman's *Slavery's Reach:*

> A slaveholding financier provided much of the capital behind the fur trade in southern and central Minnesota. Military officers, federal appointees, commuting businessmen, small farmers, banks and insurance companies, Hotel keepers and land speculators benefitted from slaveholding wealth (Lehman, 2018: 1)

And in the context of the Floyd police killings the voices for abolition have grown louder. Once again Ruth Gilmore provides insight:

> More police are not the answer to the deep structural issues of economic dispossession, state and interpersonal violence, recognizing and protecting our humanity. The answer is not replacing one repressive system with another.

In fact, a fundamental theme running through today's radical Black resistance in Minneapolis and beyond is to shift power from the police to communities. The critical resistance assertion to abolish prisons is also articulated in the push against state violence and stopping police occupation of Black communities.

The radical impulses which inform this era of Black rebellion are drawn from what I've called the long durée of Black political resistance for self-determination, liberation, and social transformation. Moreover, a powerful Black feminist intervention in today's fight back places front and center the deep inter-relationality of gender/sexuality, race, and class for Black liberation. This places Black rise-up in wider emancipatory context. The assertive demand now and is to value and respect Black lives. Youth, the economically dispossessed, the lower strata of the Black working class, some of the middle classes are core to the current struggle. Leading are women, genderqueer, gender nonconforming Black radicals, rooted in a radical Black feminist praxis, placing front and center the simultaneity of oppressions.

The current insurgency marks a shift in consciousness for many on the nature of policing and state violence. Publicly asserting, visibly and with bodies on the line in the middle of the COVID 19 pandemic, materially expressed that Black Lives Matter. This means rearticulating the capitalist racial state for human needs: to invest in education, living wages, health – germinating the seeds of a new society. For that to happen the current order must be fundamentally changed. The logical extension is the struggle for a different order. It is a society built on shared resources, social development of humanity with deep democracy and sustainability of the earth.

This is different moment, a certain kind of rupture, conjuncture. While struggle is centered on Black lives, it extends deep and across the multiple crises of the racial capitalist state. The times demand this and more. As always, the great African revolutionary Amilcar Cabral is clear about our challenges:

> our challenges are great to be organized and firmly united …
> … the struggle against our own weaknesses
> The battle against ourselves –no matter what difficulties the enemy may create – this is the most difficult of all – whether for the present or the future of our peoples.

References

Aptheker, Herbert. 1937. "American Negro Slave Revolts," *Science & Society* 1, no 4: 512–538.

Brennen Center for Justice. 2020. FBI targets a new generation of Black activists. accessed at https://www.brennancenter.org/our-work/analysis-opinion/fbi-targets-new-generation-black-activists.

Brown, Elaine. 1992. *A Taste of Power*. New York: Pantheon Books.

Bush, Rod. 1999. *We Are Not What We Seem: Black Nationalism and Class Struggle in the American Century.* New York: New York University Press.

Cha-Jua, S. K. 2000. *America's First Black Town Brooklyn, Illinois, 1830-1915,* Urbana: University of Illinois Press.

Collins, Patricia Hill. 1990. *Black Feminist Thought.* Boston: Unwin Hyman.

Cox, O. 1948. *Caste, Class and Race.* New York: Modern Reader.

Crenshaw, Kimberlee, Neil Gotanda, Gary Peller and Kendall Thomas. 1995. *Critical Theory: Key Writings that Formed the Movement,* New York: The New Press.

Davis, Angela. 1971. "Reflections on the Black Woman's Role in the Community of Slaves," *The Black Scholar* 3, no. 4: 2–15.

Davis, Angela 1981. *Women, Race and Class,* New York: Knopf.

DuBois, W. E. B. 1990. *The Souls of Black Folk,* New York: Vintage.

Feagin, Joe. 2018. *Racist America.* New York: Routledge.

Georgakas, Dan and Martin Surkin. 1998. *Detroit I Do Mind Dying: A Study in Urban Revolution.* Boston: South End Press.

Gil, R. 2014. The Mascogo/Black Seminole Diaspora: The Intertwining Borders of Citizenship, Race, and Ethnicity, *Latin American and Caribbean Ethnic Studies* 9, no 2:23–43.

Gillon, Steven M. 2018. *Separate and Unequal: Separate and Unequal: The Kerner Commission and the Unraveling of American Liberalism.* New York: Basic Books.

Gilmore, Ruth Wilson. 1993. "Terror Austerity Race Gender." In *Reading Rodney King, Reading Urban Uprising,* edited by Robert Gooding-Williams, 23–37. New York: Routledge.

Hamilton, Charles and Kwame Toure. 1992. *Black Power: The Politics of Liberation,* New York: Vintage Books.

Harris, Cheryl. 1993. Whiteness as Property. *Harvard Law Review.* Available at: https://harvardlawreview.org/1993/06/whiteness-as-property/.

Hines, Darlene, William C. Hines and Stanley Harrold. 2018. *The African American Odyssey,* New York: Pearson Educational Publishing.

Ingraham, Christopher. 2020. Racial inequality in Minneapolis is among the worst in the nation, *The Washington Post,* May 30, accessed at https://www.washingtonpost.com/business/2020/05/30/minneapolis-racial-inequality/.

Jessop, Bob. 2013. *State Power: A Strategic Relational Approach.* Cambridge: Polity Press.

Juan, E San. 1989. "Problems in the Marxist Project of Theorizing Race." *Rethinking Marxism,* no. 2 (Summer): 58–80.

Kerner Report. 2016. Princeton: Princeton University Press.

Lebowitz, Michael A. 1995. "Situating the Capitalist State," In *Marxism in the Postmodern Age,* edited by Antonio Callari, Stephen Cullenberc, and Carole Biewener, 198–207. New York: The Guilford Press.

Lehman, Christopher. 2018. *Slavery's Reach: Southern Slaveholders in the Northstar State.* St. Paul: Minnesota Historical Society.

Levin, Sam. 2017. FBI terrorism unit says 'black identity extremists' pose a violent threat, *Guardian,* October 7, Available at https://www.theguardian.com/us-news/2017/oct/06/fbi-black-identity-extremists-racial-profiling

Lui, et. al. 2006. *The Color of Wealth.* New York: The New Press.

Marx, Anthony W. 2002. M*aking Race and Nation: A comparison of South Africa, the United States and Brazil.* Cambridge: Cambridge University Press.

Mills, Charles. 1997. *The Racial Contract.* Ithaca: Cornel University Press.

MPD150. 2020. *Enough is Enough* accessed @ https://www.mpd150.com/report.

Omi, Michael and Howard Winant. 1994. *Racial Formation in the United States.* New York: Routledge.

Robinson, Cedric. 1983. *Black Marxism: The Making of the Black Radical Tradition,* London: Zed Books.

Shellow, Robert. 2018. *The Harvest of American Racism. The Political Meaning of Violence in the Summer of 1967,* Ann Arbor: University of Michigan Press.

Shilevitz, Judith. 2018. "Forgotten Feminists: Johnnie Tillmon's Battle Against "The Man" *The New York* Review accessed at https://www.nybooks.com/daily/2018/06/26/forgotten-feminisms-johnnie-tillmons-battle-against-the-man/.

Williams, Eric. 2021. *Capitalism and Slavery, ed. 3.* Durham: University of North Carolina Press.

Williams, Rhonda M. 1993. "Accumulation as Evisceration: Urban Rebellion and the new Growth Dynamics." In *Reading Rodney King, Reading Urban Uprising,* edited by Robert Gooding-Williams, 82–96. New York: Routledge.

Williams, Rhonda M. 1995. "Consenting to Whiteness: Reflections on Race and Marxian Theories of Discrimination." In *Marxism in the Postmodern Age,* edited by Antonio Callari, Stephen Cullenberc, and Carole Biewener, 301–310. New York: The Guilford Press.

CHAPTER 12

Marxism and Intersectionality

A Critical Historiography

Ashley J. Bohrer

1   Introduction[1]

In recent years, intersectionality has been discussed more than ever before. These discussions have been so frequent that some have even called it 'hegemonic' (Mann, 2013: 55). Since the 2008 financial crisis, there has also been a renewed interest in Marxism. As these two frameworks have been increasingly analyzed and considered over the past decade, they have also come into contact with one another. Marxists have criticized intersectionality scholars and vice versa. But there has also been a series of interesting and important attempts to synthesize these frameworks, forging a productive and nuanced theory that is able to respond dynamically to the complexities of oppression in the twenty-first century. In particular, these debates have significantly coalesced around questions of identity politics, or the ways in which identity can, is, and should be related to the structural conditions of capitalism. In the context of debates around identity politics, having a deeper and more nuanced understanding of the history and relationship between Marxism and intersectionality, which in some ways is the contemporary paradigm for understanding identity, is absolutely crucial for contemporary activists and academics alike.

This chapter proceeds as follows: Section 2 section describes the key tenets of intersectionality and its critiques of Marxism. While there is a vast literature of intersectionality theorists' critiques of Marxism, I focus on two charges in particular. The first is the claim that Marxism relies on binary structures to explain the world. The second is that Marxism reduces analyses of oppression to class oppression, only or primarily, and considers all other forms of domination (like sexism, racism and heteronormativity) to be merely epiphenomenal to primary class relations. While these charges are certainly true of many traditional Marxist theorists, I argue that the vibrant and rapidly transforming

---

1 This chapter is slightly altered from its original publication as "Intersectionality and Marxism: A Critical Historiography" in *Historical Materialism* 26.2 (2018) 46–74.

tradition of Marxist feminisms[2] has developed quite substantially and has proven able to incorporate these very criticisms into its theories. The third section explains the Marxist-feminist criticisms of intersectionality, which often revolve around the idea that many intersectional theories have underdeveloped analyses of class. While many intersectional theories discuss class or name it as one of the axes of oppression in the contemporary world, few delve into the specificities of structural class relations or engage in a holistic critique of capitalism. I argue that a nuanced and specific critique of capitalism as a structure is vitally necessary to theories of domination. I also address the criticisms of certain Marxist scholars that, because certain strains of intersectionality embrace 'identity politics', they are therefore, in their terms, 'bourgeois'. I argue that this criticism is misplaced, can much more accurately be levied against poststructuralist feminism, and that while intersectionality and poststructuralism certainly share common elements, their frameworks are fundamentally different. Thus, this criticism seems to be a failure on the part of Marxist feminists to actually engage with intersectionality. Since the claim that intersectionality and hence identity politics are essentially poststructuralist

---

2   I use the term 'Marxist feminisms' in a slightly different way than some other theorists. I use it to signify the many strains of and frameworks within feminist theory and activism that locate themselves in direct reference to a Marxist diagnosis of the structure of capitalism. In this way, I group what others have called 'socialist feminisms', 'communist feminisms', 'Marxist feminisms', 'anti-capitalist feminisms' and 'Marxist-anarcha feminisms' together under this heading. I do so for a few reasons: (1) The borders and boundaries between these categories are often extremely fuzzy. While Susan Archer Mann (Mann 2012), for instance, argues that there exist sharp theoretical differences between these strains, I have found that these theoretical distinctions are not always consistent, that theorists identify themselves with 'so- cialist feminism', for example, when historians of the feminist movement would call them 'Marxist feminists' and vice versa. Thus, while the thinkers inside each category hold very different positions, it is not clear to me that the names of these various traditions neatly de- lineate conceptual frameworks in any easy and unproblematic sense. (2) All of the traditions named above are in a similar position, trying to negotiate a relationship with intersectionality, and hence, for the scope of this chapter, they can be considered together. The criticism that intersectionality makes of 'Marxism' could be levied equally against those in many of the above camps. (3) While at a certain point in feminist theory, most notably during the so- called 'second wave', differences between these theories were quite pronounced, it seems as though in contemporary feminist scholarship and activism, the terms 'socialist', 'Marxist' and 'anticapitalist' are often used interchangeably, sometimes by the same theorist in one piece. Moreover, these distinctions were even more porous in the early twentieth century, when Marxism, socialism, communism, and anti-capitalism were often considered synonyms. In grouping these traditions together, I do not mean to erase the distinctions between them nor to de-legitimise the various authors' nomenclatures, but rather intend to be able to speak more broadly about theoretical trends without encumbering my writing with the list of five frameworks each time a Marxist-oriented kind of feminism is mentioned.

notions is a constant feature of the debate around identity politics, under-standing this argument is essential to grounding a clearer understanding of how identity politics is constructed than is often present in the Marxist liter-ature on the subject. The last section attempts to develop an intersectional Marxism or a Marxist theory of intersectionality, one that uses key insights from both frameworks. In doing so, I argue that Marxism needs intersectional-ity, and in its best and most-thoughtful iterations has been intersectional, even if it has not used this term. I argue further that intersectionality can benefit from a Marxist theory of capitalism. In highlighting the mutual insufficiency of these two theories on their own, I hope to move toward the development of a theoretical framework that can adequately account for relations of domina-tion and exploitation organised around race, class, gender and sexuality.

2   Intersectionality Critiques Marxism

Developed by women-of-color feminists, intersectionality sought to theorize the specific problems experienced by women of color, problems that often-involved racism, sexism, classism and heterosexism, and that were often over-looked by single-axis theories. While the term 'intersectionality' was coined by Kimberlé Crenshaw in 1989, many intersectionality theorists root their framework in the nineteenth-century writings of black women like Sojourner Truth, Anna Julia Cooper, and others, who sought to describe the exclusions and oppressions faced by Black women on account of their gender and race. Intersectionality continued to be developed throughout the twentieth century by theorists who variously identified themselves as Black womanists, Black feminists, Chicana feminists, Hispanas, Xicanistas, and sister/outsiders. In her landmark work, *Black Feminist Thought*, Patricia Hill Collins describes intersec-tionality theory as an 'analysis claiming that systems of race, social class, gen-der, sexuality, ethnicity, nation, and age form mutually constructing features of a social organization, which shape Black women's experiences and, in turn, are shaped by Black Women' (Collins, 2000: 299). As Barbara Smith explains this key insight, 'the major "isms" ... are intimately intertwined' (Smith, 1998: 112); they simply cannot be separated. Patricia Hill Collins and others frequently use the term 'matrix of domination' instead of 'intersecting oppressions.' Others use 'interlocking oppressions' or 'mutually reinforcing oppressions' to describe the same phenomena. In its most basic form, then, intersectionality is the theory that both structurally and experientially, social systems of domi-nation are linked to one another and that, in order both to understand and to change these systems, they must be considered together. Intersectionality thus submits to critique theories that treat forms of oppression separately, as well as attempts to locate one axis of oppression as primary. It is from this perspective that the most frequent criticisms of Marxism are made.

In the first place, intersectionality theorists allege that Marxists reduce all social, political, cultural, and economic antagonisms to class.[3] Some Marxist theorists do in fact omit any significant discussions of race, gender, or sexuality from their work (as, for example, Marx's *Capital* did), explaining the processes of capital accumulation, crises and dispossession in gender and race-blind terms (or discuss axes of oppression but only as epiphenomena of class).[4] This erasure of race, gender, and sexuality as relevant terms in the discussion of oppression is one tendency that intersectionality theorists, as well as feminists generally, have identified as a serious limitation of the tradition of Marxism.[5] In fact, it was due to the long history of the occlusion of women's work, lives, and experiences of violence and exploitation that Marxist feminists submitted to critique more mainstream discussions of capitalist economy and culture. In this sense, the criticism of mainstream or hegemonic Marxism as race and gender-blind is a criticism shared by both intersectionality theorists and feminists who locate themselves in the Marxist tradition.[6]

While there were and continue to be many attempts by Marxist feminists (as well as critical race scholars and postcolonial theorists) to correct this gross omission, many of these attempts proposed inadequate solutions. Some proposed a 'dual-system theory' wherein capitalism and patriarchy were distinct systems that coincided in the preindustrial era to create the system of class

---

3   For example, take the following claim by Beverly Smith (Smith and Smith 1983, p. 122) of the Combahee River Collective: there are 'people who are Marxists who say "Well, when class oppression and racism end, definitely the oppression of women and lesbians will end." ' Smith was herself a Marxist and an intersectional thinker who repeatedly submitted to critique a class-reductionist trend in Marxist organising. See also Gedalof 2013 and Alcoff 2011.

4   For example, Benn Michaels 2006.

5   While this criticism is certainly valid of many Marxist theorists, it would be misleading to erase the long history of Marxists who spoke extensively of gender, race and colonialism. Some of the major theorists of the Marxist tradition, among them Karl Marx himself as well as Friedrich Engels (cf. Engels 1942), discussed imperialism, colonialism and slavery, and in Engels's case, patriarchy. It is true that Marx's discussions of slavery and imperial- ism do not themselves constitute a theory of race, or at all reference the gendered dimen- sions of these structures. Indeed, it may be particularly problematic to give an account of colonisation and slavery that does not centre race and gender. It is true that many who wrote in the tradition of Marx and Engels ignored these dimensions in their analysis. For an analysis of Marx's stances on slavery, imperialism, and colonialism, see Anderson 2010. For more on Marx and Engels's theorisation of the oppression of women, see Brown 2012.

6   See: Hartmann 1981; Barrett 1988; Cox and Federici 1976; Dalla Costa 2008; James and Dalla Costa 1973.

and gender exploitation that characterizes the contemporary world (for example, Hartmann, 1981). These accounts, offered by theorists like Sylvia Walby (1988), while attempting a nascent proto-intersectional account of class and gender, generally said nothing of race, sexuality, or colonization, repeating the very theoretical marginalization they accused mainstream theorists of perpetrating.

Others developed a 'single-system theory' in which sexism or patriarchy and capitalism were one and the same system.[7] This insight took multiple forms: some argued that patriarchy and class-based exploitation were mutually constructing and equiprimordial features of capitalism in both its history and its logic (Federici, etc.). Others argued that patriarchy and class-based exploitation were indeed historically mutually constructing and, because they have empirically shaped and continue to shape the world around us, an analysis of both is necessary, but also that the logic of capitalism is itself gender-blind (Meiksins Wood). Gender, in these accounts, emerges as a technique of social control in the service of capitalist accumulation. In other words, this kind of theory had the benefit of being able to discuss the ways in which gender and class emerged together as forms of social control that mutually reinforced one another. However, in the Meiksins Wood iteration, it also had the effect of treating gender as a kind of epiphenomenon of the more primary social cleavage of class; class relations were the true logical core of capitalism, while gender relations were mere empirical fact – incredibly important to analyse *as empirical fact*, but ultimately of a different analytic order and existential weight. While the logical is never in these accounts expressly predicated as superior to or more fundamental than the empirical, this implication is clear.[8] In this sense, certain forms of single-system theory tended to hierarchise oppressions, placing class as the most important and primary social antagonism.

While other forms of single-systems theory did not mark this distinction between the logical and the empirical in this way, intersectional theorists have still subjected Marxist-feminist single systems theory to critique in two distinct ways. In the first place, often (though not exclusively) Marxist-feminist unitary theory focused only on two aspects of life – gender and class – in ways

---

7   For example, Vogel 1983 and Young 1981

8   This implicit denigration of the empirical in favour of the logical is itself deeply ironic, given Marx's own description of the relationship between abstract and concrete in the Grundrisse, where he argues (Marx 1993, p. 101) that one must 'ris[e] from the abstract to the concrete', suggesting that the abstract or 'logical' level of the analysis is itself a heuris- tic tool to effectively understand the concrete, the empirical, the world.

that implicitly or by omission seem to suggest that race, sexuality, ability, and nationality are of secondary or incidental importance. At the very least, they tended not to mention or treat with a sustained analysis the multiple ways in which gender as a structure and as a concept was raced and sexualized, as well as deeply embedded in histories of colonialism and imperialism. In another way, intersectional theorists subjected unitary theorists to critique for their focus on the housewife as the primary locus for understanding the relationship between gender and capitalism. Much of single-system theory accounts of domestic labor, especially in the first wave of Marxist feminism from the 1960s to the 1980s, presumed a heterosexual, single-income married couple, often with children, in ways that did not explain or incorporate analyses of queer couples, dual-income households, or of single-parent households. It was especially the latter two of these exclusions that led some prominent black feminists including Angela Davis to argue that the model of the dominant trend of Marxist Feminism of those years implicitly assumed a white, heterosexual, middle-class frame of analysis (Davis 1981: 222–44).

One of the central contentions of intersectionality as a framework is the necessity of embracing 'the working hypothesis of the equivalency between oppressions (Collins 1997: 74)'. As intersectionality historiographer Vivian May writes, 'In gender-first or class-first critiques, intersectionality's censure of hierarchy of oppressions mindsets cannot be taken up – single-axis, hierarchical models of identity and oppression remain as measures of political/theoretical adequacy (May 2014: 102)'. In other words, one of the central insights of intersectionality theory is precisely that hierarchizing oppressions itself perpetuates the marginalization of those who are often invested with the least social power. In this way, single-system theories that discuss gender (and occasionally race) only as secondary after-effects of capital relations, cannot adequately account for the specific forms of oppression faced by women of colour, working-class queers, or gender non-conforming people. These theories seem still to take white, employed, married, heterosexual men (and their wives) as the only subjects of inquiry.

Both dual-system and single-system (white) Marxist feminisms of the 1970s and 1980s tended to essentialize and homogenize the women they were discussing. This tendency, which Elizabeth Spelman calls 'the Trojan horse of feminist ethnocentrism' (Spelman 1988: x), was most visible in the largest Marxist feminist theoretico-activist group of the 1970s, the Wages for Housework Campaign, who took housewifery as the universal position of women. These accounts nearly always assume that women are in heterosexual couplings with a male breadwinner. They equate the ability to become pregnant with womanhood itself. They assume that the experiences of middle-class white women are definitive and universal determinants of womanhood itself. Audre Lorde critiques the supposed homogeneity of experience in *Sister/Outsider*:

> There is a pretense to the homogeneity of experience covered by the word sisterhood that does not in fact exist ... Certainly there are very real differences between us of race, age, and sex. But it is not those differences between us that are separating us. It is rather our refusal to recognize those differences.
>
> LORDE 1984: 115

Rather than cover over the differences between women under the guise of a 'universal sisterhood', intersectionality theorists argue that differences in experiences are caused by differential structural relations to forms of institutionalized power, and thus need to be analyzed, described and explained, as key components of feminist theorizing.

3   Marxism Critiques Intersectionality

Marxist feminists have responded to the above-articulated critiques in a variety of ways. Some have simply dismissed intersectionality (for example, Aguilar 2012); others have attempted to nuance their positions and adopt more-sophisticated understandings of the structures of domination. As I have argued elsewhere (see Bohrer 2015), Marxist feminism underwent a radical shift in its assumptions after the dissolution of the Wages for Housework campaign in North America and the disbanding of central Marxist feminist organizations like Lotta Feminista in Italy, which were producing the most developed Marxist-feminist theories in the 1970s. In particular, responding to the above-explained critiques from women of color around the world, many Marxist-feminists shifted their perspectives radically to account for race as a primary structure of oppression, neither secondary to nor epiphenomenal of class. They began also to develop situated accounts of the role of women in the global geo-political economy that recognised the simultaneity of oppressions based on race, gender, class and country of origin.[9]

---

9 It is on the basis of this turn that Chandra Talpade Mohanty names Maria Mies, one of the most widely-read Marxist feminist theorists even today, as a prime example of a white, Western scholar engaging in thoughtful work that considers race, gender, class and na- tional origin in a nuanced, situated and sensitive manner (Mohanty 1988).

Marxist-feminist theorists have not only engaged in the two above-named strategies; they have also offered critiques of intersectionality. Perhaps unsurprisingly, many of these criticisms allege that intersectionality has an underdeveloped analysis of class as a fundamental axis of oppression. Jean Ait Belkhir (2001: 160) argues that: 'Despite its place in the now familiar list – race, gender, and class – class is often the last addressed of these issues' in contemporary feminist theory. As Susan Archer Mann (2012: 112) explains, the relatively little attention paid to class is a frequent trope in criticisms of intersectionality: 'Other scholars have criticized the "theoretically impoverished concepts of class" employed by authors who claim to do race, gender, and class analyses' (Kandal 1995: 143). As Martha Gimenez (2001) explains, fear of class reductionism has led intersectional analyses to overcorrect, nearly leaving out class entirely:

> the flattening or erasure of the qualitative difference between class, race and gender in the RGC [Race, Gender and Class] perspective is the foundation for the recognition that it is important to deal with 'basic relations of domination and subordination' which now appear disembodied, outside class relations. In the effort to reject 'class reductionism,' by postulating the equivalence between class and other forms of oppression, the RGC perspective both negates the fundamental importance of class [and] is forced to acknowledge its importance by postulating some other 'basic' structures of domination.

Gimenez's critique goes farther than the underdevelopment of class; rather, Gimenez argues, intersectional analyses often have the effect of misapprehending the nature of class itself, postulating a qualitative equivalence between it and other forms of oppression where none exists. Gimenez argues that there is something distinctive about the organization of class oppression that makes it different in kind from either race or gender. We should note that 'different in kind' does not mean more fundamental or primary; rather it means that class oppression is distinctive and necessitates a different kind of treatment, politically and theoretically, than race and gender. This differential treatment requires a wholesale analysis of capitalism as a system and a structure of material relations of production and reproduction, accumulation and dispossession, which has its roots in political economy and effects in the multifaceted realms of culture, ideology and politics. I will return to this 'different kind of treatment' in the third section.

The lack of focused and sustained analysis of political economy has led some Marxists to accuse intersectionality of reinforcing certain tenets of bourgeois liberalism. In a widely read and distributed pamphlet, Eve Mitchell alleges that the focus of intersectionality on identity politics constitutes a of specifically capitalist ideas of individuality. Responding specifically to bell hooks's iteration of the critique of the homogeneity of experience so frequent in non-intersectional analyses, Mitchell (2013) writes,

> hooks is correct to say that basing an entire politics on one particular experience, or a set of particular differences, under capitalism is problematic. However, intersectionality theory replicates this problem by simply adding particular moments, or determinant points; hooks goes on to argue for race and class inclusion in a feminist analysis. Similarly, theories of an 'interlocking matrix of oppressions,' simply create a list of naturalized identities, abstracted from their material and historical context. This methodology is just as ahistorical and antisocial as Betty Friedan's.

This selection highlights two related but slightly different criticisms. In the first place, Mitchell's critique is representative of a frequent criticism of what we might call 'mathematical' intersectionality theory[10]; these are the theories that conceive of the multiple axes of oppression as additive or multiplicative, using concepts like 'triple jeopardy' to explain the position of working-class women of colour who experience class, gender, and race-based oppressions.[11] While

---

10   The descriptor 'mathematical' comes from Deborah King's analysis of intersectionality. She writes, 'most applications of the concepts of triple jeopardy have been overly simplistic in assuming that the relationships among the various discriminations are merely additive. These relationships are interpreted as equivalent to the mathematical equation, racism plus sexism plus classism equals triple jeopardy. In this instance, each discrimination has a single, direct, and independent effect on status, wherein the relative contribution of each is readily apparent.' Commenting on these mathematical notions of intersecting oppressions, Martha Gimenez (Gimenez 2001, pp. 25ff.) explains the variety of intersectionality theories that resist this kind of analysis. Her historiography is so helpful that I quote it at length: 'Authors vary in the metaphors they use to describe the nature of these intersections: e.g., triple oppression, interplay, interrelation, cumulative effects, interconnections [Belkhir 1994]; interactive, triadic relation, overlapping, interactive systems [Belkhir 1993, p. 4]; multiple jeopardy, meaning "not only several, simultaneous oppressions but also the multiplicative relations among them" [King, cited in Barnett, Brewer and Kuumba 1999, p. 14]; multiplicative, simultaneous, inter-connected systems of a whole [Barnett, Brewer and Kuumba 1999, p. 15]. Collins, however, appears to disagree with mathematical interpretations of these relationships, for she states that they (meaning race, gender and class) cannot be "added together to produce one so-called grand oppression" [Collins, cited in Barnett, Brewer and Kuumba 1999, p. 15]; it follows they cannot be multiplied either.

11   It is important to note here that while Mitchell does not simultaneously criticise the tradition of Marxist feminism, the mathematical model of oppression has also been frequently

there are certainly some intersectional theorists who deploy this framework, many intersectional theorists themselves have argued against additive and multiplicative models for their failure to highlight the mutual constitution of the structures of domination. In one example of an intersectional critique of this language, Deborah King's 'Multiple Jeopardy: The Context of Black Feminist Ideology' decries what she terms the 'pop-bead approach' where oppressions are considered separate and then added together, arguing that by considering these systems as wholly distinct, these frameworks revive the tendency to hierarchize oppressions (King 1988). As this same intervention is made by many other intersectionality theorists, Mitchell's (and others') identification of intersectionality with these mathematical models constitutes a straw-man argument, one that refuses to seriously engage with the vast intersectional literature critiquing the very position Mitchell attributes to this framework.

The second but related criticism that Mitchell levies concerns the nature of identity as it is discussed by intersectionality. Mitchell worries that identities are conceived as 'natural', 'ahistorical', and later in this essay, 'idealistic' and 'bourgeois.' While ultimately, I think this is an unhelpful criticism, I would like to reconstruct Mitchell's argument in depth, as it does point to some more nuanced and interesting questions about the nature of feminist theory, even if these questions remained undeveloped in Mitchell's piece.

Mitchell's worry about identity politics is rooted in a long history of Marxist criticism. Marxism, as a perspective grounded in historical materialism, generally views identities as effects of structural, material, and historical processes. Hence, accounts of identity that are only descriptive and do not speak about the structures enframing, creating, policing, and maintaining these identities lack, from a Marxist perspective, the crucial and necessary explanatory element of theory that would be grounded in a historical perspective of the power of structures and institutions. Politics of identity that stay only at the level of claiming a social location are seen as overly self-congratulatory and, in some ways, as reaffirming the social cleavages created by dominating structures without necessarily giving an account of the genesis, logic, organization,

---

used in this tradition. Many Marxist feminists used the language to describe the duality of class and gender oppressions. The refusal to recognise the roots of this mathematical model in the very tradition that Mitchell defends is itself a form of epistemic domination, one in which the voices and theories of women of colour are the only voices criticised for a more general tendency in theory. While I agree with Mitchell that mathematical models of oppression are not the most helpful metaphors for explain- ing the relationships between various instantiations of social domination, we should be wary of the power dynamics at play in accusing only intersectionality and not other frameworks of this problem.

history, or power of those structures. In this way, certain iterations of identity politics ground themselves in purely individual terms and reduce politics solely to an issue of claiming a position within a social totality. And when one claims this position, when, for example, I claim my social location as that of a white queer working-class American Jew, Marxists worry that without an analysis of the structures of whiteness, queerness, etc., I am treating each of these identities as natural facts, pre-existing molds into which I simply fit my individual body and history without critiquing the historical contingency of each of them. Critics of identity politics, especially those who are engaged not only in theory but also in movement-based activist work, also worry that grounding a politics in identity can have the effect of limiting the possibilities for cross group coalition-building and solidarity.

It is this history of critiquing identity politics, first formulated, we should note, by mainstream Marxists against Marxist feminisms, that is present in the background of Mitchell's analysis of intersectionality's identity politics. Because of the above-enumerated worries, Mitchell (2013) accuses intersectionality of reconfirming a certain kind of bourgeois politics: 'Since identity politics, and therefore intersectionality theory, are a bourgeois politics, the possibilities for struggle are also bourgeois. Identity politics reproduces the appearance of an alienated individual under capitalism and so struggle takes the form of equality among groups at best, or individualized forms of struggle at worst.'

While I think Marxist critiques offered above constitute incredibly important criticisms of the effects of certain strands of identity politics, I think they are submitting to critique a fundamentally different understanding of 'identity politics' than that taken in the majority of developed intersectionality theories. Take, for example, the explanation of identity politics offered by the Combahee River Collective (1977): 'this focusing upon our own oppression is embodied in the concept of identity politics. We believe that the most profound and potentially most radical politics come directly out of our own identity, as opposed to working to end someone else's oppression.' But what exactly do these theorists mean by the term 'identity politics'? Do they use it to signify an endless, congratulatory string of individual identifications, disconnected from structures and histories?

Quite simply, they do not. Rather, intersectionality theorists frequently critique this tendency in poststructuralist feminisms. In her article on the relationship between intersectionality and postmodernism, Susan Archer Mann (2013: 64–5) mobilizes Patricia Hill Collins's grounding of intersectionality inside a group-based standpoint epistemology against the postmodern position of the irreducible difference and uniqueness of each individual and hence the absolute untranslatability of an experience to any another. She writes,

> Here [in postmodern accounts of difference and identity] differences are infinite and each individual is potentially unique. In contrast, for Collins, the notion of standpoint refers to groups who have shared histories because of their shared location in relations of unequal power and privilege. They are neither groups based simply on identities chosen by individuals nor groups analytically created by demographers, bureaucrats or scholars. For her, to call for the deconstruction of all group categories in the name of critiquing essentialism is simply to move to a 'language game of politics'.[12]

It is not only Patricia Hill Collins who argues against this version of identity politics. Nikol Alexander-Floyd explains that 'women of color feminists generally support identity politics centred on complex, negotiated understandings of group interests' rather than on individual identities (2012: 11). These 'negotiated' conceptions of group-based identity politics signify the shifting, historically situated nature of oppressions, precisely the opposite of the ahistoricism and naturalization of which intersectionality theorists are accused. As Vivian May (2014: 103) argues, this gross misreading of intersectionality is itself embroiled in a politics of knowledge production, one that ignores the theoretical sensitivity and nuance that these theories elaborate:

> Pitting context versus identity ignores how intersectionality posits identity as located within, navigating across, and shaped by social structures. A more thorough reading of the literature, in any period of intersectionality's genealogy, substantiates that a 'both/and' approach to (multiple) identities contextualized within myriad social structures and cognizant of relational power dynamics within and between groups is a basic premise of intersectionality.

What, then, does 'identity politics' mean in the context of intersectionality theories? 'The most general statement of our politics', writes the Combahee River Collective, 'at the present time would be that we are actively committed to struggling against racial, sexual, heterosexual, and class oppression, and see as our particular task the development of integrated analysis and practice based

---

12   The reference here is to Collins 2004: 248 and 252–3

upon the fact that major systems of oppression are interlocking. The synthesis of these oppressions creates the conditions of our lives' (The Combahee River Collective 1977). Mitchell's accusation can only seem ludicrous in this context. The Combahee River Collective and many other intersectionality theorists mobilize their experiences of the simultaneity of oppressions rather as a starting place – not the end goal – of theory and praxis, as a window into the structures of domination from which to speak, interrogate, analyze and explain. And while it may be true that eliminating the structures of oppression is not *per se* about any one person's experience of these oppressions, ultimately, is not the goal of radical political transformation the elimination of oppression precisely *because* of its mal-effects on the lives and experiences of really existing human beings?[13]

It is from this position that intersectionality theorists rehabilitate the notion of identity politics in the service of radically transformative politics. Kimberlé Crenshaw (1995: 539) argues that defending group rather than individual identity-politics constitutes an important political tactic: 'At this point in history, a strong case can be made that the most critical resistance strategy for disempowered groups is to occupy and defend a politics of social location rather than to vacate and destroy it'. Crenshaw here points to the distinction between theory as a political strategy and theory as a supposedly value-free inquiry aimed at establishing a form of everlasting or universal truth. The argument is not that group-based identity politics forms a political truth *tout court*, but rather that *inside the particular historical context* of the exclusion and marginalization of women of color from both mainstream theory and political practice, recentering our analyses on these groups itself constitutes an intervention into sedimented structures of domination.

---

13   It might be helpful to return to Marx at this point, who argues that historical materialism contains precisely this theoretical move – to ground philosophy in real, historical individuals and their experiences. To do otherwise is to fall back into the idealist trap of German metaphysics. He writes in The German Ideology: 'In direct contrast to German philosophy which descends from heaven to earth, here we ascend from earth to heaven. That is to say, we do not set out from what men say, imagine, conceive, nor from men as narrated, thought of, imagined, conceived, in order to arrive at men in the flesh. We set out from real, active men, and on the basis of their real life-process we demonstrate the development of the ideological reflexes and echoes of this life-process ... Thinking and the products of their thinking. Life is not determined by consciousness, but consciousness by life. In the first method of approach the starting-point is consciousness taken as the living individual; in the second method, which conforms to real life, it is the real living individu- als themselves, and consciousness is considered solely as their consciousness.' (Marx and Engels 2004, p. 47.)

This regrounding of theory, when considered from the perspective of class relations, has been a hallmark of Marxist theories in political economy, history, and cultural criticism. Marxist theories recognize very well that truth is partial, produced, and situated inside historical relations of force and power. This is a patently uncontroversial claim, even for mainstream, orthodox Marxisms. Much of Marxist theorizing in the twentieth century took the form of rehabilitating disciplines from bourgeois ideology by grounding enquiry in a concern for the experiences, histories and phenomena most relevant to the working class. In this sense, what intersectionality theorists call 'subjugated knowledges' enumerated from a 'situated' standpoint is quite crucial to Marxism; the difference between these perspectives is that many of the orthodox Marxist accounts recognize only class as a situated perspective, whereas intersectionality theorists have reclaimed race, gender, sexuality and ability as positions embedded with historical perspectives that produce sites of knowledge and terrains of struggle.

4   Integrating Marxism and Intersectionality

As I have argued above, many of the mutual criticisms of intersectionality and Marxism are the result of multiple failures of communication. Intersectionality's criticisms of many Marxist positions are themselves also held by Marxist feminists and have been incorporated into contemporary scholarship. Marxist feminists' worries about identity politics would seem rather better directed toward other traditions of feminist scholarship, which, while they might discuss multiple kinds of oppression, do not share a framework with the majority of the hallmark texts of intersectionality theories. Other contentions, however, remain to be worked through. I share with many Marxist theorists a dissatisfaction with the treatment of capitalism in many intersectional theories and believe that capitalism forms one of the root causes of a network of oppressive social, political, economic and cultural relations in the contemporary world that necessitates the kind of detailed analysis that Marxism has long sought to advance. I agree also with intersectionality theorists that many treatments of capitalism have amounted at worst to vulgar class reductionism and at best to simple under-theorization of the complex racial, gendered, and sexual dynamics of power operative in the world in which we live.

I would thus like to treat the rest of this chapter as a prolegomenon to developing an intersectional theory of capitalism. As prolegomenon, I consider this account to be provisional, a gesture toward a long and complicated project that I could not hope to exhaust here. This section proceeds in two ways. First, I argue that in order to ground an intersectional theory of capitalism, it is necessary first to contest some of the reigning historiographies of both traditions that have contributed to the divergent development of these frameworks. Revisiting the work, both academic and activist, of many key figures in both traditions, I foreground the vitally important but under-discussed traditions of anti-capitalist women of color that have straddled the divide between Marxism and intersectionality. These analyses provide a foothold in the project of bridging these modes of analysis. Second, I turn critically to a consideration of capitalism as a structure, arguing that capitalism is the overarching system that gave rise[14] to patriarchy, racism, colonization and imperialism, as well as to the formation of more frequently discussed proletarian exploitation. In framing these systems as all *equally* part of capitalism, I hope to place capitalism at the centre of an intersectional theory, but one that would not take class as the privileged or primordial antagonism to be considered.

4.1 *Towards a New Historiography*

While Marxist feminism and intersectionality theories are frequently discussed separately, some of the hallmark works of women-of-colour feminisms in the twentieth and twenty-first centuries have been both intersectional and Marxist, a fact that is all too frequently downplayed in the historiography of both traditions.

Consider the following extended excerpt from the Combahee River Collective Statement (1977), one of the fundamental framing texts of intersectionality:

---

14 This claim needs further explanation. By arguing that capitalism 'gave rise' to patriarchy or racism, I do not mean that there were not, or indeed are not, forms of what we would call gender-based or race-based inequality, prejudice or subjugation before the rise of capitalism in the fifteenth century. Rather, I mean that the current forms of patriarchy and racism are coterminous with capitalism, that the very expressions and constructions of race and gender operative in our world are inseparable from capitalism. What we mean when we say 'race' is a phenomenon that is inseparable from, for example, the systems of slavery, colonialism and imperialism that formed necessary, structural elements of capitalism. The same is true of gender. Insofar as race, gender and sexuality are really-existing categories involved in systems of exploitation and oppression that structure the contemporary world, these categories were decisively constructed, changed and metamorphosed – indeed, created – through capitalism and for its ends. This does not mean that feudalism did not entail certain kinds of gender-based hierarchy, but rather that the referent of the contemporary term 'patriarchy' and all of its determinants corresponds to a series of expectations, relations, rules, stereotypes and dynamics that cannot be separated from their development through and with capitalism.

We realize that the liberation of all oppressed peoples necessitates the destruction of the political-economic systems of capitalism and imperialism as well as patriarchy. We are socialists because we believe that work must be organized for the collective benefit of those who do the work and create the products, not for the profit of the bosses. Material resources must be equally distributed among those who create the resources ... We need to articulate the real class situation of persons who are not merely raceless, sexless workers, but for whom racial and sexual oppression are significant determinants in their working/economic lives. Although we are essentially in agreement with Marx's theory as it applied to the very specific economic relationships he analyzed, we know that his analysis must be extended further in order for us to understand our specific economic situation as Black women.

The Combahee River Collective locate themselves squarely within the tradition of Marx and Marxism and consider his diagnosis of capitalism to be fundamental. Their call to *extend* Marx's analysis beyond its original scope is precisely the project that all Marxism since the nineteenth century has taken up. To be a Marxist is precisely to engage in this kind of analysis, of 'stretching' Marx's analysis, to borrow an expression from the anti-colonial thinker, Frantz Fanon, to account for the material relations of domination better than could be expected of any one thinker. Though the Combahee River Collective recognize limitations to Marx's corpus, they locate their project in the extension rather than in the rejection of his fundamental problematic – a sustained critique of capitalism.[15]

---

15   In Susan Archer Mann's Doing Feminist Theory, an exhaustive account of the history of feminist scholarship, Marxist feminism and intersectionality theories are treated as completely distinct, with separate chapters for each. Mann in a certain sense contributes to the false separation between intersectionality and Marxist/materialist/socialist feminisms by treating them separately. Though she mentions briefly at the end of her history of Marxist feminisms that all the founders of the Combahee River Collective identified as socialists, this insight appears as an afterthought, buried in the conclusion of a 40-page chapter that completely occludes the vibrant history of women-of-colour Marxist feminisms. In the same conclusion, she also mentions Angela Davis, but rather than discuss her work as a Marxist, the only sustained treatment of Davis's work comes in the chapter on intersectionality theory. I do not mean to embark on an extended critique of this one text in particular, but I do think it is necessary to make the point explicitly that intersectionality was a Marxist project, one that utilised the insights of Marxist feminism to create a new and incredibly important perspective on oppression and domination. I stress this point only to highlight that although it is a commonplace in the literature to counterpose intersectionality and Marxism, the founding texts of intersectionality reject this kind of dichotomy.

Many other women-of-color feminists who engage race, class, gender and sexuality simultaneously also position their politics as fundamentally Marxist in character. Angela Davis, Assata Shakur, Claudia Jones, Lucy Parsons and many other Black women of this tradition identified capitalism as one of the primary causes of the global system of dispossession and domination. Many of the black women active in organizations like the United States Communist Party, the Black Panthers and the Student Nonviolent Coordinating Committee identified themselves as Marxists, socialists, or anti-capitalist anarchists. Many Latina, Hispana, Chicana and Xicana feminists themselves also mobilized Marxism in the definitions of their struggles both in the mid-century and in contemporary liberation struggles like the EZLN. Martha Gimenez, cited above, and María Lugones have contributed incomparably to both Marxist theories of capitalism and intersectional theories of oppression. Transnational feminisms have long used Marxist analyses of capitalism to explain the racialized and gendered systems of disempowerment that characterized imperialism and colonialism in the global South.

White Marxists, too, have had considerable things to say about the relationships between capitalism, race and gender that are often forgotten or underthematized in contemporary histories. Rosa Luxemburg's landmark text *The Accumulation of Capital* argues that imperialism and colonization were both logically and historically necessary for the system of capitalism to function. V.I. Lenin also posited white Euro-imperialism as an inextricable part of capitalism. Even Marx himself wrote about the plight of slavery in the United States, as well as the colonization of North America, China, India and Ireland. While none of these authors had an explicit theory of race in all of its complexities and multiplicities, they did clearly have an analysis of global exploitation, dispossession and power relations that recognized the co-constitution of racialized systems of violence and capitalism. Other white Marxist theorists have proposed detailed theories of race specifically; Theodore Allen's two volume *The Invention of the White Race*, David Roediger and Elizabeth Esch's *The Production of Difference* and Jodi Melamed's *Represent and Destroy* are exemplary in this regard.

This is not to say that Marxism and intersectionality have only one shared history, or that each of these figures and texts offered exhaustive and definitive analyses of the structures in question. Rather, this alternative historiography shows that analyses of capitalism are not alien to intersectionality, and nor have extended considerations of race, gender, colonialism, and imperialism been wholly absent from Marxism. Rather, I return to these figures to emphasize that there is already a significant history, both activist and academic, of common ground and common work between these frameworks, a history that could form the basis for a more integrated theory of intersectional capitalism.

4.2 Colonial Heterosexualism and the Invention of Capitalism

By foregrounding the shared theoretical and political ground between Marxism and intersectionality, we begin to see a path for an intersectional theory of capitalism emerge, one that would offer a sustained, nuanced critique of the logic and structure of capitalism *through* an analysis of race, gender, class, sexuality, imperialism, and colonization. The reading I propose in this section is that capitalism *is just* the conjunction of these structures of dispossession. Following the important work of Silvia Federici, Anne McClintock, María Lugones and others, I argue that capitalism cannot be adequately rendered by class-only or class-primary accounts, but that economic class structure is merely one part of a complex and multifaceted system of domination in which patriarchy, white supremacy, colonization (both direct and indirect) and heterosexualism are fundamental, constitutively ineradicable, equiprimordial elements. This approach does not de-emphasize more traditional class analysis but follows the key insights of intersectionality in arguing that class, race, gender, sexuality, colonization and imperialism are constituted in and through one another in such a way that class cannot be considered the master-term of capitalist accumulation and antagonism. A truly adequate analysis of capitalism, both theoretically and historically, I argue, treats capitalism as the original synthesis of these systems of dispossession.

The wage relation has often been taken as the starting point for the analysis of capitalism. Much of Marx's account in *Capital* unpacks the historically specific emergence of the organization of labor under the wage as the major factor differentiating capitalism from the feudal economy which preceded it. As Marx and others have remarked, the invention of wage labor as a mechanism of market compulsion is one of the most historically salient changes in the modes of production. So, it is no surprise that, since the late nineteenth century, most analyses of capitalism have begun with an analysis of waged labor or have considered only wage labor.

But more recently, theorists have come to understand that the wage relation, while definitive for white European men, is only one part of the story of capitalism. As Marxist feminists have argued since the mid-twentieth century, unwaged labor forms a constitutive element of capitalism as well. Many Marxist feminists focused on what they called 'social reproduction' – the unwaged labor of cooking, cleaning, subsistence farming, bearing and rearing children, and multiple modes of affective and care work that are structurally necessary for the continuation of capitalist society, but which remain unwaged.

Social-reproduction theorists have argued that the fact that this labor, undertaken primarily by women, is unwaged, forms a structural necessity under capitalism, for it allows the capitalist to glean the benefits of reproductive labor
necessary for the waged worker to enter the formal economy without paying
for it; they argue that if all of this labor were paid, it would make the capitalist system itself insolvent.[16] This structural dependence on the unwaged labor
of women leads Maria Mies (1986) to deem social reproduction a position of
'structurally necessary super-exploitation' to which women are generally subjected and which affects women of colour and women from the global South
in particularly violent ways.

But women's work in the home was not the only form of unwaged labor on
which capitalism depends. As Domenico Losurdo (2011), Sidney Mintz (1985)
and Eric Williams (1994) have all convincingly argued, capitalism would not
have been possible without the invention of the distinctive brand of transatlantic chattel slavery that formed the basis of European economies through
the nineteenth century. Dorothy Roberts (1997), Jennifer Morgan (2004), Amy
Dru Stanley (1998) and bell hooks (1981) have further clarified the specific role
of enslaved women in the accumulative regime of capitalism, as their bodies
were violently used as a means to birth new slaves and perpetuate the regime
of slavery-based capitalism. Many enduring racializing and gendered stereotypes that still hold power in the contemporary world were generated in order
to secure this means of reproducing the institution of slavery; the hypertextu-
alization of racialized bodies served to legitimate the mass rape of enslaved
women, and later to enforce the terror of lynching when slavery was no longer
a viable social form. All of these theorists have contextualized the emergence
of race in the eighteenth century and the persistence of anti-black racism as
direct consequences of slavery.

Capitalism also would not have been possible or successful without a sustained regime of colonization. Andrea Smith (2005), Anne McClintock (1995)
and Domenico Losurdo (2011) argue that the dispossession of indigenous peoples from their lands in North America formed a necessary historical condition for the concretion of capitalism. As Quijano (2000: 538) explains, 'The vast
genocide of the Indians in the first decades of colonization was not caused principally by the violence of the conquest nor by the plagues the conquistadors

---

16   Elements of this argument have been made by a wide variety of feminist theorists, includ-
      ing Silvia Federici, Maria Mies, Giovanna Franca Dalla Costa (Dalla Costa 2008), Selma
      James and Mariarosa Dalla Costa (James and Dalla Costa 1973), Kathi Weeks (Weeks 2011),
      Nancy Fraser (Fraser 2013), Lise Vogel (Vogel 1983) and innumerable others.

brought but took place because so many American Indians were used as disposable manual labor and forced to work until death.'

Marx himself gestures toward the unwaged aspects of capitalism as being structurally necessary. In Chapter 26 of *Capital, Volume I*, Marx submits to critique Adam Smith's notion of primitive accumulation to argue that the proximate cause of capitalism was not the thrifty ingenuity of rich Europeans, but rather sustained campaigns of slaughter, enslavement, genocide and dispossession. Contemporary theorists have expanded Marx's quite succinct analysis of primitive accumulation, placing it at the center of the historical and theoretical structures of capitalism (see Mies 1986; Perelman 2000; Federici 2004).

Attempting to synthesize these different spheres of unwaged labor under capitalism, Quijano develops an analysis of what he calls the 'coloniality of power'. Maria Lugones (2007: 20) reconstructs this concept:

> In Quijano's model of global capitalist Eurocentered power, 'capitalism' refers to the structural articulation of all historically known forms of control of labor or exploitation, slavery, servitude, small independent mercantile production, wage labor, and reciprocity under the hegemony of the capital-wage labor relation. In this sense, the structuring of the disputes over control of labor are discontinuous: not all labor relations under global, Eurocentered capitalism fall under the capital/wage relation model, though this is the hegemonic model. It is important in beginning to see the reach of the coloniality of power that wage labor has been reserved almost exclusively for white Europeans. The division of labor is thoroughly 'racialized' as well as geographically differentiated. Here we see the coloniality of labor as a thorough meshing of labor and 'race'.

While the coloniality of power provides an immensely powerful analytic for the phenomena under discussion, Lugones submits Quijano's model to critique for its erasure of the gendered and sexual dynamics of colonial capital. She complicates and expands the coloniality of power to include what she calls 'heterosexualism' as a founding and constitutive element in the ruling colonial capitalist order:

> Considering critically both biological dimorphism and the position that gender socially constructs biological sex is pivotal to understand the scope, depth, and characteristics of the colonial/modern gender system. The sense is that the reduction of gender to the private, to control over sex and its resources and products is a matter of ideology, of the cognitive production of modernity that understood race as gendered and gender

as raced in particularly differential ways for Europeans/'whites' and col-
onized/'non-white' peoples. Race is no more mythical and fictional than
gender, both powerful fictions.

LUGONES 2007: 12

Lugones's analysis of the creation of the modern regimes of race, gender and
heterosexuality through the regime of colonial capital provides one of the
most nuanced accounts of the inextricably interwoven regimes of domination.
Her analysis, which focuses on the ways in which white colonizers-imposed
regimes of rationality, race, gender, sex and sexuality becomes even more powerful when conjoined with Anne McClintock's, who argues that the power relations entailed in colonization were not simply unidirectional, but rather contained incredibly important consequences for the construction of race, gender,
sex and sexuality inside white Euro-society. In her landmark text *Imperial
Leather*, McClintock (1995: 47) explains that in the nineteenth century, 'sexual
purity emerged as a controlling metaphor for racial, economic and political
power', a metaphor that while it was deployed differently for men and women,
for whites and for Blacks, had deep effects on social relations even inside colonial societies. One of the lasting effects of the heterosexualist coloniality of
power, McClintock argues, is a kind of hierarchical inventory of human beings,
one that justified not only the subjugation of non-white and colonized people,
but that of women and workers generally. In this regime, 'the English middle-
class male was placed at the pinnacle of evolutionary hierarchy. White English
middle class women followed. Domestic workers, female miners and working-
class prostitutes were stationed on the threshold between the white and black
races' (McClintock 1995: 56). What is crucial about McClintock's analysis is the
recognition that the kind of domination enacted in the colonies contained
significant effects on individuals located on all sides of these power relations.
This is not to say that these effects were the same; not at all. The discourse of
purity, for example, has never had the same effect on white women as Black
women, though it was used as a technique of domination on both. The central insight, however, is that techniques and discourses of power are *relational*;
they contain reverberating effects for the construction of subjectivity for both
the oppressed and the oppressor, as well as for those who benefit materially
from oppression but have little direct control over the processes of its concretion and maintenance (for example, white women who benefitted materially
from systems of white supremacy, but had little political, economic or social
clout in the direct organization of the institutions which created it).

The analysis of the relationality of power is the central insight of an intersectional critique of capitalism. The above analyses show that capitalism *required*

colonization and its attendant systems of racial, gender and sexual control. But what this last piece offered by McClintock is able to thematize is the way in which the central wage-relation at the heart of the European bourgeoisie/ proletariat split is itself simultaneously the cause and the effect of the regime of colonial heterosexualism. Or, to put this another way, the European class system developed in and through the regimes of racial, gendered, and sexual power of capitalist colonialism. Again, this does not mean that racialization, sexualization or gendering happened in the same way in the alleys of Paris as on the plantations of Haiti, but rather that the fate of the European working class and colonized populations cannot be considered separately from the perspective of capitalism. The profit-logic of capitalism, with its necessarily consequent ideas about reason, labor, race, gender and sexuality created both the metropole and the colonies simultaneously, and subjects on both sides of this divide were constructed, through systems of domination and exploitation, in the image of what capitalism needed to survive. That capitalism requires multiple kinds of exploitation, multiple forms of dispossession, and multiple kinds of subjects in order to gain global hegemony is corroborative evidence for Marx's fundamental diagnosis of the system's simultaneous resilience and its ultimate fragility.

5   Conclusion: Toward an Intersectional Critique of Capitalism

The intersectional critique of capitalism that I have been trying to develop departs radically from prevailing Marxist arguments about the nature of class. I argue that to claim that capitalism is the root of the modern class, gender, sexuality and race systems of oppression is not to say that class is the primary or privileged axis of oppression. Rather, Marxist analyses give the clearest analysis of certain aspects of class and also, more so than other theories, have devoted much time, effort and energy to detailing the historical and contemporary workings of capitalism. So, while I do, in this analysis, privilege capitalism as the name of the system oppressing us all, I do not hold that class, as an isolatable economic or social determination, gives us a privileged understanding of capitalism, or at least, it does not do so any more than race, gender, or sexuality. Slavery, colonialism, patriarchy, white supremacy – all these were developed in and through capitalism, at least in their modern and contemporary forms. So, when I call the 'matrix of domination' capitalism, this should not mean that economic determinations are privileged in this analysis.

I give one single name to this system because I believe it is *a coherent system*. What the very helpful, incredibly fruitful analyses of 'intersecting oppressions', the 'matrix of domination' and 'simultaneous oppressions' do not adequately render is the unity of these oppressions; to say that oppressions intersect, interact and mutually-reinforce one another is still to pose them as separate. The work of the intersectionality theorists who coined these terms themselves have argued convincingly that race, class, gender, and sexuality in fact cannot be separated and were historically concreted in and through one another. In this respect, their insights go far beyond the language they use to describe the phenomena they explain. When intersectionality scholars argue for the centrality of identity politics, they are arguing for the fundamental truth that the oppressions which have been most explicitly theorized in relation to individual identities are precisely the oppressions that must be interrogated as the basis for any structural analysis of domination in the contemporary world. In this sense, the politics of identity espoused by intersectionality, as group based, historically concreted oppressions go far beyond the experience of individual identity while also insisting that individuals and their experiences must be an ineliminable part of our theorizing. Just as Marx (1994: 113) once criticized Feuerbach for speaking of Man when he should have spoken of 'real historical men', so too our analysis of capitalism must speak of real historical people – of all genders – which means speaking of their real identities and the social locations those identities produce.

I return to Lugones (2003: 146) once more to articulate this framework. She writes,

> the image of interlocking [oppressions] is of two entirely discreet things, like two pieces of a jigsaw puzzle. I am not ready to give up the term because it is used by other women of color theorists who write in a liberatory vein about enmeshed oppressions. I think interwoven or intermeshed or enmeshed may provide better images.

I want to follow Lugones here, in not jettisoning the term 'intersectionality', as it is this vein and tradition of thinking and writing from which this project comes and it is her to whom I want to explicitly acknowledge my intellectual debt. I agree with Lugones that interwoven oppressions are the best way to render racism, exploitation, white supremacy, colonialism, heterosexism, cissexism. What I want to suggest is that if these oppressions are interwoven, then the tapestry is capitalism.[17]

---

17   I thank Gil Morejón for this incredibly insightful way of framing this intervention

References

Aguilar, Delia 2012, 'From Triple Jeopardy to Intersectionality: A Feminist Perplex', *Comparative Studies of South Asia, Africa and the Middle East*, 32, 2: 415–28.

Alcoff, Linda Martín 2011, 'An Epistemology for the Next Revolution', *Transmodernity: Journal of Peripheral Cultural Production of the Luso-Hispanic World*, 1, 2: 67–78.

Alexander-Floyd, Nikol G. 2012, 'Disappearing Acts: Reclaiming Intersectionality in the Social Sciences in a Post-Black Feminist Era', *Feminist Formations*, 24, 1: 1–25.

Allen, Theodore W. 2012, *The Invention of the White Race*, two volumes, London: Verso.

Anderson, Kevin B. 2010, *Marx at the Margins: On Nationalism, Ethnicity, and Non-Western Societies*, Chicago: University of Chicago Press.

Barnett, Bernice McNair, Rose M. Brewer and M. Bahati Kuumba 1999, 'New Directions in Race, Gender & Class Studies: African American Experiences', *Race, Gender & Class*, 6, 2, 7–28.

Belkhir, Jean 1993, 'Editor's Introduction: Integrating Race, Sex, & Class in Our Disciplines', *Race, Sex & Class*, 1, 1: 3–11.

Belkhir, Jean 1994, 'The "Failure" and Revival of Marxism on Race, Gender, & Class Issues', *Race, Sex & Class*, 2, 1: 79–107.

Belkhir, Jean Ait 2001, 'Marxism Without Apologies: Integrating Race, Gender, Class; A Working Class Approach', *Race, Gender & Class*, 8, 2: 142–71, <https://www.jstor.org/ stable/41674975>.

Benn Michaels, Walter 2006, *The Trouble with Diversity: How We Learned to Love Identity and Ignore Inequality*, New York: Holt Books.

Bohrer, Ashley 2015, 'Fanon and Feminism: The Discourse of Colonization in Italian Feminism', *Interventions: International Journal of Postcolonial Studies*, 17, 3: 378–93, <https://doi.org/10.1080/1369801X.2014.996180>.

Brown, Heather A. 2012, *Marx on Gender and the Family: A Critical Study*, Historical Materialism Book Series, Leiden: Brill.

Collins, Patricia Hill 1997, 'On Wes and Fenstermaker's Doing Difference', in *Men, Women, and Gender: Ongoing Debates*, edited by Mary Roth Walsh, New Haven, CT: Yale University Press.

Collins, Patricia Hill 2000, *Black Feminist Thought: Knowledge, Consciousness, and the Politics of Empowerment*, New York: Routledge.

Collins, Patricia Hill 2004, 'Comment on Hekman's "Truth and Method: Feminist Standpoint Theory Revisited": Where's The Power?', in *The Feminist Standpoint Reader: Intellectual and Political Controversies*, edited by Sandra Harding, New York: Routledge.

Cox, Nicole and Silvia Federici 1976, *Counter-planning from the Kitchen. Wages for Housework: A Perspective on Capital and the Left*, New York: New York Wages for Housework Committee.

Crenshaw, Kimberlé 1995, *Critical Race Theory: The Key Writings that Formed the Movement*, New York: The New Press.

Dalla Costa, Giovanna Franca 2008, *The Work of Love: The Role of Unpaid Housework as a Condition of Poverty and Violence at the Dawn of the 21st Century*, New York: Autonomedia.

Davis, Angela Y. 1981, *Women, Race, and Class*, New York: Random House.

Engels, Friedrich 1942 [1888], *The Origin of the Family, Private Property and the State, in the Light of the Researches of Lewis H. Morgan*, New York: International Publishers.

Federici, Silvia 2004, *Caliban and the Witch: Women, the Body and Primitive Accumulation*, New York: Autonomedia.

Fraser, Nancy 2013, *Fortunes of Feminism: From State-Managed Capitalism to Neoliberal Crisis*, London: Verso.

Gedalof, Irene 2013, 'Sameness and Difference in Government Equality Talk', *Ethnic and Racial Studies*, 36, 1: 117–35.

Gimenez, Martha E. 2001, 'Marxism and Class, Gender and Race: Rethinking the Trilogy', *Race, Gender & Class*, 8, 2: 23–33.

Hartmann, Heidi 1981, 'The Unhappy Marriage of Marxism and Feminism', in Sargent (ed.) 1981.

hooks, bell 1981, 'Sexism and the Black Female Slave Experience', in *Ain't I a Woman: Black Women and Feminism*, Boston, MA: South End Press.

James, Selma and Mariarosa Dalla Costa 1973, *The Power of Women and the Subversion of the Community*, Bristol: Falling Wall Press.

Kandal, Terry R. 1995, *The Woman Question in Classical Sociological Theory*, Miami: University Press of Florida.

King, Deborah K. 1988, 'Multiple Jeopardy, Multiple Consciousness: The Context of a Black Feminist Ideology', *Signs: Journal of Women in Culture and Society*, 14, 1: 42–72.

Lorde, Audre 1984, *Sister Outsider: Essays and Speeches*, Trumansburg, NY: Crossing Press.

Losurdo, Domenico 2011, *Liberalism: A Counter-History*, translated by Gregory Elliott, London: Verso.

Lugones, Maria 2003, *Pilgrimages/Peregrinajes: Theorizing Coalition against Multiple Oppressions*, Lanham, MD: Rowman & Littlefield.

Lugones, Maria 2007, 'Heterosexualism and the Colonial/Modern Gender System', *Hypatia*, 22, 1: 186–209.

Mann, Susan Archer 2012, *Doing Feminist Theory: From Modernity to Postmodernity*, Oxford: Oxford University Press.

Mann, Susan Archer 2013, 'Third Wave Feminism's Unhappy Marriage of Post-structuralism and Intersectionality Theory', *Journal of Feminist Scholarship*, 4: 54–73.

Marx, Karl 1967 [1876], *Capital: A Critique of Political Economy*, edited by Friedrich Engels, New York: International Publishers.

Marx, Karl 1993 [1857–8/1939], *Grundrisse: Foundations of the Critique of Political Economy (Rough Draft)*, translated by Martin Nicolaus, Harmondsworth: Penguin.

Marx, Karl 1994, *Selected Writings*, edited by Lawrence H. Simon, Indianapolis, IN: Hackett Publishing.

Marx, Karl and Frederick Engels 2004 [1846/1932], *The German Ideology. Part One, with Selections from Parts Two and Three and Supplementary Texts*, edited by C.J. Arthur, New York: International Publishers.

May, Vivian M. 2014, '"Speaking into the Void?": Intersectionality Critiques and Epistemic Backlash', *Hypatia*, 29, 1: 94–112.

McClintock, Anne 1995, *Imperial Leather: Race, Gender, and Sexuality in the Colonial Contest*, New York: Routledge.

Melamed, Jodi 2011, *Represent and Destroy: Rationalizing Violence in the New Racial Capitalism*, Minneapolis: University of Minnesota Press.

Mies, Maria 1986, *Patriarchy and Accumulation on a World Scale: Women in the International Division of Labour*, First Edition, London: Zed Books.

Mintz, Sidney Wilfred 1985, *Sweetness and Power: The Place of Sugar in Modern History*, New York: Viking.

Mitchell, Eve 2013, 'I Am a Woman and a Human: A Marxist Feminist Critique of Intersectionality Theory', *Libcom.org*, 12 September, available at: <https://libcom.org/library/i-am-woman-human-marxist-feminist-critique-intersectionality-theory-eve-mitchell>, accessed 26 November 2014.

Mohanty, Chandra Talpade 1988, 'Under Western Eyes: Feminist Scholarship and Colonial Discourses', *Feminist Review*, 30: 61–88.

Morgan, Jennifer L. 2004, *Laboring Women: Reproduction and Gender in New World Slavery*, Philadelphia: University of Pennsylvania Press.

Perelman, Michael 2000, *The Invention of Capitalism: Classical Political Economy and the Secret History of Primitive Accumulation*, Durham, NC: Duke University Press.

Quijano, Anibal 2000, 'Coloniality of Power, Eurocentrism, and Latin America', *Nepantla: Views from South*, 1, 3: 533–80.

Roberts, Dorothy E. 1997, *Killing the Black Body: Race, Reproduction, and the Meaning of Liberty*, New York: Pantheon Books.

Roediger, David R. and Elizabeth D. Esch 2014, *The Production of Difference: Race and the Management of Labor in U.S. History*, New York: Oxford University Press.

Smith, Andrea 2005, *Conquest: Sexual Violence and American Indian Genocide*, Cambridge, MA: South End Press.

Smith, Barbara 1998, *The Truth That Never Hurts: Writings on Race, Gender, and Freedom*, New Brunswick, NJ: Rutgers University Press.

Smith, Beverly and Barbara Smith 1983, 'Across the Kitchen Table: A Sister-to-Sister Dialogue', in *This Bridge Called My Back: Writings by Radical Women of Color*, edited by Cherrie Moraga and Gloria Anzaldúa, Second Edition, New York: Kitchen Table Press.

Spelman, Elizabeth V. 1988, *Inessential Woman: Problems of Exclusion in Feminist Thought*, Boston, MA: Beacon Press.

Stanley, Amy Dru 1998, *From Bondage to Contract: Wage Labor, Marriage, and the Market in the Age of Slave Emancipation*, Cambridge: Cambridge University Press.

The Combahee River Collective 1977, *The Combahee River Collective Statement*, April, available at: <http://circuitous.org/scraps/combahee.html>.

Vogel, Lise 1983, *Marxism and the Oppression of Women: Toward a Unitary Theory*, New Brunswick, NJ: Rutgers University Press.

Walby, Sylvia 1988, *Gender Segregation at Work*, Milton Keynes: Open University Press.

Weeks, Kathi 2011, *The Problem with Work: Feminism, Marxism, Antiwork Politics, and Postwork Imaginaries*, Durham, NC: Duke University Press.

Williams, Eric Eustace 1994, *Capitalism & Slavery*, Chapel Hill, NC: University of North Carolina Press.

Young, Iris Marion 1981, 'Beyond the Unhappy Marriage: A Critique of Dual Systems Theory', in Sargent (ed.) 1981.

CHAPTER 13

Marxism, Peasants, and the Cultural Turn

The Myth of a 'Nice' Populism

Tom Brass

All's Whiggery now, / But we old men are massed against / the world.
WILLIAM BUTLER YEATS (1933: 23)

∴

1 Introduction

The usual argument heard today, as so often in the past, is that Marxist theory is fundamentally wrong because it has always misunderstood the peasantry – and thus underestimated the enduring nature of their cultural and economic 'otherness' – in every form of society. Here this argument is reversed: it is because Marxism was right about peasants that it has posed awkward questions for those in academia who continue to study and write about agrarian change. Over the whole range of economic, ideological, and political issues, a clear-cut difference has always separated Marxist theory from agrarian populism, its main political rival where interpretations of the peasantry are concerned. This was a distinction embodied in their respective combinations of a discourse-for (what each of them endorses) and discourse-against (what each opposes). Whereas agrarian populism approved (and approves) of the kind of things and/or processes objected to by Marxism, the latter in turn disagreed (and disagrees still) with what is backed by the former.

The significance of this distinction lies in the fact that over the latter half of the twentieth century agrarian populism has resurfaced in the discourse of the 'cultural turn'. Rejecting the previous modernity/development project as part of an inappropriate Eurocentric colonial imposition on the rural sector of Third World countries, the 'new' populist postmodernism analytically re-essentialized the identity politics associated historically with 'peasantness'. A major claim made by exponents of the 'cultural turn', however, is that – unlike its earlier counter-part – the current form of populism and the grassroots movements subscribing to this ideology are politically progressive, and thus models to be followed in the future. This re-emergence and consolidation of populism, both globally and academically, is itself reflected in the attempt to recuperate specifically populist interpretations of agrarian history.

Current analyses following this line justify their approach to peasant/farmer agency by claiming that a break exists between what they accept as old/reactionary forms of agrarian populism and what they argue are modern/progressive (= 'nice') variants. This is done by insisting that issues previously encountered at the rural grassroots – such as class divisions or backwards-looking rural nostalgia and tradition – are all identities/discourses belonging to the past, and as a result are now largely absent. Instead, these historical forms are said to have been replaced currently by a forwards-looking project in the countryside that is not only different but also based on modern/realist politics and ideology; the latter reflect the changed economic demands neither seen nor rooted in the past. The impression conveyed is that 'bad' populism is somehow an anomaly, not just unconnected with but a deviation from the contemporary norm of a 'nice' populism.[1]

For its part, Marxist theory is condemned for not recognizing this transformation, and thus for continuing to apply preconceived/outmoded critiques to present-day agrarian populism. This insistence on the progressive character of modern agrarian populism is also linked to the view that Marxist critiques have yet to establish its reactionary nature, or such objections as have been made are in some sense faulty. However, it will be argued here that these claims, advanced in defense of agrarian populism, are themselves problematic, both methodologically and in terms of theory. Furthermore, it will also be argued that the Marxist critiques deemed by agrarian populism to be absent or faulty are neither.

In the presentation which follows there are three main sections, the first of which contrasts agrarian populist interpretations with Marxist positions on the peasantry, together with the way each approach is endorsed or undermined by

---

1   As well as the two main case studies examined below, a recent example of this approach is Borras (2019), who attempts unsuccessfully to make a distinction between right-wing (= 'nasty') populism and what he terms 'progressive agrarian populism', a 'nice' contemporary variant. The latter, he maintains, consists of 'people of the land' who in his opinion have a natural political inclination towards socialism, defined by him as nothing more than 'a deeply democratic and egalitarian organization of power'. Missing from this pointlessly vague definition – which could just as well apply to some forms of accumulation – is any consideration of issues such as the ownership/control of the means of production, distribution, and exchange, property relations generally, collectivization, income redistribution, and central planning, not to say class struggle aimed at seizure/control of the state.

the 'cultural turn'. Recent claims about peasant movements made in case-studies of the Russian and Indian countryside are considered in the next section, while the final section appraises critically the view contained in these same case-studies regarding the existence of a modern/progressive (= 'nice') variant of agrarian populism.

2   Peasants, Marxism, Populism

Agrarian populism has its roots in the antagonism towards Enlightenment discourse and the 1789 French Revolution expressed by Romanticism, a hostility which took the form of support for pre-revolutionary traditional forms/institutions and both the specificity and innateness of cultural/ethnic/national identity. At the center of this discourse was an essentialist concept of an homogenous smallholding peasant, whose pristine and immutable cultural 'otherness' was said to embody both Nature and nationhood. The same identity structured not only Russian populist/neo-populist ideology at the end of the nineteenth century and the beginning of the twentieth, but also Italian fascism and German Nazism. In common with this prefigurative discourse, therefore, agrarian populism is supportive of small-scale economic activity (peasant family farming, individual proprietorship, artisanry) in the countryside, and also of rural cultural forms/institutions based on this activity: family, village, regional, national, ethnic, and religious identities which are perceived as being derived from Nature.

By contrast, agrarian populism opposes large-scale economic activity (collectivization, massification), particularly urban-based forms (finance capital, industrialization, planning). It is also hostile to their accompanying institutional, relational, and systemic effects (class formation/struggle, revolution, bureaucracy, the state), all of which are regarded as inauthentic/non-natural internationalisms imposed on rural populations by external (= 'foreign') agency/processes (socialism, capitalism). Unsurprisingly in view of its essentialist perception of rural identity, the historical subject of agrarian populism is an undifferentiated peasantry, the repository of traditional culture and thus emblematic of people/nation/Nature. Equally unsurprisingly is the fact that a consequence of peasant de-essentialization as a result of separation from means of production (land) is the erosion of cultural and national identity.

Peasants were – and are – central to Marxist theory about the dynamics informing the trajectory in pursuit of modernity and systemic transition: from feudalism to capitalism, and from the latter to socialism. Hence the process of accumulation is itself premised on an agrarian transition, whereby a marketed surplus is transferred to industry. This in turn requires the differentiation of the peasantry, and its fragmentation along class lines, thereby providing accumulation with both the employer and worker. A result of capitalist development in agriculture, therefore, was the emergence of rich, middle, and poor strata: the top component became part of a rural bourgeoisie, while the bottom stratum was converted into a proletariat. Middle peasants, or petty commodity producers, were de-peasantized, and over time the majority of them also joined the ranks of landless labor. For Marxism, therefore, the historical agent of transformation is – and can only ever be – the proletariat.

In the two decades following the defeat of fascism, agrarian populism was supplanted both by bourgeois modernization theory and by Marxist approaches to Third World development. Each challenged static depictions of peasant smallholders long associated with pre-1939 analyses of rural societies in underdeveloped nations which tended to portray them as unchanging and unchangeable. Notwithstanding a shared commitment to 'progress', Marxism and bourgeois modernization theory subscribed to very different interpretations as to its systemic direction and outcome. From the 1950s to the 1970s, therefore, the object of agrarian reform policies advocated by bourgeois modernization was to generate a twofold process: by extending landownership, peasant proprietors would create a mass consumer market for commodities produced by domestic capital. For its part, Marxism viewed mobilizations by poor peasants and agricultural laborers throughout Asia and Latin America as heralding the possibility of a socialist transition.

The 1980s, however, were characterized by the academic decline of development theory itself, and in particular those approaches – such as modernization and Marxism – which adhered to notions of 'progress'. This was accompanied by the simultaneous rise of neoliberalism and postmodernism, both of which had a profound impact on the peasantry: one on its economic prospects, the other on its interpretation. Critiques of capitalism underwent a corresponding shift, away from political economy and towards culture/aesthetics, and increasingly took the form of opposition to the impact of accumulation on grassroots rural farming/tradition/culture/ethnicity. In keeping with this, class as an analytical concept was downgraded and/or replaced by non-class identity; modernity, revolution, and socialism as desirable objectives gave way to tradition, resistance, and a return to a benign (= 'nicer') capitalism.

In every respect, therefore, Marxism has been and remains the 'other' of agrarian populism. Although the Marxist critique of populism is rightly associated with the work of Lenin and Trotsky, their opposition to its discourse is prefigured in the work of Marx and Engels.[2] This kind of mid-nineteenth century populism was identified by Engels as one which sought 'to establish the rule of the aristocracy', composed of 'adherents of feudal and patriarchal society which has been or is still being daily destroyed by large-scale industry, world trade and the bourgeois society that they have both brought into existence. From the ills of present-day society this group draws on the conclusion that feudal or patriarchal society should be restored because it was free from these ills' (Engels 1976, 355). His conclusion was that 'it always gives away its real intentions every time the proletariat becomes revolutionary and communist, when it immediately allies itself with the bourgeoisie against the proletarians.'

Such a pattern remains extant, with the difference that it is now a rural bourgeoisie that seeks to gain the support of plebeian elements by invoking a shared non-class identity when engaged in struggle against rival producers. As will be seen below in the case of new farmers' movements in India, unlike Marxism – which is antagonistic to capitalism *tout court* – agrarian populism is opposed only to particular variants of capital (financial, foreign), ones moreover that in the form of largescale agribusiness enterprises compete successfully with rich peasants and commercial farmers in the market for agricultural commodities. Obtaining the political collaboration of plebeian elements requires a non-class ideology which purports to advance the cause of 'those below': in short, a pro-peasant discourse that ignores or downgrades class distinctions transecting the peasantry. It is precisely this ideology – labelled by Marxist theory as 'false consciousness' – which is not only supplied by agrarian populism, but also endorsed by postmodern, post-colonial, and post-development approaches, via arguments championing as 'progressive' and empowering cultural identities that transect class.[3]

---

2   For these critiques see Lenin (1964a) and Trotsky (1969). Marx and Engels (1976: 507ff.) had attacked agrarian populism half a century earlier, when in the *Communist Manifesto* they considered 'feudal socialism', defined thus: 'The aristocracy, in order to rally the people to them, waved the proletarian alms-bags in front for a banner ... so little do they conceal the reactionary character of their criticism that their chief accusation against the bourgeoisie amounts to this, that under the bourgeois regime a class is being developed, which is destined to cut up root and branch the old order of society'. In the sentence that follows, the underlying political fear of landowners who mobilize on the basis of agrarian populism is made clear: 'What they upbraid the bourgeoisie with is not so much that it creates a proletariat, as it creates a *revolutionary* proletariat' (original emphasis).

3   As indicated elsewhere (Brass, 2017, 2019), those holding these kinds of view subscribe to paradigms such as global labour history or every-day-forms-of-resistance, and deploy concepts like 'multitudes', 'subalterns', 'classes of labour', 'food commodity chains', 'food security', 'food sovereignty', 'land sovereignty', and 'land grabbing'.

2.1   The 'Cultural Turn' and/as the 'New' Populist Postmodernism

In order to understand the current relevance and significance of Marxist theory as the 'other' of the 'cultural turn', it is necessary to situate both approaches in the context of the development debate taking place over the last half century (and, indeed, earlier). Epistemologically, the 'cultural turn' (= 'new' populist postmodernism) encompasses a variety of frameworks, including those presented under the label of subaltern studies, ecofeminism, new social movements, everyday-forms-of resistance, post-colonialism, post-Marxism, post-development, and post-capitalism.[4] Of crucial importance, therefore, is how the 'cultural turn' represents an epistemological and political fusion of postmodernism (= identity choice) and neoliberalism (= economic choice), enabling its academic exponents to reassert the analytical validity of agrarian populism. This in turn has not just negated but reversed the political agenda informing much discussion in academia generally – and the social sciences in particular – whereby socialism was perceived as a desirable outcome of economic development.

At the root of the 'cultural turn' is the privileging by postmodern theory of language, and a corresponding deprivileging of socialism, materialism and class as illegitimate Enlightenment/Eurocentric forms of 'foundationalism' inapplicable to the rural Third World. No significance is attached to the link between language and the material conditions that give rise to or sustain a particular narrative. Indeed, it is a link the very existence – let alone the efficacy – of which postmodern theory denies. An important reason that poverty has vanished from the development agenda is, quite simply, that it has been redefined. Rather than being categorized as a problem, which is what Marxism and much modernization theory did in the 1960s and 1970s, rural poverty has been redefined by postmodernism as part of culture, and thus empowering for its grassroots subjects. Postmodernism has been able to do this for two reasons.

First, because many of those who regard themselves either as sympathetic towards socialism, or indeed as Marxists, have forgotten (or in some cases never learned) what Marxist theory actually teaches.[5] They have as a result espoused

---

4   Marxist critiques of the 'new' populist postmodernism as a result of long-standing theoretical and political engagement with the latter framework are outlined in Brass (2000, 2014), where further details about the case made in this section can be found.

5   It is noticeable when comparing the extent and range of sources cited, that measured against earlier analyses of rural transformation many texts currently attempting to situate peasant economy in terms both of a global presence and of a *longue durée* are what might be called 'research lite'. The resulting absence of depth and breadth manifests itself in numerous ways, not least in misrecognizing – and thus conflating – theoretical approaches that are politically and epistemologically incompatible.

postmodern theoretical positions (peasant essentialism, the innateness of nationalism, the desirability of grassroots ethnic empowerment, rural tradition as mobilizing discourse) that are epistemologically no different from the identity politics advocated by the political right. Postmodernists compare the nationalist discourse featuring subaltern identity to that developed in the first decade of the twentieth century, suggesting this is the way forward politically. In their view it is the model that the left should incorporate into its theory and practice because, in the present stage of capitalism, national difference and not class antagonism is the main contradiction. Against this, the crucial distinction informing the Marxist position on nationalism is best summed up by Lenin: 'Combat all national oppression? Yes, of course! Fight *for* any kind of national development, *for* "national culture" in general? – Of course not.'[6]

And second, because the reproduction of capitalism no longer depends on the consuming power of peasants in the so-called Third World. What an increasingly international capitalism wants, however, is only their capacity as workers, for two reasons. On the one hand, to produce agricultural commodities that can be exported and consumed elsewhere, an old argument made by Kautsky a century ago, and still relevant today. On the other, as migrants to form part of a globally expanding industrial reserve army, the object of which is to force down yet further wages and conditions throughout the world in what is now an international capitalist labor process.

This failure to understand the centrality of the industrial reserve army to the global accumulation project exposed the inadequacy of 'new' populist postmodern claims about the capacity of the rural economy and society effectively to resist systemic change. Namely, the truism long proclaimed by Marxism that hollowed-out petty commodity production is in the long run incompatible with the reproduction of independent smallholding proprietorship as envisaged by agrarian populism. Unlike the 1960s, when peasants were seen by varieties of modernization theory as contributing to economic development in two ways – as consumers and producers of commodities – now all that accumulation requires of them is their labor-power. However, because it does not advocate the transcendence of capitalism as a system and perceives empowerment simply in terms of re-establishing/protecting rural culture, agrarian populism is unable to address this problem.

Just as the recent past has seen attempts to divide capitalism along 'nice'/'nasty' lines, so now we are presented with an analogous distinction between

---

6 See Lenin (1964b: 35, original emphasis) and also Trotsky (1934: 908ff.). Earlier, Marx warned that a working class divided along national and/or ethnic lines undermined the solidarity necessary for a successful struggle against capital.

'nice'/'nasty' populisms. In each case the object is the same: to present a tainted economic system and/or political opposition to it as essentially benign. Such attempts insist a better populism or capitalism is possible, despite being claims that have been strongly criticized historically and currently by Marxists, who argue that a better populism or capitalism is not possible. Neoliberalism is the logical outcome of capitalist development, to which agrarian capitalism is an equally predictable form of far-right political reaction. What advocates of a 'progressive'/'nicer' populism forget, therefore, is that in subordinating ever larger portions of the globe to the market, capitalism has triggered not a class but a non-class response. The dilemma faced by the 'new' populist postmodernism underlines what by now ought to be obvious: unless the very existence of accumulation is itself questioned, capital will always succeed in using agriculture for its own purposes, notwithstanding attempts to protect/re-establish a culturally 'other' form of peasant farming.

That a concept of an undifferentiated peasantry engaged in resisting modernity/progress is central to a postmodern approach to development theory is in fact conceded by one of its main devotees. Wrongly castigating Marxism (and bourgeois economics) for failing to notice that peasants have not disappeared, therefore, Escobar objects to development *per se*, on the grounds that it is an inappropriate foundational/Eurocentric imposition on Third World nations.[7] Maintaining inaccurately that 'one never finds in these [developmentalist] accounts ... how the peasants' world may contain a different way of seeing problems and life', he proceeds to endorse what is an unambiguously populist view of the peasantry – labelled by him 'post-development' – as an alternative to capitalism.[8] Development is in his view nothing more than a failed attempt to apply Enlightenment values to Asia, Africa, and Latin America, since '[i]n the Third World, modernity is not "an unfinished project of the Enlightenment"'.

---

7   Escobar (1995: 106). Needless to say, such an objection ignores the view of Kautsky (1984) who pointed out that peasant survival is an effect neither of its supposed economic efficiency nor of the desire of smallholders themselves, but rather of the need on the part of agribusiness enterprises and/or rich peasant farmers to have continuing access to the labour-power on the peasant family farm.

8   Escobar (1995: 111). For the claims which follow, see Escobar (1995: 205, 215, 219, 221, 225). Contrary to what he thinks – that development theory in general and its Marxist variant in particular has somehow overlooked the fact that peasants have 'a different way of seeing problems and life' – no theory of development ignores the presence, the content and the distinctiveness of rural opinion. The problem is that the latter is not uniform, and consequently economic and political interests diverge, for the simple reason that different class elements at the rural grassroots (rich peasants, poor peasants, agricultural labourers) hold opposed views about crucial issues such as the role of the state, land reform, property redistribution, wage levels, etc.

Much rather, instead of development linked to the Enlightenment, Escobar invokes 'grassroots movements, local knowledge and popular power', citing as an example the capacity of smallholders in Peru to 'reinvent ... elements of longstanding peasant culture'. The resulting 'culture-specific productive strategy' is categorized by him as alternative to capitalism grounded in 'the sheer fact of cultural difference'.

The position taken by the 'new' populist postmodernism replicates the earlier response elicited by the term 'cultural cringe', a phenomenon described by its originator as 'an assumption that the domestic cultural product will be worse than the imported article', and applied by him to the positive way – verging on awe – which an erstwhile colonized nation perceives the cultural achievements of its one-time colonizer ('the centrifugal pull of the great cultural metropolises works against us').[9] Of relevance to the case made by the 'new' populist postmodernism, therefore, is not the 'cultural cringe' *per se* but rather its 'other'; the latter is a mirror image of the former, and arises as a reaction to it, thereby replacing a sense of cultural subordination with one of cultural autonomy ('the Cringe Inverted').[10] It entails a twofold process: not only the assertion by a previously colonized nation of its own ideological and cultural independence, but also and simultaneously the opposite; depriviledging the same characteristics of the earlier colonial power. Whatever is linked to the experience and/or history of colonization is *ipso facto* condemned, regardless of its wider theoretical provenance and politics, a view not so different from that of the 'new' populist postmodernism.

---

9   The term 'cultural cringe' was outlined during 1950 by Phillips (1958: 89–95) and used by him to depict the asymmetrical intellectual relationship between Australia as an ex-colony and the UK as an ex-colonizer, a link the inequality of which he described as an 'internalised inferiority complex [which] causes people to dismiss their own culture'.

10 On 'the cringe inverted' as the 'other' of 'the cultural cringe', see Phillips (1958: 89–90). An essay dealing with Australian folksong where this reverse variant is described observes (Phillips, 1979: 50): 'A generation ago, aesthetically U-minded Australians averted their eyes from the vulgarities of their country's past; today those vulgarities have become history to be sought out and cherished'. It could be argued that, in effect, there are not two but three variants of 'the cringe'. First, the privileging by the erstwhile colonized of the culture of the ex-colonizer ('your culture is so much better than ours') – the 'cringe' proper; second, the privileging in a positive way by the erstwhile colonized of their own culture ('we know and understand our own culture, you don't') – the 'cringe' inverted; and third, the privileging by the erstwhile colonized of their own critiques about the culture belonging to the ex-colonizer ('we know and understand your culture so much better than you do yourselves') – the 'cringe' relocated. The last variant, it could be argued, informs many 'new' populist postmodern analyses encountered in higher educational institutions of metropolitan capitalist nations.

Accordingly, what is significant are the following. First, that both the 'cultural cringe' and its reversal project an identity not of class but of nation. Second, in doing so, each creates a space for a discourse about related institutional forms as emblematic of long-standing national tradition, and consequently essentializing them as innate. This in turn sanctifies rival cultures as being 'authentic', a process reifying a specifically national identity of both colonizer and colonized. And third, attempts then to invoke a similar kind of 'difference' with regard to economic organization/behaviour do no more than deflect attention from the sameness of class formation/struggle imposed by the process of accumulation. The point about Marxist political economy is that its scope is international: since the rules it applies transcend frontiers, its teachings about capitalism as a system are not restricted to any one context, and cannot thus be regarded as specific – or, indeed, inapplicable – to a particular nation, region, or locality. It is precisely this element of universality that varieties of the 'new' populist postmodernism deny, rejecting not just Marxism, class analysis and socialism but also modernity as inappropriate Eurocentric models of development emanating from (and restricted to) an Enlightenment project.[11]

3 Case-Studies of the Russian and Indian Countryside

3.1 *Russia Then, India Now*

The two case studies examined here, by Henry Bernstein about rural Russia at the beginning of the twentieth century and by D.N. Dhanagare about rural India at the end of the same century, make the same kind of claims and exhibit similar contradictions. Both rely heavily on views expressed by and/ or interpretations contained in populist and/or anti-Marxist sources: Shanin (cited no less than fifty times) and Figes (cited some thirty times) in the case of Bernstein, and Laclau and Mouffe in the case of Dhanagare.[12] Each ignores alternative explanations advanced either by earlier analyses of Russian peasants in the case of Bernstein, or in the case of Dhanagare by his own previous writings on Indian farmers' movements.

---

11   As will be seen below, to some degree this is consistent with the view expressed by Dhanagare.

12   Notwithstanding his many endorsing references to the populist approaches of Shanin and Chayanov, Bernstein fails to mention, let alone to address, important critiques of them by Littlejohn (1973a, 1973b, 1977). Despite the fact that the *Journal of Peasant Studies* special issue in which the article by Bernstein appears is supposed to be about Marxism, it seems to be much rather a celebration of agrarian populism.

Replicating positions taken historically in debates about the role of agricultural production in the development process, Bernstein and Dhanagare subscribe to what might be termed broadly a 'farmer first' view. The latter has its epistemological origins in and is supportive of agrarian populist discourse/agency; it is also antagonistic towards Marxist theory which questions not just the political efficacy of a 'farmer first' approach to the study of economic development, but also claims that the current structure and political objectives of agrarian populism are progressive. Although accepting that his analysis is 'highly selective' in that it not only relies on a 'limited number of works' but also omits to address Bolshevik positions and debates about the agrarian question in Russia, Bernstein nevertheless fails to mention the outcome of such an approach: the reification of an agrarian populist narrative.[13] Unsurprisingly, this has epistemological and political implications for the object of his analysis, which is to place 'the Russian experience' in the context of 'today's global capitalism'.

About the socio-economic characteristics and mobilizing discourse of the 1980s new farmers' movement, Dhanagare is nothing if not adamant. To begin with, his central point is that farmers are not peasants, and as such both the movement itself and the demands it makes are considered as being without precedent.[14] 'For the first time in the history of protest movements in postcolonial India', he declares, 'the new farmers' movements were not only advancing new agendas but also presenting new ideas in theoretical and ideological discourses.'[15] Hence the insistence by Dhanagare (2017: 30, original emphasis) that the object of the movement was simply the realization of 'cost-based agricultural prices so that farmers (*not peasants* of the Chayanovian imagery) could compete in domestic and international markets'. This emphasis

---

13   See Bernstein (2018; 1128). Not addressing Bolshevik interpretations does not, however, prevent him (Bernstein, 2018: 1133, 1140) from dismissing Lenin in particular (see below) and, more generally, Bolshevism, both for 'ignorance of the realities of village life' because of a 'longstanding deficit in rural political work', and for not having a detailed agrarian programme. These claims about Bolshevik ignorance/absence, however, are not supported by other studies that are not Marxist – for example, Seregny (1989).

14   By the mid-1970s, therefore, (Dhanagare, 2017: 8, original emphasis), 'the Indian *peasant* had become a market-oriented *farmer*, although an overwhelming majority of them continued to be subsistence farmers, but now, less dependent on the landlord, but more dependent on the market.'

15   Dhanagare (2017: 62). The section continues: 'The ideology of the farmers' movements was a blend of economism and populism [a] calculation of the cost of farm production and the hiatus between the low support prices being offered to farmers and the rising costs of farm inputs. Such rational arguments were unheard of in the pre-independence peasant movements.'

on remunerative prices, moreover, was in his opinion proof both of a modern outlook and (consequently) of an absence of grassroots support for 'any
strong nostalgia for "tradition"' based on backwards-looking ideological
forms like nationalism, ethnicity, and caste (Dhanagare, 2017: 27). According
to Dhanagare, therefore, the sectoral divide informing the ideas of the farmers' leader in Maharashtra, Sharad Joshi – Bharat (= 'the farm sector') v. India
(= industry) – refers to nothing more than an imbalance in terms of trade
between 'the rural' and 'the urban', and is thus devoid of any backwards-looking ideological taint.[16]

Agrarian populist ideology as a mobilizing discourse is seen by Dhanagare
(2017: 32, 34-35) as wholly positive: he insists that 'in the post-modern context, populist forms of protest politics cannot be discredited', adding – like
Bernstein – that it is 'important to examine the emancipatory potential of populism as an ideology and of populist mobilization'. For this reason, Dhanagare
approves of the positive interpretations of populism by Laclau, Mouffe, and
Piccone, and – again, like Bernstein – is strongly critical of Marxists who
question its progressive credentials.[17] Hence the antagonism expressed by
Dhanagare – just as with Bernstein – towards Marxist analyses which seek to
explain the social composition and mobilizing ideology of the new farmers'
movements in terms of class interests and class struggle.[18] Given this optimism

---

16   Dhanagare (2017: 81–82, 84). Both at the outset and subsequently Dhanagare (2017: xiii,
     36–38) acknowledges the influence not just of farmer leaders/activists, but also of Sharad
     Joshi himself, described effusively by Dhanagare (2017: 80) as a 'towering leader'. A result
     of interviewing Joshi seems to be that Dhanagare (2017: 92 n.17, 231, n. 16 and n.18) has
     become increasingly drawn to his views. Many of the arguments made by Dhanagare are
     prefigured in Varshney (1995: 118–19, 137) who not only demonstrates a similar enthusi-
     asm for the leadership of Sharad Joshi but denies both that the latter represents the 'old
     agrarians' (= backwards-looking pre-1947 populist discourse) and that the new farmers'
     movements are 'class-driven'.

17   See Dhanagare (2017: 25, 27) who overlooks the fact that because they endorse populism,
     both Mouffe (2018) and Piccone also regard as positive the ideas of Carl Schmitt (2004;
     2005), the right-wing Catholic political theorist responsible for legally justifying the Nazi
     seizure of power in Germany on the grounds that it restored stability/order in the name
     of 'the people' and thus in the interests of the nation. It is perhaps significant that this
     endorsement by those who still regard themselves as politically leftist has attracted scorn
     not just from Marxists but also from those belonging to the political right. Hence the
     view expressed by one of the latter (Lévy, 2008: 87) who observes that 'a whole part of the
     Left, deprived of Marx, is now embracing Schmitt – seeking in the latter the reasons for
     thinking and acting that they can no longer find in the former. A whole segment of the
     European ... intelligentsia is marching as a single man behind the strange and ... halluci-
     natory idea that we need a Nazi thinker to help the Left out of its gridlock.'

18   Dismissive views about explanations which focus on class identity/interests/ struggle
     surface periodically throughout his analysis. Thus, for example, the view (Dhanagare,

where populist mobilizing discourse is concerned, the decline of the new farmers' movement is regarded by Dhanagare as an unanticipated – almost inexplicable – political and ideological nadir.

3.2   Old Believers?

Where Marxism is concerned, the antipathy expressed by Dhanagare and Bernstein is difficult to miss. Nearly four decades ago, Dhanagare (1983) published what was then, and what is still, an important analysis of peasant movements in India in the period immediately before and after Independence. Nevertheless, over time his political views have undergone a twofold change: to an increasingly benign view of populism and the new farmers' movements, and a correspondingly hostile perception of any Marxist critiques aimed at them. Based on what he argues is a framework informed by Gramscian hegemony, such positive/negative judgments pervade his recent analysis.

As he makes abundantly clear, the analysis of the new farmers' movements to which Dhanagare objects so strongly is a Marxist one. In what is a lengthy catalogue of shortcomings, Marxist interpretation is accused, variously, of 'failing to acknowledge the ability of populist ideological discourse to help the class-ridden agrarian hierarchy to transcend their class situations and interests'; of overlooking how rich farmers establish hegemony over middle and poor farmers 'through a populist ideological interpellation'; and, finally, of unjustifiably 'clubbing together' the Bharat v. India ideology of the new farmers' movements with 'postmodern articulations', thereby conflating subaltern historiography, eco-feminism, and new social movements with the conservatism, reaction, nationalism and populism of the BJP – all of which, claims Dhanagare, is 'far from convincing'.[19] Because of a 'theoretical and ideological commitment to orthodox Marxism', this framework is also charged by him with having too

---

2017: 16) that 'the success of the farmers' movement … cannot possibly be understood … in terms of its being the 'old' *kulak*-rich peasant movement, that is, a class-based movement', and that 'it would be naïve to brand the farmers' movement as the rich farmers' or *kulak* movement'. Much the same point is made subsequently when Dhanagare (2017: 65) claims that 'the straitjacket theoretical and conceptual categories of Marxist class analysis [are] over-simplistic'. Following Laclau, therefore, Dhanagare (2017: 27, 66) maintains 'there is a need to go beyond stereotyped but meaningless formulas such as class struggle', describing the latter as 'a fetish of "revolutionary praxis" [and] infantile adventurism'.

19   See Dhanagare (2017: 29–32), who objects to what he terms the Marxist categorization of populism, the subaltern studies approach, the new farmers' movements, ecofeminism, and new social movements as all subscribing to postmodern theory, whereas the Marxist argument is actually somewhat different. Namely, that what subaltern studies, new farmers' movements, new social movements, ecofeminism, and postmodernism actually have in common is their *populism* – not quite the same epistemological linkage as that made by

negative a view of populism: since 'populist movements have become a part of everyday life, especially in India today,' contends Dhanagare, consequently 'this phenomenon cannot be written off as a potential area of sociological enquiry'.[20] Moreover, since Marxism applies 'the nineteenth century model of European peasantry to the post-Green Revolution, market-oriented Indian farmer', which he regards as 'completely misplaced and erroneous', it misses the fact that Sharad Joshi, 'always appealed to reason and rational thinking and not to arouse emotions'.

In the case of Bernstein, negative assessments of Marxism entail a dual approach, coupling outright condemnation of some analyses with the contention that others were sympathetic to the aims of agrarian populism. Accordingly, he cites the work of Trotsky, but manages to convey the misleading impression that he, too, shared the pro-peasant ideology of populism, whereas strong opposition to the latter view was a constant theme in all that Trotsky wrote about the agrarian question in pre- and post-1917 Russia.[21] Similarly, the case made by Lenin about class formation/struggle generally, and class differentiation of the Russian peasantry in particular, is dismissed by Bernstein (2018: 1131, 1133), who follows Shanin in asserting that Lenin's analysis was not just methodologically flawed but its focus was also more on the urban worker and insufficiently on its rural counterpart. Not only is no attempt to present – let alone engage with – the methodological approach of Lenin, but this assertion overlooks the fact that historically even those strongly opposed to Marxist theory have found value in his approach. Thus, for example, writing about the Russian factory system in the late nineteenth century, Tugan-Baranovsky (1970, 302, 438–9, n.16) not only upheld Lenin's calculations and findings but also endorsed his criticisms of populist methodology and data.

The decoupling by Bernstein of peasant economic activity from Marxist theory about class differentiation and capitalist accumulation takes a number of forms, extending from on the one hand the assertion that exploitation/inequality had more to do with patriarchy than capitalism, to on the other

---

Dhanagare. Others who have subsequently made a similar connection between all these variants of populism include Roy and Borowiak (2003), Nanda (2004), and Cochrane (2007).

20   'Quite contrary to [the Marxist] negative depiction and delegitimization of populism', observes Dhanagare (2017: 32), 'Piccone [has] stressed the need to rethink the phenomena of populist ideology and movements as alternative discourse that its critics dismiss prematurely.'

21   See Bernstein (2018: 1127, 1133). The mistaken view that Trotsky subscribed to pro-peasant ideology is also found in Brenton (2016), one of the many centenary volumes purporting to assess – but the guiding theme appears simply to express hostility towards – the 1917 Russian Revolution.

the rejection of the view that *kulaks* were numerically/economically/politically significant, and the denial that they were producers (as distinct from moneylenders) and were anything more than middle peasants. Expanding on the view of Figes that exploitation within the peasantry is mainly patriarchal, Bernstein (2018: 1130, n. 9) adds: 'that is, within "traditional" structures of inequality in the *mir* rather than manifesting capitalist accumulation'. Where inequality and exploitation are found, therefore, this is merely an effect not of capital accumulation but rather of longstanding village organizational norms. Surplus appropriation is a consequence of family relations inside the peasant household (= 'patriarchal forms') and not capitalist differentiation and accumulation *per se*. This view exculpates capitalism and its rich peasant by transferring blame for exploitation/inequality onto 'traditional structures', thereby avoiding fixing this to rural capital and perhaps even denying the presence in the countryside of the accumulation process itself. Exploitation is decoupled, in part or in whole, from agrarian capitalism.

On the issue of peasant differentiation, Bernstein again follows Shanin in arguing that the rise of the *kulaks* was exaggerated, that such better-off peasants were 'never a serious political force', and that anyway 'it was difficult to distinguish *kulaks* from middle peasants'.[22] The inference is clear: by claiming that what were termed '*kulaks*' were actually no more than middle peasants, Bernstein is attempting to play down – if not deny – the existence of peasant differentiation and its negative role (both political and economic) in the pre- and post-1917 agrarian sector of Russia.[23] Not only are *kulaks* not numerous, therefore, but they are marginal to production. Contrary to what Marxists argued, Bernstein regards the presence and efficacy of *kulaks* at the rural grassroots in Russia at this conjuncture as negligible. Downplaying the presence/ role of agrarian capitalism, peasant differentiation, and *kulak*s, creates a space in turn for the claim that current variants of agrarian populism are not just different but even more 'progressive' than earlier counterparts, and for this reason should be supported politically by Marxism. Among the characteristics which are said to be specific to current variants are 'ecological farming' and 'less emphasis on property rights' (Bernstein, 2018, 1145–46).

---

22 Bernstein (2018: 1130–31). Significantly, perhaps, the same claim – that no difference existed between *kulak*s and middle peasants – was made by the Social Revolutionaries, the agrarian populist party representing the interests of peasant proprietors (Radkey, 1963: 145, 249).

23 In his words (Bernstein, 2018: 1142), therefore, 'If the problem was above all that of the predominant middle peasantry, this casts a different light on ... differentiation'.

That such antagonism extends to include additionally current Marxist analyses is evident from the denial by Bernstein that 'all agrarian populism [is] necessarily and equally "wrong" and "reactionary" '.[24] What is still lacking, therefore, is 'a critical engagement' by Marxism with 'today's agrarian populism and the diverse rural struggles it embraces', which in his opinion elicits support because it 'appears a more vital ideological and political force [that] challenges ... any Marxist agrarian politics'. Not only is the claim that 'critical engagement' is lacking incorrect, but the 'wrong'/'reactionary' label clearly refers to what Marxist criticism says about the 'new' populist postmodernism.[25] Accordingly, negative appraisals are the result not of an *a priori* Marxist approach but rather of having examined agrarian populism in terms of its economics, politics, and ideology. It is precisely because of an engagement with the claims made historically and currently by populists and populism that Marxism has time after time declared agrarian populism to be politically wrong and ideologically reactionary.

3.3   *Farmers, Peasants,* Kulaks

The supposedly theoretical shortcomings/failings/absences on the part of Marxism identified by Dhanagare and Bernstein are extremely problematic. These are anyway surprising claims to make, not least because in the case of Dhanagare evidence to the contrary is found in two places, with both of which he is familiar: not only in the earlier collected volume to which Dhanagare himself contributed, but also in his monograph. Elsewhere, therefore, he accepts what initially he denied: namely, that 'the role of gender, nature or nation/ethnicity can and, in fact, does enter into the neo-populist discourse of the new farmers' movement', a view attributed to Marxism (Dhanagare, 2017: 121–22 n. 30). Equally contradictory, Dhanagare also cites approvingly the Marxist argument concerning the central role played by non-class identities – 'those that can be shared by them' uniting rich, middle, and poor peasants – in the populist discourse of the new farmers' movement.[26] So much for the supposed failure

---

24   Bernstein (2018: 1146). For an analogous complaint see Borras (2019: 6), who objects to the fact that what he perceives as 'broadly left-wing agrarian social movements ... are often lumped together, perjoratively [by Marxism] as populist and dismissed as such.'

25   The call to back a movement or belief simply because it is 'a more vital ideological and political force' could have been advanced as a reason for shifting one's support behind the rise of fascism during the 1920s and 1930s.

26   Dhanagare (2017: 118). Lest there be any doubt as to what he agrees is the case, the citation in full goes as follows: 'It is precisely this development of a superior unity that helped a populist movement to deflect roles – of middle and poor peasants – that suggests ... "the possibility of identities/interests not only unconnected with class but also those that can be shared by them (disadvantaged otherwise in economic terms) with rich peasants

of Marxism to indicate how populist discourse is deployed in order to gain the support of those petty commodity producers who are not rich peasants.

Contrary to the assertion Dhanagare that '[a] simple class analysis of the farmers' movement in the traditional Marxist perspective would not, in our view, unfold either the secret of its mass mobilisation nor would it reveal the manner in which rich farmers succeeded in their hegemonic influence over the class alliance within the farmers' movement', therefore, class struggle requires that rich peasants – otherwise engaged in conflict with poor peasants who sell their labor-power – resort to populist discourse about sectoral and these other non-class identities specifically in order to divert attention from this class divide and its effects (Dhanagare, 2017, 16). That is, precisely 'the ability of populist ideological discourse to help the class-ridden agrarian hierarchy to transcend their class situations and interests' which he earlier claimed was missing from Marxist analysis of populism. As misplaced is the inference that Marxism advocates writing off populism 'as a potential area of sociological enquiry': much rather the opposite is the case, in that Marxism has long argued the rightwards political trajectory of much academic writing about populism makes such enquiry crucial. That Marxism is critical of populism does not mean that it ought not to be analysed, far from it. Unfortunately, however, Dhanagare mistakenly conflates being critical of populism with a desire to avoid studying it.

With one notable difference, most of the arguments made by Dhanagare are prefigured in the agrarian populist framework of Charan Singh.[27] Regarded as 'the champion of India's peasants', he – much like Dhanagare – dismissed 'Marxist thinking' as 'a pathetic but unexplained faith', arguing that 'in agriculture there are many improvements which are not sufficiently remunerative'; not only did he advocate policies such as agricultural price supports and input cost reduction, but he also opposed land ceilings, wage increases for hired labor and was antagonistic to what he termed the 'socialistic'/'collectivist' agrarian program of Nehru.[28] The main difference in approach is simply put: cultivators

---

(we-are-all-the-same by virtue of being rural-not-urban, peasants-not-workers, Hindus-not-Muslims, Maharashtrians-not-Gujaratis, Indians-not-foreigners) that populism discharges for an emerging/aspiring agrarian bourgeoisie".'

27   Proclaiming that data vindicates his view about the systemic viability of peasant economy, Singh (1964: 105) concludes in Chayanovian terms that 'these figures are an unmistakable tribute to the inherent internal strength of the system of peasant farming, its adaptability to changing circumstances, its capacity to bear the stresses of modernisation, and above all its power to endure.'

28   For these views, based largely on the peasantry in 1950s Uttar Pradesh, see Singh (1964: 25, 92, 96, 102, 336ff., 448–49). In keeping with the economic logic of the development decade, he observed (Singh, 1964: 102): 'It is high productivity per acre which is the crux of the

described by Singh as peasants are labelled farmers by Dhanagare. It is perhaps no more than a measure of this ambivalence that Dhanagare (2017: 8, 39 n.6) not only uses the words 'peasant' and 'farmer' interchangeably, but also applies to farmers the same tripartite division – rich, middle, poor – as used by Lenin to differentiate the peasantry in terms of class.

Nowhere is this more evident than in how what he wrote nearly a quarter of a century ago has metamorphosed in his most recent analysis. Then his view was that 'the peaceful assertion of *peasant* power through mass mobilization ... defines its class character', an interpretation which he accepted was 'not wholly untenable empirically' (Dhanagare 1995: 73, emphasis added). Exactly the same argument is reproduced now, but with one crucial difference: 'peasant power' has now been changed to 'farmer power' (Dhanagare 2017, 98). Further on he does indeed accept both that capitalist production in rural Maharashtra is reflected in 'the well-entrenched position of rich *peasants* in local power structures', and that 'the sugar lobby overlaps with the *kulak* lobby [which] consists of *peasant* producers who turn increasingly to cash-crop farming for market and profit' (Dhanagare 2017: 108–10, emphasis added). In short, his perception earlier was (and to some degree is still) unambiguous: that the farmers' movement was indeed no different from a peasant mobilisation, that in some sense it had a class dimension, and that empirically these characteristics accorded with reality obtaining on the ground. As presented currently, however, his view now appears to be exactly the opposite: it is a movement composed solely of farmers, all of whom are united by this identity and the economic demands to which such 'hegemony' gives rise. Indeed, Dhanagare seems at times to regard all rural producers uniformly as a species of 'economic man', striving relentlessly to enter and perform effectively in the capitalist market.

The claim by Dhanagare – like that of Bernstein – that the demand for remunerative prices is a modern phenomenon, and thus a characteristic not of peasant agency but only of farmer movements, is incorrect: he perceives a break where in reality there was none, there being significant continuities between peasant agency/organizations before and during the 1950s and the post-1980s farmers' movements. In a general sense, therefore, every agrarian producer engaged in market transactions can be said to have always been in favor of lower input costs and higher output prices. Historically, sharecroppers and tenants – no less than peasant proprietors – have pursued (and where possible organized in furtherance of) policies such as rent reduction, debt

---

matter. Once this is achieved, as it can be on small independent farms, the peasants will have more to consume and also more to sell.'

write-offs, and low-or-no-interest credit. Among the demands made by rich and middle peasant mobilizations in 1950s Andhra Pradesh, for example, was that for better provision by the state both of agricultural inputs (irrigation, electricity) and remunerative prices for their agricultural produce. In short, the economic objectives sought by the new farmers' movements during the 1980s are not as novel as Dhanagare appears to think.

Even in late nineteenth century Russia, rich peasants combined farming with trading and industrial economic activity, seeking to concentrate in their hands land, crop areas, livestock and implements. Characteristics attributed by Lenin to *kulaks* – such as usury, the production of marketable grain, all of which increased as capitalism developed – are no different from those attributed by Dhanagare to Indian farmers.[29] It is a view, moreover, with which Dhanagare (2014: 52) appears to concur, in that elsewhere he himself uses the term 'rich farmers/*kulaks*'. Before the 1939–45 war, many peasant parties in Europe were members of the Green International, the forerunner of the present-day *Vía Campesina* (the umbrella organization to which are affiliated many of the farmers' movements in India), espousing a similar agrarian populist ideology and advocating much the same kind of political and economic policies.[30] Among the latter was the demand for high output prices and low input costs, or exactly the same policy objectives – sought by peasants – as made by the new farmers' movements in 1980s India.

4   A Modern/Progressive Variant of Agrarian Populism?

4.1   Old/New Agrarian Populism?

The attempt to decouple peasant economic activity from capitalism, class differentiation, and exploitation ignores a number of things. To begin with, early twentieth century sources emphasize both the fact and extent of *kulak*

---

29   References by Lenin to these characteristics as being those of rich peasants are found throughout his collected works. In a context of capitalist agriculture, objections by a better-off tenant to *corvée* or rental payments in kind or cash, or by a sharecropper to the percentage of the product taken by the landowner, are in effect demands for lower input costs. Similarly, rural agency to end the legal capacity of a landlord to appropriate a proportion from cultivators wishing to dispose of land itself carries with it the perception of what is (and what is not) a remunerative price for this commodity.

30   Peasant parties affiliated to the Green International were nationalist and supportive of religion, but against both collectivization and the State, blamed by them for low output prices and high input costs. See Vlado Matchek, 'The International Peasant Union', *The Tablet*, 19 March 1949, pp. 180–181.

economic activity in Russia, together with rich peasant self-perception as 'benefactors'.[31] The various claims made by Bernstein, along the lines that exploitation was an effect not of accumulation but of kinship/family, that the presence of *kulaks* was exaggerated, that they were only money-lenders, essentially no different from middle peasants, and anyway posed no threat to socialist planning, is contradicted by the very sources he failed to consult: namely, early twentieth century accounts by a variety of politically different analyses. Far from being indistinguishable from middle peasants, therefore, *kulaks* were regarded as 'other', and perceived as being 'the bitterest enemies' of those at the rural grassroots: in short, opposition to *kulaks* was seen in terms of a struggle about class, and was expressed in this kind of language.[32]

On the question of the link between patriarchy and capitalism, the extent to which it is capitalist production relations that transect the peasant household, and consequently kinship and/or fictive kinship (= 'traditional structures') present in the labor process correspond also to links between an owner of the means of production (a household head possessing land) and non-owning kinsfolk (sons, daughters not having property rights).[33] Furthermore, although he accepts the presence of *kulaks*, Bernstein (2018, 1130) maintains that their

---

31   Stepniak (1905: 67, 69) notes both the reach and impact of exploitation by *kulaks*, which is 'imposed every year on millions of peasants in every region of the [Russian] empire ... Far from considering it as something to be ashamed of, the moneylenders always pose as the peasants' "benefactors"'. He concludes that it is a 'new economical regime which has struck root in Russia [and] is not only extending but acquiring permanent force ... There is no province, no district, in which the system does not extensively obtain.' In a similar vein, Mackenzie Wallace (1877: 105) reports: 'Not a few industrial villages have ... fallen under the power of the *Kulaki* ... By advancing money the Kulák may succeed in acquiring over a group of villages a power almost as unlimited as that of the proprietor in the time of serfage.'

32   Hence the following comment (Stepniak, 1905: 312–13): 'At the present day the bitterest enemies to the people are singled out from among their own ranks. They form a detached and numerous class, which has its adherents, and agents, and supporters. The hatred they inspire in millions of peasants is as legitimate as that inspired by the slave-owning nobility in times of yore. Modern hatred assumes the character of class-hatred, and extends to the whole social system, of which the rural plutocracy is the necessary outcome'. Much the same point was made by Walling (1908: 256–7), who observed that 'there is in every village a small class of peasants who have always been, and may for some time remain, loyal to the Czar. These are the privileged – the village usurers, the peasant landlords, the small merchants ... Between these and the majority of peasants there is arising the most brutal and terrible war ... From pillaging the landlords, it is a short step to pillaging the rich peasants. The latter reply where they can with a forced confiscation of the weaker peasants' goods.'

33   The way in which capitalist relations not only transected but overrode considerations of kinship in rural Russia is outlined by Stepniak (1905: 325ff.).

main economic activity is money-lending, and thus unconnected with production (= 'not to richer, more "progressive" peasant farmers, even those who might employ workers'). What he fails to note, however, is the link between moneylending and production: that rich peasants used loans to secure and maintain control over the labor-power of poor peasants, who because of debts owed to *kulak*s were compelled to work on land owned/leased by the latter.

Contrary to the argument that *kulak* economic activity was largely confined to usury, therefore, moneylending was a method whereby capitalist peasants secured both land and labor-power (= means of production). Referred to by other peasants as '*mir*-eaters', *kulaks* use money-lending for productive ends: to lower costs and increase profitability across all their economic operations in the village commune.[34] Combining 'extensive land culture' with shopkeeping and trading, therefore, *kulaks* possess not only extensive property of their own, but lease-in additional land within the *mir*.[35] The object of money-lending is also to obtain/control/cheapen the requisite labor-power for production on these rural holdings at a point in the agricultural cycle when competition for this commodity is at its height.[36] All this underlines the central dilemma the

---

34   'On the whole,' notes Stepniak (1905: 84), 'the *kulaks* and *mir*-eaters, as all observers agree, obtain by the bondage system tolerably good work. Working for a *kulak* exhausts the peasant's strength ... [e]mploying a much greater proportion of bondage work relatively to their capital than the regular landlords ... the *kulaks* and *mir*-eaters grow in numbers, riches, and power with startling rapidity'.

35   According to Stepniak (1905: 74, 75–76) some 25–33% of Cossack land – 'inalienable by law' – was in the hands of *kulaks*: 'Letting [of land] to *koulaks*, or peasant capitalists, is ... quite common and much in vogue ... At the present time, the new peasant *bourgeoisie*, the *koulaks*, legally have got into their hands vast quantities of inalienable communal land under the form of long leases'. Although only 5.4% of the population, such rich peasants have 54+ acres per household, and many possess between 270 and 810 acres 'of the richest black soil per household'. Other sources – not noticeably sympathetic to Marxism – confirm not just the increasing power and wealth of *kulaks*, but also how moneylending was used in order to get access to land. Hence the observation by Mavor (1914: 356): 'The prosperity of the *kulaki*, or well-to-do peasants, is one of the significant features of the period. The growth of this class was facilitated by the Peasants' Bank and its presence as an important fraction of the village population is noticed in all the reports from the districts ...' Similarly, Drage (1904: 120) notes that 'legal restrictions on sale of land and communal ownership, which hinder the richer peasants from extending their farms in a legal manner by the purchase of more land, force them into the position of moneylenders, in order to obtain the use of neighbouring fields ... Peasants who have been successful as farmers and invested much labour and money in their land are naturally opposed to the system of periodical redistribution, and where the number of prosperous farmers is large they are often able to prevent them.'

36   'Credit is mostly given on the security of the peasants' work, their hands being their most valuable possession', observes Stepniak (1905: 60–61, original emphasis), adding: 'It

kulaks posed for Bolshevism. Unless their increasing economic power was reined in, therefore, any attempt by the October Revolution to transform the agrarian sector of Russia would be undermined.[37]

When considering old/new agrarian populist variants, it is not the case that what is termed the 'progressive' populism of today is in certain important respects that different from its historical counterparts. This challenges the view of Bernstein (2018: 1145) that current agrarian populist mobilizations and farmers' movements, in the form of the *Via Campesina*, are 'very different' from the rural agency of early twentieth century Russia: present-day agrarian populism is for him 'very different from anything that existed a century ago'. Continuing in the same vein, he argues that 'the substance and styles of "peasant politics" have changed radically from the "heroic" period of peasant wars and their contributions to the making of modern history' (Bernstein, 2018: 1144). These claims in effect clear the ground for the main populist argument: namely, that insofar as contemporary forms of agrarian populism are different from their historical precursors, they can – and should – be regarded as 'progressive', politically speaking. Contrary to such assertions, however, the distinctions said by him to separate the old/new populisms are mostly non-existent. What remains a

---

assumes the form of payment in anticipation for work to be done in the next season ... A very important proviso [is that the] agreement never omits to mention that it retains its binding power for an indefinite number of years. Thus, if the [lender] should not require his debtor to work in the immediately following summer ... he is free to call on him to liquidate his debt in the following year, or even the year after, thus securing for himself cheap labour at a time when wages are likely to be at their *maximum*.' Many examples of wage differences between free workers hired in summer and unfree labour bonded during the winter months are provided by the same source (Stepniak, 1905: 63ff.), which notes that 'it is no uncommon thing ... to see labourers of each class working side by side, the one for ten the other for three and a half roubles per *dessiatine*.' For a similar account, see Walling (1908: 246ff.).

37   On this point see, among many others (again, not necessarily sympathetic to Bolshevism), Rosenberg (1934: 197ff., 220ff.) and Sukhanov (1955: 308). During the 1920s the Left Opposition (Serge and Sedova Trotsky, 2015: 142) warned that '[i]ndustry was still too weak to supply all the needs of the countryside, and large stocks of grain and of other primary products were accumulating in the hands of the *kulaks* ... private traders, more ingenious and flexible and also less scrupulous than the public sector, speculated in the products of socialized industry and resold them at extortionate profits; middlemen grew rich and the new capitalists were able to invest their surpluses in small businesses or to deposit them in the State Bank at a reasonably attractive rate of interest. These "NEP-men", profiteers created by the New Economic Policy, were a parasitic and demoralizing social phenomenon. Unless firm and prudent counter-measures were taken, the Opposition foresaw a multitude of evils: a conflict with the *kulaks*; industrial stagnation; food shortages in the cities and in the army; the growth of a counter-revolutionary bourgeoisie made up of *kulaks* and "NEP-men" ... and the final surrender of all the Revolution had stood for.'

constant are on the one hand the political discourses and policy objectives, and on the other robust opposition to the state and anything resembling socialism.

Hence the 'ecological' dimension invoked by current peasant and/or farmer movements is merely a continuation of the longstanding agrarian populist discourse about Nature, and how petty commodity producers have always represented this (peasant = Nature = nation), so this ideological dimension is not in fact new. Similarly, property rights are still central to the discourse and political objectives of agrarian populism today, a presence registered by slogans such as 'peasant autonomy' and 'land sovereignty' (= the moral right of peasants to individual smallholdings) and 'land grabbing' (= struggle against de-peasantization). Even the demand for higher agricultural prices – an objective currently affixed specifically to new farmers' movements – was made by peasants affiliated to the Green International, which emerged during the 1920s and was the precursor of the present-day *Via Campesina*. There *is* a difference, but not with regard to discourse/ideology. Whereas the latter has remained constant (= the agrarian myth), therefore, it is the *practice* that has changed. Nowadays academic populism is for the most part anchored in unthreatening agency (demonstrations, petitions, etc.), whilst the practice of earlier populists – the Russian intelligentsia who went to the people was not just physically and politically a riskier kind of commitment, but also one that depended on a more sustained engagement with the rural grassroots.

The political object finally emerges; Marxists and Marxism, insists Bernstein, must accept the necessity, as he sees it, of change, by including agrarian populist claims and subjects in a broadly 'progressive' anti-capitalist mobilization. To this end he advocates a 'capacity ... to change positions, that goes far beyond the comfort zone of class purism and other illusions', by, among other things, 'accepting the need for some rapprochement with the middle peasant' (Bernstein, 2018, 1146). If, as he argues, there is no difference between *kulak*s and middle peasants – that is, *kulak* ≠ rich peasant; instead, *kulak* = middle peasant – then what is advocated is clear: the inclusion within the ranks of a 'progressive' mobilization of capitalist producers, on the grounds that the peasantry is, after all, undifferentiated in terms of class.

Instead of being differentiated by class, as Marxists argued, peasants have been re-essentialized by current agrarian populism as undifferentiated smallholders – or farmers – who are authentic bearers of national/regional/local culture. In this way, homogeneous petty commodity producers have resurfaced as the eternal 'other' of capitalist development. This is the discourse informing many 'new' populist postmodern analyses currently informed by concepts such as new social movements, the subaltern, ecofeminism, post-colonialism, post-Marxism, and post-capitalism. Conceptually, the 'new' populist postmodernism replaced the disempowerment of class relations – the focus of Marxist political economy – with its opposite: the notion that, much rather, petty commodity producers in rural areas were empowered by the 'otherness' of their cultural identity. Contrary to the case made by Dhanagare, this applies also to the 'new' farmers' movements in India.

4.2   A Sense of Robust Realism?

If the economic distinction between the objectives pursued by peasant agency and farmer movements is less marked than Dhanagare imagines, then neither is the discourse used in furtherance of these ends. What he objects to is not just the application of a Chayanovian economic model to the new farmers' movements, but also to the view that such mobilization might in any way involve endorsement of a traditionalist (= backwards-looking) political ideology.[38] However, this objection is similarly contradicted by Dhanagare (2017: 107, 109 emphasis added) himself, where he states of 'the dominant class interests in rural India' that their 'political expressions and manifestations may be mediated through *caste, kinship and other similar ethnic or primordial identities*', and further that 'the sugar lobby ... is ridden with factional conflicts and competing interests, often mediated by *caste, sub-caste, clan or other similar primordial identities*'.

In short, he himself underlines the presence of the very identities which in an earlier analysis he denies as having any relevance to or purchase on the discourse of the new farmers' movements, in the process castigating those who maintained the opposite was the case. Having championed Joshi's 'modern'/ 'rational' populism, therefore, a long way into his own analysis Dhanagare (2017, 88) is suddenly confronted with what he terms 'obvious illusory and mystifying elements' in the discourse of the new farmers' movements hitherto regarded by him as progressive and 'emancipatory'. It is a discovery so at odds with his own approach that, clearly, he remains baffled by it. Ironically, the main claim – concerning the unalloyed modernity of populist discourse – is

---

38   See Dhanagare (2017: 79–80), who notes that 'while the earlier peasant movements always involved one class or class interests against the other in rural society, the new farmers' movements have not tended to divide agrarian communities on economic (class), ethnic, caste, religious or political lines. The new farmers' movements have succeeded to a reasonable measure in bringing together the entire rural agricultural population and interests ... the earlier peasant movements had streaks of restorative consciousness; they at least tacitly glorified the pastoral agrarian *gemeinschaft* feeling of solidarity, with nostalgia, idealism and romanticism of the tradition (*à la* the Chayanovian peasant in Russia had). In contrast, the new farmers' movements faced the challenges posed by processes of industrialisation and modernisation with a sense of robust realism.'

also undermined by additional evidence, provided both by its author and by others.

During the mid-1990s, therefore, Joshi not only founded the BSP (*Swatantra Bharat Paksha*) so as to participate in electoral politics, but entered into alliances with Hindu chauvinist organizations such as the BJP (*Bharatiya Janata Party*), linked to the far-right RSS (*Rashtriya Swayamsevak Sangh*), and *Shiv Sena*, a Maharashtra-based rightist political grouping. Both the latter subscribe to a *Hindutva* discourse invoking ancient cultural traditions, practices, language, and religious beliefs, a backwards-looking ideology which proclaims Indian national identity as innate and ethnically specific. Observing that Joshi's *Sanghatana* was beginning to admire the BJP, and further that the BSP was launched by him 'in an attempt to bring together all ideologically like-minded right-wing forces', Dhanagare notes further that 'impressed by Joshi's ideological articulations' *Shiv Sena* supported his bid to become an MP (2004–2010). Joshi in turn provided support for BJP-*Shiv Sena* candidates in Maharashtra (Dhanagare 2017: 217, 221–22, 226, 227).

Dhanagare perceives this development as an anomaly, a regrettable and unnecessary deviation from the otherwise promising norm of a 'modern'/ 'rational' populist ideology, hitherto deployed successfully by Joshi so as to maintain new farmers' movement 'hegemony', rather than what it was: the culmination of an entirely predictable rightwards political trajectory. Part of the difficulty is that Dhanagare (2017, 8) mistakenly equates Guha's 'subaltern category' simply with subsistence cultivation, and thus incompatible with those producers (= farmers) who grow cash-crops for the market. However, as Guha himself makes clear, his definition of subaltern includes components of an agrarian bourgeoisie – or precisely those elements which produce for the market.[39] Consequently, for Dhanagare the category 'subaltern' cannot be seen as linked epistemologically to the way in which rich peasants benefit from deploying a populist discourse.

In order to deflect from class divisions within the ranks of supporters divided by class, therefore, populism as a mobilizing discourse has of necessity to invoke other, non-class identities, or the kinds of religious/nationalist/ communal issues that historically feature most effectively in the ideology of conservatives and the far right. Misunderstanding this ideological role, due

---

39   According to Guha (1982: 8), therefore, among the social components of 'the subaltern' are 'the lesser rural gentry, impoverished landlords, rich peasants and upper middle peasants', which underlines the extent to which it is an agrarian populist category. This is one of the reasons why it is regarded by me as possessing ideological affinities with other, similar kinds of populism.

in part to his rejection of Marxist theory about false consciousness and class struggle, Dhanagare (2017, 244) attributes the decline of the farmers' movement simply to the political ambition of Joshi ('despite its initial spectacular successes, started showing symptoms of decline rather too early [because] he was obviously harboring political ambitions [and had a] hunger for power').

Quite why Joshi's complicity with the existing political system may have undermined the farmers' movement is anyway open to a different interpretation. As leader of the *Shetkari Sanghatana*, he benefited directly from the religious discourse about Bali Raj, a mythological kingdom the presence of which is a pervasive component of rural grassroots ideology in Maharashtra.[40] Contrary to the claim made by Dhanagare, this confirms the important role in the farmers' movement of traditional ideology. Moreover, insofar as his person was identified by the members of the *Shetkari Sanghatana* with the deity Bali (the demon king) at the center of this discourse, therefore, Sharad Joshi was associated with the restoration of a golden age era under King Bali. Once he joined the formal institutional structure of politics, however, Joshi in effect severed the link at the center of this myth, and thus betrayed its object: the restoration of a golden age that would be not just different from but better than the present.

5   Conclusion

Any modern defense of Marxism necessarily entails engaging with what is now a globally resurgent populism. Accordingly, the question posed currently by Marxist theory about peasants is aimed directly at its political 'other', and concerns whether populism in its historical or present-day manifestation (the 'cultural turn', the 'new' populist postmodernism) is – or, indeed, can ever be – progressive (= 'nice') in a political sense. This is an issue that has been thrown into sharp political focus by the contemporary rise of populism in Europe, Asia, and the Americas. However, the deep roots of this question, both in historical terms and in long-standing debates about the role of the agrarian structure in socio-economic transformation (and systemic transition), are not always recognized, let alone addressed. The significance of these considerations is simply put: from the late nineteenth century onwards, agrarian populism has featured centrally in important grassroots movements and mobilizations, together with the debates and disputes such agency generated.

---

40   On the perception of Sharad Joshi as King Bali, see Youngblood (2016).

Regarding the main question posed by Marxism of whether or not agrarian populism is currently as progressive as its academic supporters claim, evidence suggests otherwise. Over a whole range of issues – among them the desirability/feasibility of the rural, nationalism, ethnicity, individual private property; the undesirability/infeasibility of the urban, Marxist theory, socialism, collective agriculture, state regulation – little or no difference separates new variants of agrarian populism from their older counterparts. Like its historical precursors, therefore, current agrarian populism is opposed not to accumulation *per se* but only to particular forms of capitalism (finance, 'foreign', largescale agribusiness). The wish of present-day agrarian populism to preserve/restore peasant economy, by resisting capitalist penetration of the countryside – but without advocating the systemic transcendence of the accumulation process itself, fails to confront the irony at the heart of this process: what capital wants from peasant economy is not its produce but its role as a source of cheap labor-power. This contradiction generates in turn the anti-capitalism of the political right, in that smallholders threatened with dispossession of necessity invoke non-class identity – nationalism, ethnicity, traditional culture – as their main (or only) political defense. In their struggle to compete or survive, therefore, peasant proprietors have shifted the debate with the neoliberal State from one simply about economic (which they feel they are bound to lose) to one about 'the social' (where they perceive their winning chances are better).

Of these supporters, Bernstein makes much the same case as Dhanagare: both maintain that current populist movements are not the same as earlier ones, the object being – where peasants are concerned – to recuperate and thus to exonerate the validity of populism generally as a mobilizing ideology, at the expense of Marxist theory about such agrarian movements. Each insists that, in contrast to the past, present-day farmer/peasant agency is neither reactionary in political terms nor does it advocate a backwards looking/traditional ideology. Their reasons for thinking that contemporary populism is progressive are the same: because current peasant agency informed by agrarian populist ideology is aimed at neoliberal capitalism, consequently it cannot be regarded as backwards looking and reactionary. Both undertake a double renaming: for Bernstein, therefore, no difference exists between *kulak*s and middle peasants, whereas for Dhanagare all peasants are simply farmers.

Crucial issues such as peasant differentiation, the class position and interests of rich peasant capitalists, plus the way they structure and inform grassroots agency in the countryside are thereby downplayed or avoided. Where the interpretation of early twentieth century rural Russia is concerned, therefore, the fact that current agrarian populist approach insists – contrary to past and present Marxist views – no substantial economic and political difference separated *kulak*s from middle peasants, throws into doubt both the presence of class divisions at the rural grassroots, and thus the extent to which capitalism had penetrated the countryside. However, the shape and intensity of conflict at the level of the *mir* not only contradicts this assertion that no difference existed between the rich peasant *kulak* and the middle peasant but also suggests further that it was a *class* distinction fully recognized and opposed by all villagers involved in grassroots struggles.

That the struggle conducted by the new farmers' movements not only included better-off producers as well as those who were poorer but was also couched in terms of non-class identity does not mean that class is an inappropriate Marxist category to apply to an analysis of the new farmers' movements in India. The argument that categories such as 'peasant' and 'class' are relevant to an understanding only of pre-1947 rural agency, not to that of the new farmers' movements of the 1980s, is contradicted by evidence found in many different sources. This suggests that the difference between 'peasant' and 'farmer' in terms of characteristics and economic demands are not as stark as claimed. Furthermore, the transformation that has occurred over this period is much rather the consolidation of an agrarian capitalist stratum, an economic identity recognized by Lenin and other Marxists not just as an outcome of the accumulation process but also as compatible epistemologically with the concept 'peasant'.

Where Gramscian 'hegemony' is concerned, any view which follows uncritically the interpretation of Mouffe ends up subscribing to the notion of populism as an emancipator/progressive ideology simply as it is already constituted, rather than as a discourse possessing many reactionary components. Gramsci himself was clear that 'hegemony' entailed cultural struggle, precisely due to the fact that so much grassroots ideology was permeated by – and thus required opposition to – already existing 'common sense' discourse and concepts. In the battle over culture so as to establish 'hegemony', therefore, Gramsci – like Lenin and other Marxists (then and now) – argued that much of the ideology circulating at the rural grassroots (customs, traditions) had to be challenged and transformed, not least because it was penetrated by landlord and/or bourgeois discourse hostile to fundamental change.

Since the connection between a backwards-looking ideology (= the *sine qua non* of populist mobilization) and the forwards-looking *economic* objectives of rich peasant capitalists is misunderstood, also missed is the significance of class interests/struggle. In their pursuit of lower input costs and higher output prices, therefore, rich peasants realize that, rather than agitating for such objectives on their own, it is better to obtain the support of middle and poor peasants for these same interests, which explains the crucial role that Bharat/India played as an 'us'/'them' mobilizing discourse. Hence the Bharat/India dichotomy informing the movement enables actual/aspiring rich peasants to make a number of interrelated claims: that all agrarian strata – large, medium, and small landed proprietors, sharecroppers, tenants, sub-tenants, and peasant families generally – are united by virtue of being rural producers: that such an identity ranges them all against the urban; and, consequently, that oppression/exploitation occurs/originates *outside* the ranks of the movement itself.

Again, contrary to what is argued, there is nothing inherently 'mystifying' about the fact that the new farmers' movements subscribe to conservative and even reactionary politics, as is evident from the kind of political alliances (BJP, *Shiv Sena*) into which Sharad Joshi entered. Ironically, the similarity between the non-class identities deployed specifically as a populist mobilizing ideology in order to establish and reproduce 'hegemony', thereby avoiding political discord within the ranks of the new farmers' movements in India, and the populist discourse used by the far right have made it easier for the latter group to garner support from the former. It is precisely this process of ideological 'capture', together with the reasons for it, that a positive view of populism as an 'emancipatory' mobilizing discourse prevents one from understanding.

Against what its supporters claim, therefore, agrarian populist movements are neither inherently progressive nor nowadays so different from earlier variants. Historically and currently, populist mobilizing ideology – nowadays informing 'cultural turn' discourse – downgrades or ignores class consciousness/struggle while privileging those non- or anti-class identities (nationalism, ethnicity) which play directly into the hands of conservatism and the far right. This is precisely what Marxist critiques have always maintained was – and is still – the case.

References

Bernstein, Henry. 2018. 'The "peasant problem" in the Russian revolution(s), 1905–1929'. *The Journal of Peasant Studies* 45(5–6): 1127–1150.

Borras, S.M. 2019. 'Agrarian social movements: The absurdly difficult but not impossible agenda of defeating right-wing populism and exploring a socialist future'. *Journal of Agrarian Change*, 1–34. https://doi.org/10.1111/joac.12311.

Brass, Tom. 2000. *Peasants, Populism and Postmodernism*. London: Frank Cass.

Brass, Tom. 2014. *Class, Culture, and the Agrarian Myth*. Leiden: Brill.

Brass, Tom. 2017. *Labour Markets, Identities, Controversies: Reviews and Essays 1982–2016*. Leiden: Brill.

Brass, Tom. 2019. *Revolution and Its Alternatives: Other Marxisms, Other Empowerments, Other Priorities*. Leiden: Brill.

Brenton, Tony (ed.) 2016. *Historically Inevitable? Turning Points of the Russian Revolution*. London: Profile Books.

Cochrane, Regina. 2007. 'Rural poverty and impoverished theory: Cultural populism, ecofeminism, and global justice'. *The Journal of Peasant Studies* 34(2): 167–206.

Dhanagare, D.N. 1983. *Peasant Movements in India 1920–1950*. Delhi: Oxford University Press.

Dhanagare, D.N. 1995. 'The Class Character and Politics of the Farmers' Movement in Maharashtra during the 1980s'. In Tom Brass (ed) *New Farmers' Movements in India*. London: Frank Cass.

Dhanagare, D.N. 2014. *The Writings of D.N. Dhanagare: The Missing Tradition – Debates and Discourses in Indian Sociology*. New Delhi: Orient Blackswan.

Dhanagare, D.N. 2017. *Populism and Power: Farmers' movement in Western India, 1980–2014*. London: Routledge.

Drage, Geoffrey. 1904. *Russian Affairs*. London: John Murray.

Engels, Frederick. 1976 [1847] 'Principles of Communism', *Marx and Engels Collected Works*, Vol. 6. London: Lawrence & Wishart.

Escobar, Arturo. 1995. *Encountering Development: The Making and Unmaking of the Third World*. Princeton, NJ: Princeton University Press.

Guha, Ranajit (ed.) 1982–89. *Subaltern Studies I-VI*. New Delhi: Oxford University Press.

Kautsky, Karl. 1984 [1894/95]. 'The Competitive Capacity of Small-scale Enterprise in Agriculture'. In Athar Hussain and Keith Tribe (eds) *Paths of Development in Capitalist Agriculture*, London: Macmillan.

Lenin, V.I. 1964a. 'The Development of Capitalism in Russia [1899]'. *Collected Works, Volume 3*. Moscow: Foreign Languages Publishing House.

Lenin, V.I. 1964b. 'Critical Remarks on the National Question [1913]'. *Collected Works, Volume 20*. Moscow: Foreign Languages Publishing House.

Lévy, Bernard-Henri. 2008. *Left in Dark Times: A stand against the new barbarism*. New York: Random House.

Littlejohn, Gary. 1973a. 'The Peasantry and the Russian Revolution'. *Economy and Society* 2(1): 112–125.

Littlejohn, Gary. 1973b. 'The Russian Peasantry: A Reply to Teodor Shanin'. *Economy and Society* 2(3): 376–385.

Littlejohn, Gary. 1977. 'Peasant Economy and Society'. In Barry Hindess (ed) *Sociological Theories of the Economy*. London: The Macmillan Press, Ltd.

Mackenzie Wallace, Donald. 1877. *Russia*. London: Cassell & Company, Limited.

Marx, Karl, and Frederick Engels. 1976 [1848]. 'The Communist Manifesto'. *Marx and Engels Collected Works, Vol. 6*. London: Lawrence & Wishart.

Mavor, J. 1914. *An Economic History of Russia: Volume Two – Industry and Revolution.* London: J.M. Dent & Sons, Limited.

Mouffe, Chantal. 2018. *For a Left Populism*, London & New York: Verso.

Nanda, Meera. 2004. *Prophets Facing Backward: Postmodern Critiques of Science and Hindu Nationalism,* New Brunswick, NJ: Rutgers University Press.

Phillips, A.A. 1958. *The Australian Tradition: Studies in Colonial Culture*, Melbourne: F.W. Cheshire.

Phillips, A.A. 1979. *Responses: Selected Writings*. Balmain, NSW: Australia International Press.

Radkey, Oliver H. 1963. *The Sickle under the Hammer*. London and New York: Columbia University Press.

Rosenberg, Arthur. 1934. *A History of Bolshevism*. London: Oxford University Press.

Roy, T., and C. Borowiak. 2003. 'Against Ecofeminism: Agrarian Populism and the Splintered Subject in Rural India'. *Alternatives,* 28, pp. 57–89.

Schmitt, Carl. 2004. *Legality and Legitimacy*. Durham, NC: Duke University Press.

Schmitt, Carl. 2005. *Political Theology: Four Chapters on the Concept of Sovereignty.* Chicago, IL: The University of Chicago Press.

Seregny, S. J. 1989. *Russian Teachers and Peasant Revolution: The Politics of Education in 1905*. Bloomington, IN: Indiana University Press.

Serge, Victor, and Natalia Sedova Trotsky. 2015. *The Life and Death of Leon Trotsky*. Chicago, IL: Haymarket Books.

Singh, Charan. 1964. *India's Poverty and Its Solution*, London: Asia Publishing House.

Stepniak, S. 1905. *The Russian Peasantry: Their Agrarian Condition, Social Life and Religion.* London: George Routledge & Sons, Limited.

Sukhanov, N.N. 1955. *The Russian Revolution 1917*. London: Oxford University Press.

Trotsky, L.D. 1934. *The History of the Russian Revolution*. London: Victor Gollancz, Ltd.

Trotsky, L.D. 1969. 'The Three Conceptions of the Russian Revolution'. *Writings 1938–39*. New York: Merit Publishers.

Tugan-Baranovsky, M. I. 1970 [1898]. *The Russian Factory in the 19th Century*. Homewood, Illinois: The American Economic Association.

Varshney, Ashutosh. 1995. *Democracy, Development and the Countryside: Urban-Rural Struggles in India*, Cambridge: Cambridge University Press.

Walling, W. E. 1908. *Russia's Message*. New York: Doubleday, Page & Company.

Yeats, William Butler. 1933. *The Winding Stair and Other Poems*. London: Macmillan and Co., Limited.

Youngblood, M. (2016) *Cultivating Community: Interest, Identity, and Ambiguity in an Indian Social Mobilization*, Pasadena, CA: South Asian Studies Association.

CHAPTER 14

Marx on Social Movements

Left and Right

Lauren Langman

1   Introduction[1]

Most of the major social, political, and cultural changes of past few centuries, have been the result of social movements. Movements such as the bourgeois American and French revolutions, then socialist Russian and Chinese Communist revolutions, have changed history and impacted everyone on the face of the Earth. In the last few decades, we have seen a proliferation of social movements, progressive movements like anti-globalization movements, Arab Spring, Southern Europe and Occupy Wall Street all seemed to spearhead a global move toward more socialistic societies, especially the Pink Tide of South America. So too did cultural movements like Me-Too or Black Lives Matter impact consciousness and values but with only incremental immediate influence. But in part as a reaction to these movements came various reactionary populist counter movements, e.g., the National Rally (France), *Alternative für Deutschland*, the Tea Party, PiS, Fidesz, the BJP, and of course the rise of Trump and/or Brexit. The powerful support for these reactionary mobilizations became especially clear on January 6, 2020, when a coalition of extremist right movements attempted a coup to secure Trump's presidency.

But how do we understand the nature of these movements? The mainstream social movement theories, resource mobilization (RM) political process (PP), social constructivist (SC) or New Social Movement theory (NSM) are quite limited in understanding recent social mobilizations, especially the essential roles of political economy, class systems, legitimating ideologies crises, the use of the Internet and social media and the cultural, psychosocial and emotional impetus that engender these progressive or reactionary movements (Della Porta, 2017; Krinsky, 2013). It is ever more obvious that the old "toolkits" for understanding social movement studies no longer fit current mobilizations

---

1   The author wishes to express his most heartfelt appreciation to David Fasenfest for the considerable help offered in getting this manuscript suitable for publication. There should be a medal for editors like him whose efforts are above and beyond the call of duty.

that tend to be more spontaneous, "bottom up," as opposed to more traditional hierarchical social movement organizations for example parties, unions, or NGOs. Often, these movements have limited resources-if any, highly democratic, participatory emergent leadership rather than clear-cut leaders, and they may mobilize whether or not the political system offers opportunities (Nilsen and Cox, 2013).

For Hetland and Goodwin (2013) many seemingly cultural movements *may not seem materially based*, especially cultural movements concerned with values, motives and/or identity e.g., feminism, gay rights, civil rights etc. But that said, *such movements cannot be understood apart from the underlying political economy, namely the capitalist system*. But as they also point out, considering political economy *does mean embracing a crude economistic, determinist perspective, nor leadership by a vanguard party*. Rather, the question is mediatization, how do economic influences at the level of structure become transformed and mediated to motivate the contestations and mobilizations of particular actors. While the mainstreams of academic social movement research have generally marginalized Marxist approaches, as time wore on, between the implosions of capitalism in 2008 and again in 2020, along with greater inequality and precarity, revisiting Marxist approaches provide evermore explanatory power to the range of social movements both left and right.

While Marx did not present a theory of social mobilization, his discussions of several trends provide us some insight into how reading Marx informs social movements:

1.   The material basis of history, consciousness and action, contradiction (dialectics), class conflict, alienation and immiseration, evident in his calls for revolution, his discussions of the 18th Brumaire and civil wars in France provide important starting points

2.   Trotsky's analysis of the Russian Revolution illustrates the combination of material adversity, inept governance, and the humiliation and anger following the massive defeats in WW that mobilized peasants, workers, and the military.

3.   Gramsci's, analysis of hegemony, "wars of position" and the interregnum will help us understand the conditions of today.

4.   The Frankfurt School of Critical Theory notes the economic adversities and hardships, together with alienation, authoritarianism and mass mediated propaganda aided the Nazi mobilization in Germany.

5.   Following World War II, relative economic growth and prosperity had two consequences: the revolutionary potential of workers was attenuated, while the growing levels of security had a major impact upon certain segments of youth that would be evident in the various progressive

cultural political movements of the 1960s especially Paris 1968 and the American antiwar movements.

These post-war movements, theorized by the Situationists, Habermas, and Touraine, laid the foundation for New Social Movement theory, which, when informed by aspects of political economy, ideology, and emotions help us to understand the most important social movements of our time, the progressive ascendant left and the declining reactionary movements, authoritarian populisms, ethnoreligious nationalisms and indeed neofascism. Progressive movements, what Marcuse (1969) called "great refusals," are reactions to a variety of injustices as well as a statement about how the shallowness of capitalist culture impels visions of a "new sensibility", a preference for the "Life Instincts" rather than the "Death Instincts" within a post capitalist, humanistic society. Given this legacy of Marxist and neo-Marxist thought we can now better understand the profound importance of the dialectical struggle between the progressive versus reactionary forces of today, and while often the future may seem bleak, the telos of history, now spearheaded by progressive youth gives us hope.

2 Marx, Marxism and Movements

2.1 *Alienation and Human Suffering*

Marx's critique of capitalism begins with the alienation of the poorly paid wage labor of exploited workers who produced the "surplus value" that enriched the coffers of the capitalist class at the expense of the suffering of workers. As a small minority, the capitalists must depend upon both coercion, and consent to reproduce class relationships and reap their profits. But at the same time, the everyday life experiences under capitalism, especially in its contemporary neoliberal stage of globalization, creates a variety of economic, cultural, and emotional crises, strains, and grievances, that in turn lead to social movements. In recent years we've seen a resurgence of interest in Marxist thought as surveys[2] reveal a small majority of the young people now prefer socialism to capitalism. To be sure, most see socialism largely providing welfare state benefits of health care and education, rather collective workplace democracy and the control over the means of production. For Marx, the critique of alienation informs his subsequent concerns how capitalism is a system of domination and suffering (see Raju Das in this volume).

---

2 Saad, Lydia, 2019. "Socialism as Popular as Capitalism Among Young Adults in U.S" https://
   news.gallup.com/poll/268766/socialism-popular-capitalism-among-young-adults.aspx

   Implicit in his critique of political economy was a vision of the possible, an alternative post-capitalist world where domination was transcended, alienation overcome and people would find freedom, agency, self-knowledge, self-realization, meaningful community, recognition, and fulfillment of their basic humanity, what he called "species being." However, this humanistic view of the possible rested on a particular view of human nature and a careful reading of the *1844 Manuscripts*, as well as *The Theses on Feuerbach*, suggested notion of human nature, as kindly, benevolent, egalitarian living in harmony with each other and with Nature. (There are further hints of this view in the Engels Marx writings on the family). For Marx, perhaps as Rousseau hinted, with horticulture and the "ownership of land" we begin to see differentiations of wealth and power and small classes of men assumed greater power over other men and women in general. With advances in agricultural technology and astronomy, more efficient production of food, whether grown, fished, or herded, greater numbers of the populations were available for full time work as administrators and warriors.

   Changing material conditions refashioned behavior, "human nature" was thought to be naturally greedy, selfish, and avaricious if not aggressive. Human beings were regarded as "naturally" selfish, sinful, violent, and needed constraint by superior power. While this was an essential aspect of many theologies, Judeo-Christianity, it was also held by some Enlightenment philosophers ranging from Adam Smith celebrating self-interest, Hobbes "war of all against all" and even Freud's views of fundamentally aggressive nature. But another, more benevolent view of human nature is often obscured. Rather, for Marx, and indeed many neo-Marxists, there is a far more optimistic view of "human nature."

   Marx's view of human nature, dominated, alienated, and warped by capital, was more fully developed by Fromm (1961). "Marx's aim was ... liberation from the chains of economic determination, of restituting him in his human wholeness, of enabling him to find unity and harmony with his fellow man and with Nature." Similarly, for Geras, "Whatever else it may be, theory and socio-historical explanation, and scientific as it may be, that work [1844 Manuscripts] is a moral indictment of capital resting on the conception of essential human needs, an ethical standpoint, in other words, in which a view of human nature is involved" (Geras.1983: 83–84). As Erich Fromm put it, capitalism turned human beings into monsters. Langman (2015), following Geras (1983) argued that within the *1844 Manuscripts* and the *6th Thesis on Feuerbach*, there was an implicit notion of human nature and social psychology that was the basis of Marx's normative principles valorizing human freedom, agency, self-production in work, democratic, egalitarian community, recognition and meaning.

Dignity was the consequence overcoming domination and alienation as a basic human desire, an individual and collective emotion and fundamental right for all. Here the basic premise is that human beings seek dignity by overcoming alienation, and the movement from necessity to freedom brings agency, creative self-fulfillment in productive activities, recognition of one's fundamental humanity, and engagement with meaningful and democratic community life, within an identity granting and recognizing egalitarian community of shared meanings and the realization of their "species being" (Cf. Geras, 1983; Langman, 2015). This view can be seen in the work of a number of Frankfurt school theorists, Bloch, Benjamin, and perhaps most clearly in Eric Fromm's (1961) vision of productive character in a "sane". society" and, of special concern for social movements, Herbert Marcuse's views of "great refusals" as mobilizations inspired by and seeking to achieve a "new sensibility," one seeking freedom and fulfillment.

When conditions of alienation and domination are such that human fulfillment becomes thwarted, then people were or are denied basic human dignity. While Marx only used that term twice in the manuscripts, dignity can be seeing as the state in which alienation is overcome, Thus, we can see dignity as that state in which people can find gratification of basic human needs including creative fulfillment of themselves, dignity is not simply an individual emotion or feeling as such, but a collective condition, a normative virtue with emotional consequences in which alienation has been transcended, basic human needs are fulfilled and people and human potential realized. Otherwise said, dignity can be thought of as an emotional condition, freedom from immiseration and instead, personal satisfaction for the individual, as well a state of collective wellbeing and the goal for a post capitalist society. As Marx put it "in place of the old bourgeois society, with its classes and class antagonisms, we shall have an association, in which the free development of each is the condition for the free development of all" (Marx, 1848 1972).

2.2   Marx: From Bonapartism to the Paris Commune

Marx's primary concern with social movements was inspiring communist revolution in which the working class became conscious of itself as the universal agent of history, moved from a class in-itself to a class for-itself, and, insofar as communism represented the interests of the workers, a revolution would transform society. But the bourgeoisie, were always two steps ahead of a revolution and effectively coopted revolution by providing reforms and hegemonic ideologies. With basic entitlements, unemployment compensation and retirement benefits, 8-hour days and furthermore, the encouragement of nationalism obscured class in favor of citizenship. By the end of the 19th century and early 20th century, with industrial mass production, growing wages enabling consumerism, gave the [white] working classes sufficient "comforts" to dull revolutionary consciousnesses.

Marx's views of social movements can be found in his analysis of the *18th Brumaire*, (Marx, 1852 [1972]). the coup of Louis Bonaparte, and in the *Civil Wars in France* (Marx, 1871[1972]) . The crises of French capital circa 1847, led a coalition of financial and landowning bourgeoisie and elements of the proletariat to overthrow the of the government of Louis Philip in 1848. They established the Second Republic and Louis Bonaparte, a ne'er-do-well interloper, became its president. But limited to a single term, the bourgeoisie fearing the loss of their wealth in face of the rising proletariat, together with the rural peasantry, supported the coup d'état of Louis Bonaparte who transformed the Republic to the second Empire, proclaimed himself Emperor, and like a typical dictator, abolished democratic processes, due process, free press, thwarted democratic movements and ruled by secret police and the military. Although the working class were not the primary actors, what becomes extremely important is how this coup of an antidemocratic demagogue was strongly supported by the petty bourgeois French peasant farmers. As Marx showed, when Napoleon Bonaparte emancipated the peasants and granted them land confiscated from the aristocracy, they were transformed from a mass of peasants into a petty bourgeois class of landowners. But the divisions of property among sons over generations reduced the size of farms, yet large mortgages on their property and the tax burdens of maintaining a large army made their declining situation precarious. With little education, and poor communication networks among the rural French farmers isolated from each other, they were "like potatoes in a sack" who flocked to Louis Bonaparte in the hopes that he would renew the promises of the 1789 emancipation.

What was clear to Marx was that the petit bourgeois classes facing economic uncertainty, become bearers of reaction, critical of the existing government, and supporters of demagogues who promise the restoration of a "better time" now past. This has been true in most subsequent right populist movements that Marx called "Bonapartism[3]." While broadly supported by many classes, especially the self-interested economic elites who gain economic advantages from reactionary governments, massive support for reactionary populist movements has come from the petty bourgeois seeking a highly authoritarian, powerful, anti-democratic leader who will restore the lost Golden Age and

---

3   This, in turn, morphed into fascism, whether German Nazism, Italian Fascism, Argentinian Fascism or more recent right wing, authoritarian populisms.

punish the "enemies" of the "real people". To distract from his many failures, Louis Napoleon attacked Prussia. France was defeated, the Prussian army occupied Paris, and the weakened French government moved to Versailles as Louis Bonaparte was exiled to London.

With the expansion of capitalism, the growing numbers of increasingly immiserated working facing the repressive policies of Louis Napoleon, there was growing support for progressive forms of socialism, communism, and/or anarcho-syndicalism. The retreat of the weakend French government from Paris to Versailles enabled a coalition of progressive forces to overthrow the Paris government and establish the Paris Commune. This was a time and place of peaceful cordiality and radical equality between classes and between men and women, of toleration, cooperation, and mutual aid. In the end it was violently crushed, and the streets ran red with the blood of 30,000 communards. As Tilly (1978) noted, "... the augments Marx stated ... have stood the passage of time rather well".

2.3   *The German Ideology*

Societies are generally legitimated, sustained and reproduced by ideologies. Social movements need an ideology, a frame to understand their basic grievances, envision strategies of confrontation and envision the goal(s) of contestation. Marx's critiqued Hegel's idealism as if ideas came from "heaven down to earth." Ideologies acted like a camera obscura that inverts images, turn them upside down. Ideologies were parts of the superstructure, material conditions expressed as ideas articulated by various intellectuals, literati or priesthood that are part of the ruling class.

> The premises from which would begin are not arbitrary ones, not dogmas, but real premises from which abstraction can only be made in the imagination. They are the real individuals, their activity, and the material conditions under which they live, both those which they find already existing and those produced by their activity. These premises can thus be verified in a purely empirical way ... The materialist conception focuses on the extent to which ideologies are the expression of material factors, mainly the power of ruling class,[ancient, feudal or capitalist] to control the productions of ideas, of conceptions, of consciousness, all that "men say, imagine, conceive, and include such things as "politics, laws, morality, religion, metaphysics, etc." Ideology functions as the superstructure of a civilization: the conventions and culture that make up the dominant ideas of a society. ... Life is not determined by consciousness, but consciousness by life, ,.The ruling ideas are nothing more than the ideal expression of the dominant material relationships grasped as ideas;

hence of the relationships which make the one class the ruling one, therefore, the ideas of their dominance.

MARX, 1845 [1972] p.149-155

Ideologies are not simply ethereal emanations from the smokestacks of factories or locomotives, but rather they are systematically produced cultural legitimations and normalizations mystifying existing material conditions and power relations seen as either the will of God (s) or the general "will of the people" expressed in supposedly democratic elections. Ideologies serve to mediate between the economic base and the superstructure, culture, individual/collective consciousness that colonizes agency to elide critique, normalize and reproduce class domination. Finally, parents and other socializers, schools, mass media, national holidays, and historical celebrations, insinuate ideologies that become internalized as character and identity, and thus ideologies not only sustain elite power, but themselves act as material force acting from within. Nevertheless, domination fosters resistance and ideologies of domination foster counter ideologies of liberation-as Marxism itself embodies.

2.4   Hegemony

One of the central questions for Marxist approach to social mobilization has been the interrelated questions of mediation and mobilization, how the material conditions impact consciousness, understandings of the world, emotions and motivation serve to reproduce or change the group in power, the hegemonic bloc. Several important insights can be found in the work of Antonio Gramsci (1971), an organizer, theorist and journalist, Secretary-General of the Italian Communist Party, who worked to organize industrial workers in the North of Italy and agricultural workers in the South. From Sardinia, one of the poorest regions of Italy, he understood subalternity and interpreted the experiences of everyday life through Marx's critiques. As a communist organizer, he quickly learned how and why so many of the dominated and exploited workers actively, willingly "consented" to their subjugation rather than pursue their emancipation. It soon became evident to him how hegemony, the ideological control of culture, beliefs, values, and understandings, served as barriers to forming a social critique of existing conditions and thereby thwarting attempts to change. Taking a hint from Lenin, for whom "hegemony" was based on political leadership, Gramsci expanded the concept to show how the "historic bloc," maintained power through the ideological control of culture, despite the hardships and adversities it engendered. The "historic bloc" was not simply the property owners, but politicians and state institutions such as the legal system, and the military but included a coalition of many sectors of "civil society" such as media, education and, in the case of the *Risorgimento* of Italy at that time, the Catholic Church in political alliance.

As noted, for Marx the ideas of every society were the ideas of its ruling classes, the ideologies legitimating, normalizing and reproducing class relationships, fostered great deal of suffering, *materially* from abject poverty and precarious survival, as well as *psychoculturally*, e.g., alienation as powerlessness and the thwarting of self-fulfillment and denial of dignity. Such adversities might to lead to critiques of domination, and mobilization and contestations to achieve alternative visions of the possible. But ruling class ideologies normalized the historically arbitrary and demonized critique.

For Gramsci, every class has its intellectuals who do the actual production and dissemination of these (materially based) ideas, the literati, cultural specialists, teachers, journalists and even priests allied to the economic elites, are all collectively shaping ideas values and understandings, that "rendered the historically arbitrary as normal, natural, and in the best interests of all" -and to question the society was pathological, immature or even sinful. Catholic priests warned peasants and workers that joining unions, let alone the Communist Party, would warrant excommunication and an eternity in hell. As most Italians had been raised Catholic, Gramsci began to understand ideological power and how the ideological control of culture, beliefs, and values served as barriers to articulating social critiques of existing conditions and organizing to change.[4] Hegemony thus served to justify and legitimate class relationships creating a general "acceptance" of capitalist society. The result was the reproduction of domination through the colonization of consciousness whereby working classes saw that their "best" interests were realized by the historic bloc resulting in their "willing consent," actively reproducing their own subjugation; "consent", especially when it is experienced as chosen is always far more effective than coercion.

2.5   Gramsci's Organic Intellectuals and "Wars of Position"

How might, subalterns understand the basis of their subjugation, envision more fulfilling alternatives, and mobilize to pursue freedom democracy and autonomy? Given the power of ideology, how does one challenge those deeply held values? Gramsci understood that books, pamphlets, and speeches would only appeal to the already converted. Rather, it was the task of "organic intellectual," actors clearly from the subaltern classes yet who were also critically educated,

---

4   The psychodynamic dimension incorporated by the Frankfurt School suggested that fear of abandonment and here and now isolation from community was more salient for Catholic workers than one's fate in the afterlife.

understanding Marx, dialectics, and visions of the possible. Organizations needed intellectuals to articulate the relationship of theory and practice, both necessary for effective organizations. The organic intellectual would spearhead "wars of position," ideological struggles to persuade, enlighten and challenge the "common sense" of hegemonic discourses, to change the consciousness of the masses, and illuminate their standpoint to prepare for actual political confrontation, the "war of maneuver", undertaken in face-to-face discussions in which the starting point was the sharing of experiences.[5] They could articulate the lived experiences, the feelings and emotions subalterns could not articulate for themselves, but which exposed the illusions of hegemony and presented the truths of counter-hegemonic ideologies that would unmask the realities of class domination, alienation, and suffering. Organic intellectuals engaged in ideological struggles to change the consciousness of the masses, not through indoctrination but by sharing experiences.[6]. They would hasten the wars of maneuver, overcome domination through "wars of maneuver," and foster political confrontations that would hasten the arrival of the new society of freedom and equality

Struggles for liberation are never easy, especially since ruling classes blocs can muster a variety of strategies from increasing the wages and benefits of workers and providing entitlements, and more recently, valorizing consumerism. When these efforts begin to fail, the elites rely on racist, xenophobic, or religious tropes claiming victimization, and mobilizing fear and grievances to sustain a fading loyaly to the statsus quo through a temporary alliance between the [political-economic] elite and the [angry] mob (Arendt, 1951). Moreover, changing consciousness and ideas often depends on generational mediation, that is the changing historical context differentially impacts each generation, which maintains the ideas of earlier contexts (Manheim, 1952).[7]

---

5   As will be noted below, while for Habermas the bourgeois public spheres were places where people might freely discuss a variety of philosophical views critical of dynastic rule and largely justifying the leadership claims of the rising bourgeoisie, many contemporary mobilizations depend on the Internet in general and social media in particular as places where people may share and debate ideas.
6   This point was more fully developed by Paulo Friere (1970) who offered a critical model of education as opposed to the more typical "banking" model insinuating the "received" wisdom, hegemonic ideologies, into the minds of students normalizing domination.
7   But as will be seen below, many of the contemporary progressive movements have fostered their own "organic intellectuals" whose research and activism produces counterhegemonic analyses that prompt mobilizations.

2.6   *The Interregnum*

Gramsci's Marxism rejected "economism" as a crude and unmediated material determination of collective action and yet well understood how domination created resistance, fostering the demise and dying of capitalism and the birth of a new socialism, "The old is dying and the new cannot be born; in this interregnum a variety of morbid symptoms appear." We need only look at the current situation and its many "morbid symptoms" such as fascism, racism, homophobia, violence, and mass irrationality. We've now seen much the same pattern in many other societies, but at the same time various forms of right populism, politics of grievance and ressentiment might easily get leaders elected. Once in office, they make critical mistakes leading to their demise.[8]

Gramsci's analysis of the interregnum was quite prescient. Gilbert Ashcar (2016) finds Gramsci's analysis useful for understanding how the promises of a progressive Middle East following the Arab Spring degenerated into various wars, conflicts, and continued oppression of the people. Perhaps the clearest evidence of these morbid symptoms has been the election and (mis) administration of Donald Trump giving voice to two large segments of angry, discontented groups, some prone to verbal violence ranging from bullying and name, calling to others, more extremist, extolling physical violence culminating in the January 6 attempted coup to overturn a democratic election. Similarly, Nancy Fraser (2017) followed Gramsci's analysis, offered a critique of neoliberalism, it is inequality, precarity, and environmental despoliation, as propensities for crisis that mainstream governments cannot ameliorate and which, in turn, has led to a variety of progressive as well as reactionary mobilizations. Just as Mussolini had gained power in Italy and Hitler seized power in Germany, we've now seen much the same pattern in many other countries.

What is missing from Gramsci's analysis is the psychodynamic dimension, the extent to which hegemonic ideologies become internalized as unconscious aspects of character, anchored in the superego, illuminating the dynamics of how and why alienated workers "willingly" subjugation to authority by their exploiters. Gramsci seemed unaware of Freud's theory of psychodynamics, and the relationship of repression and desire, and fears of abandonment. That task would fall to the Frankfurt School of Critical Theory. Various forms of right-wing populist movements resonated with an internalized a rigid, sadomasochistic, politics of grievance, ressentiment, victimization and scapegoating might easily get leaders elected.

---

8   Louis Bonaparte started and lost the Franco-Prussian war, Mussolini invaded Ethiopia a big mistake Hitler attacked Poland and then Russia – even bigger mistakes, Trump ignored the reality of COVID-19, Trump lost. Bolsano used the same playbook and he is on his way out.

3   The Frankfurt School of Critical Theory

In the aftermath of the Russian Revolution and the emergence of a highly authoritarian communist party, Marxist theory moved from an emancipatory critique of domination to stressing economic determinism as an authoritarian playbook to "justify" a vanguard party as a dictatorship *over* the proletariat. Just as Koresh had critiqued the abandonment of Marx's philosophy, Lukacs emphasized the cultural implications of Marx's notion of "commodity fetishism" where the "appearance" of the commodity masked reification, the underlying social relationships of production. Informed by Weber's theories of rationality, bourgeois logic had colonized and distorted consciousness arguing that workers were unable to see themselves as a revolutionary class thereby reproducing class relationships.

In the late 1920s, Marx's *1844 Manuscripts* were discovered. At about this time, a group of Marxist scholars who believed that social, cultural, and psychological factors were as salient as economics, gathered at the University of Frankfurt to create an Institute for Social Research (ISR) devoted to developing a multi-dimensional, interdisciplinary critique of suffering (Kellner 2003). Erich Fromm and Herbert Marcuse were among the first to focus on alienation in Marx's writings on alienation, which would inform the rest of their careers.[9] The ISR scholars attempted to integrate the Marxist critique of alienation with Max Weber's theory of rationality in which Instrumental Reason became the dominant logic of advanced monopoly capital, especially the impersonal rationality embedded within the bureaucratic structures of both governance and commerce that was an essential moment of 20th Century capitalism in a cold, "disenchanted," rational world. They argued that Marx's theory of alienation had spread from the factory floor to capitalist societies in general. People of all classes were reduced to powerless, dehumanized cogs in a vast bureaucratic system which entrapped into all workers within "iron cages of rationality" reducing them to dehumanized cogs within a bureaucratic structure administered by "specialists without spirit, sensualists without hearts."

The elevation of Instrumental Reason as the organizing logic and ideological buttress of capital, ensconced in bureaucratic organizations, embedded in language and consciousness, eroded the capacity for critical thought, and much as Lukacs had argued privileged cognition over feeling, repressed instincts thwarting possibilities of emancipation and creative self-fulfillment.

---

9   See Fromm (1961) *The Sane Society*, and Herbert Marcuse (1964) *One-Dimensional Man.*

As will be noted, many of the postwar social movements were as attempts to reclaim humanity, authenticity and meaning given the sterility of the "administered society;" they would seek to recover agency and creative self-realization, and transform social relationships thwarted by the downsides of the Enlightenment (Horkheimer and Adorno, 1947; Marcuse, 1964).

In the late 1920s and early 1930s a variety of capitalist crises, bankruptcies, growing unemployment and hyperinflation, proved catastrophic for German society. For Wilhelm Reich (1933), fascism could not be understood simply in economic terms but depended on a particular authoritarian character type instilled by early, repressive, socialization, especially the repression of sexuality. Such socialization typically demanded obedience, usually instilled by physical punishment was likely to foster identification with authoritarian role models. The authoritarian family was the ideal preparation for those laboring in the industrial armies of the factories and administrative offices of monopoly capital, ensuring the compliance to superiors and "necessary" motivation for the labor required by capitalism. "Identification with the aggressor" became internalized as a rigid sadomasochistic superego most typically found among the petty bourgeoisie largely small businesspeople, artisans, and some upper echelon segments of the working classes, especially supervisors, and lower echelon state workers especially those in authoritarian organizations such as the police or the military. Thus, authoritarianism provided elective affinity for Nazi ideology and its leader.

Perhaps the best-known early study of the rise of fascism was Erich Fromm's (1941) analysis of authoritarianism as an "escape mechanism" to alleviate the anxiety of social fragmentation and powerlessness that came about with the rise of capitalism and demise of feudalism. Fromm had argued that at times of rapid social change, such as the rise of early market capitalism and breakdown of small, cohesive feudal communities, the individual became freed from traditional social ties and attachments to his/her superiors, or to family and members of the community. Meanwhile, the dominant frameworks of meanings and values provided by the Catholic Church eroded. This "freedom from" evoked anxiety due to the isolation and powerlessness that came with the fragmentation of society, and the individual became increasingly powerless against larger market forces he could neither understand or control. In turn, authoritarianism became a "mechanism of escape" from isolation, powerlessness, and meaninglessness, leading people to embrace the Reformation, one of the first of the major social movements of modernity, in which the highly authoritarian religions of Luther, Calvin and Zwingli, demanding submission to a powerful God and with clear-cut rules of behavior, quelled the anxiety of social change. For Fromm, the collapse, and crises of the German economy in the 20s, evoked fear, uncertainty, and anger, and again authoritarianism as a mechanism of escape would be evident in the mobilizations for fascism. If Fromm wrote for the wider audience, Adorno (1950) and his colleagues carried out one of the largest influential research studies of authoritarianism[10] in postwar United States. They developed what was called the F scale to measure fascist dispositions and the relationship between authoritarianism and prejudice, primarily racism and especially anti-Semitism. But authoritarianism was also associated with conventionalism, valorizing power and toughness, rigid black-white thought, intolerance of ambiguity and projectivity, a paranoid view of one's aggression seen in others. Authoritarianism remains a very powerful explanation for fascist mobilizations. In an analysis of the 2016 election, authoritarianism, as measured by some F scale items, was more likely to predict voting for Trump then the usual demographic variables such as income, education etc. (Smith and Hanley, 2018). Altemeyer (2016) made a similar observation.

3.1   *Adorno, Propaganda and Communication*
Early studies from the Frankfurt School were concerned with authoritarianism in the media; Adorno (2000) analyzed the radio speeches of the Rev. Martin Luther Thomas, who broadcast fascist messages to a large audience of the American public. While not specifically tied to Nazi propaganda, Adorno analyzed how Thomas' quasi-fascist radio broadcasts fostered a "pagan religious sect" which Adorno said was "racketeering in religion" (Adorno, 2000). The basic elements of Fascist demagoguery were 1) the "lone wolf", 2) movement and 3), the exactitude of error. "The lone wolf device is taken from the arsenal of Hitler, who always used to boast [...] about the fact that others controlled the press, the radio – everything; and that he had nothing" (Adorno, 2000, p.4). His speeches glorified, action, not specific policies. "The movement is conceived of as an end in itself, like the Nazis who always made a fetish of the term *Bewegung* ["move" or "movement"] without pointing out exactly where the *Bewegung* was going" (Adorno, 2000, P. 31). Finally, the rhetoric includes what Adorno called the "inexactitude of error" which today we would call "false facts."[11]

---

10   A compendium of the research and theory on authoritarianism has been collected and summarized by Altemeyer (1996).

11   Haverda and Halley (2019) did an analysis of Trump's speeches, and found that Adorno's analysis clearly anticipated the fascist messaging of Donald Trump. But this time, Trump was amplified by a far-reaching Internet based social media. The same can be said of Bolsinaro, Modi, Erdogan, Le Pen, Orban etc.

The figures mentioned in [Thomas's] diatribe are, of course, utterly fantastic. There is [not] the slightest corroboration of the astronomical figure of the "cost of crime" in America. To operate with fantastic figures is
an established Nazi habit. The apparent scientific exactitude of any set
of figures silences resistance against the lies hidden behind the figures.
This technique which might be called the "exactitude of error" device is
common to all fascists. Phelps, [another reactionary pastor] for instance,
has similar fantastic figures about the influx of refugees into this country.
The greatness of the figure, incidentally, acts as a psychological stimu-
lant, suggesting a general feeling of grandeur which is easily transferred
to the speaker.

ADORNO, 2000, p. 93

After the Second World War Lowenthal and Guterman (1949) systematically
showed how the "prophets of deceit" could transform economic malaise and
discontents into a politics of grievances of the victimized that shifted blame
from the economic system to "malign foreign interests," and/or traitors from
within, designated as dangerous vermin. With a nod to Carl Schmitt, the reactionary agitator needs and stokes a politics of friend and "dangerous" foes as
a threat to the very existence of the "real people," but he or she, and only here
she, can stand up to the enemies and defeat them. Moreover, s/he portrays
him/herself as being both "one of the ordinary people" and having highly
unique and special skills, being both the "corner barber" and "King Kong" that
enables him/her to "save" society from its peril. For most right-wing agitators,
that foe was likely to be Jews. or communists.[12] More recently, the foes may
include Moslems and the danger comes from racialized minorities, LGBTQ or
the "socialists" which includes all Democrats, college educated "coastal elites"
and most of the professoriate who indoctrinate youth.

The psychological appeal of fascist propaganda and agitators from to Adolf
Hitler Martin Luther Thomas established a paradigm for understanding the
postwar "culture industries" systematically producing amusement and enter-
tainment that was escapist, deceptive, and clearly propaganda exalting the
American way of life (Horkheimer and Adorno 1947). Mass culture needs to
be considered as the mass production of profit generating wish fulfillments,
compensations for the love and romance lacking in the lives of many, as exem-
plars of power and often violence appealing to the powerless, and as implicitly

---

12   For Postone following Marx, the "good" capitalists were the ones who produced goods,
      created jobs and gave us prosperity, while the finance capitalists, bankers and speculators,
      greedy Jews were parasites who suck the blood of the good producers and workers.

extolling individualism, competition and the resulting "success" expressed in the "goods life" as the reward for alienated labor. At the same time, as Marcuse (1964) put it. mass media would become the primary means of the dissemination of "one-dimensional thought" that promised rewards of competition and conformity being "repressive de-sublimation". Finally, most mainstream news outlets, owned by a handful of corporations, presents relatively "mainstream views" as "normal," while any fundamental critique of capitalism is reformist at best or altogether absent. There was very little severe criticism of Donald Trump lest corporate media lose advertisers and audiences.

3.2   Marcuse and the Great Refusals

One of the most important contributions by the Frankfurt School to the study of social movements, especially the progressive movements of the 1960s, could be found in Herbert Marcuse (1969) extolling the "Great Refusals" as collective rejections of the status quo. Inspired by Paris '68, the civil rights movements, the feminist movements, and the massive antiwar movements of the 6os, he argued that these movements were less motivated by bread-and-butter economic considerations as such, but rather by the attempt to overcome uncritical, one "dimensional thought" and realize what he called a "new sensibility" with the predominance of the life instincts over the death instincts, love, creativity and fulfillment as opposed to destructiveness and domination which thwarted needs for human freedom, fulfillment, and a humanistic social order free of domination exploitation, alienation and competition.

> In proclaiming the "permanent challenge" (la contestation permanente), the Great Refusals recognized the mark of social repression, even in the most sublime manifestations of traditional culture, even in the most spectacular manifestations of technical progress. They have again raised a specter (and this time a specter which haunts not only the bourgeoisie but all exploitative bureaucracies), the specter of a revolution which subordinates the development of productive forces and higher standards of living for the requirements of creating solidarity for the human species, for abolishing poverty and misery beyond all national frontiers and spheres of interest, for the attainment of peace.
>
> MARCUSE 1969: ix–x

As he put it, these utopian movements aimed to foster a new character type, a "new sensibility" free from the systems of capitalist domination, seeking both personal liberation and transformation of the world that would value the life instincts over the death instincts, transforming the nature of the self, relationships between people and between people and Nature. The new sensibility is the medium of social change that mediates between the political practice of changing the world and one's own drive for personal liberation (Marcuse, 1969, p. 234; Marcuse, 1970).

Moreover, and it should be noted quite presciently, Marcuse, like many other critical theorists saw that the industrial working classes, then with relatively better wages and affordable consumerism, had been incorporated into the "administered society." As C. Wright Mills had noted, organized labor had become primarily concerned with wages, benefits and working conditions and paid little attention to larger political issues besides supporting pro-labor Democrats. Indeed, in the 1960s, many workers tended to be quite racist-fearing minorities might take their job and/or lower the value of their property. Marcuse however, noting Paris 68 saw the many of the then newer progressive mobilizations on college campuses, such as, the free speech movement, the "New Left", antiwar movements and campus-based feminist conscious raising groups as well as various minority movements, such as "Black Panthers," envisioned college students and minorities were increasingly likely to be the agents of social change.

3.3   Habermas: The Public Sphere, the Life World, Legitimation Crises

As societies changes, social movements emerge or wane, as do theories to explain these movements. Habermas, a second-generation Frankfurt School theorist, had shown that with the emergence of "civil society," came bourgeois "public spheres in which educated, male, bourgeois elites, 'free individuals,' discussed and debated various aspects of political philosophy (Habermas, 1989). The "free-speech situations" enabled "undistorted communication" which led to consensus and in turn "public opinion" that became a political force. These "public spheres," as open spaces of "undistorted communication" and the possibility of rational consensus to discuss relevant issues and political questions again appeared in the 60s and 70s as feminists, gays, antiwar activists gathered to share views and experiences. With the postwar prosperity, bourgeois democracy was not problematic, as wages rose and workers enjoyed consumerism, they were not longer agents of resistance indeed, they opposed change. For Habermas (1981), these new social movements were less concerned with classical labor capital conflicts, rather, "the new conflicts manifested in sub-institutional, extra-parliamentary forms of protest. The underlying deficits reflect a reification of communicative spheres of action; the media of money and power are not sufficient to circumvent this reification" (Habermas, 1981, p. 49). The new struggles would be over lifestyles, identities and values, culture as the primary locus of crisis and struggle

Habermas bridged cultural Marxism with phenomenology and differentiated between the larger "system" and the individual "life worlds" of identity and experience which had been colonized by Instrumental Reason-objectifying and dehumanizing the subject. Social movements emerged at the seams between the "life worlds" of experience and the system to overcome alienation, domination, and dehumanization. They were more concerned with questions of the colonization of the life world that was fostering identities that were shallow, inauthentic and conformist at best, reproducing hierarchies of domination at worst. These new social movements would assert communicatively rational action in the new "public spheres" critical of the agendas of the state and the economy. At this point he updated Marxist critique of alienation, but like the first generation of the Frankfurt school, it is no longer simply a matter of wage labor, but the domination of Instrumental Reason as the regulatory principle of both advanced capitalism and the modern State.[13]

Such movements were especially likely when late capitalism faced legitimation crises (Habermas, 1975). Capitalism, as Marx had shown, is inherently crisis prone and occurs when 1) the economic system fails to sustain growth and does not "fairly" distributes resources for all; 2) the political system fails to provide conditions for economic growth, regulate businesses, and provide rights, entitlements, and legal systems to secure justice and grant legitimacy to the system; 3) the cultural system the was unable to provide meaningful identities, lifestyles and values Habermas argued that crises in any of these spheres could migrate from the level of the system to the lifeworld of individual/collective identities and motivation. At such times, these crises might both foster withdrawal of loyalty to the system and evoke powerful emotions from fear and anxiety to anger and aggression, that would open people's minds to alternatives and mobilize to achieve them.

4 Social Movements, Old and New

The post war decades of Keynesian economic growth witnessed the explosion of mass consumption and proliferation of mass media, especially television. This was a time of relatively tranquility but hiding beneath the surface,

---

13 NB! At this point, while Habermas pays more attention to the cultural and psychosocial consequences of late capitalism, he still retains a space for the impact of political economy. As will be noted, the concern with political economy waned and social movement theory until the rise of the anti-globalization movements and this becomes especially clear in contemporary progressive mobilizations.

a great deal of alienation, discontent, and disenchantment was brewing. Looking back, this period was an incubator for the conditions for movements that would later erupt.[14] But note, in part due to the affluence of the postwar era, as the critique of political economy had shaded into the background, and while these newer social movements contested on the cultural terrains, the fundamental issues remain tied to an underlying economic system, but while wealth and possessions produced comforts, "keeping up with the Joneses" was a constant source of anxiety, consumerism provided only shallow transitory meanings and ersatz gratifications while "inauthentic" conformity, was neither self– fulfilling, nor intrinsically gratifying or socially meaningful. But all "good things" must come to end.

By the end of the 60s, imports from Japan and Germany cost less than American made products, American factories were shuttered, and a new "Rust Belt," and urban "wasteland" spread across the heart of industrial America, initiating economic declines in many parts of the country, impacting both workers and small businesses. The full employment policies under Keynesian programs created inflation, a squeeze on profits, and a shift by business to support pro-business and anti-labor candidates. This marked the beginning of a period of economic hardship, and duress for many as real income stagnated, people's lives were burdened by rising debt, and the ensuing economic crises precipitated several movements, both progressive and reactionary. Ronald Reagan was elected president, he soon busted PATCO, and the economic ideas of Von Mise and Hayek moved from the margins of economic theory to the mainstream, thanks in part to Milton Friedman and promises of "trickle down" economic policies to benefit all but primarily benefited business.[15] Neoliberalism with its promises of affluence for all became widely embraced.[16] Clinton subsequently pronounced "the end of big government" and negotiated NAFTA – a hint of what was to come.

To understand the social movements over the past several decades, both the progressive moments and the emergence of right-wing populism we reflect on two factors that emerge out of Marx's analysis of capitalism: the role of

---

14   We are not ignoring the earlier history of movement like unionization drives and civil rights struggles. Most African Americans were aware of the Montgomery bus boycott in 1955 and other events led to the turning point and the Civil Rights Act of 1964

15   A similar outcome was in the UK, with Thatcher's election and her assault on the mine workers' unions.

16   For an excellent history of the rise and fall of Milton Friedman and neoliberalism see https://newrepublic.com/article/162623/milton-friedman-legacy-biden-government-spending?utm_campaign=fund&utm_medium=email&utm_source=newsletter

culture and the importance of character. As the Frankfurt School argued, the intertwining of monopoly capital and Instrumental Reason were "taken for granted" as "common sense", providing consumer abundance, but a dehumanized shallow life. There was little critique of the repression, conformity, consumerism, materialism, and superficiality of the culture.[17] Such values served to reproduce the capitalist system. While the neo-Marxist critiques had little had little direct impact on American sociology, a number of scholars such as David Riesman, C. Wright Mills, William Kornhauser, Seymour Lipset or Robert Nisbet observed the alienation, fragmentation, detachment/loneliness, conformity, homogenization and apathy of postwar "mass society" For some however, especially Kornhauser (1959) and Lipset and Raab (1970) these were the very conditions that led to right wing extremism, especially when many of the newly rich, facing "status inconsistency" (affluence but without the cultural capital of "old money") could never be fully accepted into the upper classes so they embraced fervent patriotism and economic conservatism. Others feared the loss of economic status and an apparent upward mobility of immigrants and minorities, and/or were convinced that progressive political movements meant a takeover of the country and the appropriation of their "hard earned wealth."

If the early studies of authoritarianism saw how that character structure was initially shaped in family life, other observers suggested the changing socialization styles led to a major change in social character. Following World War II, between economic security and the expert advice regarding child-rearing, there were changes in character. Wolfenstein (1951) called this the move from obedience qua impulse control, to enjoyment, the emergence of the "fun morality" Inglehart (1971) argued that the economic security after the war led parents to be more comfortable and more lenient in their child rearing practices, echoing Reich's views that less punitive, less authoritarian, more empathic parenting resulted in greater concern with a child's development than with his/her obedience to authority that would lead to the embrace of post-materialist values. One early observer, Turner (1976) saw the locus of "real selfhood" moving from an "institution locus," that is ambition, morality, and altruism, to one of "impulse" with a focus on one's feelings and relations to other. For Lakoff 1996) the family, is the cauldron of social specifically moral politics, unconscious worldviews, in which the "strict father" orientation stresses individualism, self-reliance and toughness, often instilled through

---

17   This is not to suggest there was no critique, but the most vocal sociological critic, C. Wright Mills, had very limited impact on the profession – though he did inspire many of the activist youth of the 60s. See Langman, 2021.

physical punishment, leading to conservative world views. Meanwhile, "empathic parenting" encourages the child's freedom and curiosity, his/her sensitivity to other people's needs and care for other people that leads to progressive worldviews. Socialization and in turn social character were changing, and as Inglehart (1971) suggested, during the 60's many youths had begun to embrace "post-materialist values" seeking intrinsic gratification and realms of creativity rather than external rewards.[18] There was an explosion of counter cultures repudiated conformity, repressive norms and "inauthenticity", while other youth promoted progressive social movements and cultures that challenged various forms of domination especially over identities and values.

4.1   *Emerging Progressive Movements and a New Social Consciousness*
The 1960s witnessed a series of system challenging contentious movements spearheaded by activist middle class often college educated youth and/or minority youth who were propelling civil rights movements in marches and sit-ins, organizing massive anti-Vietnam War mobilizations, advocating second wave feminisms, sexual liberation, gay rights and early concerns about the environment and pollution. There were cultural movements, not revolutionary struggles, which revealed the alienation from the capitalist system and struggles against the indifference of governments to popular will. These movements shifted the traditional focus of progressive movements from economic interests (labor, suffrage, wages) to focus on changing lifestyles, values, and identities to overcome alienation, domination, and repressive conformity. This came to a heard by the end of the 1960s a cultural moment embraced political challenges.

Radicalized by protesting the Algerian and the Vietnam wars, in 1968 Nantes University students reacted to the horrendous conditions of the factory workers in nearby French defense factories. They staged protests supporting the workers' actions, protests which quickly spread to other French universities. They were soon joined by the labor unions and the Communist Party (PFC), eventually attracting 1/3 of the French population who joined in the movements. These students led mobilizations included the radical Situationists, who owed as much to the aesthetic transgressions of Dada or Surrealism as to Marxism. While critical of capitalist alienation deforming everyday life, especially given the triumph of semiotics in advertising and consumerism in the "society of spectacles" where illusions were sacred. they saw your criticized

---

18   As a survey researcher, he did not offer a theoretical explanation, but it seems as if one consequence of a growing capitalist economy is fostering a character type to see if that would challenge its norms.

socialism as B-O-R-I-N-G (Du Bord, 1970). For Du Bord, the spectacle had colonized social relationships, while passive identification with the spectacle supplanted genuine activity. It is not a collection of images, instead, it is a social relation between people, mediated by images. Contemporary life has become impoverished, authenticity no longer exists. Their forms of resistance, aesthetic spectacles in the streets, *détournements* (reversals of meanings) that involved using spectacular images and language to disrupt the flow of the spectacle. Weaponizing cobblestones from the street, did not "fit" within the usual social movement frameworks. Their own carnivalesque performativity was expressed in street theater and outrageous signage, "Be realistic, demand the impossible." The situationists had a considerable influence on the French student rebellion of 1968 and indeed, many of the more recent mobilizations, for example the slut walks.

Echoing what Marcuse (1969, 1970) had said about "great refusals" and the aesthetic, Boltanski and Chiapello (2005) emphasized the significance of artistic critique in the French student mobilizations of 1968 which were:

> ... were primarily motivated by a desire to overcome the disenchantment, the lack of authenticity, the misery of everyday life', the dehumanization of the world under the rule of scientific-technical knowledge and technocracy ... the loss of autonomy, the absence of creativity, and the different forms of oppression, characterizing the modern world.
>
> BOLTANSKI and CHIAPELLO, 2005, p. 245

Meanwhile in Prague, then under the domination of the USSR, the economy had been in serious decline; there was growing opposition to the government and President Novotny was forced to resign. The reformist government of Alexander Dubček, came to power and attempted to create a "socialism with a human face" granting the Czechoslovakian citizens greater rights and decentralizing the economy. The Soviet Union balked at this liberalization and sent half a million troops to quell the liberalization movement. Massive spontaneous protests and various kinds of "civilian resistance" lasted for eight months.

The antiwar movement in the United States consisted of protests, often on college campuses, marches, and massive demonstrations in Washington. These movements were for the most part a bottom-up movement without a central organization fostering mobilizations, out of which emerged SDS, Students for a Democratic Society. Across college campuses, "teach ins" explained the nature of American imperialism, the history of the intervention, the false flag justification, and the massive slaughter (body counts) of innocent civilians. By 1967 the cost of the war in dollars and in American lives began to shift public opinion to

322

LANGMAN

oppose the war. Opposition culminated in protests at the Democratic national convention in Chicago. While the massive protests did little to immediately change the direction of American policy, in retrospect, it had a major impact on the nature of political consciousness and the notion of what was possible. President Johnson did not seek re-election. Richard Nixon, running promises of law and order, clamping down on protests and with dog whistles for racism, called the Southern Strategy.[19] It worked, Nixon was elected president.

The social movements of the final decades of the 20th Century would most appropriately be considered progressive and broadly classified as on the Left. Clearly there were tendencies that anticipated the more authoritarian and populist movements on the Right, social rumblings associate with the "Silent Majority" and local socially or fiscally conservative efforts at local control of school boards, municipal governments, and anti-property tax initiatives. They would eventually morph into full-fledged popular movements on the Right. These various movements of the late-1960s and into the end of the century could not be very well understood by dominant frameworks theorizing social movements like resource mobilization, political opportunity, or even structural strain theories. Moreover, even though the Paris and Prague mobilizations were prompted by economic forces, these movements were not the classically framed Marxist movements in which workers demanded better pay, improved working conditions and benefits rather, most Czechoslovak citizens rejected the authoritarian politics and called for reform or social transformation.

The new generation of Frankfurt School scholars had been moving further and further away from considerations of the economy to cultural conncers as initiated by Habermas. That trend was further developed by Touraine (1981) and students like Castells and Melucci attempted to develop New Social Movement theory (NSM) relevant for postindustrial society.in the aftermath of the movements of 1968. The primary feature of these mobilizations was the shift away from hierarichal movement organizations, unions, political parties, or even progressive NGOs with recognized leaders pursuing specific interests (labor, suffrage, government policies). They were replaced by spontaneous, "bottom up" rhizomatic movements with emergent democratic leadership, quite different than the existing bureaucratic social movement organizations. These rhizomatic eruptions of youth sought to forge new collective identities to overcome alienation, thwarted selfhood and social fragmentation via the

---

19   This strategy was the early emergence of an anti-Black reaction to the gains of the Civil Rights movement culminating in the 1964 act providing protections against racism. Five decades later this coalition forms the basis for opposition to contemporary racial justice efforts like Black Lives Matter.

transformation of identities, lifestyles and values through movements and demonstrations in the public sphere rather than through the goal of directly impacting government policies by electoral politics. Moreover, as was seen in many of the mobilizations, especially occupations such a Occupy Wall Street, they attempted to enact in everyday life the very kinds of identities and social relationships they would like to see characteristic of the future society as a whole.

It is beyond the scope of this chapter to explore in greater detail the major new social movements that transformed society and motivated the oppositional reactions that now are characterized as the populism from the Right. While nascent in the 1960s, we again see many progressive movements and contestations that were revived and spearheaded by the 1960s generation of young people: civil rights/minority rights, feminism, LGBT rights environmentalism, and a call for an egalitarian democratic humanistic society. Most of the mass protests of that time took place on the cultural terrains, rarely if ever calling for a re-evaluation of how society organizes production and distribution. Nevertheless, these strains and crises of the times, the banality and superficiality of conformist consumerism, poverty, enduring racism, and sexism led to growing interests in neo-Marxism in general and in Critical Theory more specifically. The most widely known social critic of that time, C. Wright Mills, showed that people holding jobs, whether blue-, pink- or white-collar, were alienated and routinized while the power elite was (and remains) indifferent to popular sentiments (see Langman, 2021). At the end of the day, these moments revealed the inequality, indifference by the state, and the powerlessness, fragmentation, and emptiness of neoliberal capitalism

Recent actions by young people call for progressive social change and, in many cases exhibit growing support for socialism as a system that promotes more democratic humanistic values. By the end of the 20th century, the growing inequality due to global neo liberalism, to governmental indifference or inaction while supporting elites, pointed to a failed consumer culture. Rejecting economically based extrinsic rewards and seeking to transform cultural values movements emerged that targeted inequality, precarity, and privatization required a revisiting and updating of the arguments provided by Marx 150 years earlier. As Masquelier (2013) put it:

> despite a self-proclaimed formulation of critique from the standpoint of culture, first-generation critical theory could play a key role in (1) capturing the social malaise engendered by neoliberal capitalism; and (2) informing the practice of resistance in contemporary capitalist societies

through a re-evaluation of its own stance towards organized labor and
the critique of political economy elaborate.

MASQUELIER, 2013, p. 396

Following, the WTO protests, the Arab Spring, Occupy Wall Street it became
evident that social movement theory, even NSM, needed a paradigmatic shift
to understand the 21st Century mobilizations. These spontaneous, movements,
often organized and mobilized in "virtual public spheres" of the Internet,
enabled "internetworked social movements" (Langman, 2005). These mobilizations, occupations, were more likely to take place in the "public spheres",
especially squares like Tahrir or Syntagma, or in parks, OWS or Gezi to impact
consciousness, rather than engage in electoral politics. The basic goals of these
newer social movements were to overcome powerlessness, social fragmentation, and the meaninglessness and emptiness of "hegemonic" identities based
on conformity, homogeneity, consumerism and civic privatism, as well as economic inequalities to foster a more humane society that would enable the freedom and self-fulfillment hoped for by Marx.

With the explosion of subsequent social movements of the late 20th and
early 21st centuries, rooted in alienation as domination and powerlessness,
social fragmentation, and the denial of recognition, often expressed as indig-
nation, the NSM perspectives were useful, but NSM needed to pay more attention to aspects of the political economy. Similarly, whereas for Habermas
emotions were a consequence of legitimation crises fostering mobilizations,
emotions did not play a major role in the early articulations of NSM theory.
Yet after Arab Spring, Castells' (2012) analysis noted the anger prompting these
movements and hopes of changing society. The work of this author, and his
colleagues suggested that the goals of such movements, overcoming alienation and domination were "mobilizing for dignity" (Langman, 2015; Langman,
Benski et al. 2013).

4.2   Right Wing Mobilizations

Perhaps the most imminent danger facing the United States and indeed many
other countries has been the upsurge of a variety of right-wing authoritarian
populisms, ethno-religious nationalisms, and even some neofascist movements that may indeed shade into genuine fascism. And as we witnessed on
January 6, 2021, several of the more extremist factions in these movements,
often with members with military backgrounds, *are well armed, and potentially
quite dangerous.* How do we understand these movements? We should first
note that a common theme in most of these contemporary movements is an

animosity toward the government with a claim that corrupt elites are acting in ways contrary to the wishes and often wallets of "the people." As Marx
pointed out, the coup d'état of Louis Napoleon was largely supported by a rural
population facing economic hardships. The impact of economic duress organizes protests, some may become violent. But most of the right wing populists
today are neither poor nor working class, but an anxious, authoritarian lower
middle class impelled by racism and sexism as well as pocket book issues The
embrace of right-wing authoritarian populisms must begin by understanding
that it is a symptom of pain-and-suffering, anxiety and anger, fear, and rage.

Marx's initial foray into social movements was the 1851 coup of Louis
Napoleon who could not run for president and led a movement to overthrow-
ing the government. His support came from financial and land-owning elites
and from petit bourgeois farmers facing economic decline and hardship turning to a seemingly powerful hero to alleviate their hardships. Marx stresses
the larger context of either immediate economic crises or longer-term economic declines to understand social movements. The global Depression after
the stock market collapse caused massive bankruptcies, unemployment, and
hyperinflation in Germany led to the collapse of the Weimar government and
a 20th Century "Bonapartism" in the rise of Hitler's Nazi Party. Anti-Semitism
was weaponized by the Nazis to feed on public misery, blaming Jews for the
economic collapse. Reactionary populism resonates with underlying authoritarian character traits, joining such mobilizations empowers the victimized,
assuages the aggrieved, target aggression;the Nazi party provided a pseudo-
gemeinschaft based on unconscious ties to the powerful leader, the ego ideal
of the group. The leader was like everyman but a superman, the fusion of
King Kong and the corner barber. He exchanged his "love" for their obedience,
cementing social ties for the alienated by membership in a valorized group.
Hitler, a charismatic "rabble rouser," from the lower middle classes, spoke to
their grievances, their victimization and anger; he targeted the blameworthy Jew and promised relief using new means of mass media, film and radio,
between the endless martial music, massive rallies with torchlight parades of
precision marching, and emotion evoking films such as *The Eternal Jew* and
Triumph of the Will, what Kellner (2003) has called "media spectacles" had a
major consequence in mobilizing support for Hitler.

The Marxist approach to reactionary social movements thus argues that
the starting point must be political economy and its crises, but at the same
time, these crises must consider class and cultural factors, ideologies or frames,
as well as psychological factors primarily emotions, such as anger, shame
aggression and especially *ressentiment* that have led to embrace of various

authoritarian populisms, ethno-religious nationalisms etc.[20] However, the impact of the political economy might be mediated through various cultural changes, for example civil rights movements, feminist mobilizations, gay-rights struggles and other agendas that generate negative and at times visceral reaction. Consequently, these cultural challenges often spur reactionary social movements that defended long standing values and ideologies, identities, and lifestyles of a segment of the otherwise aggrieved public. For example, the mobilizations against the war in Vietnam angered a certain kind of "my country right or wrong" crude patriotism voiced by many that were strongly anti-Communist and so opposed to the antiwar movement. Civil rights movements challenged long term racism both structurally and individually precipitating so-called "white rage" as American right-wing movements mobilized out of fear and anger (Anderson, 2016). Feminism challenged patriarchy, "male superiority" and systems of domination over women threatening male egos that fed into the "defense of the family" and opposition to LGBTQ rights. These cultural and social psychological factors fed reactionary social mobilization in ways initially developed by the Frankfurt School scholars. Their concerns with authoritarianism as an ideology, as a character structure and as the themes embedded in a variety of mass media informs similar factors are now at play in the contemporary right-wing mobilizations.

4.3   *It's More Than the Economy, Stupid*

Large segment of the population supported, and still supports, Donald Trump with his authoritarianism, narcissism, incompetence, and chaotic policies that adversely impacted the US society. His mishandling of the COVID-19 crisis and the record deaths that followed, including among his loyal supporters, cost him his re-election. Much the same could be said of leaders like Bolsonaro in Brazil or Modi in India. While they promote unsubstantiated paranoid beliefs to their followers, the anger and vitriol of their supporters are unlikely to see policies emerge that reverse the conditions feeding their anger. The intense anxiety and uncertainty of social change, coupled with powerlessness and isolation, has fostered authoritarianism as a palliative. Challenges to their identities,

---

20   There are number of Marxist critics who have claimed a direct relationship between the rise of neoliberalism and its economic adversities, but as has been made clear in this essay, crude economic determinism can little explain how people can so vehemently embrace political leaders and causes that may not only endanger their livelihoods and identities, but as we've seen in the past year, most authoritarian governments, United States, Brazil, India, have poorly handled the Corona pandemic and many deaths have occurred among supporters.

values, and lifestyles has led many to the embrace of authoritarian leaders' irrational, paranoid beliefs, and the extreme form of authoritarian aggression, necrophilia, the love of death and destruction (Fromm, 1967).

Support for right-wing mobilizations cannot simply be explained by looking at what drives economic interests (Frank, 2004). Contemporary right-wing mobilizations, including the election of Trump in particular, echo many of the earlier studies on the rise of fascism, especially authoritarianism (Altemeyer, 2016; Smith and Hanley, 2018). In 2016, the media analysis suggested that Trump supporters were primarily the working classes who faced income loss because of globalization, automation, and neoliberal policies of austerity. *But careful analyses revealed that Trump's base of support was primarily lower middle class, mostly small business owners and lower echelon state officials, (police, military) typically with no more than a high school education but with higher than average annual incomes.* A slight majority of better paid members of the white working classes also voted for Trump whose motivation came from a combination of racism and xenophobia fueled by the fear that they will lose jobs to "unqualified" African Americans or immigrants. As much of the research has shown, for most of the reactionary base, cultural issues such as racism, sexism or religion have been more salient than economic hardship per se. And for several rich Republicans, support for Trump and tax cuts and lax regulation of commerce or environmental safeguards were typical.

Most right authoritarian populist movements have several features in common. Almost 100 years ago, Carl Schmitt (2007 [1932]) decried liberal democracies that don't represent the "will of the [true] people," who are in fundamental conflict their enemies. Only a strong, powerful leader can best realize the will of the ordinary, "authentic people" and s/he adroitly uses electoral politics to gain power, and subsequently uses that power to erode democratic freedoms and subvert the democratic process and practices that undermined the "people." They are generally anti-pluralistic, anti-democratic, anti-elitist intolerant and authoritarian (Mueller, 2016). Reactionaries typically feel that their moral community of "the real people" have been victimized by political and cultural elites; their own interests, values and identities have been ignored, challenged, or subverted by self-serving, indifferent, inapt and/ or corrupt elites who use their wealth and power to support "unpopular" economic, social, political outcomes, including rigging elections to secure "unpopular" and often cosmopolitan agenda. A common complaint is that the policies of corrupt, establishment elites have enabled subaltern Others, like "pushy" women, "inferior" minorities of color, "perverted" gays and even undocumented immigrant "criminals" to prosper at the expense of the average people.

In the US, cultural changes initiated in the 60's, feminism, gay rights, multiculturalism, and even secularism are now much more acceptable to most Americans but face strong opposition by a segment of the population who feel most threatened by these changes. Demographic changes due to historical immigration patterns, and the increasing percentage of the population represented by African Americans, Latino/as, Asian Americans, and others pose what many see as an existential threat, "extinction anxiety" threatening their identities, values, lifestyles, and political power at a time of increased economic anxiety. For Rich:

> .... this loss of ontological security is crucial in accounting for the growing environment of political, social, and cultural tension roiling across the liberal democratic world. It posits that the drive to alleviate the existential angst and uncertainty of the current moment has, at its most extreme, produced a myriad of rejectionist 'fighting identities' that have demonstrated growing salience and appeal in expanding audiences.
>
> RICH, 2021

Trump stoked these anxieties and played on their fears, anxieties, grievances, and feelings of victimization. As noted, Altemeyer (2016) suggested and Smith and Hanley (2018) demonstrated in their analysis of 150,000 voters, authoritarian sympathies were more likely to predict voting for Trump than any of the other demographic variables, measures of racism, patriarchy, aggression, and bullying were more salient than economic anxiety per se.

A recurrent theme in many of the ethnographic studies of right-wing populism has been the feeling that many people, typically from rural or exurban locale, often with no more than a high school education have been being "left behind" by the recent economic change favoring financialization and high technologies, along with demographic changes and influxes of immigrants, and cultural changes toward more progressive social values, have stoked fear and anger which have precipitated cultural backlashes throughout much of the world (Norris and Inglehart, 2019). One aspect of populist anger is seeming challenges to traditional, authoritarian identities s can be seen in "replacement" theory which "explains" how some French, the right wing followers of Marine Le Pen, fear that Moslems will take over their country and destroy French culture and its *laïcité*, its secularism, separation of Church and State. As Mitchell described the far right:

> Its basic contours are this: "indigenous" white populations, and their cultures, societies, and institutions, are being replaced by a tide of racial

others – Black people, Africans and Muslims. Moreover, this is happening not because of any natural demographic trend, but because enemies within have willed it, not only through weakness but through a suicidal, self-hating malice towards the civilization of which they are a part.

MITCHELL, 2020[21]

This replacement theory, thus argues, triggers a very primal fear of "extinction anxiety," a powerful existential anxiety over the fragilely and future of one's very identity, values and lifestyles based on essentialist, fixe notions of white identity, gender identity and Christianity that face challenges, decline, and perhaps demise.[22] The fear of death and annihilation is one of the most powerful human motivators (Becker, 1973). Various reactionary mobilizations play on this fear, and like caged animals, many violently lash out in order to defend their cultures and identities through whatever means are necessary.

Closely tied to the fear of replacement rooted in the fear of death, is the role of shame as pivotal emotion of contemporary societies where principles of competition and market exchange have spread from the economy to all domains of life (Bauman 1998). Here, "shame implies a nonmoral negative self-evaluation. Note that "nonmoral" is not synonym to "immoral". By "nonmoral" we mean that shame is not focused on responsibility issues ... it is rather concerned with a perceived discrepancy between one's actual and one's ideal self" (Miceli and Castelfranchi, 2018. p.712). In capitalist societies, one's esteem is typically based on the evaluations of others based upon the standards or criteria of recognition which most often reflect one's economic fortunes. This has become especially salient in the past several years in which neoliberalism, has made recognition and status *seem as solely due to individual efforts*, when, indeed, neoliberalism with its valorization of wealth based on its inequality, while at the same time its policies and practices, deregulation, export substitution, automation, financialization and/or privatization of resources and services like education, has made it much more difficult for individuals to find economic security let alone mobility and we now find wide spread precarity,

---

21   https://www.theguardian.com/commentisfree/2020/jun/10/attacks-protesters-enemies
      -western-culture-traction-far-right

22   More recently, Chauncey de Vega (2018) has argued that "Conservatives – and especially
      Trumpists ... are filled with dread, anger and fear about their future. In Charleston, the
      chanted 'Jews will not replace us.' While they often hide their sentiments behind words
      such as "tradition" and "culture," on a fundamental level, white conservatives believe that to
      be a real American requires a person to be first and foremost white, [male] and Christian".
      https://www.salon.com/2018/06/26/what-fuels-white-anxiety-the-baffling-hypocrisies
      -behind-white-paranoia-politics/

with gig jobs such as ride share, food delivery, short term consultancies, episodic employment etc. (cf. Standing, 2011). Precarity is problematic, even for many that are economically well off at the moment, especially the lower middle class business owners easily buffeted by market forces. The real or anticipated losses stemming from the larger political economy, but for which individuals blame themselves leads to shame as a "failure" of self, a denigrated identity that may be as painful, if not more so than the fear of the death of one's identity (cf. Maygar-Hass, 2020) Anticipatory shame thus has an adverse quality with negative implications for the self and one's esteem. This is because it signals an expected loss rather than a possible loss or social exclusion (Miceli and Castelfranchi, 2018). Scheff (1994) has argued that unconscious, unacknowledged shame is a master emotion, giving rise to violent aggression and the quest for revenge as a defense. This shame, humiliation was a factor precipitating both the Russian revolution and rise of German Fascism. Salmelal and von Scheve (2018) suggest th:

> "authoritarian populist mobilizations are characterized by repressed shame that transforms fear and insecurity into anger, resentment, and hatred against perceived enemies" of the precarious self,. Left-wing populism, in turn, associates more with acknowledged shame that allows individuals to self-identify as aggrieved and humiliated by neoliberal policies and their advocates. The latter type of shame holds emancipatory potential as it allows individuals to establish bonds with others who feel the same, whereas repressors remain in their shame or seek bonds from repression-mediated defensive anger and hatred.
>
> SALMELAL and VON SDGEVE 2018, p.434

Today, one of the consequences of this current or anticipated "failure of the self," based on negative social recognition evokes the shame as and humiliation of a "discrepant self" and thus animosity toward nefarious elites held responsible, as well as racist white rage, sexism, xenophobia, and even homophobia, attacks seen a retribution againt those deemed responsible for the erosion of heretofore status providing essentialist identities of race, gender, gender orientation and nation.

The real and/or potential shame of potential loss of privileged identities and social status, especially among the lower middle cases, disposes anger and rage toward the "threats" to one's identity and challenges that shades into *ressentiment*. Following Nietzsche (1897[1996]), *ressentiment* has a specific meaning, not simply disdaining or not liking something or someone, but an intense, "instinctive reaction," a visceral loathing and disgust and the desire for punitive revenge toward illegitimate elites and subaltern upstarts or whomever is responsible for the suffering endured by challenges to their identities, status and esteem.[23] For Nietzsche, *resssentiment* was a reaction of the poor, weak and powerless, enslaved Jews toward their rich, powerful, Roman conquerors.

For Salmela and von Scheve (2018), *ressentiment* explains how negative emotions – fear and insecurity, in particular – transformed through repressed shame into anger, resentment and hatred towards perceived 'enemies' of the self and associated social groups. This *ressentiment* motivates right populisms anger toward existing, indifferent, onerous, if not traitorous political and cultural elites, typically more affluent, cosmopolitan urbanites who ignore if not malign the concerns and values of the "real people," and whose liberal social values secular cultures and identities challenge heretofore seeming fixed, privileged, status granting "superior" identities, are eroding. Thus anger, vitriol, and disdain toward blameworthy "establishment" elites who deserve sadistic punishment as well as dangerous subalterns from below, thieves, rapists, terrorists, thugs and above all, dedicated communists who threaten their precious status. Authoritarian populisms would displace the corrupt elites with strong leaders who would defend the "of the "real people" and restore a now lost Golden Age. *Ressentiment*, is undergirded by sadomasochistic authoritarian aggression that seeks to cruelly punish if not destroy the enemy, and ultimately begins to shade into what Fromm (1967) called necrophilia, malignant aggression, as the reaction to thwarted selfhood and in turn the love of death, dying, and destruction that is clearly evident in the morbid symptoms of our age, e.g. rampant bullying, the chants at reactionary gatherings, shootings and beatings of African Americans, Jews, Moslems, Asians etc., bombing and/or defacing of Churches, synagogues, or mosques.

5   Conclusion

Marx offered insights about social movements, strongly advocating socialist revolution guided by Communist parties as the voices of workers, and celebrated in the more anarchistic, spontaneous Paris Commune. He did not offer a comprehensive theory of social mobilizations yet provided us with valuable insights on reactionary events and the movements that supported them. For Marx, Bonapartism anticipated the causes and class dynamics of fascism and

---

23   While the right is prone to conspiracies, we must note that *both* neoliberalism and more
      socially progressive culture were due to the polices of many elites both Republican and
      Democratic in the US, but not much different elsewhere, e.g., Labor and Tories, in UK.

contemporary authoritarian populisms in late capitalism. Rereading the *18th Brumaire* points to a prescient Marx as he anticipated the rise of Hitler and even the ascendence of leaders like Trump, Bolsonaro, and Modi along with other contemporary right-wing populists. Similarly, he celebrated the rise and demise of the Paris Commune as the first egalitarian socialist revolution where women played a major activist role.[24] Surely a model for the future.

The Frankfurt School critical theorists were the first scholars to read and were informed by the *1844 Manuscripts*. Gramsci showed the powerful role of hegemony and ideological control of culture that sustains dominant social class control, the hegemonic bloc, but he also noted how domination created resistance and the necessity for "organic intellectuals" to "wage wars of position" articulating counter-hegemonic critiques attuned to the experiences of the subalterns. The basic goals of newer social movements were to overcome alienation, powerlessness, social fragmentation, the meaninglessness, and emptiness of "hegemonic" identities based on conformity, homogeneity, consumerism and civic privatism. While impacted by economic inequalities, these movements sought to foster a more humane society that would enable the freedom, and self-fulfillment hoped for by Marx and Hegel. The goals of such movements, overcoming alienation and domination, were exercises in "mobilizing for dignity" (Langman, 2015; Langman, Benski et al., 2013).

It is often said that the skies go darkest before dawn[25], and I would like to conclude by suggesting that despite the seeming power of the various right-wing populisms/reactionary nationalisms in power today, the growing number of progressive youths, suggest a strong note of optimism. We might begin to note that the various progressive mobilizations of the 1960s (and some arising much earlier) have not only endured but withstood the intense resistance from reactionary segments of society. While their progressive values mobilized a backlash electing conservative Republicans, a new permutation of social character was emergent, described philosophically by Marcuse as a "new sensibility," psychoanalytically by Fromm as a "productive character" or by academics as "post-material," "mini dimensional" or "Protean." This can be viewed as the opposite polarity of the authoritarian, valuing equality over hierarchy, stressing personal and collective freedom over domination, individual creative with fulfillment over conformity to the group and being open to new experiences rather than dogmatic binary "either/or" thinking.

---

24   Some might argue that is was not led by a Communist party and may have been more anarcho-syndalist,
25   A more pessimistic reading is that it grows darker before it goes pitch black!

Given cohort flows and the generational mediation of social change described by Mannheim (1952), the most likely result of new, and increasingly progressive generations shaped by different historical conditions will eventually displace older generations with entrenched, conservative, if not reactionary values. Today's millennials are far more accepting of racial and ethnic diversity, are more gender fluid, and very concerned with new existential threats like climate change. They are less interested in supporting conservative or reactionary agendas that focus on retaining (or even returning to) past privileged social organizations. Right-wing reactionary social movements struggle against demographic, economic and social tides. As we look ahead for a generation or two, contemporary young people will presage an even more progressive future. January 6, 2021 may well mark the intersection of a declining right-wing effort that lost the presidency, lost court cases, and failed in the attempted coup as an ascendant new generation was mobilizing and organizing to elect an African American and a Jewish senator in Georgia, heretofore an extremely conservative state. There may be short-term reverses as reaction backlash movements may well succeed in slowing the course of historical transformation (after all, over 70 million people voted to keep Trump in office!). Global warming and the environmental despoliation threaten the very future of humanity, but the dialectic of history presented in the writings of Karl Marx points to the growing power of progressive forces, notwithstanding short-term mobilizations of right-wing populisms, as the only hope for human survival.

References

Adorno, Theodor, et al. 1950. *The Authoritarian Personality*. New York: Harper and Row.

Adorno, Theodor. 2000. *The Psychological Technique of Martin Luther Thomas' Radio Addresses*. Stanford, CA: Stanford University Press.

Altemeyer, Bob. 1996. *The Authoritarian Specter*. Cambridge, MA: Harvard University Press.

Altemeyer, Bob. 2016. Donald Trump and Authoritarian Followers. https://www.daily kos.com/stories/2016/3/2/1494504/-A-word-from-Dr-Bob-Altemeyer-on-Donald -Trump-and-Authoritarian-Followers.

Anderson, Carol. 2016. *White Rage: The Unspoken Truth of Our Racial Divide*. London, UK: Bloomsbury Publishing.

Arendt, Hannah. 1951. *The Orignis of Totalitarianism*. New York, NY: Harcourt Brace and Co.

Ashcar, Gilbert. 2016. *Morbid Symptoms: Relapse in the Arab Uprising*. Stanford, CA: Stanford University Press.

Bauman, Zygmunt, 1998. *Globalization: The Human Consequences*. London, UK: Politiy Press.

Becker, Ernst. 1973. *The Denial of Death*. New York, NY: Simon & Schuster.

Boltanski, Luv and Eve Chiapello. 2005. *The New Spirit of Capitalism*. London, UK: Verso.

Castells. Manuel. 2012. *Networks of Outrage and Hope: Social Movements in the Internet Age*. UK: Polity Press.

De Bord, Guy, 1967 [1970]. *Society of the Spectacle*. Detroit, MI: Red and Black Press.

Della Porta, Donatella 2017. Political economy and social movement studies: The class basis of anti-austerity protests *Anthropological Theory*, Vol. 174 453–473.

de Vega. Chauncey. 2018. What Fuels White Anxiety. https://www.salon.com/2018/06/26/what-fuels-white-anxiety-the-baffling-hypocrisies-behind-white-paranoia-politics/.

Frank, Thomas. 2004. *What's the Matter with Kansas*. New York, NY: Metropolitan Books.

Fraser, Nancy. 2021. "American Interregnum." *New Left Review*. https://newleftreview.org/sidecar/posts/american-interregnum.

Friere, Paulo. 1970. *Pedagogy of the Oppressed*. New York, NY: Herder and Herder.

Fromm, Erich. 1941. *Escape from Freedom*. New York, NY: Farrar & Rinehart.

Fromm, Erich. 1961. *Marx's Concept of Man*. New York, NY: Frederick Ungar Publishing.

Fromm, Erich. 1967. *The Anatomy of Human Destructiveness*. New York, NY: Henry Holt and Company.

Geras, Norman. 1983. *Marx and Human Nature: Refutation of a Legend.* London, UK: Verso.

Gramsci, Antonio. 1971. *Selections from the Prison Notebooks*. New York, NY: International Publishers.

Habermas, Jurgen. 1981. "New Social Movements." *Telos*, September, vol. 49, pp. 33–37.

Habermas, Jurgen 19 75 *Legitimation Crises*. Boston, MA: Beacon Press.

Habermas, Jurgen. 1989 The *Structural Transformation of the Public Sphere*. Cambridge, MA: MIT Press.

Haverda, Myra, and Jeff Halley. 2019. "Trump's 2016 Presidential Campaign and Adorno's Psychological Technique: Content Analyses of Authoritarian Populism." *Triple C*. 17(2):18–36.

Hetland, Gabriel. and Jeffry Goodwin. 2013. "The Strange Disappearance Of Capitalism From Social Movement Studies". In: Barker C, Cox L, Krinsky J and Nilsen AG eds. *Marxism and Social Movements*. Leiden, The Netherlands: Brill, pp. 83–102.

Horkheimer, Max and Theodore Adorno, 1947. *The Dialectic of Enlightenment*.

Inglehart. Ronald 1971. "The Silent Revolution in Europe: Intergenerational Change in Post-industrial Societies." *American Political Science Review*, 65 (December): 991–1017.

Kellner, Douglas. 2003. *Media Spectacle*. New York, NY: Routledge.

Kornhauser, William. 1959. *The Politics of Mass Society*. Glencoe, IL: the Free Press.

Krinsky, John 2013. "Marxism and the Politics of Possibility: beyond Academic Boundaries". In: Barker C, Cox L, Krinsky J and Nilsen AG eds. *Marxism and Social Movements*. Leiden, The Netherlands: Brill, pp 103–124.

Lakoff, George. (1996) *Moral Politics: What Conservatives Know That Liberals Don't.* Chicago, IL: University of Chicago Press.

Langman, Lauren. 2005. "From Virtual Public Spheres to Internetworked Social Movements." *Sociological Theory*, Vol. 23, No. 1 pp. 42–74.

Langman, Lauren. 2015. "Political Economy and the Normative: Marx on Human Nature and the Quest for Dignity.", in Michael Thompson Ed. *Constructing Marxist Ethics: Critique, Normativity, Praxis*. Leiden, the Netherlands Brill, pp. 59 to 85.

Langman, Lauren, Tova Benski et al. 2013. "From the Streets and Squares To Social Movement Studies: What Have We Learned". *Current Sociology* 61(4): 525–540.

Langman, Lauren. 2021, "History and Biography in the 21st Century." in Jon Frauley, ed. *The Routledge International Handbook of C. Wright Mills Studies*. New York, NY: Routledge Publishers.

Lipset, Seymour Martin and Earl Raab. 1970. *The Politics of Unreason: Right-Wing Extremism in America, 1790–1970*. New York: Harper & Row, Publishers, 1970.

Lowenthal, Leo and Norbert Guterman. 1949. *Prophets of Deceit*. New York NY: Harper & Brothers.

Manheim, Karl. 1952. "The Problem of Generations". In P. Kecskemeti ed. *Essays on the Sociology of Knowledge*. London: Routledge and Kegan Paul. pp. 276–320.

Miceli, Cristiano and Cristiano Castelfranchi, 2018. "Contempt and Disgust: the Dmotions of Disrespect". *Journal for the Theory of Social Behavior*, Volume 48, Issue 2 pp. 205–229.

Marcuse, Herbert 1964 *One-Dimensional Man*. Boston: Beacon Press.

Marcuse, Herbert. 1969 *Essay on Liberation*. Boston: Beacon Press.

Marcuse, Herbert, *The New Sensibility*, 1970 You Tube https://www.youtube.com/watch?v=TBWiiFtqq84.

Marx, Karl. 1844 [1972]. "The Economic and Philosophical Manuscripts (Paris Manuscripts)." in Robert Tucker ed. *The Marx Engels Reader*. New York, NY: W. W. Norton and Company. Pp. 469-500.

Marx, Karl. 1848 [1972]. "The Manifesto of the Communist Party." in Robert Tucker ed. *The Marx Engels Reader*. New York, NY: W. W. Norton and Company. Pp. 55–125.

Marx, Karl. 1845 [1972] "The German Ideology." in Robert Tucker ed. *The Marx Engels Reader*. New York, NY: W. W. Norton and Company. Pp. 146–202.

Marx, Karl. 1852 [1972]. "The 18th Brumaire of Louis Bonaparte", in Robert Tucker ed. *The Marx Engels Reader*. New York, NY: W. W. Norton and Company. Pp. 594–617.

Marx, Karl. 1871[1972] "The Civil War in France." in Robert Tucker ed. *The Marx Engels Reader*. New York, NY: W. W. Norton and Company. 618–652.

Masquelier, Charles. 2013. "Critical Theory and Contemporary Social Movements: Conceptualizing Resistance in The Neoliberal Age." *European Journal of Social Theory*, Vol 16(4): 395–41.

Maygar-Hass, Veronika. 2020. "Shame as An Anthropological, Historical and Social Emotion." in *Shame and Social Work*. Frost, Elizabeth, Magyar-Haas Veronika, Holger Schoneville and Sicora, Alessandro. eds. Bristol, UK: Policy Press. pp. 55–77.

Miceli, Maria and Cristiano Castelfranchi. 2018. "Reconsidering the Differences Between Shame and Guilt." *European Journal of Psychology*. Aug; 14(3): 710–733.

Mitchell, Peter. 2020. "To the Far Right, attacks on Protesters as Enemies of 'Western Culture' Are a Gift." *The Guardian* https://www.theguardian.com/commentisfree/2020/jun/10/attacks-protesters-enemies-western- culture-traction-far-right.

Mueller, Jan-Werner. 2016. *What Is Populism?* Philadelphia, PA: University of Pennsylvania Press.

Nietzsche, Frederic. 1897 [1996]. *The Genealogy of Morals*. Cambridge, UK; Cambridge University Press.

Nilsen, Alf G. and Lawrence Cox, 2013, In: Barker C, Cox L, Krinsky J. and Nilsen AG. eds *Marxism and Social Movements*. Leiden, The Netherlands: Brill, pp. 63–82.

Norris, Pippa and Ronald Inglehart. 2019. *Cultural Backlash: Trump, Brexit, and Authoritarian Populism*. New York: Cambridge University Press.

Reich Wilhelm 1933[1946]. *The Mass Psychology of Fascism*. New York, NY: Orgone Institute Press.

Rich, Ben. (2021). Political Extremism, Conflict identities and the Search for Ontological Security in Contemporary Established Democracies. *Academia Letters*, Article 602. https://doi.org/10.20935/AL602.

Saad, Lydia, 2019. "Socialism as Popular as Capitalism Among Young Adults in U.S" https://news.gallup.com/poll/268766/socialism-popular-capitalism-among-young-adults.aspx.

Salmela, Mikko and Christian von Scheve. 2018. "Emotional Roots of Right-Wing Political Populism." *Social Science Information*. Vol 56, Issue 4, PP. 434–454.

Scheff, Thomas. 1994. *Bloody Revenge: Nationalism, War, and Emotion*. New York, NY: Routledge.

Schmitt, Carl 2007. *The Concept of the Political*. Chicago, IL: University of Chicago Press.

Smith, David and Eric Hanley. 2018. "The Anger Games: Who Voted for Donald Trump in the 2016 Election, and Why?" *Current Sociology*. Vol 44, Issue 2. 2) Pp. 195–212.

Standing, Guy, 2011. *The Precariat*. London, UK: Bloomsbury Academic.

Tilly, Charles.1978. From Mobilization to Revolution. Reading, MA: Addison-Wesley.

Touraine, Alain 1981 *The Voice and the Eye. An Analysis of Social Movements*. Cambridge: Cambridge University Press.

Turner, R Ralph, 1976. "The Real Self: from Institution to Impulse." *American Journal of Sociology*, Volume 81, Number 5, March, pp. 989–1016.

Wolfenstein, Martha 1951. "The emergence of the fun morality." *Journal of Social Issues*, Volume7, Issue 4, Fall. pp. 15–25.

Index

www.ingramcontent.com/pod-product-compliance
Lightning Source LLC
Chambersburg PA
CBHW070901030426
42336CB00014BA/2283